Department of
and Social Affa
Statistics Divisic

MW01048471

World
Statistics
Pocketbook
2014 edition

United Nations, New York, 2014

The **Department of Economic and Social Affairs** of the United Nations Secretariat is a vital interface between global policies in the economic, social and environmental spheres and national action. The Department works in three main interlinked areas: (i) it compiles, generates and analyses a wide range of economic, social and environmental data and information on which States Members of the United Nations draw to review common problems and to take stock of policy options; (ii) it facilitates the negotiations of Member States in many intergovernmental bodies on joint courses of action to address ongoing or emerging global challenges; and (iii) it advises interested Governments on the ways and means of translating policy frameworks developed in United Nations conferences and summits into programmes at the country level and, through technical assistance, helps build national capacities.

Note
The designations employed and the presentation of material in this publication do not imply the expression of any opinion whatsoever on the part of the Secretariat of the United Nations concerning the legal status of any country, territory, city or area or of its authorities, or concerning the delimitation of its frontiers or boundaries.

The term "country" as used in this publication also refers, as appropriate, to territories or areas.

Visit the United Nations World Wide Web site on the Internet:
For the Department of Economic and Social Affairs,
    http://www.un.org/esa/desa/
For statistics and statistical publications,
    http://unstats.un.org/unsd/
For UN publications, https://unp.un.org/

ST/ESA/STAT/SER.V/38
United Nations Publication
Sales No. E.14.XVII.4
ISBN-13: 978-92-1-161586-9
eISBN: 978-92-1-056657-5

Contents

Country profiles

Contents (*continued*)

Contents (*continued*)

Introduction

The *World Statistics Pocketbook* is an annual compilation of key economic, social and environmental indicators, presented in one-page profiles. This edition includes country profiles for 217 countries or areas of the world. Prepared by the United Nations Statistics Division of the Department of Economic and Social Affairs, it responds to General Assembly resolution 2626 (XXV), in which the Secretary-General is requested to supply basic national data that will increase international public awareness of countries' development efforts.

The indicators shown are selected from the wealth of international statistical information compiled regularly by the Statistics Division and the Population Division of the United Nations, the statistical services of the United Nations specialized agencies and other international organizations and institutions. Special recognition is gratefully given for their assistance in continually providing data.

Time period

This issue of the *World Statistics Pocketbook* covers various years from 2005 to 2014. For the economic indicators, in general, three years - 2005, 2010 and 2012 - are shown, unless otherwise indicated. Due to space limitations, data for one year only are shown for the indicators in the social and environmental categories. For the six social indicators for which the range of years 2010-2015 is shown, the data refer to projections. When other ranges of years are shown, the data refer to the most recent year available within that range.

Organization of the Pocketbook

The country tables or profiles are presented alphabetically according to countries' names in English and contain the available data for the following broad categories:

- *General information:* includes each country's location by geographical region, currency, surface area, population and population density, capital city and United Nations membership date

- *Economic indicators:* includes national accounts (Gross domestic product (GDP), GDP growth rate, GDP per capita, gross national income per capita and gross fixed capital formation), exchange rates, balance of payments, consumer price index, production indices (industrial, agricultural and food), unemployment, employment, labour force participation, tourist arrivals, energy production, mobile-cellular telephone subscribers and internet users

- *Trade:* contains the value of total exports, imports and the trade balance as well as the countries' main trading partners

- *Social indicators:* includes population (growth rates, urban percentage, age groups and sex ratios), life expectancy, infant mortality rate, total fertility rate, contraceptive prevalence, international migrant stock, refugees, education (expenditure and enrolment), intentional homicides and female participation in national parliaments

*   *Environmental indicators:* includes threatened species, forested area, CO_2 emission estimates, energy consumption per capita and climatological information.

The complete set of indicators, listed by category and in the order in which they appear in the profiles, is shown at the beginning of the country profile section. Not all indicators are shown for each country or area due to different degrees of data availability.

The technical notes section, which follows the country profile pages, contains brief descriptions of the concepts and methodologies used in the compilation of the indicators as well as information on the statistical sources for the indicators. Readers interested in longer time-series data or more detailed descriptions of the concepts or methodologies should consult the primary sources of the data and the references listed in the section following the technical notes.

The index of indicators, at the back of this publication, lists the complete set of indicators in alphabetical order and shows the category in which each is presented in the country profiles along with the pages on which information on the concepts, definitions and the data sources are given. As noted above, the number of indicators actually shown for the countries varies according to data availability.

Note

The present *World Statistics Pocketbook, 2014 edition* (Series V, No. 38) is an update of the previous edition which was released in 2013 and entitled *World Statistics Pocketbook 2013 edition* (Series V, No. 37).

* * *

The *World Statistics Pocketbook* is prepared annually by the Statistical Services Branch of the Statistics Division, Department of Economic and Social Affairs of the United Nations Secretariat. The programme manager is Jacob Assa, the editor is Heather Page, and the software developer is Salomon Cameo. Comments on this publication are welcome and may be sent by e-mail to statistics@un.org.

Symbols, abbreviations and conversion factors

The following symbols and abbreviations have been used in the *World Statistics Pocketbook*:

...	Data not available
–	Magnitude zero
<	Magnitude not zero, but less than half of the unit employed
–<	Magnitude not zero, but negative and less than half of the unit employed
000	Thousands
°C	Degrees Celsius
%	Percentage
60+	Aged sixty years and over
.	Decimal figures are always preceded by a period (.)
CFA	Coopération financière en Afrique centrale
CIF	Cost, Insurance and Freight
CO_2	Carbon dioxide
CPI	Consumer price index
f	Females
FOB	Free on board
GDP	Gross domestic product
GNI	Gross national income
ILO	International Labour Organization
ISIC	International Standard Industrial Classification
ISO	International Organization for Standardization
ITU	International Telecommunication Union
km	Kilometres
m	Males
mt	Metric tons
N & C Ame	North and Central America
nes	Not elsewhere specified
S. America	South America
SAR	Special Administrative Region
UN	United Nations
UNESCO	United Nations Educational, Scientific and Cultural Organization
UNHCR	Office of the United Nations High Commissioner for Refugees
UNSD	United Nations Statistics Division
US$	United States dollars
WMO	World Meteorological Organization

The metric system of weights and measures has been employed in the *World Statistics Pocketbook*. The equivalents of the basic British Imperial and United States weights and measures are as follows:

Area	1 square kilometre	= 0.386102 square mile
Weight or mass	1 ton	= 1.102311 short tons or
		= 0.987207 long ton
	1 kilogram	= 35.273962 avoirdupois ounces
		= 2.204623 avoirdupois pounds
Distance	1 kilometre	= 0.621371 mile
	1 millimetre	= 0.039 inch
Temperature	°C	= (°F - 32) × 5/9

Country profile information and indicator list*

General information
Region
Currency
Surface area (square kilometres)
Population in 2012 (estimated, 000)
Population density in 2012 (per square kilometre)
Capital city and population in 2011 (000)
United Nations membership date

Economic indicators
GDP: Gross domestic product (million current US$)
GDP: Growth rate at constant 2005 prices (annual %)
GDP per capita (current US$)
GNI: Gross national income per capita (current US$)
Gross fixed capital formation (% of GDP)
Exchange rates (national currency per US$)
Balance of payments, current account (million US$)
CPI: Consumer price index (2000=100)
Industrial production index (2005=100)
Agricultural production index (2004-2006=100)
Food production index (2004-2006=100)
Unemployment (% of labour force)
Employment in industrial sector (% of employed)
Employment in agricultural sector (% of employed)
Labour force participation, adult female population (%)
Labour force participation, adult male population (%)
Tourist arrivals at national borders (000)
Energy production, primary (000 mt oil equivalent)
Mobile-cellular telephone subscriptions, total (per 100 inhabitants)
Individuals using the Internet (%)

Trade
Total trade (exports, imports and balance, million US$)
Major trading partners (exports and imports, %)

Social indicators
Population growth rate (average annual %)
Urban population growth rate (average annual %)
Rural population growth rate (average annual %)
Urban population (%)
Population aged 0-14 years (%)
Population aged 60+ years (females and males, % of total)
Sex ratio (males per 100 females)
Life expectancy at birth (females and males, years)
Infant mortality rate (per 1 000 live births)
Fertility rate, total (live births per woman)
Contraceptive prevalence (ages 15-49, %)
International migrant stock (000 and % of total population)
Refugees and others of concern to UNHCR
Education: Government expenditure (% of GDP)
Education: Primary and secondary gross enrolment ratio (females and males per 100)
Education: Female third-level students (% of total)
Intentional homicides (females and males, per 100 000)
Seats held by women in national parliaments (%)

Environmental indicators
Threatened species
Forested area (% of land area)
CO_2 emission estimates (000 metric tons and metric tons per capita)
Energy consumption per capita (kilograms oil equivalent)
Precipitation in the capital city, total mean (millimetres)
Temperature in the capital city, mean °C (minimum and maximum)

* The complete set of information and indicators listed here may not be shown for each country or area depending upon data availability.

Country profiles

Afghanistan

Region	Southern Asia
Currency	Afghani (AFN)
Surface area (square kilometres)	652 864
Population in 2012 (estimated, 000)	29 825
Population density in 2012 (per square kilometre)	45.7
Capital city and population in 2011 (000)	Kabul (3 097)
United Nations membership date	19 November 1946

Economic indicators	2005	2010	2012
GDP: Gross domestic product (million current US$)	6 622	16 078	20 364
GDP: Growth rate at constant 2005 prices (annual %)	9.9	3.2	5.2
GDP per capita (current US$)	266.4	566.2	682.8
GNI: Gross national income per capita (current US$)	266.8	566.6	684.5
Gross fixed capital formation (% of GDP)	21.8	17.5	15.2
Exchange rates (national currency per US$)[a]	50.41	45.27	52.14
Balance of payments, current account (million US$)	−1 673[b]	−2 795	−7 286
Agricultural production index (2004-2006=100)	106	116	122
Food production index (2004-2006=100)	106	116	122
Labour force participation, adult female pop. (%)	13.9	15.4	15.7
Labour force participation, adult male pop. (%)	80.7	80.1	79.7
Energy production, primary (000 mt oil equivalent)	85	577	...
Mobile-cellular subscriptions (per 100 inhabitants)	4.4	41.4[c]	53.9[c]
Individuals using the Internet (%)	1.2	4.0[c]	5.5[c]

Total trade		Major trading partners			2012
	(million US$)	(% of exports)[d]			(% of imports)[d]
Exports	428.9	Pakistan	47.0	Areas nes	50.0
Imports	6 205.0	Areas nes	28.7	Pakistan	14.2
Balance	−5 776.1	India	16.3	China	11.5

Social indicators		
Population growth rate (average annual %)	2010-2015	2.4
Urban population growth rate (average annual %)	2010-2015	4.4
Rural population growth rate (average annual %)	2010-2015	2.7
Urban population (%)	2013	24.1
Population aged 0-14 years (%)	2013	46.6
Population aged 60+ years (females and males, % of total)	2013	4.2/3.6
Sex ratio (males per 100 females)	2013	102.9
Life expectancy at birth (females and males, years)	2010-2015	62.0/59.5
Infant mortality rate (per 1 000 live births)	2010-2015	67.3
Fertility rate, total (live births per woman)	2010-2015	5.0
Contraceptive prevalence (ages 15-49, %)	2006-2012	21.8
International migrant stock (000 and % of total population)	mid-2013	105.1/0.3
Refugees and others of concern to UNHCR	mid-2013	1 503 161
Education: Primary-secondary gross enrolment ratio (f/m per 100)	2006-2012	61.2/92.8
Education: Female third-level students (% of total)	2006-2012	24.3
Intentional homicides (females and males, per 100 000)[e]	2008-2010	0.9/3.8
Seats held by women in national parliaments (%)	2014	27.7

Environmental indicators		
Threatened species	2013	36
Forested area (% of land area)	2011	2.1
CO$_2$ emission estimates (000 metric tons and metric tons per capita)	2010	8 229/0.3
Energy consumption per capita (kilograms oil equivalent)	2010	90.0
Precipitation in the capital city, total mean (millimetres)		312[f]
Temperature in the capital city, mean °C (minimum and maximum)		4.3/19.6[f]

a Principal rate. b 2008. c ITU estimate. d See technical notes. e Estimates. f Based on monthly averages for the period 1956-1983.

Albania

Region	Southern Europe
Currency	Lek (ALL)
Surface area (square kilometres)	28 748
Population in 2012 (estimated, 000)	3 162
Population density in 2012 (per square kilometre)	110.0
Capital city and population in 2011 (000)	Tirana (419)
United Nations membership date	14 December 1955

Economic indicators	2005	2010	2012
GDP: Gross domestic product (million current US$)	8 159	11 762	12 044
GDP: Growth rate at constant 2005 prices (annual %)	5.8	3.8	1.3
GDP per capita (current US$)	2 552.6	3 733.7	3 809.0
GNI: Gross national income per capita (current US$)	2 603.7	3 707.7	3 813.4
Gross fixed capital formation (% of GDP)	37.0	31.1	32.6
Exchange rates (national currency per US$)[a]	103.58	104.00	105.85
Balance of payments, current account (million US$)	−571	−1 353	−1 314
CPI: Consumer price index (2000=100)	117	135	142
Industrial production index (2005=100)[b]	100	140	126[c]
Agricultural production index (2004-2006=100)	98	119	132
Food production index (2004-2006=100)	98	119	132
Employment in industrial sector (% of employed)[b]	13.5[d]	20.8[e]	...
Employment in agricultural sector (% of employed)[b]	58.5[d]	41.5[e]	...
Labour force participation, adult female pop. (%)	48.3	45.2	45.0
Labour force participation, adult male pop. (%)	68.9	65.3	65.4
Tourist arrivals at national borders (000)[fgh]	748	2 417	3 514
Energy production, primary (000 mt oil equivalent)	915	1 420	...
Mobile-cellular subscriptions (per 100 inhabitants)	48.7	84.0[i]	108.5
Individuals using the Internet (%)	6.0	45.0	54.7[i]

Total trade		Major trading partners				2012
	(million US$)	(% of exports)			(% of imports)	
Exports	1 967.9	Italy	51.1	Italy	31.9	
Imports	4 879.8	Spain	9.2	Greece	9.5	
Balance	−2 911.9	Serbia	8.9	China	6.4	

Social indicators		
Population growth rate (average annual %)	2010-2015	0.3
Urban population growth rate (average annual %)	2010-2015	2.3
Rural population growth rate (average annual %)	2010-2015	−2.0
Urban population (%)	2013	55.6
Population aged 0-14 years (%)	2013	20.6
Population aged 60+ years (females and males, % of total)	2013	15.9/14.7
Sex ratio (males per 100 females)	2013	100.5
Life expectancy at birth (females and males, years)	2010-2015	80.5/74.5
Infant mortality rate (per 1 000 live births)	2010-2015	14.4
Fertility rate, total (live births per woman)	2010-2015	1.8
Contraceptive prevalence (ages 15-49, %)	2006-2012	69.3
International migrant stock (000 and % of total population)[j]	mid-2013	96.8/3.1
Refugees and others of concern to UNHCR	mid-2013	7 631
Education: Government expenditure (% of GDP)	2006-2012	3.3
Education: Primary-secondary gross enrolment ratio (f/m per 100)	2006-2012	79.0/81.1[k]
Education: Female third-level students (% of total)	2006-2012	55.7
Intentional homicides (females and males, per 100 000)	2008-2010	1.9/7.5
Seats held by women in national parliaments (%)	2014	20.0

Environmental indicators		
Threatened species	2013	109
Forested area (% of land area)	2011	28.3
CO$_2$ emission estimates (000 metric tons and metric tons per capita)	2010	4 280/1.3
Energy consumption per capita (kilograms oil equivalent)	2010	525.0

a Market rate. b The indices are shown in terms of ISIC Rev.3. c 2011. d Official estimates. e Age group 15 to 64 years. f Arrivals of non-resident visitors at national borders. g Excludes nationals residing abroad. h Includes in transit visitors. i ITU estimate. j Data refer to foreign citizens. k 2001.

Algeria

Region	Northern Africa
Currency	Algerian Dinar (DZD)
Surface area (square kilometres)	2 381 741
Population in 2012 (estimated, 000)	38 482
Population density in 2012 (per square kilometre)	16.2
Capital city and population in 2011 (000)	Algiers (2 916)
United Nations membership date	8 October 1962

Economic indicators	2005	2010	2012
GDP: Gross domestic product (million current US$)	103 198	161 783	207 021
GDP: Growth rate at constant 2005 prices (annual %)	5.9	3.6	2.6
GDP per capita (current US$)	3 038.7	4 365.1	5 379.7
GNI: Gross national income per capita (current US$)	2 887.9	4 191.5	5 165.5
Gross fixed capital formation (% of GDP)	22.4	36.2	32.6
Exchange rates (national currency per US$)[a]	73.38	74.94	78.10
Balance of payments, current account (million US$)	21 180	12 146	12 247
CPI: Consumer price index (2000=100)	117	146	169
Agricultural production index (2004-2006=100)	99	125	144
Food production index (2004-2006=100)	99	125	144
Employment in industrial sector (% of employed)	26.0[bcd]	33.1[e]	30.9[ef]
Employment in agricultural sector (% of employed)	20.7[bcd]	11.7[e]	10.8[ef]
Labour force participation, adult female pop. (%)	12.9	14.6	15.0
Labour force participation, adult male pop. (%)	72.5	71.1	71.9
Tourist arrivals at national borders (000)[gh]	1 443	2 070	2 634
Energy production, primary (000 mt oil equivalent)	189 329	172 110	...
Mobile-cellular subscriptions (per 100 inhabitants)	41.5	92.4	103.3[i]
Individuals using the Internet (%)	5.8	12.5	15.2[i]

Total trade		Major trading partners			2012
	(million US$)		(% of exports)		(% of imports)
Exports	71 865.7	Italy	16.0	France	12.8
Imports	50 369.4	United States	15.0	China	11.8
Balance	21 496.3	Spain	10.9	Italy	10.3

Social indicators

Population growth rate (average annual %)	2010-2015	1.8
Urban population growth rate (average annual %)	2010-2015	2.5
Rural population growth rate (average annual %)	2010-2015	−1.9
Urban population (%)	2013	74.7
Population aged 0-14 years (%)	2013	27.8
Population aged 60+ years (females and males, % of total)	2013	7.7/7.1
Sex ratio (males per 100 females)	2013	102.3
Life expectancy at birth (females and males, years)	2010-2015	72.6/69.4
Infant mortality rate (per 1 000 live births)	2010-2015	26.4
Fertility rate, total (live births per woman)	2010-2015	2.8
Contraceptive prevalence (ages 15-49, %)	2006-2012	61.4
International migrant stock (000 and % of total population)[jk]	mid-2013	270.4/0.7
Refugees and others of concern to UNHCR	mid-2013	96 043[l]
Education: Government expenditure (% of GDP)	2006-2012	4.3
Education: Primary-secondary gross enrolment ratio (f/m per 100)	2006-2012	104.2/104.7
Education: Female third-level students (% of total)	2006-2012	59.0
Intentional homicides (females and males, per 100 000)[m]	2008-2010	4.1/10.4
Seats held by women in national parliaments (%)	2014	31.6

Environmental indicators

Threatened species	2013	111
Forested area (% of land area)	2011	0.6
CO_2 emission estimates (000 metric tons and metric tons per capita)	2010	123 374/3.5
Energy consumption per capita (kilograms oil equivalent)	2010	1 138.0
Precipitation in the capital city, total mean (millimetres)		598[n]
Temperature in the capital city, mean °C (minimum and maximum)		11.9/23.7[n]

a Official rate. b 2004. c The indices are shown in terms of ISIC Rev.3. d September. e Fourth quarter. f 2011. g Arrivals of non-resident visitors at national borders. h Includes nationals residing abroad. i ITU estimate. j Data refer to foreign citizens. k Includes refugees. l According to the Government of Algeria, there are an estimated 165,000 Sahrawi refugees in the Tindouf camps. m Estimates. n Based on monthly averages for the period 1976-2005.

American Samoa

Region	Oceania-Polynesia
Currency	U.S. Dollar (USD)
Surface area (square kilometres)	199
Population in 2012 (estimated, 000)	55
Population density in 2012 (per square kilometre)	277.0
Capital city and population in 2011 (000)	Pago Pago (65)

Economic indicators	2005	2010	2012
CPI: Consumer price index (2000=100)[a]	122	130[b]	...
Agricultural production index (2004-2006=100)	107	106	98
Food production index (2004-2006=100)	107	106	98
Tourist arrivals at national borders (000)	24	23	22
Mobile-cellular subscriptions (per 100 inhabitants)	3.6[c]	...	...

Social indicators		
Population growth rate (average annual %)	2010-2015	—<
Urban population growth rate (average annual %)	2010-2015	1.9
Rural population growth rate (average annual %)	2010-2015	−1.9
Urban population (%)	2013	93.7
Population aged 0-14 years (%)[de]	2013	34.8
Population aged 60+ years (females and males, % of total)[de]	2013	8.5/7.3
Sex ratio (males per 100 females)[de]	2013	103.2
Life expectancy at birth (females and males, years)[d]	2010-2015	75.9/69.3[f]
Infant mortality rate (per 1 000 live births)[d]	2010-2015	14.9[g]
Fertility rate, total (live births per woman)[d]	2010-2015	3.1[g]
International migrant stock (000 and % of total population)	mid-2013	41.8/75.9

Environmental indicators		
Threatened species	2013	89
Forested area (% of land area)	2011	88.4

a Excludes rent. b 2007. c 2004. d Data compiled by the Secretariat of the Pacific Community Demography Programme. e De facto estimate. f 2000. g 2010.

Andorra

Region	Southern Europe
Currency	Euro (EUR)
Surface area (square kilometres)	468
Population in 2012 (estimated, 000)	78
Population density in 2012 (per square kilometre)	167.4
Capital city and population in 2011 (000)	Andorra la Vella (24)
United Nations membership date	28 July 1993

Economic indicators	2005	2010	2012
GDP: Gross domestic product (million current US$)	3 190	3 406	3 222
GDP: Growth rate at constant 2005 prices (annual %)	6.9	−5.0	−1.6
GDP per capita (current US$)	39 274.7	43 722.1	41 122.2
GNI: Gross national income per capita (current US$)	39 274.7	43 722.1	41 122.2
Gross fixed capital formation (% of GDP)	29.4	23.7	21.1
Exchange rates (national currency per US$)[a]	0.85	0.75	0.76
CPI: Consumer price index (2000=100)[b]	113	126	131
Tourist arrivals at national borders (000)[c]	2 418	1 808	2 238
Energy production, primary (000 mt oil equivalent)	7	9	...
Mobile-cellular subscriptions (per 100 inhabitants)	82.9	77.2	74.3[d]
Individuals using the Internet (%)	37.6	81.0	86.4[d]

Social indicators		
Population growth rate (average annual %)	2010-2015	0.8
Urban population growth rate (average annual %)	2010-2015	0.9
Rural population growth rate (average annual %)	2010-2015	5.5
Urban population (%)	2013	86.2
Population aged 0-14 years (%)[efg]	2013	14.8[h]
Population aged 60+ years (females and males, % of total)[efg]	2013	18.6/18.0[h]
Sex ratio (males per 100 females)[efg]	2013	104.6[h]
Fertility rate, total (live births per woman)[e]	2010-2015	1.3[i]
International migrant stock (000 and % of total population)[j]	mid-2013	45.1/56.9
Education: Female third-level students (% of total)	2006-2012	60.9
Seats held by women in national parliaments (%)	2014	50.0

Environmental indicators		
Threatened species	2013	12
Forested area (% of land area)	2011	34.0
CO$_2$ emission estimates (000 metric tons and metric tons per capita)	2010	517/6.1
Energy consumption per capita (kilograms oil equivalent)	2010	2 606.0

a Market rate. b Index base 2001=100. c 2009: Methodology revised; data not strictly comparable. d ITU estimate. e Data compiled by the United Nations Demographic Yearbook system. f Data refer to the latest available census. g De jure estimate. h 2011. i 2010. j Data refer to foreign citizens.

Angola

Region	Middle Africa
Currency	Kwanza (AOA)
Surface area (square kilometres)	1 246 700
Population in 2012 (estimated, 000)	20 821
Population density in 2012 (per square kilometre)	16.7
Capital city and population in 2011 (000)	Luanda (5 068)
United Nations membership date	1 December 1976

Economic indicators	2005	2010	2012
GDP: Gross domestic product (million current US$)	32 811	82 513	116 308
GDP: Growth rate at constant 2005 prices (annual %)	20.5	3.5	6.8
GDP per capita (current US$)	1 983.2	4 220.8	5 586.2
GNI: Gross national income per capita (current US$)	1 803.8	4 044.2	5 405.5
Gross fixed capital formation (% of GDP)	8.3	15.3	15.2
Exchange rates (national currency per US$)[a]	80.78	92.64	95.83
Balance of payments, current account (million US$)	5 138	7 506	13 851
CPI: Consumer price index (2000=100)[b]	1 846	3 438[c]	4 302
Agricultural production index (2004-2006=100)	102	166	151
Food production index (2004-2006=100)	102	165	149
Labour force participation, adult female pop. (%)	64.4	62.7	63.1
Labour force participation, adult male pop. (%)	76.3	77.0	76.9
Tourist arrivals at national borders (000)	210	425	528
Energy production, primary (000 mt oil equivalent)	63 896	90 408	...
Mobile-cellular subscriptions (per 100 inhabitants)	9.8	46.7[d]	48.6[d]
Individuals using the Internet (%)	1.1	10.0[d]	16.9[d]

Social indicators		
Population growth rate (average annual %)	2010-2015	3.1
Urban population growth rate (average annual %)	2010-2015	4.0
Rural population growth rate (average annual %)	2010-2015	0.8
Urban population (%)	2013	60.7
Population aged 0-14 years (%)	2013	47.5
Population aged 60+ years (females and males, % of total)	2013	4.2/3.5
Sex ratio (males per 100 females)	2013	98.3
Life expectancy at birth (females and males, years)	2010-2015	53.2/50.2
Infant mortality rate (per 1 000 live births)	2010-2015	96.2
Fertility rate, total (live births per woman)	2010-2015	5.9
Contraceptive prevalence (ages 15-49, %)	2006-2012	6.2[e]
International migrant stock (000 and % of total population)[f]	mid-2013	87.4/0.4
Refugees and others of concern to UNHCR	mid-2013	43 960
Education: Government expenditure (% of GDP)	2006-2012	3.5
Education: Primary-secondary gross enrolment ratio (f/m per 100)	2006-2012	72.2/112.9
Education: Female third-level students (% of total)	2006-2012	27.4
Intentional homicides (females and males, per 100 000)[g]	2008-2010	7.7/30.5
Seats held by women in national parliaments (%)	2014	36.8

Environmental indicators		
Threatened species	2013	126
Forested area (% of land area)	2011	46.8
CO_2 emission estimates (000 metric tons and metric tons per capita)	2010	30 393/1.6
Energy consumption per capita (kilograms oil equivalent)	2010	307.0
Temperature in the capital city, mean °C (minimum and maximum)		22.3/27.7[h]

a Official rate. b Luanda. c Series linked to former series. d ITU estimate. e 2001. f Includes refugees. g Estimates. h Based on monthly averages for the period 1961-1990.

Antigua and Barbuda

Region	Caribbean
Currency	E.C. Dollar (XCD)
Surface area (square kilometres)	442
Population in 2012 (estimated, 000)	89
Population density in 2012 (per square kilometre)	201.5
Capital city and population in 2011 (000)	St. John's (27)
United Nations membership date	11 November 1981

Economic indicators	2005	2010	2012
GDP: Gross domestic product (million current US$)	997	1 136	1 176
GDP: Growth rate at constant 2005 prices (annual %)	6.1	−7.1	2.3
GDP per capita (current US$)	12 079.9	13 017.3	13 207.2
GNI: Gross national income per capita (current US$)	11 570.7	12 656.3	12 740.1
Gross fixed capital formation (% of GDP)	29.4	36.9	30.7
Exchange rates (national currency per US$)[a]	2.70	2.70	2.70
Balance of payments, current account (million US$)	−171	−167	−79
CPI: Consumer price index (2000=100)	110	123	131
Agricultural production index (2004-2006=100)	95	112	117
Food production index (2004-2006=100)	95	112	117
Employment in industrial sector (% of employed)[bc]	15.6	15.6[d]	...
Employment in agricultural sector (% of employed)[bc]	2.8	2.8[d]	...
Tourist arrivals at national borders (000)[e]	245[f]	230[f]	247
Mobile-cellular subscriptions (per 100 inhabitants)	102.5	189.4	198.6
Individuals using the Internet (%)[g]	27.0	47.0	59.0

Total trade	Major trading partners				2012
(million US$)	(% of exports)		(% of imports)		
Exports	29.0	United States	22.1	United States	50.1
Imports	339.5	United Kingdom	18.6	United Kingdom	6.1
Balance	−310.5	Barbados	9.7	China	5.7

Social indicators		
Population growth rate (average annual %)	2010-2015	1.0
Urban population growth rate (average annual %)	2010-2015	1.0
Rural population growth rate (average annual %)	2010-2015	1.0
Urban population (%)	2013	29.8
Population aged 0-14 years (%)	2013	25.0
Population aged 60+ years (females and males, % of total)	2013	10.8/9.5
Sex ratio (males per 100 females)	2013	91.5
Life expectancy at birth (females and males, years)	2010-2015	78.2/73.4
Infant mortality rate (per 1 000 live births)	2010-2015	8.5
Fertility rate, total (live births per woman)	2010-2015	2.1
Contraceptive prevalence (ages 15-49, %)[h]	2006-2012	52.6[i]
International migrant stock (000 and % of total population)	mid-2013	28.7/31.9
Refugees and others of concern to UNHCR	mid-2013	0[j]
Education: Government expenditure (% of GDP)	2006-2012	2.6
Education: Primary-secondary gross enrolment ratio (f/m per 100)	2006-2012	100.4/105.6
Education: Female third-level students (% of total)[k]	2006-2012	68.0
Seats held by women in national parliaments (%)	2014	10.5

Environmental indicators		
Threatened species	2013	44
Forested area (% of land area)	2011	22.3
CO_2 emission estimates (000 metric tons and metric tons per capita)	2010	513/5.8
Energy consumption per capita (kilograms oil equivalent)	2010	1 935.0[l]
Precipitation in the capital city, total mean (millimetres)		1 052[m]
Temperature in the capital city, mean °C (minimum and maximum)		23.9/29.6[n]

a Official rate. **b** Official estimates. **c** The indices are shown in terms of ISIC Rev.3. **d** 2008. **e** Excludes nationals residing abroad. **f** Air arrivals. **g** ITU estimate. **h** Age group 15 to 44 years. **i** 1988. **j** Value is zero, not available or not applicable. **k** National estimate. **l** UNSD estimate. **m** Based on monthly averages for the period 1960-1995. **n** Based on monthly averages for the period 1969-1995.

Argentina

Region	South America
Currency	Argentine Peso (ARS)
Surface area (square kilometres)	2 780 400
Population in 2012 (estimated, 000)	41 087
Population density in 2012 (per square kilometre)	14.8
Capital city and population in 2011 (000)	Buenos Aires (13 528)
United Nations membership date	24 October 1945

Economic indicators	2005	2010	2012
GDP: Gross domestic product (million current US$)	183 196	370 263	477 028
GDP: Growth rate at constant 2005 prices (annual %)	9.2	9.2	1.9
GDP per capita (current US$)	4 740.1	9 170.8	11 610.2
GNI: Gross national income per capita (current US$)	4 579.5	8 919.2	11 363.5
Gross fixed capital formation (% of GDP)	21.5	22.0	21.8
Exchange rates (national currency per US$)[a]	3.01	3.96	4.90
Balance of payments, current account (million US$)	5 274	1 360	22
CPI: Consumer price index (2000=100)[b]	162	249	301
Agricultural production index (2004-2006=100)	103	116	107
Food production index (2004-2006=100)	103	116	106
Unemployment (% of labour force)[cd]	11.5	7.7	7.2
Employment in industrial sector (% of employed)	23.5[efgh]	23.2[eij]	23.4[ijk]
Employment in agricultural sector (% of employed)	1.1[efgh]	1.3[eij]	0.6[ijk]
Labour force participation, adult female pop. (%)	48.7	47.0	47.3
Labour force participation, adult male pop. (%)	76.5	74.9	75.0
Tourist arrivals at national borders (000)	3 823	5 325	5 585
Energy production, primary (000 mt oil equivalent)	86 732	78 934	...
Mobile-cellular subscriptions (per 100 inhabitants)	57.3	132.9[l]	142.5
Individuals using the Internet (%)	17.7	45.0[l]	55.8[l]

Total trade		Major trading partners			2012
	(million US$)		(% of exports)		(% of imports)
Exports	80 927.1	Brazil	20.4	Brazil	26.1
Imports	68 507.5	Chile	6.3	China	14.5
Balance	12 419.6	China	6.2	United States	12.4

Social indicators

Population growth rate (average annual %)	2010-2015	0.9
Urban population growth rate (average annual %)	2010-2015	1.0
Rural population growth rate (average annual %)	2010-2015	−1.2
Urban population (%)	2013	92.8
Population aged 0-14 years (%)	2013	24.2
Population aged 60+ years (females and males, % of total)	2013	17.2/13.0
Sex ratio (males per 100 females)	2013	95.8
Life expectancy at birth (females and males, years)	2010-2015	79.8/72.5
Infant mortality rate (per 1 000 live births)	2010-2015	11.4
Fertility rate, total (live births per woman)	2010-2015	2.2
Contraceptive prevalence (ages 15-49, %)	2006-2012	78.9[m]
International migrant stock (000 and % of total population)	mid-2013	1 885.7/4.6
Refugees and others of concern to UNHCR	mid-2013	4 748
Education: Government expenditure (% of GDP)	2006-2012	5.8
Education: Primary-secondary gross enrolment ratio (f/m per 100)	2006-2012	106.1/102.2
Education: Female third-level students (% of total)	2006-2012	59.5
Intentional homicides (females and males, per 100 000)	2008-2010	1.0/5.4
Seats held by women in national parliaments (%)	2014	36.6

Environmental indicators

Threatened species	2013	242
Forested area (% of land area)	2011	10.7
CO$_2$ emission estimates (000 metric tons and metric tons per capita)	2010	180 364/4.5
Energy consumption per capita (kilograms oil equivalent)	2010	1 753.0
Precipitation in the capital city, total mean (millimetres)		1 215[n]
Temperature in the capital city, mean °C (minimum and maximum)		13.5/22.5[n]

a Official rate. b Metropolitan areas. c Main cities or metropolitan areas. d 2006: Break in series; data not strictly comparable. e The indices are shown in terms of ISIC Rev.3. f Age group 10 years and over. g Second semester. h 28 urban agglomerations. i Average of quarterly estimates. j 31 urban agglomerations. k Break in series; data not strictly comparable. l ITU estimate. m 2004-2005. n Based on monthly averages for the period 1961-1990.

Armenia

Region	Western Asia
Currency	Dram (AMD)
Surface area (square kilometres)	29 743
Population in 2012 (estimated, 000)	2 969
Population density in 2012 (per square kilometre)	99.8
Capital city and population in 2011 (000)	Yerevan (1 116)
United Nations membership date	2 March 1992

Economic indicators	2005	2010	2012
GDP: Gross domestic product (million current US$)	4 900	9 260	9 950
GDP: Growth rate at constant 2005 prices (annual %)	13.9	2.2	7.2
GDP per capita (current US$)	1 625.4	3 124.8	3 351.3
GNI: Gross national income per capita (current US$)	1 669.4	3 239.1	3 479.7
Gross fixed capital formation (% of GDP)	29.8	33.4	23.7
Exchange rates (national currency per US$)[a]	450.19	363.44	403.58
Balance of payments, current account (million US$)	−52	−1 373	−1 108
CPI: Consumer price index (2000=100)	117	154	169
Agricultural production index (2004-2006=100)	103	102	122
Food production index (2004-2006=100)	103	102	122
Employment in industrial sector (% of employed)	15.9[bc]	17.4	16.7[d]
Employment in agricultural sector (% of employed)	46.2[bc]	38.6	38.9[d]
Labour force participation, adult female pop. (%)	52.0	50.9	51.6
Labour force participation, adult male pop. (%)	69.6	72.3	73.4
Tourist arrivals at national borders (000)	319	684	843
Energy production, primary (000 mt oil equivalent)	386	434	...
Mobile-cellular subscriptions (per 100 inhabitants)	10.4	125.0	106.9
Individuals using the Internet (%)	5.3	25.0[e]	39.2[e]

Total trade		Major trading partners			2012
	(million US$)	(% of exports)		(% of imports)	
Exports	1 428.1	Russian Federation	19.5	Russian Federation	24.7
Imports	4 266.9	Germany	10.7	China	9.3
Balance	−2 838.8	Bulgaria	9.1	Iran	5.1

Social indicators		
Population growth rate (average annual %)	2010-2015	0.2
Urban population growth rate (average annual %)	2010-2015	0.3
Rural population growth rate (average annual %)	2010-2015	0.1
Urban population (%)	2013	64.2
Population aged 0-14 years (%)	2013	20.3
Population aged 60+ years (females and males, % of total)	2013	16.7/12.1
Sex ratio (males per 100 females)	2013	105.9
Life expectancy at birth (females and males, years)	2010-2015	77.9/71.2
Infant mortality rate (per 1 000 live births)	2010-2015	19.0
Fertility rate, total (live births per woman)	2010-2015	1.7
Contraceptive prevalence (ages 15-49, %)	2006-2012	54.9
International migrant stock (000 and % of total population)[f]	mid-2013	317.0/10.7
Refugees and others of concern to UNHCR	mid-2013	9 807
Education: Government expenditure (% of GDP)	2006-2012	3.2
Education: Primary-secondary gross enrolment ratio (f/m per 100)	2006-2012	105.6/92.1
Education: Female third-level students (% of total)	2006-2012	56.0
Intentional homicides (females and males, per 100 000)	2008-2010	1.5/4.0
Seats held by women in national parliaments (%)	2014	10.7

Environmental indicators		
Threatened species	2013	40
Forested area (% of land area)	2011	9.1
CO_2 emission estimates (000 metric tons and metric tons per capita)	2010	4 217/1.4
Energy consumption per capita (kilograms oil equivalent)	2010	693.0[g]
Precipitation in the capital city, total mean (millimetres)		277
Temperature in the capital city, mean °C (minimum and maximum)		5.5/18.2

a Official rate. **b** Official estimates. **c** The indices are shown in terms of ISIC Rev.3. **d** 2011. **e** ITU estimate.
f Includes refugees. **g** UNSD estimate.

Aruba

Region	Caribbean
Currency	Aruban Guilder (AWG)
Surface area (square kilometres)	180
Population in 2012 (estimated, 000)	102
Population density in 2012 (per square kilometre)	568.8
Capital city and population in 2011 (000)	Oranjestad (37)

Economic indicators	2005	2010	2012
GDP: Gross domestic product (million current US$)	2 331	2 391	2 544
GDP: Growth rate at constant 2005 prices (annual %)	1.2	−3.3	−1.2
GDP per capita (current US$)	23 302.8	23 529.5	24 852.2
GNI: Gross national income per capita (current US$)	21 888.0	22 112.8	23 367.3
Gross fixed capital formation (% of GDP)	32.1	28.9	26.0
Exchange rates (national currency per US$)[a]	1.79	1.79	1.79
Balance of payments, current account (million US$)	105	−437	124
CPI: Consumer price index (2000=100)	117	139	146
Employment in industrial sector (% of employed)	20.3[bcde]	...	...
Employment in agricultural sector (% of employed)	0.7[bcde]	...	...
Tourist arrivals at national borders (000)	733	824	904
Energy production, primary (000 mt oil equivalent)[f]	121	124	...
Mobile-cellular subscriptions (per 100 inhabitants)	102.4	122.6[g]	124.3[g]
Individuals using the Internet (%)[g]	25.4	62.0	74.0

Total trade		Major trading partners			2012
	(million US$)	(% of exports)			(% of imports)[h]
Exports	173.1	Colombia	39.3	United States	46.4
Imports	1 259.8	Venezuela	29.3	Netherlands	11.5
Balance	−1 086.7	United States	13.0	Areas nes	8.5

Social indicators		
Population growth rate (average annual %)	2010-2015	0.5
Urban population growth rate (average annual %)	2010-2015	0.5
Rural population growth rate (average annual %)	2010-2015	0.2
Urban population (%)	2013	47.0
Population aged 0-14 years (%)	2013	19.4
Population aged 60+ years (females and males, % of total)	2013	18.4/15.8
Sex ratio (males per 100 females)	2013	90.9
Life expectancy at birth (females and males, years)	2010-2015	77.8/72.9
Infant mortality rate (per 1 000 live births)	2010-2015	14.8
Fertility rate, total (live births per woman)	2010-2015	1.7
International migrant stock (000 and % of total population)	mid-2013	36.0/34.9
Refugees and others of concern to UNHCR	mid-2013	6
Education: Government expenditure (% of GDP)	2006-2012	6.0
Education: Primary-secondary gross enrolment ratio (f/m per 100)	2006-2012	101.8/101.0
Education: Female third-level students (% of total)	2006-2012	58.0

Environmental indicators		
Threatened species	2013	24
Forested area (% of land area)	2011	2.3
CO$_2$ emission estimates (000 metric tons and metric tons per capita)	2010	2 319/21.6
Energy consumption per capita (kilograms oil equivalent)	2010	2 336.0[f]
Precipitation in the capital city, total mean (millimetres)		472[i]
Temperature in the capital city, mean °C (minimum and maximum)		25.9/31.5[i]

a Official rate. b 2007. c The indices are shown in terms of ISIC Rev.3. d October. e Break in series; data not strictly comparable. f UNSD estimate. g ITU estimate. h See technical notes. i Based on monthly averages for the period 1981-2010.

Australia

Region	Oceania
Currency	Australian Dollar (AUD)
Surface area (square kilometres)	7 692 024 [a]
Population in 2012 (estimated, 000)	23 050 [b]
Population density in 2012 (per square kilometre)	3.0
Capital city and population in 2011 (000)	Canberra (399)
United Nations membership date	1 November 1945

Economic indicators	2005	2010	2012
GDP: Gross domestic product (million current US$)	759 823	1 287 782	1 564 419
GDP: Growth rate at constant 2005 prices (annual %)	3.0	2.4	2.9
GDP per capita (current US$)	37 027.1	57 478.8	67 869.3
GNI: Gross national income per capita (current US$)	35 589.5	55 261.6	66 051.7
Gross fixed capital formation (% of GDP)	27.9	26.5	28.2
Exchange rates (national currency per US$) [c]	1.36	0.98	0.96
Balance of payments, current account (million US$)	−41 729	−37 176	−57 038
CPI: Consumer price index (2000=100)	116	134	141
Industrial production index (2005=100) [d]	100	112	118
Agricultural production index (2004-2006=100)	108	100	117
Food production index (2004-2006=100)	108	102	117
Unemployment (% of labour force)	5.0	5.2	5.2
Employment in industrial sector (% of employed) [e]	21.3 [f]	21.1 [gh]	...
Employment in agricultural sector (% of employed) [e]	3.6 [f]	3.3 [gh]	...
Labour force participation, adult female pop. (%)	57.0	58.8	58.8
Labour force participation, adult male pop. (%)	72.2	72.5	71.9
Tourist arrivals at national borders (000) [ij]	5 499	5 885	6 146
Energy production, primary (000 mt oil equivalent) [k]	277 441	309 315	...
Mobile-cellular subscriptions (per 100 inhabitants)	90.3	101.0	106.2
Individuals using the Internet (%)	63.0 [l]	76.0 [m]	82.4 [m]

Total trade		Major trading partners			2012
	(million US$)	(% of exports)			(% of imports)
Exports	256 242.9	China	29.6	China	18.4
Imports	250 464.8	Japan	19.4	United States	11.7
Balance	5 778.1	Republic of Korea	8.0	Japan	7.9

Social indicators		
Population growth rate (average annual %) [b]	2010-2015	1.3
Urban population growth rate (average annual %) [b]	2010-2015	1.5
Rural population growth rate (average annual %) [b]	2010-2015	−0.1
Urban population (%) [b]	2013	89.5
Population aged 0-14 years (%) [b]	2013	19.1
Population aged 60+ years (females and males, % of total) [b]	2013	20.8/18.7
Sex ratio (males per 100 females) [b]	2013	99.1
Life expectancy at birth (females and males, years) [b]	2010-2015	84.7/80.2
Infant mortality rate (per 1 000 live births) [b]	2010-2015	3.9
Fertility rate, total (live births per woman) [b]	2010-2015	1.9
Contraceptive prevalence (ages 15-49, %) [n]	2006-2012	72.3 [o]
International migrant stock (000 and % of total population) [b]	mid-2013	6 468.6/27.7
Refugees and others of concern to UNHCR	mid-2013	55 301 [p]
Education: Government expenditure (% of GDP)	2006-2012	5.6
Education: Primary-secondary gross enrolment ratio (f/m per 100)	2006-2012	116.1/119.7
Education: Female third-level students (% of total)	2006-2012	56.4
Intentional homicides (females and males, per 100 000)	2008-2010	1.3/3.3
Seats held by women in national parliaments (%)	2014	26.0

Environmental indicators		
Threatened species [q]	2013	896
Forested area (% of land area)	2011	19.3
CO_2 emission estimates (000 metric tons and metric tons per capita)	2010	372 775/16.7
Energy consumption per capita (kilograms oil equivalent) [k]	2010	5 502.0
Precipitation in the capital city, total mean (millimetres)		629 [r]
Temperature in the capital city, mean °C (minimum and maximum)		6.4/19.5 [r]

a Excludes Norfolk Island. b Includes Christmas, Cocos (Keeling) and Norfolk Islands. c Market rate. d Average of 12 months ending 30 June of the year stated. e Average of quarterly estimates. f The indices are shown in terms of ISIC Rev.3. g 2009. h Break in series; data not strictly comparable. i Arrivals of non-resident visitors at national borders. j Excludes nationals residing abroad and crew members. k Excludes the overseas territories. l Age group 15 years and over. m ITU estimate. n Age group 18 to 44 years. o 2005. p Refugee population refers to the end of 2012. q Excludes Christmas and Cocos (Keeling) Islands. r Based on monthly averages for the period 1939-2002.

Austria

Region	Western Europe
Currency	Euro (EUR)
Surface area (square kilometres)	83 871
Population in 2012 (estimated, 000)	8 464
Population density in 2012 (per square kilometre)	100.9
Capital city and population in 2011 (000)	Vienna (1 720)
United Nations membership date	14 December 1955

Economic indicators

	2005	2010	2012
GDP: Gross domestic product (million current US$)	304 984	377 680	394 458
GDP: Growth rate at constant 2005 prices (annual %)	2.4	1.8	0.9
GDP per capita (current US$)	37 018.8	44 951.6	46 604.4
GNI: Gross national income per capita (current US$)	36 659.6	44 984.3	46 316.9
Gross fixed capital formation (% of GDP)	22.0	20.8	22.0
Exchange rates (national currency per US$)[a]	0.85	0.75	0.76
Balance of payments, current account (million US$)	6 245	13 149	6 394
CPI: Consumer price index (2000=100)	111	121	128
Industrial production index (2005=100)	100	110	118
Agricultural production index (2004-2006=100)	101	100	101
Food production index (2004-2006=100)	101	100	101
Unemployment (% of labour force)[b]	5.2	4.4	4.3
Employment in industrial sector (% of employed)	27.5[cd]	24.9[e]	26.2[e]
Employment in agricultural sector (% of employed)	5.5[cd]	5.2[e]	4.9[e]
Labour force participation, adult female pop. (%)	51.2	53.9	54.6
Labour force participation, adult male pop. (%)	67.3	67.7	67.7
Tourist arrivals at national borders (000)[f]	19 952	22 004	24 151
Energy production, primary (000 mt oil equivalent)	6 067	6 659	...
Mobile-cellular subscriptions (per 100 inhabitants)	105.3	145.8	161.2
Individuals using the Internet (%)[g]	58.0	75.2	81.0

Total trade	Major trading partners				2012
	(million US$)	(% of exports)		(% of imports)	
Exports	158 821.0	Germany	30.0	Germany	36.8
Imports	169 663.2	Italy	6.3	Italy	6.1
Balance	–10 842.2	Switzerland	5.3	Switzerland	5.3

Social indicators

Population growth rate (average annual %)	2010-2015	0.4
Urban population growth rate (average annual %)	2010-2015	0.5
Rural population growth rate (average annual %)	2010-2015	−0.5
Urban population (%)	2013	68.1
Population aged 0-14 years (%)	2013	14.5
Population aged 60+ years (females and males, % of total)	2013	26.1/21.3
Sex ratio (males per 100 females)	2013	95.4
Life expectancy at birth (females and males, years)	2010-2015	83.5/78.5
Infant mortality rate (per 1 000 live births)	2010-2015	3.1
Fertility rate, total (live births per woman)	2010-2015	1.5
Contraceptive prevalence (ages 15-49, %)[h]	2006-2012	50.9[i]
International migrant stock (000 and % of total population)	mid-2013	1 333.8/15.7
Refugees and others of concern to UNHCR	mid-2013	73 957[j]
Education: Government expenditure (% of GDP)	2006-2012	5.9
Education: Primary-secondary gross enrolment ratio (f/m per 100)	2006-2012	97.2/100.1
Education: Female third-level students (% of total)	2006-2012	53.4
Intentional homicides (females and males, per 100 000)	2008-2010	1.3/2.3
Seats held by women in national parliaments (%)	2014	33.3

Environmental indicators

Threatened species	2013	107
Forested area (% of land area)	2011	47.2
CO_2 emission estimates (000 metric tons and metric tons per capita)	2010	66 842/8.0
Energy consumption per capita (kilograms oil equivalent)	2010	3 317.0
Precipitation in the capital city, total mean (millimetres)		620[k]
Temperature in the capital city, mean °C (minimum and maximum)		6.7/14.5[k]

a Market rate. b Age group 15 to 74 years. c The indices are shown in terms of ISIC Rev.3. d Excludes conscripts. e European Labour Force Survey (Eurostat). f Arrivals of non-resident tourists in all types of accommodation establishments. g Age group 16 to 74 years. h Age group 20 to 49 years. i 1995-1996. j Refugee figure relates to the end of 2012. k Based on monthly averages for the period 1971-2000.

Azerbaijan

Region	Western Asia
Currency	Azerbaijan Manat (AZN)
Surface area (square kilometres)	86 600
Population in 2012 (estimated, 000)	9 309[a]
Population density in 2012 (per square kilometre)	107.5
Capital city and population in 2011 (000)	Baku (2 123)
United Nations membership date	2 March 1992

Economic indicators	2005	2010	2012
GDP: Gross domestic product (million current US$)	13 245	52 906	68 727
GDP: Growth rate at constant 2005 prices (annual %)	28.0	4.6	2.1
GDP per capita (current US$)	1 546.8	5 817.2	7 382.9
GNI: Gross national income per capita (current US$)	1 370.3	5 468.9	6 877.8
Gross fixed capital formation (% of GDP)	41.3	18.2	21.9
Exchange rates (national currency per US$)[b]	0.92	0.80	0.78
Balance of payments, current account (million US$)	167	15 040	14 976
CPI: Consumer price index (2000=100)	125	204	...
Industrial production index (2005=100)	100	200	186
Agricultural production index (2004-2006=100)	104	118	132
Food production index (2004-2006=100)	103	122	137
Unemployment (% of labour force)	5.7[c]	5.7	5.3
Employment in industrial sector (% of employed)	12.1[de]	13.7[f]	14.3[f]
Employment in agricultural sector (% of employed)	39.3[de]	38.2[f]	37.7[f]
Labour force participation, adult female pop. (%)	59.6	61.8	62.5
Labour force participation, adult male pop. (%)	69.2	67.4	68.9
Tourist arrivals at national borders (000)	693	1 280	1 986
Energy production, primary (000 mt oil equivalent)	28 101	67 370[g]	...
Mobile-cellular subscriptions (per 100 inhabitants)	26.1	99.1	107.5
Individuals using the Internet (%)	8.0	46.0[h]	54.2[i]

Total trade		Major trading partners			2012
(million US$)		(% of exports)			(% of imports)
Exports	23 827.2	Italy	23.3	Turkey	15.8
Imports	9 641.7	India	7.9	Russian Federation	14.3
Balance	14 185.5	France	7.5	Germany	8.1

Social indicators		
Population growth rate (average annual %)[a]	2010-2015	1.1
Urban population growth rate (average annual %)[a]	2010-2015	1.6
Rural population growth rate (average annual %)[a]	2010-2015	0.7
Urban population (%)[a]	2013	54.1
Population aged 0-14 years (%)[a]	2013	22.2
Population aged 60+ years (females and males, % of total)[a]	2013	9.7/7.4
Sex ratio (males per 100 females)[a]	2013	98.8
Life expectancy at birth (females and males, years)[a]	2010-2015	73.8/67.5
Infant mortality rate (per 1 000 live births)[a]	2010-2015	39.6
Fertility rate, total (live births per woman)[a]	2010-2015	1.9
Contraceptive prevalence (ages 15-49, %)	2006-2012	51.1
International migrant stock (000 and % of total population)[aj]	mid-2013	323.8/3.4
Refugees and others of concern to UNHCR	mid-2013	605 548
Education: Government expenditure (% of GDP)	2006-2012	2.4
Education: Primary-secondary gross enrolment ratio (f/m per 100)[k]	2006-2012	97.2/99.2
Education: Female third-level students (% of total)	2006-2012	50.0
Intentional homicides (females and males, per 100 000)	2008-2010	6.7/23.6
Seats held by women in national parliaments (%)	2014	15.6

Environmental indicators		
Threatened species	2013	48
Forested area (% of land area)	2011	11.3
CO_2 emission estimates (000 metric tons and metric tons per capita)	2010	45 694/5.0
Energy consumption per capita (kilograms oil equivalent)	2010	1 255.0
Precipitation in the capital city, total mean (millimetres)		210[l]
Temperature in the capital city, mean °C (minimum and maximum)		12.0/18.1[l]

a Includes Nagorno-Karabakh. **b** Official rate. **c** 2008. **d** Official estimates. **e** The indices are shown in terms of ISIC Rev.3. **f** December. **g** UNSD estimate. **h** Age group 7 years and over. **i** ITU estimate. **j** Includes refugees. **k** National estimate. **l** Based on monthly averages for the period 1971-1990.

Bahamas

Region	Caribbean
Currency	Bahamian Dollar (BSD)
Surface area (square kilometres)	13 943
Population in 2012 (estimated, 000)	372
Population density in 2012 (per square kilometre)	26.7
Capital city and population in 2011 (000)	Nassau (254)
United Nations membership date	18 September 1973

Economic indicators	2005	2010	2012
GDP: Gross domestic product (million current US$)	7 706	7 771	8 043
GDP: Growth rate at constant 2005 prices (annual %)	3.4	0.2	2.5
GDP per capita (current US$)	23 416.9	21 557.0	21 623.9
GNI: Gross national income per capita (current US$)	23 021.9	20 981.3	21 101.7
Gross fixed capital formation (% of GDP)	24.2	23.4	28.6
Balance of payments, current account (million US$)	−701	−814	−1 500
CPI: Consumer price index (2000=100)	110	125	129[a]
Agricultural production index (2004-2006=100)	99	126	132
Food production index (2004-2006=100)	99	126	132
Employment in industrial sector (% of employed)[b]	17.8[c]	16.0[cde]	12.9[af]
Employment in agricultural sector (% of employed)[b]	3.5[c]	2.9[cde]	3.7[af]
Labour force participation, adult female pop. (%)	67.7	69.2	69.3
Labour force participation, adult male pop. (%)	77.8	79.3	79.3
Tourist arrivals at national borders (000)	1 608	1 370	1 422
Mobile-cellular subscriptions (per 100 inhabitants)	71.3	124.9	72.3[g]
Individuals using the Internet (%)[g]	25.0	43.0	71.8

Total trade		Major trading partners			2012
	(million US$)		(% of exports)		(% of imports)[h]
Exports	828.7	United States	81.6	United States	84.5
Imports	3 646.5	Germany	3.4	Trinidad and Tobago	3.9
Balance	−2 817.8	France	3.2	Areas nes	2.6

Social indicators		
Population growth rate (average annual %)	2010-2015	1.5
Urban population growth rate (average annual %)	2010-2015	1.4
Rural population growth rate (average annual %)	2010-2015	−0.1
Urban population (%)	2013	84.6
Population aged 0-14 years (%)	2013	21.3
Population aged 60+ years (females and males, % of total)	2013	13.0/10.3
Sex ratio (males per 100 females)	2013	95.8
Life expectancy at birth (females and males, years)	2010-2015	78.1/72.0
Infant mortality rate (per 1 000 live births)	2010-2015	9.1
Fertility rate, total (live births per woman)	2010-2015	1.9
Contraceptive prevalence (ages 15-49, %)[i]	2006-2012	61.7[j]
International migrant stock (000 and % of total population)	mid-2013	61.3/16.3
Refugees and others of concern to UNHCR	mid-2013	89
Education: Government expenditure (% of GDP)[k]	2006-2012	2.9[l]
Education: Primary-secondary gross enrolment ratio (f/m per 100)	2006-2012	101.6/98.1
Intentional homicides (females and males, per 100 000)	2008-2010	5.8/46.6
Seats held by women in national parliaments (%)	2014	13.2

Environmental indicators		
Threatened species	2013	71
Forested area (% of land area)	2011	51.5
CO_2 emission estimates (000 metric tons and metric tons per capita)	2010	2 462/7.2
Energy consumption per capita (kilograms oil equivalent)	2010	2 401.0
Precipitation in the capital city, total mean (millimetres)		1 396[m]
Temperature in the capital city, mean °C (minimum and maximum)		20.7/28.9[m]

a 2011. b The indices are shown in terms of ISIC Rev.3. c April. d 2009. e Break in series; data not strictly comparable. f May. g ITU estimate. h See technical notes. i Age group 15 to 44 years. j 1988. k UNESCO estimate. l 2000. m Based on monthly averages for the period 1971-2000.

Bahrain

Region	Western Asia
Currency	Bahraini Dinar (BHD)
Surface area (square kilometres)	767
Population in 2012 (estimated, 000)	1 318
Population density in 2012 (per square kilometre)	1 718.2
Capital city and population in 2011 (000)	Manama (262)
United Nations membership date	21 September 1971

Economic indicators	2005	2010	2012
GDP: Gross domestic product (million current US$)	15 969	25 713	30 362
GDP: Growth rate at constant 2005 prices (annual %)	6.8	4.3	3.4
GDP per capita (current US$)	18 156.0	20 545.8	23 039.4
GNI: Gross national income per capita (current US$)	17 686.1	18 649.5	20 127.7
Gross fixed capital formation (% of GDP)	25.7	26.1	19.5
Exchange rates (national currency per US$)[a]	0.38	0.38	0.38
Balance of payments, current account (million US$)	1 474	770	2 938
CPI: Consumer price index (2000=100)	105	120	123
Industrial production index (2005=100)[b]	100	120	121
Agricultural production index (2004-2006=100)	92	115	169
Food production index (2004-2006=100)	92	115	169
Employment in industrial sector (% of employed)[c]	15.0[bde]	35.3[fg]	...
Employment in agricultural sector (% of employed)[c]	0.8[bde]	1.1[fg]	...
Labour force participation, adult female pop. (%)	36.3	39.3	39.4
Labour force participation, adult male pop. (%)	83.4	87.2	87.2
Tourist arrivals at national borders (000)[h]	6 313	11 952	6 732[i]
Energy production, primary (000 mt oil equivalent)	16 759	18 560	...
Mobile-cellular subscriptions (per 100 inhabitants)	105.8	124.2	156.2
Individuals using the Internet (%)	21.3	55.0	88.0[j]

Total trade		Major trading partners		2012
	(million US$)[i]	(% of exports)[i]		(% of imports)[i]
Exports	22 561.9	...	Saudi Arabia	45.9
Imports	17 643.3	...	China	7.7
Balance	4 918.6	...	Brazil	7.1

Social indicators		
Population growth rate (average annual %)	2010-2015	1.7
Urban population growth rate (average annual %)	2010-2015	2.2
Rural population growth rate (average annual %)	2010-2015	1.5
Urban population (%)	2013	88.8
Population aged 0-14 years (%)	2013	21.0
Population aged 60+ years (females and males, % of total)	2013	4.4/3.1
Sex ratio (males per 100 females)	2013	164.4
Life expectancy at birth (females and males, years)	2010-2015	77.4/75.8
Infant mortality rate (per 1 000 live births)	2010-2015	6.9
Fertility rate, total (live births per woman)	2010-2015	2.1
Contraceptive prevalence (ages 15-49, %)	2006-2012	61.8[k]
International migrant stock (000 and % of total population)[l]	mid-2013	729.4/54.8
Refugees and others of concern to UNHCR	mid-2013	341
Education: Government expenditure (% of GDP)	2006-2012	2.9
Education: Primary-secondary gross enrolment ratio (f/m per 100)	2006-2012	101.6/99.7[m]
Education: Female third-level students (% of total)	2006-2012	59.2
Intentional homicides (females and males, per 100 000)	2008-2010	0.0/0.0
Seats held by women in national parliaments (%)	2014	10.0

Environmental indicators		
Threatened species	2013	33
Forested area (% of land area)	2011	0.7
CO_2 emission estimates (000 metric tons and metric tons per capita)	2010	24 182/19.2
Energy consumption per capita (kilograms oil equivalent)	2010	8 369.0
Precipitation in the capital city, total mean (millimetres)		71[n]
Temperature in the capital city, mean °C (minimum and maximum)		23.0/30.1[n]

a Official rate. b The indices are shown in terms of ISIC Rev.3. c Break in series; data not strictly comparable. d 2004. e November. f Population census. g April. h Arrivals of non-resident visitors at national borders. i 2011. j Age group 15 years and over. k 1995. l Data refer to foreign citizens. m 1999. n Based on monthly averages for the period 1961-1990.

Bangladesh

Region	Southern Asia
Currency	Taka (BDT)
Surface area (square kilometres)	147 570
Population in 2012 (estimated, 000)	154 695
Population density in 2012 (per square kilometre)	1 048.3
Capital city and population in 2011 (000)	Dhaka (15 391)
United Nations membership date	17 September 1974

Economic indicators	2005	2010	2012
GDP: Gross domestic product (million current US$)	64 989	112 412	127 195
GDP: Growth rate at constant 2005 prices (annual %)	6.0	5.8	6.5
GDP per capita (current US$)	454.0	743.8	822.2
GNI: Gross national income per capita (current US$)	472.7	805.2	892.8
Gross fixed capital formation (% of GDP)	26.8	26.7	28.7
Exchange rates (national currency per US$)[a]	66.21	70.75	79.85
Balance of payments, current account (million US$)	−176	2 106	2 648
CPI: Consumer price index (2000=100)[b]	127	183	221
Industrial production index (2005=100)[cd]	100	148	190
Agricultural production index (2004-2006=100)	103	129	107
Food production index (2004-2006=100)	103	130	105
Employment in industrial sector (% of employed)	14.5[ce]	...	...
Employment in agricultural sector (% of employed)	48.1[ce]	...	...
Labour force participation, adult female pop. (%)	55.5	56.9	57.3
Labour force participation, adult male pop. (%)	85.0	84.2	84.1
Tourist arrivals at national borders (000)	208	303	...
Energy production, primary (000 mt oil equivalent)	12 262	18 967	...
Mobile-cellular subscriptions (per 100 inhabitants)	6.4	45.7	63.8
Individuals using the Internet (%)[f]	0.2	3.7	6.3

Social indicators		
Population growth rate (average annual %)	2010-2015	1.2
Urban population growth rate (average annual %)	2010-2015	3.0
Rural population growth rate (average annual %)	2010-2015	0.6
Urban population (%)	2013	29.4
Population aged 0-14 years (%)	2013	30.0
Population aged 60+ years (females and males, % of total)	2013	6.8/7.2
Sex ratio (males per 100 females)	2013	102.4
Life expectancy at birth (females and males, years)	2010-2015	71.3/69.8
Infant mortality rate (per 1 000 live births)	2010-2015	32.4
Fertility rate, total (live births per woman)	2010-2015	2.2
Contraceptive prevalence (ages 15-49, %)	2006-2012	61.2
International migrant stock (000 and % of total population)[g]	mid-2013	1 396.5/0.9
Refugees and others of concern to UNHCR	mid-2013	231 146
Education: Government expenditure (% of GDP)	2006-2012	2.2
Education: Primary-secondary gross enrolment ratio (f/m per 100)[h]	2006-2012	80.8/73.7
Education: Female third-level students (% of total)	2006-2012	40.5
Intentional homicides (females and males, per 100 000)[i]	2008-2010	4.3/12.4
Seats held by women in national parliaments (%)	2014	20.0

Environmental indicators		
Threatened species	2013	130
Forested area (% of land area)	2011	11.1
CO$_2$ emission estimates (000 metric tons and metric tons per capita)	2010	56 107/0.4
Energy consumption per capita (kilograms oil equivalent)	2010	159.0
Precipitation in the capital city, total mean (millimetres)		2 154[j]
Temperature in the capital city, mean °C (minimum and maximum)		21.5/30.6[j]

a Principal rate. **b** Government officials. **c** The indices are shown in terms of ISIC Rev.3. **d** Average of 12 months ending 30 June of the year stated. **e** Year ending in June of the year indicated. **f** ITU estimate. **g** Includes refugees. **h** National estimate. **i** Estimates. **j** Based on monthly averages for the period 1971-2000.

Barbados

Region	Caribbean
Currency	Barbados Dollar (BBD)
Surface area (square kilometres)	430
Population in 2012 (estimated, 000)	283
Population density in 2012 (per square kilometre)	658.7
Capital city and population in 2011 (000)	Bridgetown (122)
United Nations membership date	9 December 1966

Economic indicators	2005	2010	2012
GDP: Gross domestic product (million current US$)	3 908	4 245	4 533
GDP: Growth rate at constant 2005 prices (annual %)	4.0	0.2	0.7
GDP per capita (current US$)	14 285.7	15 139.7	16 004.3
GNI: Gross national income per capita (current US$)	13 583.0	13 969.7	14 739.2
Gross fixed capital formation (% of GDP)	18.9	14.0	16.3
Exchange rates (national currency per US$)[a]	2.00	2.00	2.00
Balance of payments, current account (million US$)	−466	−218	...
CPI: Consumer price index (2000=100)	113	149	170
Industrial production index (2005=100)[b]	100	88	81
Agricultural production index (2004-2006=100)	106	92	97
Food production index (2004-2006=100)	106	92	97
Unemployment (% of labour force)	9.1	10.8	11.6
Employment in industrial sector (% of employed)	17.3[cd]	19.6[ef]	19.4[e]
Employment in agricultural sector (% of employed)	3.3[cd]	2.8[ef]	2.8[e]
Labour force participation, adult female pop. (%)	65.0	65.9	65.9
Labour force participation, adult male pop. (%)	76.4	76.7	76.7
Tourist arrivals at national borders (000)	548	532	536
Energy production, primary (000 mt oil equivalent)	90	60	...
Mobile-cellular subscriptions (per 100 inhabitants)	76.2	128.1	126.4[g]
Individuals using the Internet (%)[g]	52.5	68.1	73.3

Total trade	Major trading partners		2012
(million US$)	(% of exports)[h]		(% of imports)
Exports 566.4	United States	26.3	United States 31.0
Imports 1 767.8	Areas nes	24.1	Trinidad and Tobago 28.9
Balance −1 201.4	Trinidad and Tobago	11.5	Suriname 6.2

Social indicators

Population growth rate (average annual %)	2010-2015	0.5
Urban population growth rate (average annual %)	2010-2015	1.4
Rural population growth rate (average annual %)	2010-2015	−0.7
Urban population (%)	2013	45.4
Population aged 0-14 years (%)	2013	18.9
Population aged 60+ years (females and males, % of total)	2013	18.0/14.3
Sex ratio (males per 100 females)	2013	99.6
Life expectancy at birth (females and males, years)	2010-2015	77.7/72.9
Infant mortality rate (per 1 000 live births)	2010-2015	10.1
Fertility rate, total (live births per woman)	2010-2015	1.9
Contraceptive prevalence (ages 15-49, %)[i]	2006-2012	55.0[j]
International migrant stock (000 and % of total population)	mid-2013	32.3/11.3
Refugees and others of concern to UNHCR	mid-2013	2
Education: Government expenditure (% of GDP)	2006-2012	7.5
Education: Primary-secondary gross enrolment ratio (f/m per 100)[k]	2006-2012	107.5/102.7
Education: Female third-level students (% of total)	2006-2012	69.1
Intentional homicides (females and males, per 100 000)	2008-2010	7.3/15.5
Seats held by women in national parliaments (%)	2014	16.7

Environmental indicators

Threatened species	2013	44
Forested area (% of land area)	2011	19.4
CO_2 emission estimates (000 metric tons and metric tons per capita)	2010	1 502/5.5
Energy consumption per capita (kilograms oil equivalent)	2010	1 655.0

a Official rate. **b** The indices are shown in terms of ISIC Rev.3. **c** 2004. **d** The indices are shown in terms of ISIC Rev.2. **e** Average of quarterly estimates. **f** Break in series; data not strictly comparable. **g** ITU estimate. **h** See technical notes. **i** Age group 15 to 44 years. **j** 1988. **k** National estimate.

Belarus

Region	Eastern Europe
Currency	Belarussian Ruble (BYR)
Surface area (square kilometres)	207 600
Population in 2012 (estimated, 000)	9 405
Population density in 2012 (per square kilometre)	45.3
Capital city and population in 2011 (000)	Minsk (1 861)
United Nations membership date	24 October 1945

Economic indicators	2005	2010	2012
GDP: Gross domestic product (million current US$)	30 210	55 221	63 259
GDP: Growth rate at constant 2005 prices (annual %)	9.4	7.7	1.5
GDP per capita (current US$)	3 125.8	5 818.2	6 726.1
GNI: Gross national income per capita (current US$)	3 131.6	5 695.7	6 561.9
Gross fixed capital formation (% of GDP)	26.5	39.3	32.9
Exchange rates (national currency per US$)[a]	2 152.00	3 000.00	8 570.00
Balance of payments, current account (million US$)	459	−8 280	−1 688
CPI: Consumer price index (2000=100)	384[b]	623[c]	...
Industrial production index (2005=100)[d]	100	146	168
Agricultural production index (2004-2006=100)	98	117	121
Food production index (2004-2006=100)	98	117	121
Unemployment (% of labour force)[e]	...	1.2	0.6
Labour force participation, adult female pop. (%)	50.8	49.5	49.9
Labour force participation, adult male pop. (%)	62.8	61.7	62.7
Tourist arrivals at national borders (000)[f]	91	120	119
Energy production, primary (000 mt oil equivalent)	2 542	2 487	...
Mobile-cellular subscriptions (per 100 inhabitants)	41.7	107.7	112.1
Individuals using the Internet (%)[g]	16.2[h]	31.8	46.9

Total trade		Major trading partners			2012
	(million US$)		(% of exports)		(% of imports)
Exports	46 059.9	Russian Federation	35.1	Russian Federation	58.8
Imports	46 404.4	Netherlands	16.4	Germany	5.9
Balance	−344.5	Ukraine	12.1	China	5.1

Social indicators		
Population growth rate (average annual %)	2010-2015	−0.5
Urban population growth rate (average annual %)	2010-2015	0.2
Rural population growth rate (average annual %)	2010-2015	−2.0
Urban population (%)	2013	75.9
Population aged 0-14 years (%)	2013	15.3
Population aged 60+ years (females and males, % of total)	2013	23.8/14.6
Sex ratio (males per 100 females)	2013	86.6
Life expectancy at birth (females and males, years)	2010-2015	75.7/64.1
Infant mortality rate (per 1 000 live births)	2010-2015	5.6
Fertility rate, total (live births per woman)	2010-2015	1.5
Contraceptive prevalence (ages 15-49, %)	2006-2012	72.6[i]
International migrant stock (000 and % of total population)	mid-2013	1 085.4/11.6
Refugees and others of concern to UNHCR	mid-2013	7 002
Education: Government expenditure (% of GDP)	2006-2012	5.2
Education: Primary-secondary gross enrolment ratio (f/m per 100)	2006-2012	102.6/105.0
Education: Female third-level students (% of total)[j]	2006-2012	56.9
Intentional homicides (females and males, per 100 000)	2008-2010	3.8/6.5
Seats held by women in national parliaments (%)	2014	26.6

Environmental indicators		
Threatened species	2013	22
Forested area (% of land area)	2011	42.7
CO$_2$ emission estimates (000 metric tons and metric tons per capita)	2010	62 171/6.5
Energy consumption per capita (kilograms oil equivalent)	2010	2 783.0
Precipitation in the capital city, total mean (millimetres)		677[k]
Temperature in the capital city, mean °C (minimum and maximum)		2.1/9.9[k]

a Official rate. **b** Annual average is the weighted mean of monthly data. **c** Series linked to former series. **d** The indices are shown in terms of ISIC Rev.3. **e** Official estimates. **f** Organized tourism. **g** Age group 16 years and over. **h** 2006. **i** 2005. **j** National estimate. **k** Based on monthly averages for the period 1971-2000.

Belgium

Region	Western Europe
Currency	Euro (EUR)
Surface area (square kilometres)	30 528
Population in 2012 (estimated, 000)	11 060
Population density in 2012 (per square kilometre)	362.3
Capital city and population in 2011 (000)	Brussels (1 486)[a]
United Nations membership date	27 December 1945

Economic indicators	2005	2010	2012
GDP: Gross domestic product (million current US$)	377 350	471 586	483 342
GDP: Growth rate at constant 2005 prices (annual %)	1.8	2.4	−0.3
GDP per capita (current US$)	35 910.5	43 101.6	43 706.9
GNI: Gross national income per capita (current US$)	36 145.8	43 949.0	44 125.5
Gross fixed capital formation (% of GDP)	20.7	20.0	20.7
Exchange rates (national currency per US$)[b]	0.85	0.75	0.76
Balance of payments, current account (million US$)	7 703	8 468	−9 698
CPI: Consumer price index (2000=100)	111	123	131
Industrial production index (2005=100)	100	117	119
Agricultural production index (2004-2006=100)	100	101	100
Food production index (2004-2006=100)	100	101	100
Unemployment (% of labour force)[c]	8.4	8.3	7.5
Employment in industrial sector (% of employed)[d]	24.7[e]	23.4	21.8
Employment in agricultural sector (% of employed)[d]	2.0[e]	1.4	1.2
Labour force participation, adult female pop. (%)	45.6	47.6	46.9
Labour force participation, adult male pop. (%)	61.3	60.6	59.4
Tourist arrivals at national borders (000)[f]	6 747	7 186	7 591
Energy production, primary (000 mt oil equivalent)	4 321	4 788	...
Mobile-cellular subscriptions (per 100 inhabitants)	92.2	113.5[gh]	119.4
Individuals using the Internet (%)	55.8[i]	75.0	82.0[j]

Total trade

	(million US$)
Exports	446 854.4
Imports	437 882.7
Balance	8 971.7

Major trading partners 2012

(% of exports)		(% of imports)	
Germany	17.4	Netherlands	20.7
France	15.6	Germany	14.1
Netherlands	12.5	France	10.5

Social indicators		
Population growth rate (average annual %)	2010-2015	0.4
Urban population growth rate (average annual %)	2010-2015	0.3
Rural population growth rate (average annual %)	2010-2015	−0.9
Urban population (%)	2013	97.6
Population aged 0-14 years (%)	2013	17.0
Population aged 60+ years (females and males, % of total)	2013	26.1/21.0
Sex ratio (males per 100 females)	2013	96.4
Life expectancy at birth (females and males, years)	2010-2015	83.0/77.9
Infant mortality rate (per 1 000 live births)	2010-2015	3.2
Fertility rate, total (live births per woman)	2010-2015	1.9
Contraceptive prevalence (ages 15-49, %)	2006-2012	74.6[k]
International migrant stock (000 and % of total population)[l]	mid-2013	1 159.8/10.4
Refugees and others of concern to UNHCR	mid-2013	27 599[m]
Education: Government expenditure (% of GDP)	2006-2012	6.6
Education: Primary-secondary gross enrolment ratio (f/m per 100)	2006-2012	104.2/106.0
Education: Female third-level students (% of total)	2006-2012	55.3
Intentional homicides (females and males, per 100 000)	2008-2010	1.5/2.2
Seats held by women in national parliaments (%)	2014	41.3

Environmental indicators		
Threatened species	2013	31
Forested area (% of land area)	2011	22.4
CO$_2$ emission estimates (000 metric tons and metric tons per capita)	2010	108 857/10.2
Energy consumption per capita (kilograms oil equivalent)	2010	3 790.0
Precipitation in the capital city, total mean (millimetres)		820[n]
Temperature in the capital city, mean °C (minimum and maximum)		6.7/13.9[n]

a Demographic Yearbook 2012. b Market rate. c Age group 15 to 64 years. d European Labour Force Survey (Eurostat). e The indices are shown in terms of ISIC Rev.3. f Arrivals of non-resident tourists in all types of accommodation establishments. g Number of active clients. h Includes mobile virtual network operator. i ITU estimate. j Age group 16 to 74 years. k 2004. l Data refer to foreign citizens. m Refugee figure relates to the end of 2012. n Based on monthly averages for the period 1971-2000.

Belize

Region	Central America
Currency	Belize Dollar (BZD)
Surface area (square kilometres)	22 966
Population in 2012 (estimated, 000)	324
Population density in 2012 (per square kilometre)	14.1
Capital city and population in 2011 (000)	Belmopan (14)
United Nations membership date	25 September 1981

Economic indicators	2005	2010	2012
GDP: Gross domestic product (million current US$)	1 114	1 398	1 554
GDP: Growth rate at constant 2005 prices (annual %)	3.0	3.9	19.7
GDP per capita (current US$)	4 097.6	4 529.9	4 795.5
GNI: Gross national income per capita (current US$)	3 646.4	4 016.7	4 380.2
Gross fixed capital formation (% of GDP)	18.5	15.3	19.0
Exchange rates (national currency per US$)[a]	2.00	2.00	2.00
Balance of payments, current account (million US$)	−151	−46	−28
CPI: Consumer price index (2000=100)	113	128	132
Agricultural production index (2004-2006=100)	96	92	95
Food production index (2004-2006=100)	96	92	95
Employment in industrial sector (% of employed)	17.9[bcde]	...	...
Employment in agricultural sector (% of employed)	19.5[bcde]	...	...
Labour force participation, adult female pop. (%)	44.8	48.8	49.1
Labour force participation, adult male pop. (%)	80.8	82.1	82.3
Tourist arrivals at national borders (000)	237	242	277
Energy production, primary (000 mt oil equivalent)	6	238	...
Mobile-cellular subscriptions (per 100 inhabitants)	34.2[f]	62.3[gh]	50.6[gi]
Individuals using the Internet (%)	9.2	14.0[f]	25.0[f]

Total trade		Major trading partners			2012
	(million US$)	(% of exports)		(% of imports)	
Exports	340.4	United States	46.3	United States	29.3
Imports	880.3	United Kingdom	22.8	Curaçao	14.1
Balance	−539.9	Netherlands	7.6	China	12.5

Social indicators		
Population growth rate (average annual %)	2010-2015	2.4
Urban population growth rate (average annual %)	2010-2015	1.5
Rural population growth rate (average annual %)	2010-2015	2.3
Urban population (%)	2013	44.3
Population aged 0-14 years (%)	2013	33.9
Population aged 60+ years (females and males, % of total)	2013	6.2/5.8
Sex ratio (males per 100 females)	2013	99.8
Life expectancy at birth (females and males, years)	2010-2015	77.0/70.8
Infant mortality rate (per 1 000 live births)	2010-2015	12.9
Fertility rate, total (live births per woman)	2010-2015	2.7
Contraceptive prevalence (ages 15-49, %)	2006-2012	34.3
International migrant stock (000 and % of total population)[j]	mid-2013	50.9/15.3
Refugees and others of concern to UNHCR	mid-2013	92
Education: Government expenditure (% of GDP)	2006-2012	6.6
Education: Primary-secondary gross enrolment ratio (f/m per 100)	2006-2012	103.1/102.7
Education: Female third-level students (% of total)	2006-2012	62.4
Intentional homicides (females and males, per 100 000)	2008-2010	10.1/73.5
Seats held by women in national parliaments (%)	2014	3.1

Environmental indicators		
Threatened species	2013	103
Forested area (% of land area)	2011	60.7
CO$_2$ emission estimates (000 metric tons and metric tons per capita)	2010	421/1.4
Energy consumption per capita (kilograms oil equivalent)	2010	573.0[k]
Precipitation in the capital city, total mean (millimetres)		2 020[l]
Temperature in the capital city, mean °C (minimum and maximum)		20.3/30.9[l]

a Official rate. b The indices are shown in terms of ISIC Rev.3. c Age group 14 years and over. d April. e Break in series; data not strictly comparable. f ITU estimate. g December. h Includes Mobile GSM and AMPS Post and Pre Mobile Base. i Includes Mobile GSM and Pre Mobile Base. j Includes refugees. k UNSD estimate. l Based on monthly averages for the period 1980-2003.

Benin

Region	Western Africa
Currency	CFA Franc (XOF)
Surface area (square kilometres)	114 763
Population in 2012 (estimated, 000)	10 051
Population density in 2012 (per square kilometre)	87.6
Capital city and population in 2011 (000)	Porto-Novo (315)[a]
United Nations membership date	20 September 1960

Economic indicators	2005	2010	2012
GDP: Gross domestic product (million current US$)	4 358	6 558	7 557
GDP: Growth rate at constant 2005 prices (annual %)	2.9	2.6	5.4
GDP per capita (current US$)	532.6	689.6	751.9
GNI: Gross national income per capita (current US$)	529.0	691.5	750.0
Gross fixed capital formation (% of GDP)	19.4	20.5	19.9
Exchange rates (national currency per US$)[b]	556.04	490.91	497.16
Balance of payments, current account (million US$)	−226	−530	−516[c]
CPI: Consumer price index (2000=100)[d]	115	134[e]	147
Industrial production index (2005=100)[f]	100	129	139
Agricultural production index (2004-2006=100)	102	115	134
Food production index (2004-2006=100)	102	122	138
Labour force participation, adult female pop. (%)	66.2	67.3	67.5
Labour force participation, adult male pop. (%)	78.7	78.4	78.3
Tourist arrivals at national borders (000)	176	199	220
Mobile-cellular subscriptions (per 100 inhabitants)	7.8	79.9	89.9
Individuals using the Internet (%)	1.3	3.1	3.8[g]

Total trade[h]		Major trading partners			2012
	(million US$)[h]	(% of exports)[h]			(% of imports)[h]
Exports	434.5	Nigeria	48.5	France	16.3
Imports	1 494.3	China	11.6	China	12.6
Balance	−1 059.8	India	5.2	Togo	10.9

Social indicators

Population growth rate (average annual %)	2010-2015	2.7
Urban population growth rate (average annual %)	2010-2015	4.1
Rural population growth rate (average annual %)	2010-2015	1.5
Urban population (%)	2013	46.2
Population aged 0-14 years (%)	2013	42.8
Population aged 60+ years (females and males, % of total)	2013	5.2/4.0
Sex ratio (males per 100 females)	2013	99.3
Life expectancy at birth (females and males, years)	2010-2015	60.6/57.8
Infant mortality rate (per 1 000 live births)	2010-2015	68.7
Fertility rate, total (live births per woman)	2010-2015	4.9
Contraceptive prevalence (ages 15-49, %)	2006-2012	17.0
International migrant stock (000 and % of total population)[i][j]	mid-2013	234.2/2.3
Refugees and others of concern to UNHCR	mid-2013	5 233
Education: Government expenditure (% of GDP)	2006-2012	5.4
Education: Primary-secondary gross enrolment ratio (f/m per 100)	2006-2012	74.2/93.4
Education: Female third-level students (% of total)	2006-2012	21.2
Intentional homicides (females and males, per 100 000)[k]	2008-2010	4.9/25.6
Seats held by women in national parliaments (%)	2014	8.4

Environmental indicators

Threatened species	2013	69
Forested area (% of land area)	2011	40.0
CO_2 emission estimates (000 metric tons and metric tons per capita)	2010	5 185/0.6
Energy consumption per capita (kilograms oil equivalent)	2010	178.0
Precipitation in the capital city, total mean (millimetres)[d]		1 308[l]
Temperature in the capital city, mean °C (minimum and maximum)[d]		24.3/30.1[l]

a Porto-Novo is the constitutional capital and Cotonou is the seat of government. b Official rate. c 2011.
d Cotonou. e Series linked to former series. f The indices are shown in terms of ISIC Rev.3. g ITU estimate.
h 2010. i Data refer to foreign-born and foreign citizens. j Includes refugees. k Estimates. l Based on WMO
Climatological Normals (CLINO) for the period 1961-1990.

Bermuda

Region	Northern America
Currency	Bermuda Dollar (BMD)
Surface area (square kilometres)	53
Population in 2012 (estimated, 000)	65
Population density in 2012 (per square kilometre)	1 230.5
Capital city and population in 2011 (000)	Hamilton (11)

Economic indicators	2005	2010	2012
GDP: Gross domestic product (million current US$)	4 868	5 757	5 593
GDP: Growth rate at constant 2005 prices (annual %)	1.7	−2.2	−1.3
GDP per capita (current US$)	75 902.1	88 642.7	85 762.3
GNI: Gross national income per capita (current US$)	93 848.1	110 779.9	105 170.6
Gross fixed capital formation (% of GDP)	19.6	18.8	18.8
Balance of payments, current account (million US$)	1 252[a]	696	771
CPI: Consumer price index (2000=100)	116	136	143
Agricultural production index (2004-2006=100)	98	116	120
Food production index (2004-2006=100)	98	116	120
Employment in industrial sector (% of employed)	12.1[bcd]	...	...
Employment in agricultural sector (% of employed)	1.7[bce]	...	...
Tourist arrivals at national borders (000)[f]	270	232	232
Mobile-cellular subscriptions (per 100 inhabitants)	82.2	135.8[g]	139.6[g]
Individuals using the Internet (%)	65.5	84.2[g]	91.3[g]

Total trade	Major trading partners				2012
(million US$)	(% of exports)[h]		(% of imports)	
Exports	9.6	United States	55.2	United States	69.3
Imports	866.9	Areas nes	31.3	Canada	11.1
Balance	−857.3	United Kingdom	7.3	United Kingdom	3.7

Social indicators

Population growth rate (average annual %)	2010-2015	0.2
Urban population growth rate (average annual %)	2010-2015	0.2
Rural population growth rate (average annual %)	2010-2015	0.0
Urban population (%)	2013	100.0
Population aged 0-14 years (%)[ijkl]	2013	16.4[m]
Population aged 60+ years (females and males, % of total)[ijkl]	2013	20.9/17.5[m]
Sex ratio (males per 100 females)[ijkl]	2013	92.5[m]
Life expectancy at birth (females and males, years)[i]	2010-2015	82.4/77.2[n]
Fertility rate, total (live births per woman)[i]	2010-2015	1.8[n]
International migrant stock (000 and % of total population)	mid-2013	19.1/29.2
Education: Government expenditure (% of GDP)	2006-2012	2.6
Education: Primary-secondary gross enrolment ratio (f/m per 100)	2006-2012	86.0/80.2
Education: Female third-level students (% of total)	2006-2012	66.4

Environmental indicators

Threatened species	2013	56
Forested area (% of land area)	2011	20.0
CO$_2$ emission estimates (000 metric tons and metric tons per capita)	2010	476/7.3
Energy consumption per capita (kilograms oil equivalent)	2010	2 413.0[o]
Precipitation in the capital city, total mean (millimetres)		1 410[p]
Temperature in the capital city, mean °C (minimum and maximum)		19.6/24.4[p]

a 2006. b 2004. c The indices are shown in terms of ISIC Rev.2. d Excludes mining and quarrying. e Break in series; data not strictly comparable. f Air arrivals. g ITU estimate. h See technical notes. i Data compiled by the United Nations Demographic Yearbook system. j Data refer to the latest available census. k Census, de jure, complete tabulation. l Bermuda is 100% urban. m 2010. n 2012. o UNSD estimate. p Based on monthly averages for the period 1949-1999.

Bhutan

Region	Southern Asia
Currency	Ngultrum (BTN)
Surface area (square kilometres)	38 394
Population in 2012 (estimated, 000)	742
Population density in 2012 (per square kilometre)	19.3
Capital city and population in 2011 (000)	Thimphu (99)
United Nations membership date	21 September 1971

Economic indicators	2005	2010	2012
GDP: Gross domestic product (million current US$)	819	1 585	1 861
GDP: Growth rate at constant 2005 prices (annual %)	7.1	11.7	4.6
GDP per capita (current US$)	1 259.0	2 211.4	2 508.9
GNI: Gross national income per capita (current US$)	1 241.2	2 112.3	2 386.0
Gross fixed capital formation (% of GDP)	53.4	59.9	64.0
Exchange rates (national currency per US$)[a]	45.06	44.81	54.78
Balance of payments, current account (million US$)	−38[b]	−142	−350
CPI: Consumer price index (2000=100)	117	156	188
Agricultural production index (2004-2006=100)	106	95	110
Food production index (2004-2006=100)	106	95	110
Employment in industrial sector (% of employed)[c]	17.2[def]	6.7[g]	8.6[g]
Employment in agricultural sector (% of employed)[c]	43.6[def]	59.5[g]	62.2[g]
Labour force participation, adult female pop. (%)	63.5	65.9	66.4
Labour force participation, adult male pop. (%)	77.6	76.0	76.9
Tourist arrivals at national borders (000)[h]	14	41	105
Energy production, primary (000 mt oil equivalent)	287	692	...
Mobile-cellular subscriptions (per 100 inhabitants)	5.5	54.3	74.7
Individuals using the Internet (%)	3.9	13.6[i]	25.4[j]

Total trade		Major trading partners			2012
	(million US$)[k]		(% of exports)[k]		(% of imports)[k]
Exports	453.0	India	75.7	India	72.3
Imports	1 051.7	China, Hong Kong SAR	16.2	Republic of Korea	6.0
Balance	−598.7	Bangladesh	5.8	Singapore	3.8

Social indicators

Population growth rate (average annual %)	2010-2015	1.6
Urban population growth rate (average annual %)	2010-2015	3.7
Rural population growth rate (average annual %)	2010-2015	0.3
Urban population (%)	2013	37.1
Population aged 0-14 years (%)	2013	28.1
Population aged 60+ years (females and males, % of total)	2013	6.6/7.3
Sex ratio (males per 100 females)	2013	116.1
Life expectancy at birth (females and males, years)	2010-2015	68.4/67.7
Infant mortality rate (per 1 000 live births)	2010-2015	30.7
Fertility rate, total (live births per woman)	2010-2015	2.3
Contraceptive prevalence (ages 15-49, %)	2006-2012	65.6
International migrant stock (000 and % of total population)	mid-2013	50.9/6.8
Education: Government expenditure (% of GDP)	2006-2012	4.7
Education: Primary-secondary gross enrolment ratio (f/m per 100)	2006-2012	95.6/92.6
Education: Female third-level students (% of total)	2006-2012	39.8
Intentional homicides (females and males, per 100 000)[l]	2008-2010	3.5/5.9
Seats held by women in national parliaments (%)	2014	8.5

Environmental indicators

Threatened species	2013	62
Forested area (% of land area)	2011	84.9
CO_2 emission estimates (000 metric tons and metric tons per capita)	2010	476/0.7
Energy consumption per capita (kilograms oil equivalent)	2010	418.0
Precipitation in the capital city, total mean (millimetres)[m]		799[n]
Temperature in the capital city, mean °C (minimum and maximum)[m]		14.0/24.3[n]

a Official rate. **b** 2006. **c** The indices are shown in terms of ISIC Rev.3. **d** Population census. **e** May. **f** Break in series; data not strictly comparable. **g** March to April. **h** From 2010, regional high end tourists are included in the total figures. **i** Country estimate. **j** ITU estimate. **k** 2011. **l** Estimates. **m** Wangdi Phodrang. **n** Based on monthly averages for the period 1990-2005.

Bolivia (Plurinational State of)

Region	South America
Currency	Boliviano (BOB)
Surface area (square kilometres)	1 098 581
Population in 2012 (estimated, 000)	10 496
Population density in 2012 (per square kilometre)	9.6
Capital city and population in 2011 (000)	Sucre (307) [a]
United Nations membership date	14 November 1945

Economic indicators	2005	2010	2012
GDP: Gross domestic product (million current US$)	9 549	19 650	27 035
GDP: Growth rate at constant 2005 prices (annual %)	4.4	4.1	5.2
GDP per capita (current US$)	1 020.8	1 934.7	2 575.7
GNI: Gross national income per capita (current US$)	989.0	1 849.4	2 379.0
Gross fixed capital formation (% of GDP)	13.0	16.6	18.2
Exchange rates (national currency per US$) [b]	8.04	6.99	6.91
Balance of payments, current account (million US$)	622	874	2 138
CPI: Consumer price index (2000=100) [c]	117	160	183
Agricultural production index (2004-2006=100)	100	120	128
Food production index (2004-2006=100)	100	120	128
Unemployment (% of labour force) [de]	...	6.0	...
Employment in industrial sector (% of employed) [d]	19.4 [f]	20.0 [gh]	...
Employment in agricultural sector (% of employed) [d]	38.6 [f]	32.1 [gh]	...
Labour force participation, adult female pop. (%)	61.1	63.7	64.1
Labour force participation, adult male pop. (%)	81.5	80.9	80.9
Tourist arrivals at national borders (000) [i]	524	807	1 114
Energy production, primary (000 mt oil equivalent)	14 269	16 347	...
Mobile-cellular subscriptions (per 100 inhabitants)	26.5	72.3	92.6
Individuals using the Internet (%)	5.2	22.4 [j]	34.2 [j]

Total trade	Major trading partners				2012
	(million US$)	(% of exports)			(% of imports)
Exports	11 793.4	Brazil	31.1	Brazil	18.4
Imports	8 281.0	Argentina	17.9	China	13.1
Balance	3 512.4	United States	14.8	Argentina	13.1

Social indicators		
Population growth rate (average annual %)	2010-2015	1.6
Urban population growth rate (average annual %)	2010-2015	2.2
Rural population growth rate (average annual %)	2010-2015	0.3
Urban population (%)	2013	67.7
Population aged 0-14 years (%)	2013	34.9
Population aged 60+ years (females and males, % of total)	2013	8.1/6.7
Sex ratio (males per 100 females)	2013	99.8
Life expectancy at birth (females and males, years)	2010-2015	69.3/64.9
Infant mortality rate (per 1 000 live births)	2010-2015	39.1
Fertility rate, total (live births per woman)	2010-2015	3.3
Contraceptive prevalence (ages 15-49, %)	2006-2012	60.5
International migrant stock (000 and % of total population)	mid-2013	154.3/1.5
Refugees and others of concern to UNHCR	mid-2013	744
Education: Government expenditure (% of GDP)	2006-2012	6.9
Education: Primary-secondary gross enrolment ratio (f/m per 100)	2006-2012	85.9/86.5
Education: Female third-level students (% of total) [k]	2006-2012	45.0
Intentional homicides (females and males, per 100 000) [l]	2008-2010	1.1/5.3
Seats held by women in national parliaments (%)	2014	25.4

Environmental indicators		
Threatened species	2013	212
Forested area (% of land area)	2011	52.5
CO$_2$ emission estimates (000 metric tons and metric tons per capita)	2010	15 444/1.5
Energy consumption per capita (kilograms oil equivalent)	2010	561.0

a La Paz is the capital and the seat of government; Sucre is the legal capital and the seat of the judiciary. b Market rate. c Urban areas. d Age group 10 years and over. e Main cities or metropolitan areas. f The indices are shown in terms of ISIC Rev.3. g 2009. h The indices are shown in terms of ISIC Rev.2. i 2006-2012: Preliminary data. j ITU estimate. k National estimate. l Estimates.

Bosnia and Herzegovina

Region	Southern Europe
Currency	Convertible Mark (BAM)
Surface area (square kilometres)	51 209
Population in 2012 (estimated, 000)	3 834
Population density in 2012 (per square kilometre)	74.9
Capital city and population in 2011 (000)	Sarajevo (389)
United Nations membership date	22 May 1992

Economic indicators	2005	2010	2012
GDP: Gross domestic product (million current US$)	10 947	16 775	17 319
GDP: Growth rate at constant 2005 prices (annual %)	3.9	0.7	−0.7
GDP per capita (current US$)	2 821.6	4 361.7	4 517.2
GNI: Gross national income per capita (current US$)	2 942.4	4 415.1	4 572.5
Gross fixed capital formation (% of GDP)	27.8	19.3	20.9
Exchange rates (national currency per US$)[a]	1.66	1.46	1.48
Balance of payments, current account (million US$)	−1 844	−1 029	−1 633
CPI: Consumer price index (2000=100)[b]	100	118	122[cd]
Agricultural production index (2004-2006=100)	98	107	99
Food production index (2004-2006=100)	98	108	100
Employment in industrial sector (% of employed)[ef]	30.7[g]	31.0	30.3
Employment in agricultural sector (% of employed)[ef]	20.6[g]	19.7	20.5
Labour force participation, adult female pop. (%)	31.7	34.0	34.1
Labour force participation, adult male pop. (%)	56.5	57.2	57.2
Tourist arrivals at national borders (000)[h]	217	365	439
Energy production, primary (000 mt oil equivalent)	5 945	6 858	...
Mobile-cellular subscriptions (per 100 inhabitants)	42.2	82.7	89.5
Individuals using the Internet (%)	21.3	52.0	65.4[i]

Total trade		Major trading partners			2012
	(million US$)	(% of exports)			(% of imports)
Exports	5 161.8	Germany	15.4	Croatia	14.4
Imports	10 019.1	Croatia	14.8	Germany	11.3
Balance	−4 857.3	Italy	12.0	Russian Federation	9.8

Social indicators		
Population growth rate (average annual %)	2010-2015	−0.1
Urban population growth rate (average annual %)	2010-2015	0.9
Rural population growth rate (average annual %)	2010-2015	−1.3
Urban population (%)	2013	49.3
Population aged 0-14 years (%)	2013	15.7
Population aged 60+ years (females and males, % of total)	2013	23.1/18.6
Sex ratio (males per 100 females)	2013	95.4
Life expectancy at birth (females and males, years)	2010-2015	78.8/73.7
Infant mortality rate (per 1 000 live births)	2010-2015	7.6
Fertility rate, total (live births per woman)	2010-2015	1.3
Contraceptive prevalence (ages 15-49, %)	2006-2012	35.7
International migrant stock (000 and % of total population)[jk]	mid-2013	23.2/0.6
Refugees and others of concern to UNHCR	mid-2013	167 714
Education: Female third-level students (% of total)	2006-2012	55.5
Intentional homicides (females and males, per 100 000)	2008-2010	0.8/3.1
Seats held by women in national parliaments (%)	2014	21.4

Environmental indicators		
Threatened species	2013	80
Forested area (% of land area)	2011	42.8
CO$_2$ emission estimates (000 metric tons and metric tons per capita)	2010	31 100/8.3
Energy consumption per capita (kilograms oil equivalent)	2010	2 298.0
Precipitation in the capital city, total mean (millimetres)		931[l]
Temperature in the capital city, mean °C (minimum and maximum)		4.8/15.0[l]

a Market rate. b Index base 2005=100. c 2011. d Series linked to former series. e April. f The indices are shown in terms of ISIC Rev.3. g 2006. h Arrivals of non-resident tourists in all types of accommodation establishments. i ITU estimate. j Estimates. k Includes refugees. l Based on monthly averages for the period 1961-1990.

Botswana

Region	Southern Africa
Currency	Pula (BWP)
Surface area (square kilometres)	582 000
Population in 2012 (estimated, 000)	2 004
Population density in 2012 (per square kilometre)	3.4
Capital city and population in 2011 (000)	Gaborone (202)
United Nations membership date	17 October 1966

Economic indicators	2005	2010	2012
GDP: Gross domestic product (million current US$)	9 931	13 747	14 411
GDP: Growth rate at constant 2005 prices (annual %)	4.6	8.6	3.7
GDP per capita (current US$)	5 294.4	6 980.4	7 191.4
GNI: Gross national income per capita (current US$)	4 863.0	6 883.8	6 994.0
Gross fixed capital formation (% of GDP)	25.3	31.3	36.1
Exchange rates (national currency per US$)[a]	5.51	6.44	7.77
Balance of payments, current account (million US$)	1 634	−298	−1 077
CPI: Consumer price index (2000=100)	146	227	265
Agricultural production index (2004-2006=100)	101	124	142
Food production index (2004-2006=100)	101	124	143
Employment in industrial sector (% of employed)	15.2[bcde]	...	...
Employment in agricultural sector (% of employed)	29.9[bcde]	...	...
Labour force participation, adult female pop. (%)	71.1	71.7	71.8
Labour force participation, adult male pop. (%)	80.9	81.3	81.5
Tourist arrivals at national borders (000)	1 474	2 145	...
Energy production, primary (000 mt oil equivalent)	689	692	...
Mobile-cellular subscriptions (per 100 inhabitants)	30.1	117.8	150.1[f]
Individuals using the Internet (%)	3.3[g]	6.0	11.5[g]

Total trade		Major trading partners			2012
	(million US$)	(% of exports)			(% of imports)
Exports	5 971.2	United Kingdom	60.7	South Africa	62.8
Imports	8 025.3	South Africa	13.1	United Kingdom	16.8
Balance	−2 054.1	Israel	5.4	Namibia	5.7

Social indicators

Population growth rate (average annual %)	2010-2015	0.9
Urban population growth rate (average annual %)	2010-2015	2.1
Rural population growth rate (average annual %)	2010-2015	−0.7
Urban population (%)	2013	63.0
Population aged 0-14 years (%)	2013	33.5
Population aged 60+ years (females and males, % of total)	2013	6.9/4.8
Sex ratio (males per 100 females)	2013	101.2
Life expectancy at birth (females and males, years)	2010-2015	46.5/48.0
Infant mortality rate (per 1 000 live births)	2010-2015	31.8
Fertility rate, total (live births per woman)	2010-2015	2.6
Contraceptive prevalence (ages 15-49, %)[h]	2006-2012	52.8
International migrant stock (000 and % of total population)[i]	mid-2013	146.5/7.3
Refugees and others of concern to UNHCR	mid-2013	3 496
Education: Government expenditure (% of GDP)	2006-2012	9.5
Education: Primary-secondary gross enrolment ratio (f/m per 100)[j]	2006-2012	95.3/94.9
Education: Female third-level students (% of total)	2006-2012	53.2
Intentional homicides (females and males, per 100 000)[k]	2008-2010	11.1/34.1
Seats held by women in national parliaments (%)	2014	9.5

Environmental indicators

Threatened species	2013	22
Forested area (% of land area)	2011	19.8
CO$_2$ emission estimates (000 metric tons and metric tons per capita)	2010	5 229/2.6
Energy consumption per capita (kilograms oil equivalent)	2010	910.0
Precipitation in the capital city, total mean (millimetres)		552[l]
Temperature in the capital city, mean °C (minimum and maximum)		13.3/28.6[l]

a Official rate. **b** 2006. **c** The indices are shown in terms of ISIC Rev.3. **d** Age group 12 years and over. **e** Excludes conscripts. **f** December. **g** ITU estimate. **h** Age group 12 to 49 years. **i** Data refer to foreign citizens. **j** UNESCO estimate. **k** Estimates. **l** Based on monthly averages for the period 1971-2000.

Brazil

Region	South America
Currency	Real (BRL)
Surface area (square kilometres)	8 514 877
Population in 2012 (estimated, 000)	198 656
Population density in 2012 (per square kilometre)	23.3
Capital city and population in 2011 (000)	Brasília (3 813)
United Nations membership date	24 October 1945

Economic indicators	2005	2010	2012
GDP: Gross domestic product (million current US$)	882 044	2 143 035	2 254 109
GDP: Growth rate at constant 2005 prices (annual %)	3.2	7.5	0.9
GDP per capita (current US$)	4 738.5	10 978.1	11 346.8
GNI: Gross national income per capita (current US$)	4 602.6	10 780.0	11 169.4
Gross fixed capital formation (% of GDP)	15.9	19.5	18.1
Exchange rates (national currency per US$)[a]	2.34	1.69	2.05
Balance of payments, current account (million US$)	13 985	−47 273	−54 246
CPI: Consumer price index (2000=100)	151	190	214
Industrial production index (2005=100)[b]	100	115	112
Agricultural production index (2004-2006=100)	99	122	127
Food production index (2004-2006=100)	99	123	127
Unemployment (% of labour force)[cd]	9.9	6.7	5.5
Employment in industrial sector (% of employed)	21.4[bce]	22.1[bcfg]	21.9[hij]
Employment in agricultural sector (% of employed)	20.5[bce]	17.0[bcfg]	15.3[hij]
Labour force participation, adult female pop. (%)	58.9	59.4	59.5
Labour force participation, adult male pop. (%)	82.1	81.1	80.9
Tourist arrivals at national borders (000)	5 358	5 161	5 677
Energy production, primary (000 mt oil equivalent)	138 589	176 286	...
Mobile-cellular subscriptions (per 100 inhabitants)	46.4	101.0[k]	125.2
Individuals using the Internet (%)	21.0[l]	40.7[l]	49.9[m]

Total trade		Major trading partners			2012
	(million US$)	(% of exports)			(% of imports)
Exports	242 579.8	China	17.0	China	15.3
Imports	223 149.1	United States	11.1	United States	14.6
Balance	19 430.7	Argentina	7.4	Argentina	7.4

Social indicators		
Population growth rate (average annual %)	2010-2015	0.9
Urban population growth rate (average annual %)	2010-2015	1.2
Rural population growth rate (average annual %)	2010-2015	−1.0
Urban population (%)	2013	85.2
Population aged 0-14 years (%)	2013	24.1
Population aged 60+ years (females and males, % of total)	2013	12.2/10.1
Sex ratio (males per 100 females)	2013	96.8
Life expectancy at birth (females and males, years)	2010-2015	77.5/70.2
Infant mortality rate (per 1 000 live births)	2010-2015	19.5
Fertility rate, total (live births per woman)	2010-2015	1.8
Contraceptive prevalence (ages 15-49, %)	2006-2012	80.3
International migrant stock (000 and % of total population)	mid-2013	599.7/0.3
Refugees and others of concern to UNHCR	mid-2013	13 429
Education: Government expenditure (% of GDP)	2006-2012	5.8
Education: Female third-level students (% of total)	2006-2012	56.8
Intentional homicides (females and males, per 100 000)	2008-2010	5.4/54.7
Seats held by women in national parliaments (%)	2014	8.6

Environmental indicators		
Threatened species	2013	937
Forested area (% of land area)	2011	61.2
CO_2 emission estimates (000 metric tons and metric tons per capita)	2010	419 411/2.2
Energy consumption per capita (kilograms oil equivalent)	2010	930.0
Precipitation in the capital city, total mean (millimetres)		1 552[n]
Temperature in the capital city, mean °C (minimum and maximum)		16.1/26.6[n]

a Market rate. **b** The indices are shown in terms of ISIC Rev.3. **c** Age group 10 years and over. **d** Main cities or metropolitan areas. **e** September. **f** 2009. **g** August. **h** 2011. **i** The indices are shown in terms of ISIC Rev.2. **j** Break in series; data not strictly comparable. **k** Methodology revised. **l** Age group 10 years and over using the Internet within the last 3 months. **m** ITU estimate. **n** Based on monthly averages for the period 1961-1990.

British Virgin Islands

Region	Caribbean
Currency	U.S. Dollar (USD)
Surface area (square kilometres)	151
Population in 2012 (estimated, 000)	28
Population density in 2012 (per square kilometre)	186.0
Capital city and population in 2011 (000)	Road Town (10)

Economic indicators	2005	2010	2012
GDP: Gross domestic product (million current US$)	870	894	909
GDP: Growth rate at constant 2005 prices (annual %)	14.3	1.3	−4.5
GDP per capita (current US$)	37 550.2	32 839.9	32 375.2
GNI: Gross national income per capita (current US$)	34 701.5	30 011.4	29 436.4
Gross fixed capital formation (% of GDP)	24.0	23.9	23.9
CPI: Consumer price index (2000=100)	110	...	...
Agricultural production index (2004-2006=100)	100	102	104
Food production index (2004-2006=100)	100	102	104
Tourist arrivals at national borders (000)	337	330	351
Mobile-cellular subscriptions (per 100 inhabitants)	92.0[a]	204.5	205.5
Individuals using the Internet (%)	...	37.0	...

Social indicators		
Population growth rate (average annual %)	2010-2015	1.1
Urban population growth rate (average annual %)	2010-2015	1.5
Rural population growth rate (average annual %)	2010-2015	0.6
Urban population (%)	2013	41.1
International migrant stock (000 and % of total population)	mid-2013	9.1/32.3
Refugees and others of concern to UNHCR	mid-2013	1
Education: Government expenditure (% of GDP)	2006-2012	4.4
Education: Primary-secondary gross enrolment ratio (f/m per 100)[b]	2006-2012	99.5/102.1
Education: Female third-level students (% of total)	2006-2012	64.7

Environmental indicators		
Threatened species	2013	52
Forested area (% of land area)	2011	24.3
CO$_2$ emission estimates (000 metric tons and metric tons per capita)	2010	117/5.0
Energy consumption per capita (kilograms oil equivalent)	2010	1 639.0[c]

a 2007. b National estimate. c UNSD estimate.

Brunei Darussalam

Region	South-Eastern Asia
Currency	Brunei Dollar (BND)
Surface area (square kilometres)	5 765
Population in 2012 (estimated, 000)	412
Population density in 2012 (per square kilometre)	71.5
Capital city and population in 2011 (000)	Bandar Seri Begawan (16)
United Nations membership date	21 September 1984

Economic indicators	2005	2010	2012
GDP: Gross domestic product (million current US$)	9 531	12 371	16 954
GDP: Growth rate at constant 2005 prices (annual %)	0.4	2.6	1.0
GDP per capita (current US$)	25 913.6	30 882.3	41 126.6
GNI: Gross national income per capita (current US$)	25 913.6	31 032.3	41 326.3
Gross fixed capital formation (% of GDP)	11.4	15.9	13.6
Exchange rates (national currency per US$)[a]	1.66	1.29	1.22
Balance of payments, current account (million US$)	4 033	3 977[b]	...
CPI: Consumer price index (2000=100)	101	105[c]	108
Industrial production index (2005=100)[d]	100	88	88
Agricultural production index (2004-2006=100)	87	113	136
Food production index (2004-2006=100)	87	114	136
Labour force participation, adult female pop. (%)	55.1	53.5	52.9
Labour force participation, adult male pop. (%)	77.8	76.1	75.6
Tourist arrivals at national borders (000)[e]	126	214	209
Energy production, primary (000 mt oil equivalent)	21 407	19 651	...
Mobile-cellular subscriptions (per 100 inhabitants)	64.1	109.1	113.8
Individuals using the Internet (%)	36.5	53.0[f]	60.3[f]

Total trade		Major trading partners			2012
	(million US$)	(% of exports)			(% of imports)
Exports	13 000.8	Japan	44.1	Singapore	23.5
Imports	3 572.2	Republic of Korea	15.7	Malaysia	19.9
Balance	9 428.6	India	8.9	China	11.4

Social indicators		
Population growth rate (average annual %)	2010-2015	1.4
Urban population growth rate (average annual %)	2010-2015	2.1
Rural population growth rate (average annual %)	2010-2015	0.1
Urban population (%)	2013	76.7
Population aged 0-14 years (%)	2013	25.3
Population aged 60+ years (females and males, % of total)	2013	7.6/7.4
Sex ratio (males per 100 females)	2013	102.7
Life expectancy at birth (females and males, years)	2010-2015	80.4/76.6
Infant mortality rate (per 1 000 live births)	2010-2015	4.2
Fertility rate, total (live births per woman)	2010-2015	2.0
International migrant stock (000 and % of total population)	mid-2013	206.2/49.4
Refugees and others of concern to UNHCR	mid-2013	20 524
Education: Government expenditure (% of GDP)	2006-2012	3.3
Education: Primary-secondary gross enrolment ratio (f/m per 100)	2006-2012	101.9/102.0
Education: Female third-level students (% of total)	2006-2012	61.9
Intentional homicides (females and males, per 100 000)	2008-2010	</<

Environmental indicators		
Threatened species	2013	187
Forested area (% of land area)	2011	71.8
CO_2 emission estimates (000 metric tons and metric tons per capita)	2010	9 153/22.9
Energy consumption per capita (kilograms oil equivalent)	2010	9 393.0
Precipitation in the capital city, total mean (millimetres)		2 913
Temperature in the capital city, mean °C (minimum and maximum)		23.3/31.8

a Market rate. **b** 2009. **c** Series linked to former series. **d** The indices are shown in terms of ISIC Rev.3. **e** Air arrivals. **f** ITU estimate.

Bulgaria

Region	Eastern Europe
Currency	Lev (BGN)
Surface area (square kilometres)	110 900
Population in 2012 (estimated, 000)	7 278
Population density in 2012 (per square kilometre)	65.6
Capital city and population in 2011 (000)	Sofia (1 174)
United Nations membership date	14 December 1955

Economic indicators	2005	2010	2012
GDP: Gross domestic product (million current US$)	28 894	47 727	50 972
GDP: Growth rate at constant 2005 prices (annual %)	6.4	0.4	0.8
GDP per capita (current US$)	3 760.7	6 459.0	7 003.8
GNI: Gross national income per capita (current US$)	3 756.9	6 330.4	6 841.8
Gross fixed capital formation (% of GDP)	25.8	22.8	21.4
Exchange rates (national currency per US$)[a]	1.66	1.47	1.48
Balance of payments, current account (million US$)	−3 347	−796	−735
CPI: Consumer price index (2000=100)	130	178	191
Industrial production index (2005=100)	100	98	103
Agricultural production index (2004-2006=100)	91	105	99
Food production index (2004-2006=100)	91	106	100
Unemployment (% of labour force)[bc]	10.1	10.2	12.3
Employment in industrial sector (% of employed)[d]	34.2[e]	33.3	31.3
Employment in agricultural sector (% of employed)[d]	8.9[e]	6.8	6.4
Labour force participation, adult female pop. (%)	44.6	47.5	47.8
Labour force participation, adult male pop. (%)	56.3	59.5	58.8
Tourist arrivals at national borders (000)	4 837	6 047	6 541
Energy production, primary (000 mt oil equivalent)	6 661	6 926	...
Mobile-cellular subscriptions (per 100 inhabitants)	80.7	136.1	145.7
Individuals using the Internet (%)[f]	20.0	46.2	55.2

Total trade		Major trading partners			2012
	(million US$)		(% of exports)		(% of imports)
Exports	26 698.8	Germany	10.2	Russian Federation	20.2
Imports	32 743.1	Turkey	9.4	Germany	9.7
Balance	−6 044.3	Italy	8.5	Italy	6.6

Social indicators		
Population growth rate (average annual %)	2010-2015	−0.8
Urban population growth rate (average annual %)	2010-2015	0.1
Rural population growth rate (average annual %)	2010-2015	−2.8
Urban population (%)	2013	74.3
Population aged 0-14 years (%)	2013	13.7
Population aged 60+ years (females and males, % of total)	2013	29.8/22.8
Sex ratio (males per 100 females)	2013	94.5
Life expectancy at birth (females and males, years)	2010-2015	77.2/69.9
Infant mortality rate (per 1 000 live births)	2010-2015	9.0
Fertility rate, total (live births per woman)	2010-2015	1.5
Contraceptive prevalence (ages 15-49, %)[g]	2006-2012	63.4[h]
International migrant stock (000 and % of total population)	mid-2013	84.1/1.2
Refugees and others of concern to UNHCR	mid-2013	4 998[i]
Education: Government expenditure (% of GDP)	2006-2012	4.1
Education: Primary-secondary gross enrolment ratio (f/m per 100)	2006-2012	93.9/97.3
Education: Female third-level students (% of total)	2006-2012	55.1
Intentional homicides (females and males, per 100 000)	2008-2010	2.0/6.2
Seats held by women in national parliaments (%)	2014	24.6

Environmental indicators		
Threatened species	2013	84
Forested area (% of land area)	2011	36.7
CO$_2$ emission estimates (000 metric tons and metric tons per capita)	2010	44 642/6.0
Energy consumption per capita (kilograms oil equivalent)	2010	1 958.0
Precipitation in the capital city, total mean (millimetres)		571[j]
Temperature in the capital city, mean °C (minimum and maximum)		5.0/15.1[j]

a Market rate. b Age group 15 to 74 years. c 2011: Break in series; data not strictly comparable. d European Labour Force Survey (Eurostat). e The indices are shown in terms of ISIC Rev.3. f Age group 16 to 74 years. g Age group 20 to 44 years. h 1997-1998. i Refugee figure relates to the end of 2012. j Based on monthly averages for the period 1961-1990.

Burkina Faso

Region	Western Africa
Currency	CFA Franc (XOF)
Surface area (square kilometres)	272 967
Population in 2012 (estimated, 000)	16 460
Population density in 2012 (per square kilometre)	60.3
Capital city and population in 2011 (000)	Ouagadougou (2 053)
United Nations membership date	20 September 1960

Economic indicators	2005	2010	2012
GDP: Gross domestic product (million current US$)	5 463	8 993	10 687
GDP: Growth rate at constant 2005 prices (annual %)	8.7	8.4	6.2
GDP per capita (current US$)	407.0	578.7	649.3
GNI: Gross national income per capita (current US$)	403.8	563.5	643.7
Gross fixed capital formation (% of GDP)	19.7	22.8	27.2
Exchange rates (national currency per US$)[a]	556.04	490.91	497.16
Balance of payments, current account (million US$)	−634	−181	...
CPI: Consumer price index (2000=100)[b]	116	131[c]	140
Agricultural production index (2004-2006=100)	103	115	121
Food production index (2004-2006=100)	103	122	128
Employment in industrial sector (% of employed)	3.1[def]	...	...
Employment in agricultural sector (% of employed)	84.8[def]	...	...
Labour force participation, adult female pop. (%)	76.9	77.2	77.1
Labour force participation, adult male pop. (%)	90.4	90.3	90.1
Tourist arrivals at national borders (000)[g]	245	274	238[h]
Energy production, primary (000 mt oil equivalent)	9	10	...
Mobile-cellular subscriptions (per 100 inhabitants)	4.5	34.7	57.1
Individuals using the Internet (%)	0.5	2.4[i]	3.7[i]

Total trade	Major trading partners				2012
	(million US$)[h]		(% of exports)[h]		(% of imports)[h]
Exports	2 312.4	Switzerland	69.2	France	12.1
Imports	2 406.4	South Africa	10.3	Côte d'Ivoire	10.7
Balance	−94.0	Singapore	4.7	China	9.8

Social indicators		
Population growth rate (average annual %)	2010-2015	2.8
Urban population growth rate (average annual %)	2010-2015	6.0
Rural population growth rate (average annual %)	2010-2015	1.8
Urban population (%)	2013	28.2
Population aged 0-14 years (%)	2013	45.5
Population aged 60+ years (females and males, % of total)	2013	4.6/3.1
Sex ratio (males per 100 females)	2013	98.9
Life expectancy at birth (females and males, years)	2010-2015	56.7/55.5
Infant mortality rate (per 1 000 live births)	2010-2015	69.8
Fertility rate, total (live births per woman)	2010-2015	5.7
Contraceptive prevalence (ages 15-49, %)	2006-2012	16.2
International migrant stock (000 and % of total population)[j]	mid-2013	697.0/4.1
Refugees and others of concern to UNHCR	mid-2013	51 191
Education: Government expenditure (% of GDP)	2006-2012	3.4
Education: Primary-secondary gross enrolment ratio (f/m per 100)	2006-2012	53.7/58.8
Education: Female third-level students (% of total)	2006-2012	32.6
Intentional homicides (females and males, per 100 000)[k]	2008-2010	3.3/32.9
Seats held by women in national parliaments (%)	2014	18.9

Environmental indicators		
Threatened species	2013	28
Forested area (% of land area)	2011	20.4
CO2 emission estimates (000 metric tons and metric tons per capita)	2010	1 682/0.1
Energy consumption per capita (kilograms oil equivalent)	2010	36.0[l]
Precipitation in the capital city, total mean (millimetres)		744[m]
Temperature in the capital city, mean °C (minimum and maximum)		21.9/34.9[m]

a Official rate. b Ouagadougou. c Series linked to former series. d Core Welfare Indicators Questionnaire (World Bank). e The indices are shown in terms of ISIC Rev.3. f Break in series; data not strictly comparable. g Arrivals of non-resident tourists in hotels and similar establishments. h 2011. i ITU estimate. j Includes refugees. k Estimates. l UNSD estimate. m Based on monthly averages for the period 1971-2000.

Burundi

Region	Eastern Africa
Currency	Burundi Franc (BIF)
Surface area (square kilometres)	27 834
Population in 2012 (estimated, 000)	9 850
Population density in 2012 (per square kilometre)	353.9
Capital city and population in 2011 (000)	Bujumbura (605)
United Nations membership date	18 September 1962

Economic indicators	2005	2010	2012
GDP: Gross domestic product (million current US$)	1 117	2 084	2 257
GDP: Growth rate at constant 2005 prices (annual %)	−0.9	3.9	5.2
GDP per capita (current US$)	143.8	225.8	229.2
GNI: Gross national income per capita (current US$)	141.5	224.6	228.6
Gross fixed capital formation (% of GDP)	18.4	18.9	20.2
Exchange rates (national currency per US$)[a]	997.78	1 232.50	1 546.07
Balance of payments, current account (million US$)	−6	−301	−255
CPI: Consumer price index (2000=100)[b]	145	161[c]	...
Agricultural production index (2004-2006=100)	98	111	100
Food production index (2004-2006=100)	100	113	99
Labour force participation, adult female pop. (%)	83.4	83.0	83.2
Labour force participation, adult male pop. (%)	81.9	81.5	81.8
Tourist arrivals at national borders (000)[d]	148	142[e]	...
Energy production, primary (000 mt oil equivalent)	10	17	...
Mobile-cellular subscriptions (per 100 inhabitants)	2.1	20.0[f]	25.7[g]
Individuals using the Internet (%)	0.5	1.0	1.2[f]

Total trade		Major trading partners		2012
	(million US$)	(% of exports)		(% of imports)
Exports	242.7	... Italy	17.6	
Imports	1 003.1	... Saudi Arabia	8.2	
Balance	−760.4	... Belgium	7.9	

Social indicators

Population growth rate (average annual %)	2010-2015	3.2
Urban population growth rate (average annual %)	2010-2015	4.5
Rural population growth rate (average annual %)	2010-2015	1.6
Urban population (%)	2013	11.5
Population aged 0-14 years (%)	2013	44.6
Population aged 60+ years (females and males, % of total)	2013	4.1/3.8
Sex ratio (males per 100 females)	2013	97.6
Life expectancy at birth (females and males, years)	2010-2015	55.8/52.0
Infant mortality rate (per 1 000 live births)	2010-2015	87.0
Fertility rate, total (live births per woman)	2010-2015	6.1
Contraceptive prevalence (ages 15-49, %)	2006-2012	21.9
International migrant stock (000 and % of total population)[h]	mid-2013	254.5/2.5
Refugees and others of concern to UNHCR	mid-2013	131 656
Education: Government expenditure (% of GDP)	2006-2012	5.8
Education: Primary-secondary gross enrolment ratio (f/m per 100)	2006-2012	79.6/85.2
Education: Female third-level students (% of total)	2006-2012	35.4
Intentional homicides (females and males, per 100 000)[i]	2008-2010	10.3/33.7
Seats held by women in national parliaments (%)	2014	30.5

Environmental indicators

Threatened species	2013	59
Forested area (% of land area)	2011	6.6
CO_2 emission estimates (000 metric tons and metric tons per capita)	2010	308/0.0
Energy consumption per capita (kilograms oil equivalent)	2010	14.0
Precipitation in the capital city, total mean (millimetres)		786[j]
Temperature in the capital city, mean °C (minimum and maximum)		18.7/29.6[j]

a Official rate. **b** Bujumbura. **c** 2007. **d** Includes nationals residing abroad. **e** Break in series. **f** ITU estimate. **g** December. **h** Includes refugees. **i** Estimates. **j** Based on monthly averages for the period 1961-1990.

Cabo Verde[a]

Region	Western Africa
Currency	Cabo Verde Escudo (CVE)
Surface area (square kilometres)	4 033
Population in 2012 (estimated, 000)	494
Population density in 2012 (per square kilometre)	122.6
Capital city and population in 2011 (000)	Praia (132)
United Nations membership date	16 September 1975

Economic indicators	2005	2010	2012
GDP: Gross domestic product (million current US$)	1 105	1 664	1 903
GDP: Growth rate at constant 2005 prices (annual %)	6.5	1.5	4.3
GDP per capita (current US$)	2 309.4	3 413.3	3 849.8
GNI: Gross national income per capita (current US$)	2 229.4	3 262.7	3 731.4
Gross fixed capital formation (% of GDP)	34.1	45.2	39.3
Exchange rates (national currency per US$)[b]	93.47	82.53	83.58
Balance of payments, current account (million US$)	−41	−223	−209
CPI: Consumer price index (2000=100)	105	127	136
Agricultural production index (2004-2006=100)	98	127	134
Food production index (2004-2006=100)	98	127	134
Labour force participation, adult female pop. (%)	48.0	50.4	51.1
Labour force participation, adult male pop. (%)	83.0	83.1	83.5
Tourist arrivals at national borders (000)[c]	198	336	482
Energy production, primary (000 mt oil equivalent)	1	0	...
Mobile-cellular subscriptions (per 100 inhabitants)	17.3	75.0	84.2
Individuals using the Internet (%)	6.1	30.0[d]	34.7[d]

Total trade		Major trading partners			2012
	(million US$)		(% of exports)[e]		(% of imports)
Exports	55.8	Spain	71.9	Portugal	39.9
Imports	754.8	Portugal	15.1	Netherlands	12.5
Balance	−699.0	Areas nes	5.7	United States	9.3

Social indicators		
Population growth rate (average annual %)	2010-2015	0.8
Urban population growth rate (average annual %)	2010-2015	2.1
Rural population growth rate (average annual %)	2010-2015	−1.1
Urban population (%)	2013	64.1
Population aged 0-14 years (%)	2013	29.5
Population aged 60+ years (females and males, % of total)	2013	8.7/5.7
Sex ratio (males per 100 females)	2013	99.3
Life expectancy at birth (females and males, years)	2010-2015	78.7/70.9
Infant mortality rate (per 1 000 live births)	2010-2015	17.2
Fertility rate, total (live births per woman)	2010-2015	2.3
Contraceptive prevalence (ages 15-49, %)	2006-2012	61.3[f]
International migrant stock (000 and % of total population)	mid-2013	14.9/3.0
Education: Government expenditure (% of GDP)	2006-2012	5.0
Education: Primary-secondary gross enrolment ratio (f/m per 100)	2006-2012	103.8/100.0
Education: Female third-level students (% of total)	2006-2012	57.3
Intentional homicides (females and males, per 100 000)[g]	2008-2010	4.8/21.9
Seats held by women in national parliaments (%)	2014	20.8

Environmental indicators		
Threatened species	2013	51
Forested area (% of land area)	2011	21.0
CO$_2$ emission estimates (000 metric tons and metric tons per capita)	2010	355/0.7
Energy consumption per capita (kilograms oil equivalent)	2010	233.0
Precipitation in the capital city, total mean (millimetres)[h]		70[i]
Temperature in the capital city, mean °C (minimum and maximum)[h]		23.5/23.5[ij]

a Previously listed as Cape Verde. b Official rate. c Arrivals of non-resident tourists in hotels and similar establishments. d ITU estimate. e See technical notes. f 2005. g Estimates. h Sal. i Based on WMO Climatological Normals (CLINO) for the period 1961-1990. j Refers to average temperature.

Cambodia

Region	South-Eastern Asia
Currency	Riel (KHR)
Surface area (square kilometres)	181 035
Population in 2012 (estimated, 000)	14 865
Population density in 2012 (per square kilometre)	82.1
Capital city and population in 2011 (000)	Phnom Penh (1 550)
United Nations membership date	14 December 1955

Economic indicators	2005	2010	2012
GDP: Gross domestic product (million current US$)	6 293	11 242	14 038
GDP: Growth rate at constant 2005 prices (annual %)	13.2	6.0	7.3
GDP per capita (current US$)	471.2	782.6	944.4
GNI: Gross national income per capita (current US$)	403.4	745.6	898.6
Gross fixed capital formation (% of GDP)	18.9	16.2	17.4
Exchange rates (national currency per US$)[a]	4 112.00	4 051.00	3 995.00
Balance of payments, current account (million US$)	−307	−772	−1 208
CPI: Consumer price index (2000=100)[b]	114	165	179
Agricultural production index (2004-2006=100)	105	148	175
Food production index (2004-2006=100)	105	148	175
Employment in industrial sector (% of employed)[cd]	...	16.2	18.6
Employment in agricultural sector (% of employed)[cd]	...	54.2	51.0
Labour force participation, adult female pop. (%)	76.1	79.0	78.9
Labour force participation, adult male pop. (%)	85.8	86.3	86.5
Tourist arrivals at national borders (000)[e]	1 422	2 508	3 584
Energy production, primary (000 mt oil equivalent)	4	2	...
Mobile-cellular subscriptions (per 100 inhabitants)	8.0	57.7	132.0
Individuals using the Internet (%)	0.3	1.3	4.9[f]

Total trade		Major trading partners			2012
	(million US$)	(% of exports)			(% of imports)
Exports	7 838.1	United States	25.9	China	30.6
Imports	7 062.6	China, Hong Kong SAR	21.5	Viet Nam	13.3
Balance	775.5	Singapore	8.7	Thailand	12.8

Social indicators		
Population growth rate (average annual %)	2010-2015	1.8
Urban population growth rate (average annual %)	2010-2015	2.1
Rural population growth rate (average annual %)	2010-2015	1.0
Urban population (%)	2013	20.3
Population aged 0-14 years (%)	2013	31.1
Population aged 60+ years (females and males, % of total)	2013	9.0/6.7
Sex ratio (males per 100 females)	2013	95.3
Life expectancy at birth (females and males, years)	2010-2015	74.2/68.8
Infant mortality rate (per 1 000 live births)	2010-2015	40.6
Fertility rate, total (live births per woman)	2010-2015	2.9
Contraceptive prevalence (ages 15-49, %)	2006-2012	50.5
International migrant stock (000 and % of total population)	mid-2013	75.6/0.5
Refugees and others of concern to UNHCR	mid-2013	87
Education: Government expenditure (% of GDP)	2006-2012	2.6
Education: Primary-secondary gross enrolment ratio (f/m per 100)[g]	2006-2012	81.1/88.6
Education: Female third-level students (% of total)	2006-2012	37.6
Intentional homicides (females and males, per 100 000)[h]	2008-2010	3.9/39.9
Seats held by women in national parliaments (%)	2014	20.3

Environmental indicators		
Threatened species	2013	234
Forested area (% of land area)	2011	56.5
CO$_2$ emission estimates (000 metric tons and metric tons per capita)	2010	4 177/0.3
Energy consumption per capita (kilograms oil equivalent)	2010	97.0
Precipitation in the capital city, total mean (millimetres)		1 636[i]
Temperature in the capital city, mean °C (minimum and maximum)		23.8/32.5[i]

a Market rate. **b** Phnom Penh. **c** Age group 15 to 64 years. **d** Social-economic survey. **e** Arrivals by all means of transport. **f** ITU estimate. **g** UNESCO estimate. **h** Estimates. **i** Based on monthly averages for the period 1997-2001.

Cameroon

Region	Middle Africa
Currency	CFA Franc (XAF)
Surface area (square kilometres)	475 650
Population in 2012 (estimated, 000)	21 700
Population density in 2012 (per square kilometre)	45.6
Capital city and population in 2011 (000)	Yaoundé (2 432)
United Nations membership date	20 September 1960

Economic indicators	2005	2010	2012
GDP: Gross domestic product (million current US$)	16 588	23 623	26 094
GDP: Growth rate at constant 2005 prices (annual %)	2.3	3.2	5.3
GDP per capita (current US$)	914.6	1 145.4	1 202.5
GNI: Gross national income per capita (current US$)	880.4	1 121.3	1 134.2
Gross fixed capital formation (% of GDP)	17.7	19.0	21.9
Exchange rates (national currency per US$)[a]	556.04	490.91	497.16
Balance of payments, current account (million US$)	−493	−856	−956
CPI: Consumer price index (2000=100)	111	129	133[b]
Industrial production index (2005=100)[c]	100	102	112
Agricultural production index (2004-2006=100)	103	139	148
Food production index (2004-2006=100)	102	143	152
Employment in industrial sector (% of employed)[d]	14.1[e]	12.6	...
Employment in agricultural sector (% of employed)[d]	55.7[e]	53.3	...
Labour force participation, adult female pop. (%)	62.1	63.3	63.6
Labour force participation, adult male pop. (%)	76.2	76.5	76.7
Tourist arrivals at national borders (000)[f]	451[g]	573	817
Energy production, primary (000 mt oil equivalent)	4 902	3 993	...
Mobile-cellular subscriptions (per 100 inhabitants)	12.8	44.1	64.0
Individuals using the Internet (%)	1.4	4.3[h]	5.7[h]

Total trade		Major trading partners				2012
	(million US$)		(% of exports)			(% of imports)
Exports	4 275.0	China	15.3	Nigeria		17.8
Imports	6 515.1	Portugal	11.8	France		11.9
Balance	−2 240.1	Netherlands	11.3	China		10.4

Social indicators		
Population growth rate (average annual %)	2010-2015	2.5
Urban population growth rate (average annual %)	2010-2015	3.2
Rural population growth rate (average annual %)	2010-2015	0.9
Urban population (%)	2013	53.2
Population aged 0-14 years (%)	2013	43.0
Population aged 60+ years (females and males, % of total)	2013	5.2/4.5
Sex ratio (males per 100 females)	2013	100.0
Life expectancy at birth (females and males, years)	2010-2015	56.0/53.7
Infant mortality rate (per 1 000 live births)	2010-2015	73.5
Fertility rate, total (live births per woman)	2010-2015	4.8
Contraceptive prevalence (ages 15-49, %)	2006-2012	23.4
International migrant stock (000 and % of total population)	mid-2013	291.8/1.3
Refugees and others of concern to UNHCR	mid-2013	110 065
Education: Government expenditure (% of GDP)	2006-2012	3.2
Education: Primary-secondary gross enrolment ratio (f/m per 100)	2006-2012	75.2/86.5
Education: Female third-level students (% of total)	2006-2012	42.2
Intentional homicides (females and males, per 100 000)[i]	2008-2010	13.9/25.6
Seats held by women in national parliaments (%)	2014	31.1

Environmental indicators		
Threatened species	2013	639
Forested area (% of land area)	2011	41.7
CO_2 emission estimates (000 metric tons and metric tons per capita)	2010	7 229/0.4
Energy consumption per capita (kilograms oil equivalent)	2010	121.0
Precipitation in the capital city, total mean (millimetres)		1 541[j]
Temperature in the capital city, mean °C (minimum and maximum)		19.8/28.5[j]

a Official rate. b 2011. c The indices are shown in terms of ISIC Rev.3. d Age group 10 years and over. e Break in series; data not strictly comparable. f Arrivals of non-resident visitors at national borders. g 2006. h ITU estimate. i Estimates. j Based on monthly averages for the period 1971-2000.

Canada

Region	Northern America
Currency	Canadian Dollar (CAD)
Surface area (square kilometres)	9 984 670
Population in 2012 (estimated, 000)	34 838
Population density in 2012 (per square kilometre)	3.5
Capital city and population in 2011 (000)	Ottawa-Gatineau (1 208)[a]
United Nations membership date	9 November 1945

Economic indicators	2005	2010	2012
GDP: Gross domestic product (million current US$)	1 164 179	1 614 072	1 821 445
GDP: Growth rate at constant 2005 prices (annual %)	3.2	3.4	1.7
GDP per capita (current US$)	36 095.1	47 297.1	52 283.3
GNI: Gross national income per capita (current US$)	35 352.6	46 379.7	51 346.5
Gross fixed capital formation (% of GDP)	22.0	23.3	24.1
Exchange rates (national currency per US$)[b]	1.16	1.00	1.00
Balance of payments, current account (million US$)	21 910	−56 626	−62 256
CPI: Consumer price index (2000=100)	112	122	128
Industrial production index (2005=100)[c]	100	88	92[d]
Agricultural production index (2004-2006=100)	102	102	103
Food production index (2004-2006=100)	102	103	104
Unemployment (% of labour force)	6.8	8.0	7.2
Employment in industrial sector (% of employed)[ce]	22.0	21.5[f]	...
Employment in agricultural sector (% of employed)[ce]	2.7	2.4[f]	...
Labour force participation, adult female pop. (%)	60.9	61.8	61.6
Labour force participation, adult male pop. (%)	72.6	71.5	71.2
Tourist arrivals at national borders (000)	18 771	16 219	16 344
Energy production, primary (000 mt oil equivalent)	388 916	384 541	...
Mobile-cellular subscriptions (per 100 inhabitants)	52.7	75.9	75.7[g]
Individuals using the Internet (%)	71.7[h]	80.3[hi]	86.8[g]

Total trade		Major trading partners			2012
	(million US$)	(% of exports)		(% of imports)	
Exports	453 380.9	United States	74.5	United States	50.6
Imports	462 369.2	China	4.3	China	11.0
Balance	−8 988.3	United Kingdom	4.1	Mexico	5.5

Social indicators		
Population growth rate (average annual %)	2010-2015	1.0
Urban population growth rate (average annual %)	2010-2015	1.1
Rural population growth rate (average annual %)	2010-2015	0.4
Urban population (%)	2013	80.9
Population aged 0-14 years (%)	2013	16.4
Population aged 60+ years (females and males, % of total)	2013	22.7/19.7
Sex ratio (males per 100 females)	2013	98.5
Life expectancy at birth (females and males, years)	2010-2015	83.5/79.3
Infant mortality rate (per 1 000 live births)	2010-2015	4.4
Fertility rate, total (live births per woman)	2010-2015	1.7
Contraceptive prevalence (ages 15-49, %)[j]	2006-2012	74.0[k]
International migrant stock (000 and % of total population)	mid-2013	7 284.1/20.7
Refugees and others of concern to UNHCR	mid-2013	190 673[l]
Education: Government expenditure (% of GDP)	2006-2012	5.5
Education: Primary-secondary gross enrolment ratio (f/m per 100)	2006-2012	100.1/101.2
Education: Female third-level students (% of total)	2006-2012	56.0[m]
Intentional homicides (females and males, per 100 000)	2008-2010	0.9/2.7
Seats held by women in national parliaments (%)	2014	25.1

Environmental indicators		
Threatened species	2013	86
Forested area (% of land area)	2011	34.1
CO$_2$ emission estimates (000 metric tons and metric tons per capita)	2010	498 729/14.7
Energy consumption per capita (kilograms oil equivalent)	2010	6 519.0
Precipitation in the capital city, total mean (millimetres)		943[n]
Temperature in the capital city, mean °C (minimum and maximum)		1.1/10.9[n]

a The capital is Ottawa. b Market rate. c The indices are shown in terms of ISIC Rev.3. d 2011. e Excludes residents of the Territories and indigenous persons living on reserves. f 2008. g ITU estimate. h Age group 16 years and over. i Methodology revised; data not strictly comparable. j Age group 18 to 44 years. k 2002. l Refugee population refers to the end of 2012. m 2000. n Based on monthly averages for the period 1971-2000.

Cayman Islands

Region	Caribbean		
Currency	Cayman Islands Dollar (KYD)		
Surface area (square kilometres)	264		
Population in 2012 (estimated, 000)	58		
Population density in 2012 (per square kilometre)	218.1		
Capital city and population in 2011 (000)	George Town (28)		

Economic indicators	2005	2010	2012
GDP: Gross domestic product (million current US$)	3 042	3 249	3 393
GDP: Growth rate at constant 2005 prices (annual %)	6.5	−2.9	0.9
GDP per capita (current US$)	62 558.1	58 531.9	58 942.3
GNI: Gross national income per capita (current US$)	56 667.9	53 020.7	53 392.5
Gross fixed capital formation (% of GDP)	22.4	22.4	22.4
Exchange rates (national currency per US$)[a]	...	...	0.82[b]
CPI: Consumer price index (2000=100)	117	125	128
Agricultural production index (2004-2006=100)	94	105	113
Food production index (2004-2006=100)	94	105	113
Employment in industrial sector (% of employed)[cd]	22.2	19.1[e]	...
Employment in agricultural sector (% of employed)[cd]	1.7	1.9[e]	...
Tourist arrivals at national borders (000)[f]	168	288	322
Mobile-cellular subscriptions (per 100 inhabitants)[g]	154.9	177.7	168.3
Individuals using the Internet (%)	38.0	66.0	74.1[h]

Social indicators		
Population growth rate (average annual %)	2010-2015	1.5
Urban population growth rate (average annual %)	2010-2015	0.8
Rural population growth rate (average annual %)	2010-2015	0.0
Urban population (%)	2013	100.0
Population aged 0-14 years (%)[ijk]	2013	18.3[l]
Population aged 60+ years (females and males, % of total)[ijkm]	2013	6.6/5.2[l]
Sex ratio (males per 100 females)[ijk]	2013	95.8[l]
Life expectancy at birth (females and males, years)[in]	2010-2015	83.8/76.3[o]
International migrant stock (000 and % of total population)	mid-2013	33.7/57.6
Refugees and others of concern to UNHCR	mid-2013	3
Education: Primary-secondary gross enrolment ratio (f/m per 100)	2006-2012	97.3/106.2[p]
Education: Female third-level students (% of total)	2006-2012	68.9

Environmental indicators		
Threatened species	2013	40
Forested area (% of land area)	2011	52.9
CO$_2$ emission estimates (000 metric tons and metric tons per capita)	2010	590/10.5
Energy consumption per capita (kilograms oil equivalent)	2010	3 496.0
Precipitation in the capital city, total mean (millimetres)		1 429[q]
Temperature in the capital city, mean °C (minimum and maximum)		22.2/30.3[q]

a UN operational exchange rate. b August 2012. c October. d The indices are shown in terms of ISIC Rev. 3. e 2008. f Air arrivals. g Year-end mobile handsets in operation. h ITU estimate. i Data compiled by the United Nations Demographic Yearbook system. j Data refer to the latest available census. k De jure estimate. l 2012. m Population aged 65 years and older. n Data are based on a small number of deaths. o 2006. p 1999. q Based on monthly averages for the period 1981-2010.

Central African Republic

Region	Middle Africa
Currency	CFA Franc (XAF)
Surface area (square kilometres)	622 984
Population in 2012 (estimated, 000)	4 525
Population density in 2012 (per square kilometre)	7.3
Capital city and population in 2011 (000)	Bangui (740)
United Nations membership date	20 September 1960

Economic indicators	2005	2010	2012
GDP: Gross domestic product (million current US$)	1 350	1 986	2 184
GDP: Growth rate at constant 2005 prices (annual %)	2.4	3.0	4.0
GDP per capita (current US$)	340.9	456.6	482.7
GNI: Gross national income per capita (current US$)	338.6	455.5	448.6
Gross fixed capital formation (% of GDP)	9.8	14.1	14.7
Exchange rates (national currency per US$)[a]	556.04	490.91	497.16
CPI: Consumer price index (2000=100)[bc]	112	138	...
Industrial production index (2005=100)[d]	100	126	144
Agricultural production index (2004-2006=100)	99	114	121
Food production index (2004-2006=100)	99	113	119
Labour force participation, adult female pop. (%)	71.5	72.5	72.5
Labour force participation, adult male pop. (%)	85.4	85.2	85.1
Tourist arrivals at national borders (000)[e]	12	54	...
Energy production, primary (000 mt oil equivalent)	12	12[f]	...
Mobile-cellular subscriptions (per 100 inhabitants)	2.5	22.3	23.4
Individuals using the Internet (%)	0.3[g]	2.0	3.0[g]

Total trade		Major trading partners			2012
	(million US$)[h]		(% of exports)[h]		(% of imports)[h]
Exports	103.9	France	26.3	France	31.7
Imports	214.7	Japan	15.0	Japan	13.6
Balance	−110.8	Cameroon	9.7	Cameroon	7.7

Social indicators		
Population growth rate (average annual %)	2010-2015	2.0
Urban population growth rate (average annual %)	2010-2015	2.6
Rural population growth rate (average annual %)	2010-2015	1.6
Urban population (%)	2013	39.6
Population aged 0-14 years (%)	2013	39.8
Population aged 60+ years (females and males, % of total)	2013	6.3/5.1
Sex ratio (males per 100 females)	2013	96.9
Life expectancy at birth (females and males, years)	2010-2015	51.8/48.0
Infant mortality rate (per 1 000 live births)	2010-2015	93.3
Fertility rate, total (live births per woman)	2010-2015	4.4
Contraceptive prevalence (ages 15-49, %)	2006-2012	19.0
International migrant stock (000 and % of total population)[i]	mid-2013	134.2/2.9
Refugees and others of concern to UNHCR	mid-2013	226 336
Education: Government expenditure (% of GDP)	2006-2012	1.3
Education: Primary-secondary gross enrolment ratio (f/m per 100)	2006-2012	46.4/66.1
Education: Female third-level students (% of total)	2006-2012	26.9
Intentional homicides (females and males, per 100 000)[j]	2008-2010	14.4/44.5

Environmental indicators		
Threatened species	2013	44
Forested area (% of land area)	2011	36.2
CO_2 emission estimates (000 metric tons and metric tons per capita)	2010	264/0.1
Energy consumption per capita (kilograms oil equivalent)	2010	23.0[f]

a Official rate. b Excludes rent. c Bangui. d The indices are shown in terms of ISIC Rev.3. e Air arrivals to Bangui only. f UNSD estimate. g ITU estimate. h 2011. i Data refer to foreign citizens. j Estimates.

Chad

Region	Middle Africa
Currency	CFA Franc (XAF)
Surface area (square kilometres)	1 284 000
Population in 2012 (estimated, 000)	12 448
Population density in 2012 (per square kilometre)	9.7
Capital city and population in 2011 (000)	N'Djamena (1 079)
United Nations membership date	20 September 1960

Economic indicators	2005	2010	2012
GDP: Gross domestic product (million current US$)	5 873	8 919	10 183
GDP: Growth rate at constant 2005 prices (annual %)	7.9	14.6	5.9
GDP per capita (current US$)	586.5	761.0	818.1
GNI: Gross national income per capita (current US$)	330.4	480.8	493.8
Gross fixed capital formation (% of GDP)	20.3	22.7	22.2
Exchange rates (national currency per US$)[a]	556.04	490.91	497.16
CPI: Consumer price index (2000=100)[b]	126	147	...
Industrial production index (2005=100)[c]	100	79	73
Agricultural production index (2004-2006=100)	104	104	126
Food production index (2004-2006=100)	104	110	131
Labour force participation, adult female pop. (%)	64.2	64.1	64.0
Labour force participation, adult male pop. (%)	79.4	79.2	79.2
Tourist arrivals at national borders (000)	46[d]	71	...
Energy production, primary (000 mt oil equivalent)	8 899	6 278	...
Mobile-cellular subscriptions (per 100 inhabitants)	2.2	25.6[e]	35.5[f]
Individuals using the Internet (%)	0.4	1.7[g]	2.1[g]

Social indicators		
Population growth rate (average annual %)	2010-2015	3.0
Urban population growth rate (average annual %)	2010-2015	3.0
Rural population growth rate (average annual %)	2010-2015	2.5
Urban population (%)	2013	22.0
Population aged 0-14 years (%)	2013	48.4
Population aged 60+ years (females and males, % of total)	2013	4.1/3.5
Sex ratio (males per 100 females)	2013	100.3
Life expectancy at birth (females and males, years)	2010-2015	51.9/50.1
Infant mortality rate (per 1 000 live births)	2010-2015	95.8
Fertility rate, total (live births per woman)	2010-2015	6.3
Contraceptive prevalence (ages 15-49, %)	2006-2012	2.8[h]
International migrant stock (000 and % of total population)[i]	mid-2013	439.1/3.4
Refugees and others of concern to UNHCR	mid-2013	509 009
Education: Government expenditure (% of GDP)	2006-2012	2.6
Education: Primary-secondary gross enrolment ratio (f/m per 100)	2006-2012	49.8/71.4
Education: Female third-level students (% of total)	2006-2012	19.1
Intentional homicides (females and males, per 100 000)[j]	2008-2010	7.9/23.8
Seats held by women in national parliaments (%)	2014	14.9

Environmental indicators		
Threatened species	2013	35
Forested area (% of land area)	2011	9.1
CO$_2$ emission estimates (000 metric tons and metric tons per capita)	2010	469/0.0
Energy consumption per capita (kilograms oil equivalent)	2010	7.0[k]
Precipitation in the capital city, total mean (millimetres)		510[l]
Temperature in the capital city, mean °C (minimum and maximum)		20.8/30.5[m]

a Official rate. b N'Djamena. c The indices are shown in terms of ISIC Rev.3. d 2006. e December. f July. g ITU estimate. h 2004. i Includes refugees. j Estimates. k UNSD estimate. l January to November only. m Based on monthly averages for the period 1961-1990.

Chile

Region	South America
Currency	Chilean Peso (CLP)
Surface area (square kilometres)	756 102
Population in 2012 (estimated, 000)	17 465
Population density in 2012 (per square kilometre)	23.1
Capital city and population in 2011 (000)	Santiago (6 034)
United Nations membership date	24 October 1945

Economic indicators	2005	2010	2012
GDP: Gross domestic product (million current US$)	123 056	217 556	268 314
GDP: Growth rate at constant 2005 prices (annual %)	6.2	5.8	5.6
GDP per capita (current US$)	7 532.0	12 684.9	15 363.1
GNI: Gross national income per capita (current US$)	6 902.4	11 831.8	14 637.7
Gross fixed capital formation (% of GDP)	21.5	21.1	24.1
Exchange rates (national currency per US$)[a]	514.21	468.37	478.60
Balance of payments, current account (million US$)	1 449	3 224	−9 497
CPI: Consumer price index (2000=100)	114[b]	101[c]	108[c]
Agricultural production index (2004-2006=100)	100	109	113
Food production index (2004-2006=100)	100	109	113
Unemployment (% of labour force)	9.2	8.1[d]	6.4
Employment in industrial sector (% of employed)[e]	23.0[f]	23.0	23.4[dg]
Employment in agricultural sector (% of employed)[e]	13.2[f]	10.6	10.3[dg]
Labour force participation, adult female pop. (%)	38.3	46.8	49.0
Labour force participation, adult male pop. (%)	73.0	74.3	74.6
Tourist arrivals at national borders (000)	2 027	2 801	3 554
Energy production, primary (000 mt oil equivalent)	4 670	4 448	...
Mobile-cellular subscriptions (per 100 inhabitants)	64.8	116.0	138.5
Individuals using the Internet (%)[hi]	31.2	45.0	61.4

Total trade	Major trading partners				2012
(million US$)	(% of exports)			(% of imports)	
Exports	78 277.0	China	23.3	United States	22.9
Imports	79 461.5	United States	12.3	China	18.2
Balance	−1 184.5	Japan	10.7	Argentina	6.6

Social indicators

Population growth rate (average annual %)	2010-2015	0.9
Urban population growth rate (average annual %)	2010-2015	1.1
Rural population growth rate (average annual %)	2010-2015	−1.1
Urban population (%)	2013	89.6
Population aged 0-14 years (%)	2013	21.1
Population aged 60+ years (females and males, % of total)	2013	15.6/12.8
Sex ratio (males per 100 females)	2013	97.9
Life expectancy at birth (females and males, years)	2010-2015	82.6/77.0
Infant mortality rate (per 1 000 live births)	2010-2015	5.9
Fertility rate, total (live births per woman)	2010-2015	1.8
Contraceptive prevalence (ages 15-49, %)[j]	2006-2012	64.2
International migrant stock (000 and % of total population)	mid-2013	398.3/2.3
Refugees and others of concern to UNHCR	mid-2013	2 078
Education: Government expenditure (% of GDP)	2006-2012	4.1
Education: Primary-secondary gross enrolment ratio (f/m per 100)	2006-2012	95.3/95.5
Education: Female third-level students (% of total)	2006-2012	51.6
Intentional homicides (females and males, per 100 000)	2008-2010	1.9/12.3
Seats held by women in national parliaments (%)	2014	15.8

Environmental indicators

Threatened species	2013	179
Forested area (% of land area)	2011	21.9
CO$_2$ emission estimates (000 metric tons and metric tons per capita)	2010	72 199/4.2
Energy consumption per capita (kilograms oil equivalent)	2010	1 463.0
Precipitation in the capital city, total mean (millimetres)		313
Temperature in the capital city, mean °C (minimum and maximum)		8.3/22.5

a Principal rate. **b** Santiago. **c** Index base 2009=100. **d** Break in series; data not strictly comparable. **e** The indices are shown in terms of ISIC Rev.2. **f** Fourth quarter. **g** 2011. **h** ITU estimate. **i** Age group 5 years and over. **j** Age group 15 to 44 years.

China[a]

Region	Eastern Asia
Currency	Yuan Renminbi (CNY)
Surface area (square kilometres)	9 596 961
Population in 2012 (estimated, 000)	1 377 065
Population density in 2012 (per square kilometre)	143.5
Capital city and population in 2011 (000)	Beijing (15 594)
United Nations membership date	24 October 1945

Economic indicators	2005	2010	2012
GDP: Gross domestic product (million current US$)	2 287 238	5 949 786	8 358 400
GDP: Growth rate at constant 2005 prices (annual %)	11.3	10.4	7.7
GDP per capita (current US$)	1 735.2	4 375.4	6 069.7
GNI: Gross national income per capita (current US$)	1 699.9	4 342.2	5 957.5
Gross fixed capital formation (% of GDP)	39.6	45.6	46.1
Exchange rates (national currency per US$)[b]	8.07	6.62	6.29
Balance of payments, current account (million US$)	132 378	237 810	193 139
CPI: Consumer price index (2000=100)	107	124	133
Agricultural production index (2004-2006=100)	100	120	127
Food production index (2004-2006=100)	100	121	128
Unemployment (% of labour force)[cd]	1.9	2.9	2.8
Employment in industrial sector (% of employed)[cde]	23.8	28.7	29.5[f]
Employment in agricultural sector (% of employed)[cde]	44.8	36.7	34.8[f]
Labour force participation, adult female pop. (%)	66.5	63.5	63.8
Labour force participation, adult male pop. (%)	79.5	77.6	78.1
Tourist arrivals at national borders (000)	46 809	55 664	57 725
Energy production, primary (000 mt oil equivalent)	1 439 360	1 980 266	...
Mobile-cellular subscriptions (per 100 inhabitants)	30.1	64.0	81.3[g]
Individuals using the Internet (%)	8.5	34.3	42.3[g]

Total trade		Major trading partners			2012
	(million US$)	(% of exports)			(% of imports)
Exports	2 048 782.3	United States	17.2	Japan	9.8
Imports	1 818 199.3	China, Hong Kong SAR	15.8	Republic of Korea	9.3
Balance	230 583.0	Japan	7.4	China	7.9[h]

Social indicators

Population growth rate (average annual %)	2010-2015	0.6
Urban population growth rate (average annual %)[i]	2010-2015	2.9
Rural population growth rate (average annual %)[i]	2010-2015	−2.3
Urban population (%)	2013	53.2
Population aged 0-14 years (%)	2013	18.0
Population aged 60+ years (females and males, % of total)	2013	14.6/13.3
Sex ratio (males per 100 females)	2013	107.6
Life expectancy at birth (females and males, years)	2010-2015	76.6/74.0
Infant mortality rate (per 1 000 live births)	2010-2015	13.0
Fertility rate, total (live births per woman)	2010-2015	1.7
Contraceptive prevalence (ages 15-49, %)	2006-2012	84.6
International migrant stock (000 and % of total population)	mid-2013	848.5/0.1
Refugees and others of concern to UNHCR	mid-2013	301 357[k]
Education: Government expenditure (% of GDP)	2006-2012	1.9[l]
Education: Primary-secondary gross enrolment ratio (f/m per 100)	2006-2012	103.7/103.4
Education: Female third-level students (% of total)	2006-2012	50.2
Intentional homicides (females and males, per 100 000)	2008-2010	1.0/2.2
Seats held by women in national parliaments (%)	2014	23.4

Environmental indicators

Threatened species	2013	958
Forested area (% of land area)	2011	22.5
CO_2 emission estimates (000 metric tons and metric tons per capita)	2010	8 280 112/6.2
Energy consumption per capita (kilograms oil equivalent)	2010	1 534.0
Precipitation in the capital city, total mean (millimetres)		578[m]
Temperature in the capital city, mean °C (minimum and maximum)		6.5/17.7

a For statistical purposes, the data for China do not include Hong Kong SAR, Macao SAR or Taiwan Province of China, unless otherwise indicated. **b** Principal rate. **c** Official estimates. **d** Age group 16 years and over. **e** December. **f** 2011. **g** ITU estimate. **h** Data refer to returned goods or goods resulting from outward processing, i.e. minor processing or, in general, operations which do not change the country of origin. When these goods come back they are recorded as re-imports and the country of origin is the country itself. **i** Excludes Hong Kong SAR and Macao SAR of China. **j** Estimates. **k** The 300,000 Vietnamese refugees are well integrated and in practice receive protection from the Government of China. **l** 1999. **m** Based on monthly averages for the period 1961-1990.

China, Hong Kong SAR

Region	Eastern Asia
Currency	Hong Kong Dollar (HKD)
Surface area (square kilometres)	1 104
Population in 2012 (estimated, 000)	7 148
Population density in 2012 (per square kilometre)	6 475.1
Capital city and population in 2011 (000)	Hong Kong (7 122)

Economic indicators	2005	2010	2012
GDP: Gross domestic product (million current US$)	181 569	228 697	263 259
GDP: Growth rate at constant 2005 prices (annual %)	7.4	6.8	1.5
GDP per capita (current US$)	26 327.0	32 441.5	36 827.2
GNI: Gross national income per capita (current US$)	26 466.2	33 127.9	37 611.4
Gross fixed capital formation (% of GDP)	21.4	21.8	26.4
Exchange rates (national currency per US$)[a]	7.75	7.77	7.75
Balance of payments, current account (million US$)	21 575	16 070	6 067
CPI: Consumer price index (2000=100)	94	104	114
Agricultural production index (2004-2006=100)	99	56	58
Food production index (2004-2006=100)	99	56	58
Unemployment (% of labour force)	5.6	4.3	3.3
Employment in industrial sector (% of employed)	15.1[bc]	11.4[de]	11.6[de]
Employment in agricultural sector (% of employed)[c]	0.3[b]	0.2[df]	...
Labour force participation, adult female pop. (%)	51.7	51.8	51.6
Labour force participation, adult male pop. (%)	71.2	68.4	68.0
Tourist arrivals at national borders (000)	14 773	20 085	23 770
Mobile-cellular subscriptions (per 100 inhabitants)	125.5	195.6	227.9
Individuals using the Internet (%)[g]	56.9	72.0	72.8

Total trade		Major trading partners			2012
	(million US$)	(% of exports)			(% of imports)
Exports	492 907.5	China	57.7	China	45.5
Imports	553 486.5	United States	8.9	Japan	7.7
Balance	−60 579.0	Japan	3.8	Singapore	6.3

Social indicators

Population growth rate (average annual %)	2010-2015	0.7
Urban population growth rate (average annual %)	2010-2015	1.0
Rural population growth rate (average annual %)	2010-2015	0.0
Urban population (%)	2013	100.0
Population aged 0-14 years (%)	2013	11.7
Population aged 60+ years (females and males, % of total)	2013	19.9/20.4
Sex ratio (males per 100 females)	2013	87.9
Life expectancy at birth (females and males, years)	2010-2015	86.4/80.3
Infant mortality rate (per 1 000 live births)	2010-2015	1.9
Fertility rate, total (live births per woman)	2010-2015	1.1
Contraceptive prevalence (ages 15-49, %)	2006-2012	79.5
International migrant stock (000 and % of total population)	mid-2013	2 804.8/38.9
Refugees and others of concern to UNHCR	mid-2013	1 427
Education: Government expenditure (% of GDP)	2006-2012	3.5
Education: Primary-secondary gross enrolment ratio (f/m per 100)	2006-2012	103.2/104.4
Education: Female third-level students (% of total)	2006-2012	51.0

Environmental indicators

Threatened species	2013	58
CO$_2$ emission estimates (000 metric tons and metric tons per capita)	2010	36 259/5.1
Energy consumption per capita (kilograms oil equivalent)	2010	1 697.0
Precipitation in the capital city, total mean (millimetres)		2 398[h]
Temperature in the capital city, mean °C (minimum and maximum)		21.4/25.6[h]

a Market rate. b The indices are shown in terms of ISIC Rev.2. c Excludes marine and institutional populations. d Average of quarterly estimates. e Excludes the institutional population. f 2008. g Age group 10 years and over. h Based on monthly averages for the period 1981-2010.

China, Macao SAR

Region	Eastern Asia
Currency	Pataca (MOP)
Surface area (square kilometres)	30
Population in 2012 (estimated, 000)	557
Population density in 2012 (per square kilometre)	18 559.4
Capital city and population in 2011 (000)	Macao (556)

Economic indicators	2005	2010	2012
GDP: Gross domestic product (million current US$)	11 793	28 360	43 582
GDP: Growth rate at constant 2005 prices (annual %)	8.6	27.5	10.0
GDP per capita (current US$)	25 189.8	53 046.0	78 275.1
GNI: Gross national income per capita (current US$)	23 584.1	47 340.6	71 387.1
Gross fixed capital formation (% of GDP)	25.8	12.5	13.4
Exchange rates (national currency per US$)[a]	7.99	8.02	7.98
Balance of payments, current account (million US$)	2 962	12 180	18 710
CPI: Consumer price index (2000=100)	99	124	139
Industrial production index (2005=100)[b]	100	45	42
Agricultural production index (2004-2006=100)	100	95	88
Food production index (2004-2006=100)	100	95	88
Unemployment (% of labour force)[cd]	4.1	2.8	2.0
Employment in industrial sector (% of employed)[b]	25.0[e]	16.0[cfgh]	...
Employment in agricultural sector (% of employed)[b]	0.1[e]	0.0[cfh]	...
Labour force participation, adult female pop. (%)	59.0	65.7	65.9
Labour force participation, adult male pop. (%)	74.3	77.2	77.5
Tourist arrivals at national borders (000)[ij]	9 014	11 926	13 578
Mobile-cellular subscriptions (per 100 inhabitants)	110.7	206.4	284.3
Individuals using the Internet (%)	34.9	55.2[k]	64.3[l]

Total trade		Major trading partners			2012
	(million US$)	(% of exports)[m]		(% of imports)	
Exports	1 020.5	China, Hong Kong SAR	39.7	China	32.3
Imports	8 982.1	Areas nes	36.4	China, Hong Kong SAR	11.4
Balance	−7 961.6	China	11.0	France	8.7

Social indicators		
Population growth rate (average annual %)	2010-2015	1.8
Urban population growth rate (average annual %)	2010-2015	2.0
Rural population growth rate (average annual %)	2010-2015	0.0
Urban population (%)	2013	100.0
Population aged 0-14 years (%)	2013	12.4
Population aged 60+ years (females and males, % of total)	2013	13.3/13.6
Sex ratio (males per 100 females)	2013	92.6
Life expectancy at birth (females and males, years)	2010-2015	82.5/78.1
Infant mortality rate (per 1 000 live births)	2010-2015	4.1
Fertility rate, total (live births per woman)	2010-2015	1.1
International migrant stock (000 and % of total population)	mid-2013	333.3/58.8
Refugees and others of concern to UNHCR	mid-2013	6
Education: Government expenditure (% of GDP)	2006-2012	2.7
Education: Primary-secondary gross enrolment ratio (f/m per 100)	2006-2012	95.9/97.8
Education: Female third-level students (% of total)	2006-2012	51.5

Environmental indicators		
Threatened species	2013	10
CO_2 emission estimates (000 metric tons and metric tons per capita)	2010	1 030/1.9
Energy consumption per capita (kilograms oil equivalent)	2010	1 152.0
Precipitation in the capital city, total mean (millimetres)		2 123[n]
Temperature in the capital city, mean °C (minimum and maximum)		20.2/25.2[n]

a Market rate. **b** The indices are shown in terms of ISIC Rev.3. **c** Age group 16 years and over. **d** 2009; Break in series; data not strictly comparable. **e** Age group 14 years and over. **f** 2009. **g** Excludes mining and quarrying. **h** Break in series; data not strictly comparable. **i** Country estimate. **j** From 2008, data does not include other non-residents (workers, students, etc.). **k** Age group 3 years and over. **l** ITU estimate. **m** See technical notes. **n** Based on monthly averages for the period 1971-2000.

Colombia

Region	South America
Currency	Colombian Peso (COP)
Surface area (square kilometres)	1 141 748
Population in 2012 (estimated, 000)	47 704
Population density in 2012 (per square kilometre)	41.8
Capital city and population in 2011 (000)	Bogotá (8 744)
United Nations membership date	5 November 1945

Economic indicators	2005	2010	2012
GDP: Gross domestic product (million current US$)	146 566	287 018	369 813
GDP: Growth rate at constant 2005 prices (annual %)	4.7	4.0	4.0
GDP per capita (current US$)	3 394.0	6 179.8	7 752.2
GNI: Gross national income per capita (current US$)	3 309.2	5 959.9	7 442.6
Gross fixed capital formation (% of GDP)	19.7	21.9	23.9
Exchange rates (national currency per US$)[a]	2 284.22	1 989.88	1 771.54
Balance of payments, current account (million US$)	−1 886	−8 919	−12 124
CPI: Consumer price index (2000=100)[b]	140	177	191
Agricultural production index (2004-2006=100)	99	102	108
Food production index (2004-2006=100)	99	104	111
Unemployment (% of labour force)[c]	11.8	11.8	10.4
Employment in industrial sector (% of employed)[de]	20.3	19.6	20.9
Employment in agricultural sector (% of employed)[de]	21.4	18.4	16.9
Labour force participation, adult female pop. (%)	53.0	55.3	55.7
Labour force participation, adult male pop. (%)	81.0	79.7	79.7
Tourist arrivals at national borders (000)	933	1 405	2 175
Energy production, primary (000 mt oil equivalent)	76 092	102 790	...
Mobile-cellular subscriptions (per 100 inhabitants)	50.8	96.1	103.2
Individuals using the Internet (%)	11.0	36.5[f]	49.0[f]

Total trade		Major trading partners			2012
	(million US$)	(% of exports)		(% of imports)	
Exports	60 273.6	United States	36.9	United States	24.3
Imports	58 087.9	China	5.5	China	16.5
Balance	2 185.7	Spain	4.9	Mexico	11.0

Social indicators		
Population growth rate (average annual %)	2010-2015	1.3
Urban population growth rate (average annual %)	2010-2015	1.7
Rural population growth rate (average annual %)	2010-2015	0.2
Urban population (%)	2013	75.9
Population aged 0-14 years (%)	2013	27.7
Population aged 60+ years (females and males, % of total)	2013	10.4/8.6
Sex ratio (males per 100 females)	2013	96.7
Life expectancy at birth (females and males, years)	2010-2015	77.6/70.3
Infant mortality rate (per 1 000 live births)	2010-2015	16.3
Fertility rate, total (live births per woman)	2010-2015	2.3
Contraceptive prevalence (ages 15-49, %)	2006-2012	79.1
International migrant stock (000 and % of total population)	mid-2013	129.6/0.3
Refugees and others of concern to UNHCR	mid-2013	4 744 410
Education: Government expenditure (% of GDP)	2006-2012	4.5
Education: Primary-secondary gross enrolment ratio (f/m per 100)	2006-2012	100.5/98.0
Education: Female third-level students (% of total)	2006-2012	52.2
Intentional homicides (females and males, per 100 000)	2008-2010	5.3/63.3
Seats held by women in national parliaments (%)	2014	12.1

Environmental indicators		
Threatened species	2013	730
Forested area (% of land area)	2011	54.4
CO_2 emission estimates (000 metric tons and metric tons per capita)	2010	75 618/1.7
Energy consumption per capita (kilograms oil equivalent)	2010	546.0
Precipitation in the capital city, total mean (millimetres)		799[g]
Temperature in the capital city, mean °C (minimum and maximum)		7.4/16.0[g]

a Official rate. **b** Low income group. **c** Nonstandard age coverage. **d** Age group 12 years and over. **e** The indices are shown in terms of ISIC Rev.2. **f** Age group 5 years and over. **g** Based on monthly averages for the period 1971-2000.

Comoros

Region	Eastern Africa
Currency	Comoros Franc (KMF)
Surface area (square kilometres)	2 235
Population in 2012 (estimated, 000)	718
Population density in 2012 (per square kilometre)	321.0
Capital city and population in 2011 (000)	Moroni (54)
United Nations membership date	12 November 1975

Economic indicators	2005	2010	2012
GDP: Gross domestic product (million current US$)	387	530	616
GDP: Growth rate at constant 2005 prices (annual %)	4.2	2.0	2.5
GDP per capita (current US$)	644.3	776.6	858.3
GNI: Gross national income per capita (current US$)	642.5	792.1	830.4
Gross fixed capital formation (% of GDP)	9.3	12.7	14.0
Exchange rates (national currency per US$)[a]	417.03	368.18	372.87
Agricultural production index (2004-2006=100)	96	113	112
Food production index (2004-2006=100)	96	114	112
Labour force participation, adult female pop. (%)	32.5	34.6	35.0
Labour force participation, adult male pop. (%)	79.6	80.2	80.2
Tourist arrivals at national borders (000)	26	15	19[b]
Mobile-cellular subscriptions (per 100 inhabitants)	2.4	22.5	32.3[c]
Individuals using the Internet (%)[c]	2.0	5.1	6.0

Total trade		Major trading partners			2012
	(million US$)[d]		(% of exports)[d]		(% of imports)[d]
Exports	12.6	France	43.7	United Arab Emirates	29.4
Imports	181.5	Singapore	23.8	France	21.4
Balance	−168.9	Netherlands	6.3	Pakistan	14.7

Social indicators		
Population growth rate (average annual %)	2010-2015	2.4
Urban population growth rate (average annual %)	2010-2015	2.8
Rural population growth rate (average annual %)	2010-2015	2.4
Urban population (%)	2013	28.2
Population aged 0-14 years (%)	2013	42.1
Population aged 60+ years (females and males, % of total)	2013	4.9/4.2
Sex ratio (males per 100 females)	2013	101.5
Life expectancy at birth (females and males, years)	2010-2015	62.2/59.4
Infant mortality rate (per 1 000 live births)	2010-2015	67.2
Fertility rate, total (live births per woman)	2010-2015	4.7
Contraceptive prevalence (ages 15-49, %)	2006-2012	25.7[e]
International migrant stock (000 and % of total population)	mid-2013	12.5/1.7
Refugees and others of concern to UNHCR	mid-2013	0[f]
Education: Government expenditure (% of GDP)	2006-2012	7.6
Education: Primary-secondary gross enrolment ratio (f/m per 100)	2006-2012	92.8/100.2
Education: Female third-level students (% of total)	2006-2012	45.0
Intentional homicides (females and males, per 100 000)[g]	2008-2010	7.9/16.4
Seats held by women in national parliaments (%)	2014	3.0

Environmental indicators		
Threatened species	2013	104
Forested area (% of land area)	2011	1.4
CO_2 emission estimates (000 metric tons and metric tons per capita)	2010	139/0.2
Energy consumption per capita (kilograms oil equivalent)	2010	64.0[h]
Precipitation in the capital city, total mean (millimetres)		2 700
Temperature in the capital city, mean °C (minimum and maximum)		21.2/29.5

a Official rate. **b** 2011. **c** ITU estimate. **d** 2009. **e** 2000. **f** Value is zero, not available or not applicable. **g** Estimates. **h** UNSD estimate.

Congo

Region	Middle Africa
Currency	CFA Franc (XAF)
Surface area (square kilometres)	342 000
Population in 2012 (estimated, 000)	4 337
Population density in 2012 (per square kilometre)	12.7
Capital city and population in 2011 (000)	Brazzaville (1 611)
United Nations membership date	20 September 1960

Economic indicators	2005	2010	2012
GDP: Gross domestic product (million current US$)	6 087	12 281	14 763
GDP: Growth rate at constant 2005 prices (annual %)	7.6	8.7	6.8
GDP per capita (current US$)	1 718.1	2 986.8	3 404.0
GNI: Gross national income per capita (current US$)	1 246.1	2 365.3	2 816.1
Gross fixed capital formation (% of GDP)	24.2	29.7	32.8
Exchange rates (national currency per US$)[a]	556.04	490.91	497.16
Balance of payments, current account (million US$)	696	−2 181[b]	...
CPI: Consumer price index (2000=100)[cd]	110	139[e]	145
Agricultural production index (2004-2006=100)	100	125	132
Food production index (2004-2006=100)	100	125	132
Employment in industrial sector (% of employed)	20.6[fgh]	...	...
Employment in agricultural sector (% of employed)	35.4[fgh]	...	...
Labour force participation, adult female pop. (%)	67.5	68.3	68.4
Labour force participation, adult male pop. (%)	71.7	72.8	72.9
Tourist arrivals at national borders (000)[i]	35	101	204
Energy production, primary (000 mt oil equivalent)	12 798	16 326	...
Mobile-cellular subscriptions (per 100 inhabitants)	15.8	92.0	101.2
Individuals using the Internet (%)[j]	1.5	5.0	6.1

Total trade		Major trading partners			2012
	(million US$)[k]	(% of exports)[k]			(% of imports)[k]
Exports	6 917.6	China	20.9	Angola	15.0
Imports	4 369.4	Angola	13.1	France	12.2
Balance	2 548.2	France	12.5	Singapore	10.1

Social indicators		
Population growth rate (average annual %)	2010-2015	2.6
Urban population growth rate (average annual %)	2010-2015	2.8
Rural population growth rate (average annual %)	2010-2015	1.0
Urban population (%)	2013	64.5
Population aged 0-14 years (%)	2013	42.5
Population aged 60+ years (females and males, % of total)	2013	5.5/4.8
Sex ratio (males per 100 females)	2013	100.0
Life expectancy at birth (females and males, years)	2010-2015	60.1/57.2
Infant mortality rate (per 1 000 live births)	2010-2015	63.6
Fertility rate, total (live births per woman)	2010-2015	5.0
Contraceptive prevalence (ages 15-49, %)	2006-2012	44.7
International migrant stock (000 and % of total population)	mid-2013	431.5/9.7
Refugees and others of concern to UNHCR	mid-2013	70 736
Education: Government expenditure (% of GDP)	2006-2012	6.2
Education: Primary-secondary gross enrolment ratio (f/m per 100)	2006-2012	82.5/82.2
Education: Female third-level students (% of total)	2006-2012	38.5
Intentional homicides (females and males, per 100 000)[i]	2008-2010	13.5/48.0
Seats held by women in national parliaments (%)	2014	7.4

Environmental indicators		
Threatened species	2013	109
Forested area (% of land area)	2011	65.6
CO$_2$ emission estimates (000 metric tons and metric tons per capita)	2010	2 026/0.5
Energy consumption per capita (kilograms oil equivalent)	2010	162.0

a Official rate. **b** 2007. **c** Brazzaville. **d** African population. **e** Series linked to former series. **f** Core Welfare Indicators Questionnaire (World Bank). **g** The indices are shown in terms of ISIC Rev.2. **h** June to August. **i** Arrivals of non-resident tourists in hotels and similar establishments. **j** ITU estimate. **k** 2010. **l** Estimates.

Cook Islands

Region	Oceania-Polynesia
Currency	New Zealand Dollar (NZD)
Surface area (square kilometres)	236 [a]
Population in 2012 (estimated, 000)	21 [a]
Population density in 2012 (per square kilometre)	87.0
Capital city and population in 2011 (000)	Avarua (...) [b]

Economic indicators	2005	2010	2012
GDP: Gross domestic product (million current US$)	183	257	306
GDP: Growth rate at constant 2005 prices (annual %)	−1.1	−2.9	3.0
GDP per capita (current US$)	9 410.7	12 653.0	14 917.7
GNI: Gross national income per capita (current US$)	9 410.7	12 653.0	14 917.7
Gross fixed capital formation (% of GDP)	13.1	12.3	12.3
Exchange rates (national currency per US$) [c]	1.46	1.31	1.22
CPI: Consumer price index (2000=100) [d]	118	144	...
Agricultural production index (2004-2006=100)	100	104	98
Food production index (2004-2006=100)	100	104	98
Tourist arrivals at national borders (000)	88	104	122

Total trade	Major trading partners				2012
(million US$) [e]		(% of exports) [e]			(% of imports) [e]
Exports	3.1	Japan	58.1	New Zealand	77.1
Imports	109.3	China	16.1	Fiji	10.0
Balance	−106.2	United States	6.5	Australia	5.3

Social indicators		
Population growth rate (average annual %)	2010-2015	0.5
Urban population growth rate (average annual %)	2010-2015	0.9
Rural population growth rate (average annual %)	2010-2015	−0.4
Urban population (%)	2013	74.0
Population aged 0-14 years (%) [fg]	2013	28.5
Population aged 60+ years (females and males, % of total) [fg]	2013	13.0/12.2
Sex ratio (males per 100 females) [fg]	2013	100.0
Life expectancy at birth (females and males, years) [fg]	2010-2015	79.8/73.6 [hi]
Infant mortality rate (per 1 000 live births) [fg]	2010-2015	7.0 [hi]
Fertility rate, total (live births per woman) [fg]	2010-2015	2.8 [e]
Contraceptive prevalence (ages 15-49, %)	2006-2012	43.2 [j]
International migrant stock (000 and % of total population)	mid-2013	3.2/15.7
Education: Government expenditure (% of GDP)	2006-2012	3.3
Education: Primary-secondary gross enrolment ratio (f/m per 100) [k]	2006-2012	99.6/89.8
Education: Female third-level students (% of total)	2006-2012	52.8

Environmental indicators		
Threatened species	2013	63
Forested area (% of land area)	2011	64.6
CO_2 emission estimates (000 metric tons and metric tons per capita)	2010	70/3.5
Energy consumption per capita (kilograms oil equivalent)	2010	1 159.0 [l]

a Excludes Niue. **b** Population estimates for Avarua are not available. **c** UN operational exchange rate.
d Rarotonga. **e** 2011. **f** Data compiled by the Secretariat of the Pacific Community Demography Programme.
g Resident population only. **h** 2006-2012. **i** Preliminary. **j** 1999. **k** National estimate. **l** UNSD estimate.

Costa Rica

Region	Central America
Currency	Costa Rica Colon (CRC)
Surface area (square kilometres)	51 100
Population in 2012 (estimated, 000)	4 805
Population density in 2012 (per square kilometre)	94.0
Capital city and population in 2011 (000)	San José (1 515)
United Nations membership date	2 November 1945

Economic indicators	2005	2010	2012
GDP: Gross domestic product (million current US$)	19 965	36 298	45 107
GDP: Growth rate at constant 2005 prices (annual %)	5.9	5.0	5.1
GDP per capita (current US$)	4 621.4	7 773.2	9 387.0
GNI: Gross national income per capita (current US$)	4 440.6	7 563.1	9 128.8
Gross fixed capital formation (% of GDP)	18.7	19.8	20.2
Exchange rates (national currency per US$)[a]	496.68	512.97	508.20
Balance of payments, current account (million US$)	−981	−1 281	−2 376
CPI: Consumer price index (2000=100)[b]	170	268	293
Agricultural production index (2004-2006=100)	98	110	119
Food production index (2004-2006=100)	98	112	120
Unemployment (% of labour force)	...	...	10.1
Employment in industrial sector (% of employed)	21.6[cde]	19.5[cd]	19.5[e]
Employment in agricultural sector (% of employed)	15.2[cde]	15.0[cd]	13.4[e]
Labour force participation, adult female pop. (%)	44.0	46.1	46.4
Labour force participation, adult male pop. (%)	80.5	78.9	79.0
Tourist arrivals at national borders (000)	1 679	2 100	2 343
Energy production, primary (000 mt oil equivalent)	681	756	...
Mobile-cellular subscriptions (per 100 inhabitants)	25.6	65.1	128.3
Individuals using the Internet (%)	22.1[f]	36.5[g]	47.5[g]

Total trade		Major trading partners			2012
	(million US$)		(% of exports)		(% of imports)
Exports	11 250.8	United States	38.3	United States	51.9
Imports	18 356.0	Netherlands	7.6	China	7.9
Balance	−7 105.2	Panama	5.2	Mexico	6.5

Social indicators

Population growth rate (average annual %)	2010-2015	1.4
Urban population growth rate (average annual %)	2010-2015	2.1
Rural population growth rate (average annual %)	2010-2015	<
Urban population (%)	2013	65.6
Population aged 0-14 years (%)	2013	23.5
Population aged 60+ years (females and males, % of total)	2013	11.2/9.9
Sex ratio (males per 100 females)	2013	103.2
Life expectancy at birth (females and males, years)	2010-2015	82.1/77.7
Infant mortality rate (per 1 000 live births)	2010-2015	8.5
Fertility rate, total (live births per woman)	2010-2015	1.8
Contraceptive prevalence (ages 15-49, %)	2006-2012	82.2
International migrant stock (000 and % of total population)[h]	mid-2013	419.6/8.6
Refugees and others of concern to UNHCR	mid-2013	21 600
Education: Government expenditure (% of GDP)	2006-2012	6.3
Education: Primary-secondary gross enrolment ratio (f/m per 100)	2006-2012	105.3/103.4
Education: Female third-level students (% of total)	2006-2012	54.6
Intentional homicides (females and males, per 100 000)	2008-2010	2.6/18.8
Seats held by women in national parliaments (%)	2014	38.6

Environmental indicators

Threatened species	2013	315
Forested area (% of land area)	2011	51.5
CO_2 emission estimates (000 metric tons and metric tons per capita)	2010	7 764/1.7
Energy consumption per capita (kilograms oil equivalent)	2010	670.0
Precipitation in the capital city, total mean (millimetres)		1 866[i]
Temperature in the capital city, mean °C (minimum and maximum)		16.2/24.9[j]

a Market rate. b Central area. c The indices are shown in terms of ISIC Rev.2. d Age group 12 years and over. e July. f Age group 5 years and over. g Age group 5 years and over using the Internet within the last 3 months. h Includes refugees. i Based on monthly averages for the period 1888-1997. j Based on monthly averages for the period 1961-1982.

Côte d'Ivoire

Region	Western Africa
Currency	CFA Franc (XOF)
Surface area (square kilometres)	322 463
Population in 2012 (estimated, 000)	19 840
Population density in 2012 (per square kilometre)	61.5
Capital city and population in 2011 (000)	Yamoussoukro (966)[a]
United Nations membership date	20 September 1960

Economic indicators	2005	2010	2012
GDP: Gross domestic product (million current US$)	17 085	22 920	24 406
GDP: Growth rate at constant 2005 prices (annual %)	1.7	2.4	8.6
GDP per capita (current US$)	982.2	1 207.8	1 230.2
GNI: Gross national income per capita (current US$)	914.3	1 163.2	1 184.7
Gross fixed capital formation (% of GDP)	9.2	9.0	12.5
Exchange rates (national currency per US$)[b]	556.04	490.91	497.16
Balance of payments, current account (million US$)	40	465	...
CPI: Consumer price index (2000=100)[cd]	117	133[e]	139[f]
Industrial production index (2005=100)[g]	100	103	124
Agricultural production index (2004-2006=100)	100	104	115
Food production index (2004-2006=100)	98	106	118
Labour force participation, adult female pop. (%)	50.6	52.0	52.2
Labour force participation, adult male pop. (%)	82.2	81.7	81.5
Tourist arrivals at national borders (000)[h]	182[i]	252	289
Energy production, primary (000 mt oil equivalent)	3 757	3 337	...
Mobile-cellular subscriptions (per 100 inhabitants)	13.0	79.0	96.3
Individuals using the Internet (%)	1.0	2.1[j]	2.4[j]

Total trade		Major trading partners			2012
	(million US$)	(% of exports)			(% of imports)
Exports	10 861.0	Netherlands	8.7	Nigeria	25.7
Imports	9 769.7	United States	8.1	France	12.4
Balance	1 091.3	Nigeria	8.0	China	7.3

Social indicators		
Population growth rate (average annual %)	2010-2015	2.3
Urban population growth rate (average annual %)	2010-2015	3.6
Rural population growth rate (average annual %)	2010-2015	0.7
Urban population (%)	2013	52.8
Population aged 0-14 years (%)	2013	41.3
Population aged 60+ years (females and males, % of total)	2013	4.7/5.5
Sex ratio (males per 100 females)	2013	104.0
Life expectancy at birth (females and males, years)	2010-2015	51.4/49.7
Infant mortality rate (per 1 000 live births)	2010-2015	75.3
Fertility rate, total (live births per woman)	2010-2015	4.9
Contraceptive prevalence (ages 15-49, %)	2006-2012	12.9
International migrant stock (000 and % of total population)[k]	mid-2013	2 446.2/12.0
Refugees and others of concern to UNHCR	mid-2013	759 275
Education: Government expenditure (% of GDP)	2006-2012	4.6
Education: Primary-secondary gross enrolment ratio (f/m per 100)[l]	2006-2012	45.2/65.4[m]
Education: Female third-level students (% of total)	2006-2012	33.8
Intentional homicides (females and males, per 100 000)[n]	2008-2010	17.6/94.5
Seats held by women in national parliaments (%)	2014	9.4

Environmental indicators		
Threatened species	2013	217
Forested area (% of land area)	2011	32.7
CO$_2$ emission estimates (000 metric tons and metric tons per capita)	2010	5 800/0.3
Energy consumption per capita (kilograms oil equivalent)	2010	126.0

a Yamoussoukro is the capital and Abidjan is the seat of government. **b** Official rate. **c** Abidjan. **d** African population. **e** Series linked to former series. **f** 2011. **g** The indices are shown in terms of ISIC Rev.3. **h** Arrivals of non-resident visitors at national borders. **i** 2007. **j** ITU estimate. **k** Data refer to foreign-born and foreign citizens. **l** UNESCO estimate. **m** 2002. **n** Estimates.

Croatia

Region	Southern Europe
Currency	Kuna (HRK)
Surface area (square kilometres)	56 594
Population in 2012 (estimated, 000)	4 307
Population density in 2012 (per square kilometre)	76.1
Capital city and population in 2011 (000)	Zagreb (686)
United Nations membership date	22 May 1992

Economic indicators	2005	2010	2012
GDP: Gross domestic product (million current US$)	44 821	58 895	56 447
GDP: Growth rate at constant 2005 prices (annual %)	4.3	−2.3	−2.0
GDP per capita (current US$)	10 212.5	13 576.5	13 104.6
GNI: Gross national income per capita (current US$)	9 996.0	13 190.2	12 647.2
Gross fixed capital formation (% of GDP)	24.7	20.8	19.2
Exchange rates (national currency per US$)[a]	6.23	5.57	5.73
Balance of payments, current account (million US$)	−2 460	−929	−186
CPI: Consumer price index (2000=100)	114	133	141
Industrial production index (2005=100)	100	99	92
Agricultural production index (2004-2006=100)	98	100	88
Food production index (2004-2006=100)	98	100	88
Unemployment (% of labour force)[b]	12.6	11.8	15.8
Employment in industrial sector (% of employed)	28.6[cd]	27.3[e]	27.4[e]
Employment in agricultural sector (% of employed)	17.3[cd]	14.9[e]	13.7[e]
Labour force participation, adult female pop. (%)	46.3	45.7	44.8
Labour force participation, adult male pop. (%)	61.3	59.1	58.5
Tourist arrivals at national borders (000)[f]	7 743	9 111	10 369
Energy production, primary (000 mt oil equivalent)	3 653	3 963	...
Mobile-cellular subscriptions (per 100 inhabitants)	82.2	111.9[g]	113.3
Individuals using the Internet (%)[h]	33.1	56.6	63.0

Total trade		Major trading partners			2012
	(million US$)		(% of exports)		(% of imports)
Exports	12 369.0	Italy	15.3	Italy	16.9
Imports	20 834.3	Bosnia-Herzegovina	12.8	Germany	12.7
Balance	−8 465.3	Germany	10.2	Russian Federation	7.6

Social indicators		
Population growth rate (average annual %)	2010-2015	−0.4
Urban population growth rate (average annual %)	2010-2015	0.3
Rural population growth rate (average annual %)	2010-2015	−0.9
Urban population (%)	2013	58.4
Population aged 0-14 years (%)	2013	14.9
Population aged 60+ years (females and males, % of total)	2013	28.3/21.6
Sex ratio (males per 100 females)	2013	93.2
Life expectancy at birth (females and males, years)	2010-2015	80.3/73.6
Infant mortality rate (per 1 000 live births)	2010-2015	5.1
Fertility rate, total (live births per woman)	2010-2015	1.5
Contraceptive prevalence (ages 15-49, %)[i]	2006-2012	58.0[j]
International migrant stock (000 and % of total population)[k]	mid-2013	757.0/17.7
Refugees and others of concern to UNHCR	mid-2013	24 059
Education: Government expenditure (% of GDP)	2006-2012	4.3
Education: Primary-secondary gross enrolment ratio (f/m per 100)	2006-2012	98.1/95.7
Education: Female third-level students (% of total)	2006-2012	57.3
Intentional homicides (females and males, per 100 000)	2008-2010	1.1/1.2
Seats held by women in national parliaments (%)	2014	23.8

Environmental indicators		
Threatened species	2013	156
Forested area (% of land area)	2011	34.4
CO_2 emission estimates (000 metric tons and metric tons per capita)	2010	20 866/4.7
Energy consumption per capita (kilograms oil equivalent)	2010	1 904.0
Precipitation in the capital city, total mean (millimetres)		856
Temperature in the capital city, mean °C (minimum and maximum)		5.4/15.7

a Market rate. b Age group 15 to 74 years. c The indices are shown in terms of ISIC Rev.3. d Excludes conscripts. e European Labour Force Survey (Eurostat). f Arrivals of non-resident tourists in all types of accommodation establishments. g ITU estimate. h Age group 16 to 74 years. i Age group 15 to 44 years. j 1970. k Includes refugees.

Cuba

Region	Caribbean
Currency	Cuban Peso (CUP)[a]
Surface area (square kilometres)	109 884
Population in 2012 (estimated, 000)	11 271
Population density in 2012 (per square kilometre)	102.6
Capital city and population in 2011 (000)	Havana (2 116)
United Nations membership date	24 October 1945

Economic indicators	2005	2010	2012
GDP: Gross domestic product (million current US$)	42 644	64 328	71 017
GDP: Growth rate at constant 2005 prices (annual %)	11.2	2.4	3.0
GDP per capita (current US$)	3 776.5	5 702.0	6 300.8
GNI: Gross national income per capita (current US$)	3 720.4	5 608.6	6 197.7
Gross fixed capital formation (% of GDP)	9.0	10.6	9.9
CPI: Consumer price index (2000=100)	109	125[b]	...
Agricultural production index (2004-2006=100)	97	88	95
Food production index (2004-2006=100)	97	88	95
Employment in industrial sector (% of employed)[cd]	19.1[e]	17.0	17.1[f]
Employment in agricultural sector (% of employed)[cd]	20.2[e]	18.5	19.7[f]
Labour force participation, adult female pop. (%)	38.7	43.1	43.3
Labour force participation, adult male pop. (%)	67.2	70.1	70.1
Tourist arrivals at national borders (000)[g]	2 261	2 507	2 815
Energy production, primary (000 mt oil equivalent)	3 953	4 200	...
Mobile-cellular subscriptions (per 100 inhabitants)	1.2	8.9	15.0
Individuals using the Internet (%)	9.7[h]	15.9[h]	25.6[i]

Social indicators		
Population growth rate (average annual %)	2010-2015	−0.1
Urban population growth rate (average annual %)	2010-2015	−0.1
Rural population growth rate (average annual %)	2010-2015	<
Urban population (%)	2013	75.1
Population aged 0-14 years (%)	2013	16.2
Population aged 60+ years (females and males, % of total)	2013	19.6/17.4
Sex ratio (males per 100 females)	2013	101.1
Life expectancy at birth (females and males, years)	2010-2015	81.2/77.2
Infant mortality rate (per 1 000 live births)	2010-2015	4.5
Fertility rate, total (live births per woman)	2010-2015	1.5
Contraceptive prevalence (ages 15-49, %)	2006-2012	72.6
International migrant stock (000 and % of total population)	mid-2013	16.2/0.1
Refugees and others of concern to UNHCR	mid-2013	374
Education: Government expenditure (% of GDP)	2006-2012	12.9
Education: Primary-secondary gross enrolment ratio (f/m per 100)	2006-2012	94.4/94.8
Education: Female third-level students (% of total)	2006-2012	60.1
Intentional homicides (females and males, per 100 000)	2008-2010	2.2/7.2
Seats held by women in national parliaments (%)	2014	48.9

Environmental indicators		
Threatened species	2013	331
Forested area (% of land area)	2011	27.3
CO$_2$ emission estimates (000 metric tons and metric tons per capita)	2010	38 333/3.4
Energy consumption per capita (kilograms oil equivalent)	2010	1 074.0
Precipitation in the capital city, total mean (millimetres)		1 189[j]
Temperature in the capital city, mean °C (minimum and maximum)		21.6/28.8[j]

a The national currency of Cuba is the Cuban Peso (CUP). The convertible peso (CUC) is used by foreigners and tourists in Cuba. b 2008. c The indices are shown in terms of ISIC Rev.2. d Age group 17 to 59 for males and age group 17 to 54 for females. e December. f 2011. g Air arrivals. h Includes users of the international network and also those having access only to the Cuban network. i ITU estimate. j Based on WMO Climatological Normals (CLINO) for the period 1961-1990.

Cyprus[a]

Region	Western Asia
Currency	Euro (EUR)[b]
Surface area (square kilometres)	9 251
Population in 2012 (estimated, 000)	1 129[c]
Population density in 2012 (per square kilometre)	122.0
Capital city and population in 2011 (000)	Nicosia (253)
United Nations membership date	20 September 1960

Economic indicators	2005	2010	2012
GDP: Gross domestic product (million current US$)	16 902	23 053	22 768
GDP: Growth rate at constant 2005 prices (annual %)	3.9	1.3	−2.4
GDP per capita (current US$)	22 298.5	28 680.3	26 462.4
GNI: Gross national income per capita (current US$)	21 372.4	27 756.1	25 580.3
Gross fixed capital formation (% of GDP)	19.4	19.1	13.7
Exchange rates (national currency per US$)	0.48[de]	0.75[fg]	0.76[fg]
Balance of payments, current account (million US$)	−971	−2 309	−1 577
CPI: Consumer price index (2000=100)	115	129	137
Industrial production index (2005=100)	100	100	83
Agricultural production index (2004-2006=100)	98	83	83
Food production index (2004-2006=100)	98	84	83
Unemployment (% of labour force)[hi]	5.3	6.3	11.8
Employment in industrial sector (% of employed)[j]	24.1[k]	20.4	20.2
Employment in agricultural sector (% of employed)[j]	4.6[k]	3.8	2.9
Labour force participation, adult female pop. (%)	53.6	57.1	55.8
Labour force participation, adult male pop. (%)	73.1	71.3	70.8
Tourist arrivals at national borders (000)	2 470	2 173	2 465
Energy production, primary (000 mt oil equivalent)	0	9	...
Mobile-cellular subscriptions (per 100 inhabitants)	75.8	93.7	98.4
Individuals using the Internet (%)[l]	32.8	53.0	61.0

Total trade		Major trading partners			2012
	(million US$)	(% of exports)[m]			(% of imports)
Exports	1 826.0	Greece	20.3	Greece	21.2
Imports	7 376.9	Bunkers	18.7	Israel	11.8
Balance	−5 550.9	United Kingdom	8.9	Italy	8.2

Social indicators		
Population growth rate (average annual %)[c]	2010-2015	1.1
Urban population growth rate (average annual %)[c]	2010-2015	1.4
Rural population growth rate (average annual %)[c]	2010-2015	0.4
Urban population (%)[c]	2013	70.9
Population aged 0-14 years (%)[c]	2013	17.0
Population aged 60+ years (females and males, % of total)[c]	2013	18.8/15.7
Sex ratio (males per 100 females)[c]	2013	104.4
Life expectancy at birth (females and males, years)[c]	2010-2015	81.8/77.8
Infant mortality rate (per 1 000 live births)[c]	2010-2015	3.7
Fertility rate, total (live births per woman)[c]	2010-2015	1.5
International migrant stock (000 and % of total population)[c]	mid-2013	207.3/18.2
Refugees and others of concern to UNHCR	mid-2013	7 188[n]
Education: Government expenditure (% of GDP)	2006-2012	7.3
Education: Primary-secondary gross enrolment ratio (f/m per 100)[o]	2006-2012	96.7/96.3
Education: Female third-level students (% of total)	2006-2012	49.8
Intentional homicides (females and males, per 100 000)	2008-2010	1.3/2.2
Seats held by women in national parliaments (%)	2014	12.5

Environmental indicators		
Threatened species	2013	57
Forested area (% of land area)	2011	18.8
CO$_2$ emission estimates (000 metric tons and metric tons per capita)	2010	7 702/7.0
Energy consumption per capita (kilograms oil equivalent)	2010	2 102.0
Precipitation in the capital city, total mean (millimetres)		342[p]
Temperature in the capital city, mean °C (minimum and maximum)		13.7/26.5[p]

a Data generally refer to the government-controlled area unless otherwise indicated. b Beginning 1 January 2008, the Cyprus Pound (CYP) was replaced by the euro (1 EUR=0.585274 CYP). c Includes Northern Cyprus. d Official rate. e Cyprus Pound (CYP). f Market rate. g Euro. h Age group 15 to 74 years. i 2009: Break in series; data not strictly comparable. j European Labour Force Survey (Eurostat). k The indices are shown in terms of ISIC Rev.3. l Age group 16 to 74 years. m See technical notes. n UNHCR's assistance activities for internally displaced persons in Cyprus ended in 1999. o National estimate. p Based on monthly averages for the period 2002-2011.

Czech Republic

Region	Eastern Europe
Currency	Czech Koruna (CZK)
Surface area (square kilometres)	78 866
Population in 2012 (estimated, 000)	10 660
Population density in 2012 (per square kilometre)	135.2
Capital city and population in 2011 (000)	Prague (1 276)
United Nations membership date	19 January 1993

Economic indicators	2005	2010	2012
GDP: Gross domestic product (million current US$)	130 066	198 494	196 446
GDP: Growth rate at constant 2005 prices (annual %)	6.8	2.5	−1.0
GDP per capita (current US$)	12 713.4	18 808.0	18 428.3
GNI: Gross national income per capita (current US$)	12 177.5	17 394.4	17 063.0
Gross fixed capital formation (% of GDP)	25.9	24.6	23.2
Exchange rates (national currency per US$)[a]	24.59	18.75	19.06
Balance of payments, current account (million US$)	−1 210	−7 602	−4 731
CPI: Consumer price index (2000=100)	112	129	135
Industrial production index (2005=100)	100	110	116
Agricultural production index (2004-2006=100)	100	91	89
Food production index (2004-2006=100)	100	91	89
Unemployment (% of labour force)[bc]	7.9	7.3	7.0
Employment in industrial sector (% of employed)	39.5[d]	38.0[e]	38.1[ef]
Employment in agricultural sector (% of employed)	4.0[d]	3.1[e]	3.1[ef]
Labour force participation, adult female pop. (%)	50.6	49.2	50.1
Labour force participation, adult male pop. (%)	68.7	68.0	67.8
Tourist arrivals at national borders (000)	9 404	8 629	8 908
Energy production, primary (000 mt oil equivalent)	26 843	24 136	...
Mobile-cellular subscriptions (per 100 inhabitants)	115.2	123.6	122.8[g]
Individuals using the Internet (%)[h]	35.3	68.8	75.0

Total trade		Major trading partners			2012
	(million US$)	(% of exports)			(% of imports)
Exports	156 422.7	Germany	31.4	Germany	25.5
Imports	139 726.8	Slovakia	9.1	China	11.2
Balance	16 695.9	Poland	6.1	Poland	7.1

Social indicators		
Population growth rate (average annual %)	2010-2015	0.4
Urban population growth rate (average annual %)	2010-2015	0.2
Rural population growth rate (average annual %)	2010-2015	0.4
Urban population (%)	2013	73.4
Population aged 0-14 years (%)	2013	14.9
Population aged 60+ years (females and males, % of total)	2013	26.6/20.7
Sex ratio (males per 100 females)	2013	96.9
Life expectancy at birth (females and males, years)	2010-2015	80.6/74.5
Infant mortality rate (per 1 000 live births)	2010-2015	2.6
Fertility rate, total (live births per woman)	2010-2015	1.6
Contraceptive prevalence (ages 15-49, %)[i]	2006-2012	72.0[j]
International migrant stock (000 and % of total population)[k]	mid-2013	432.8/4.0
Refugees and others of concern to UNHCR	mid-2013	4 892
Education: Government expenditure (% of GDP)	2006-2012	4.3
Education: Primary-secondary gross enrolment ratio (f/m per 100)	2006-2012	98.3/98.2
Education: Female third-level students (% of total)	2006-2012	57.2
Intentional homicides (females and males, per 100 000)	2008-2010	0.7/1.1
Seats held by women in national parliaments (%)	2014	19.5

Environmental indicators		
Threatened species	2013	46
Forested area (% of land area)	2011	34.4
CO$_2$ emission estimates (000 metric tons and metric tons per capita)	2010	111 660/10.6
Energy consumption per capita (kilograms oil equivalent)	2010	3 350.0
Precipitation in the capital city, total mean (millimetres)		526[l]
Temperature in the capital city, mean °C (minimum and maximum)		3.6/12.5[l]

a Official rate. **b** Age group 15 to 74 years. **c** 2011: Break in series; data not strictly comparable. **d** The indices are shown in terms of ISIC Rev.3. **e** European Labour Force Survey (Eurostat). **f** Break in series; data not strictly comparable. **g** Includes subscriptions to WiFi hotspots. **h** Age group 16 to 74 years. **i** Age group 15 to 44 years. **j** 1997. **k** Data refer to foreign citizens. **l** Based on monthly averages for the period 1961-1990.

Democratic People's Republic of Korea

Region	Eastern Asia		
Currency	North Korean Won (KPW)		
Surface area (square kilometres)	120 538		
Population in 2012 (estimated, 000)	24 763		
Population density in 2012 (per square kilometre)	205.4		
Capital city and population in 2011 (000)	P'yongyang (2 843)		
United Nations membership date	17 September 1991		

Economic indicators	2005	2010	2012
GDP: Gross domestic product (million current US$)	13 031	13 945	14 411
GDP: Growth rate at constant 2005 prices (annual %)	3.8	−0.5	0.3
GDP per capita (current US$)	547.9	569.8	582.6
GNI: Gross national income per capita (current US$)	546.6	570.4	582.8
Exchange rates (national currency per US$)[a]	141.00	98.10[b]	98.95
Agricultural production index (2004-2006=100)	101	98	94
Food production index (2004-2006=100)	101	98	93
Labour force participation, adult female pop. (%)	73.5	72.5	72.3
Labour force participation, adult male pop. (%)	86.1	84.3	84.2
Energy production, primary (000 mt oil equivalent)	23 187	21 657	...
Mobile-cellular subscriptions (per 100 inhabitants)	...	1.8	6.9[c]

Social indicators		
Population growth rate (average annual %)	2010-2015	0.5
Urban population growth rate (average annual %)	2010-2015	0.6
Rural population growth rate (average annual %)	2010-2015	0.1
Urban population (%)	2013	60.6
Population aged 0-14 years (%)	2013	21.7
Population aged 60+ years (females and males, % of total)	2013	15.2/9.7
Sex ratio (males per 100 females)	2013	95.6
Life expectancy at birth (females and males, years)	2010-2015	73.3/66.3
Infant mortality rate (per 1 000 live births)	2010-2015	22.0
Fertility rate, total (live births per woman)	2010-2015	2.0
Contraceptive prevalence (ages 15-49, %)	2006-2012	68.6[d]
International migrant stock (000 and % of total population)[e]	mid-2013	46.8/0.2
Intentional homicides (females and males, per 100 000)[e]	2008-2010	3.7/27.1
Seats held by women in national parliaments (%)	2014	15.6

Environmental indicators		
Threatened species	2013	62
Forested area (% of land area)	2011	46.0
CO$_2$ emission estimates (000 metric tons and metric tons per capita)	2010	71 565/2.9
Energy consumption per capita (kilograms oil equivalent)	2010	788.0
Precipitation in the capital city, total mean (millimetres)		940[f]
Temperature in the capital city, mean °C (minimum and maximum)		5.6/15.7[f]

a UN operational exchange rate. b December 2010. c ITU estimate. d 2002. e Estimates. f Based on monthly averages for the period 1971-2000.

Democratic Republic of the Congo

Region	Middle Africa
Currency	Congo Franc (CDF)
Surface area (square kilometres)	2 344 858
Population in 2012 (estimated, 000)	65 705
Population density in 2012 (per square kilometre)	28.0
Capital city and population in 2011 (000)	Kinshasa (8 798)
United Nations membership date	20 September 1960

Economic indicators	2005	2010	2012
GDP: Gross domestic product (million current US$)	7 191	13 190	18 823
GDP: Growth rate at constant 2005 prices (annual %)	7.8	7.2	7.2
GDP per capita (current US$)	133.1	212.1	286.5
GNI: Gross national income per capita (current US$)	125.5	199.9	263.2
Gross fixed capital formation (% of GDP)	20.0	21.9	28.2
Exchange rates (national currency per US$)[a]	431.28	915.13	915.18
Balance of payments, current account (million US$)	−389	−2 174	−1 696
Agricultural production index (2004-2006=100)	100	101	109
Food production index (2004-2006=100)	100	102	109
Labour force participation, adult female pop. (%)	71.0	70.7	70.7
Labour force participation, adult male pop. (%)	73.1	73.1	73.2
Tourist arrivals at national borders (000)	61	81[b]	186[c]
Energy production, primary (000 mt oil equivalent)	2 002	1 900	...
Mobile-cellular subscriptions (per 100 inhabitants)	4.8[d]	17.9	28.0
Individuals using the Internet (%)	0.2[e]	0.7[f]	1.7[e]

Social indicators		
Population growth rate (average annual %)	2010-2015	2.7
Urban population growth rate (average annual %)	2010-2015	4.2
Rural population growth rate (average annual %)	2010-2015	1.8
Urban population (%)	2013	35.4
Population aged 0-14 years (%)	2013	45.0
Population aged 60+ years (females and males, % of total)	2013	4.9/4.1
Sex ratio (males per 100 females)	2013	98.7
Life expectancy at birth (females and males, years)	2010-2015	51.6/48.1
Infant mortality rate (per 1 000 live births)	2010-2015	108.6
Fertility rate, total (live births per woman)	2010-2015	6.0
Contraceptive prevalence (ages 15-49, %)	2006-2012	17.7
International migrant stock (000 and % of total population)[g]	mid-2013	446.9/0.7
Refugees and others of concern to UNHCR	mid-2013	3 320 080
Education: Government expenditure (% of GDP)	2006-2012	2.5
Education: Primary-secondary gross enrolment ratio (f/m per 100)	2006-2012	71.2/89.3
Education: Female third-level students (% of total)	2006-2012	35.4
Intentional homicides (females and males, per 100 000)[h]	2008-2010	7.8/35.8
Seats held by women in national parliaments (%)	2014	10.6

Environmental indicators		
Threatened species	2013	314
Forested area (% of land area)	2011	67.9
CO$_2$ emission estimates (000 metric tons and metric tons per capita)	2010	3 037/0.0
Energy consumption per capita (kilograms oil equivalent)	2010	23.0

a Market rate. b Air arrivals only. c 2011. d Includes inactive subscriptions. e ITU estimate. f Country estimate. g Includes refugees. h Estimates.

Denmark

Region	Northern Europe
Currency	Danish Krone (DKK)
Surface area (square kilometres)	43 094 [a]
Population in 2012 (estimated, 000)	5 598 [a]
Population density in 2012 (per square kilometre)	129.9
Capital city and population in 2011 (000)	Copenhagen (1 206)
United Nations membership date	24 October 1945

Economic indicators	2005	2010	2012
GDP: Gross domestic product (million current US$)	257 676	313 139	314 889
GDP: Growth rate at constant 2005 prices (annual %)	2.4	1.6	−0.4
GDP per capita (current US$)	47 561.9	56 411.7	56 252.6
GNI: Gross national income per capita (current US$)	48 225.1	57 728.8	57 927.7
Gross fixed capital formation (% of GDP)	19.7	17.0	17.1
Exchange rates (national currency per US$) [b]	6.32	5.61	5.66
Balance of payments, current account (million US$)	11 104	18 183	18 750
CPI: Consumer price index (2000=100)	110	122	129
Industrial production index (2005=100)	100	86	88
Agricultural production index (2004-2006=100)	101	101	102
Food production index (2004-2006=100)	101	101	102
Unemployment (% of labour force) [c]	4.8	7.5	7.5
Employment in industrial sector (% of employed) [d]	23.4 [e]	19.6 [f]	19.7 [f]
Employment in agricultural sector (% of employed) [d]	2.8 [e]	2.4 [f]	2.6 [f]
Labour force participation, adult female pop. (%)	60.5	59.8	59.1
Labour force participation, adult male pop. (%)	71.4	69.1	67.5
Tourist arrivals at national borders (000) [gh]	9 178	8 744	8 068
Energy production, primary (000 mt oil equivalent) [a]	29 772	21 193	...
Mobile-cellular subscriptions (per 100 inhabitants)	100.6	115.7 [i]	118.0
Individuals using the Internet (%) [j]	82.7	88.7	93.0

Total trade		Major trading partners			2012
	(million US$) [a]	(% of exports) [ak]		(% of imports) [a]	
Exports	106 126.0	Germany	14.1	Germany	20.7
Imports	92 296.8	Sweden	12.7	Sweden	13.4
Balance	13 829.2	Areas nes	9.4	Netherlands	7.3

Social indicators		
Population growth rate (average annual %)	2010-2015	0.4
Urban population growth rate (average annual %)	2010-2015	0.5
Rural population growth rate (average annual %)	2010-2015	−0.7
Urban population (%)	2013	87.2
Population aged 0-14 years (%)	2013	17.6
Population aged 60+ years (females and males, % of total)	2013	25.7/22.5
Sex ratio (males per 100 females)	2013	98.5
Life expectancy at birth (females and males, years)	2010-2015	81.4/77.2
Infant mortality rate (per 1 000 live births)	2010-2015	3.4
Fertility rate, total (live births per woman)	2010-2015	1.9
Contraceptive prevalence (ages 15-49, %) [l]	2006-2012	78.0 [m]
International migrant stock (000 and % of total population)	mid-2013	556.8/9.9
Refugees and others of concern to UNHCR	mid-2013	17 424 [n]
Education: Government expenditure (% of GDP)	2006-2012	8.7
Education: Primary-secondary gross enrolment ratio (f/m per 100)	2006-2012	110.1/109.4
Education: Female third-level students (% of total)	2006-2012	58.1
Intentional homicides (females and males, per 100 000)	2008-2010	0.5/0.9
Seats held by women in national parliaments (%)	2014	39.1

Environmental indicators		
Threatened species	2013	37
Forested area (% of land area)	2011	12.9
CO$_2$ emission estimates (000 metric tons and metric tons per capita)	2010	46 265/8.4
Energy consumption per capita (kilograms oil equivalent) [a]	2010	2 848.0
Precipitation in the capital city, total mean (millimetres)		525 [o]
Temperature in the capital city, mean °C (minimum and maximum)		5.0/11.1 [o]

a Excludes Faeroe Islands and Greenland. b Market rate. c Age group 15 to 66 years. d Age group 15 to 74 years. e The indices are shown in terms of ISIC Rev.3. f European Labour Force Survey (Eurostat). g Arrivals of non-resident tourists in all types of accommodation establishments. h 2011: Methodology revised. i Break in comparability. j Age group 16 to 74 years. k See technical notes. l Age group 15 to 44 years. m 1988. n Refugee population refers to the end of 2012. o Based on monthly averages for the period 1961-1990.

Djibouti

Region	Eastern Africa
Currency	Djibouti Franc (DJF)
Surface area (square kilometres)	23 200
Population in 2012 (estimated, 000)	860
Population density in 2012 (per square kilometre)	37.1
Capital city and population in 2011 (000)	Djibouti (496)
United Nations membership date	20 September 1977

Economic indicators	2005	2010	2012
GDP: Gross domestic product (million current US$)	709	1 129	1 361
GDP: Growth rate at constant 2005 prices (annual %)	3.2	3.5	4.7
GDP per capita (current US$)	912.5	1 353.2	1 583.1
GNI: Gross national income per capita (current US$)	998.8	1 444.8	1 690.2
Gross fixed capital formation (% of GDP)	16.6	17.5	19.4
Exchange rates (national currency per US$)[a]	177.72	177.72	177.72
Balance of payments, current account (million US$)	20	50	−122
Agricultural production index (2004-2006=100)	95	119	135
Food production index (2004-2006=100)	95	119	135
Labour force participation, adult female pop. (%)	33.3	35.6	36.1
Labour force participation, adult male pop. (%)	66.1	66.7	67.3
Tourist arrivals at national borders (000)[b]	30	53[c]	...
Mobile-cellular subscriptions (per 100 inhabitants)	5.5	18.6	22.7[d]
Individuals using the Internet (%)	1.0	6.5	8.3[d]

Total trade		Major trading partners			2012
	(million US$)[e]	(% of exports)[e]		(% of imports)[e]	
Exports	363.7	Ethiopia	35.4	France	30.5
Imports	647.6	France	20.1	United Arab Emirates	18.5
Balance	−283.9	Somalia	11.9	Saudi Arabia	6.0

Social indicators		
Population growth rate (average annual %)	2010-2015	1.5
Urban population growth rate (average annual %)	2010-2015	2.0
Rural population growth rate (average annual %)	2010-2015	1.5
Urban population (%)	2013	77.2
Population aged 0-14 years (%)	2013	33.7
Population aged 60+ years (females and males, % of total)	2013	6.4/5.6
Sex ratio (males per 100 females)	2013	100.9
Life expectancy at birth (females and males, years)	2010-2015	63.2/60.0
Infant mortality rate (per 1 000 live births)	2010-2015	55.3
Fertility rate, total (live births per woman)	2010-2015	3.4
Contraceptive prevalence (ages 15-49, %)	2006-2012	17.8
International migrant stock (000 and % of total population)[f]	mid-2013	123.5/14.2
Refugees and others of concern to UNHCR	mid-2013	23 412
Education: Government expenditure (% of GDP)	2006-2012	8.4
Education: Primary-secondary gross enrolment ratio (f/m per 100)	2006-2012	49.8/59.4
Education: Female third-level students (% of total)	2006-2012	39.9
Intentional homicides (females and males, per 100 000)[g]	2008-2010	0.6/6.2
Seats held by women in national parliaments (%)	2014	12.7

Environmental indicators		
Threatened species	2013	93
Forested area (% of land area)	2011	<
CO_2 emission estimates (000 metric tons and metric tons per capita)	2010	539/0.6
Energy consumption per capita (kilograms oil equivalent)	2010	177.0[h]
Precipitation in the capital city, total mean (millimetres)		164[i]
Temperature in the capital city, mean °C (minimum and maximum)		25.9/33.9[i]

a Official rate. b Arrivals of non-resident tourists in hotels and similar establishments. c 2008. d ITU estimate. e 2009. f Includes refugees. g Estimates. h UNSD estimate. i Based on monthly averages for the period 1961-1990.

Dominica

Region	Caribbean
Currency	E.C. Dollar (XCD)
Surface area (square kilometres)	751
Population in 2012 (estimated, 000)	72
Population density in 2012 (per square kilometre)	95.5
Capital city and population in 2011 (000)	Roseau (14)
United Nations membership date	18 December 1978

Economic indicators	2005	2010	2012
GDP: Gross domestic product (million current US$)	362	482	499
GDP: Growth rate at constant 2005 prices (annual %)	−0.5	2.1	−1.5
GDP per capita (current US$)	5 126.0	6 766.4	6 958.2
GNI: Gross national income per capita (current US$)	4 715.0	6 631.9	6 709.8
Gross fixed capital formation (% of GDP)	20.2	21.4	22.3
Exchange rates (national currency per US$)[a]	2.70	2.70	2.70
Balance of payments, current account (million US$)	−76	−81	−55
CPI: Consumer price index (2000=100)[b]	106	122[c]	126
Agricultural production index (2004-2006=100)	95	111	116
Food production index (2004-2006=100)	95	112	117
Tourist arrivals at national borders (000)	79	77	79
Energy production, primary (000 mt oil equivalent)	2	2	...
Mobile-cellular subscriptions (per 100 inhabitants)	75.4	155.8[d]	161.5
Individuals using the Internet (%)	38.5[e]	47.5	55.2[e]

Total trade		Major trading partners			2012
	(million US$)	(% of exports)			(% of imports)[f]
Exports	37.0	Trinidad and Tobago	18.6	United States	36.8
Imports	211.9	Jamaica	16.2	Trinidad and Tobago	17.0
Balance	−174.9	Saint Kitts and Nevis	14.3	Areas nes	8.6

Social indicators		
Population growth rate (average annual %)	2010-2015	0.4
Urban population growth rate (average annual %)	2010-2015	0.2
Rural population growth rate (average annual %)	2010-2015	−0.4
Urban population (%)	2013	67.4
Population aged 0-14 years (%)[ghi]	2013	29.5[j]
Population aged 60+ years (females and males, % of total)[ghi]	2013	15.1/11.7[j]
Sex ratio (males per 100 females)[ghi]	2013	103.7[j]
Life expectancy at birth (females and males, years)[g]	2010-2015	78.2/73.8[k]
Contraceptive prevalence (ages 15-49, %)[l]	2006-2012	49.8[m]
International migrant stock (000 and % of total population)	mid-2013	6.4/8.9
Refugees and others of concern to UNHCR	mid-2013	0[n]
Education: Government expenditure (% of GDP)[o]	2006-2012	5.0[p]
Education: Primary-secondary gross enrolment ratio (f/m per 100)	2006-2012	107.0/104.3
Seats held by women in national parliaments (%)	2014	12.9

Environmental indicators		
Threatened species	2013	53
Forested area (% of land area)	2011	59.2
CO$_2$ emission estimates (000 metric tons and metric tons per capita)	2010	136/2.0
Energy consumption per capita (kilograms oil equivalent)	2010	690.0[q]
Precipitation in the capital city, total mean (millimetres)[r]		2 575[s]
Temperature in the capital city, mean °C (minimum and maximum)[r]		23.1/29.3[s]

a Official rate. b Index base 2001=100. c Series linked to former series. d Estimate. e ITU estimate. f See technical notes. g Data compiled by the United Nations Demographic Yearbook system. h Data refer to the latest available census. i De facto estimate. j 2006. k 2008. l Age group 15 to 44 years. m 1987. n Value is zero, not available or not applicable. o UNESCO estimate. p 1999. q UNSD estimate. r Melville Hall airport. s Based on monthly averages for the period 1971-1990.

Dominican Republic

Region	Caribbean
Currency	Dominican Peso (DOP)
Surface area (square kilometres)	48 192
Population in 2012 (estimated, 000)	10 277
Population density in 2012 (per square kilometre)	213.2
Capital city and population in 2011 (000)	Santo Domingo (2 191)
United Nations membership date	24 October 1945

Economic indicators	2005	2010	2012
GDP: Gross domestic product (million current US$)	33 431	50 980	58 898
GDP: Growth rate at constant 2005 prices (annual %)	9.3	7.8	3.9
GDP per capita (current US$)	3 578.1	5 089.5	5 731.2
GNI: Gross national income per capita (current US$)	3 377.9	4 923.1	5 512.0
Gross fixed capital formation (% of GDP)	16.4	16.3	16.3
Exchange rates (national currency per US$)[a]	34.88	37.93	40.36
Balance of payments, current account (million US$)	−473	−4 330	−4 037
CPI: Consumer price index (2000=100)	230	314	353
Industrial production index (2005=100)[b]	100	114	123
Agricultural production index (2004-2006=100)	99	127	133
Food production index (2004-2006=100)	99	129	135
Unemployment (% of labour force)[c]	17.9	14.3	14.7
Employment in industrial sector (% of employed)[d]	22.3[c]	14.9[c]	17.8[efg]
Employment in agricultural sector (% of employed)[d]	14.6[c]	12.0[c]	14.5[efg]
Labour force participation, adult female pop. (%)	49.0	51.0	51.2
Labour force participation, adult male pop. (%)	80.5	78.9	78.7
Tourist arrivals at national borders (000)[hi]	3 691	4 125	4 563
Energy production, primary (000 mt oil equivalent)	164	122	...
Mobile-cellular subscriptions (per 100 inhabitants)	39.1	89.6	88.8
Individuals using the Internet (%)	11.5	31.4[j]	45.0[j]

Total trade	Major trading partners				2012
	(million US$)	(% of exports)		(% of imports)	
Exports	6 902.5	United States	56.0	United States	38.6
Imports	19 200.5	Haiti	14.3	China	10.0
Balance	−12 298.0	China	5.2	Venezuela	6.3

Social indicators		
Population growth rate (average annual %)	2010-2015	1.2
Urban population growth rate (average annual %)	2010-2015	2.0
Rural population growth rate (average annual %)	2010-2015	−0.7
Urban population (%)	2013	70.8
Population aged 0-14 years (%)	2013	30.2
Population aged 60+ years (females and males, % of total)	2013	9.5/8.9
Sex ratio (males per 100 females)	2013	100.1
Life expectancy at birth (females and males, years)	2010-2015	76.6/70.3
Infant mortality rate (per 1 000 live births)	2010-2015	25.6
Fertility rate, total (live births per woman)	2010-2015	2.5
Contraceptive prevalence (ages 15-49, %)	2006-2012	72.9
International migrant stock (000 and % of total population)	mid-2013	402.5/3.9
Refugees and others of concern to UNHCR	mid-2013	211 481[k]
Education: Government expenditure (% of GDP)	2006-2012	2.2
Education: Primary-secondary gross enrolment ratio (f/m per 100)	2006-2012	90.1/91.0
Education: Female third-level students (% of total)	2006-2012	61.3[l]
Intentional homicides (females and males, per 100 000)	2008-2010	3.2/22.0
Seats held by women in national parliaments (%)	2014	20.8

Environmental indicators		
Threatened species	2013	143
Forested area (% of land area)	2011	40.8
CO$_2$ emission estimates (000 metric tons and metric tons per capita)	2010	20 947/2.1
Energy consumption per capita (kilograms oil equivalent)	2010	672.0
Precipitation in the capital city, total mean (millimetres)		1 447[m]
Temperature in the capital city, mean °C (minimum and maximum)		21.5/30.4[m]

a Principal rate. **b** The indices are shown in terms of ISIC Rev.3. **c** Age group 10 years and over. **d** The indices are shown in terms of ISIC Rev.2. **e** 2011. **f** April to June. **g** Break in series; data not strictly comparable. **h** Air arrivals. **i** Includes nationals residing abroad. **j** ITU estimate. **k** Includes estimated number of individuals resident in the country who belong to the first generation born on Dominican territory to Haitian migrant parents. **l** 2003. **m** Based on monthly averages for the period 1961-1990.

Ecuador

Region	South America
Currency	U.S. Dollar (USD)
Surface area (square kilometres)	256 369
Population in 2012 (estimated, 000)	15 492
Population density in 2012 (per square kilometre)	60.4
Capital city and population in 2011 (000)	Quito (1 622)
United Nations membership date	21 December 1945

Economic indicators	2005	2010	2012
GDP: Gross domestic product (million current US$)	41 507	69 555	87 495
GDP: Growth rate at constant 2005 prices (annual %)	5.3	3.5	5.1
GDP per capita (current US$)	3 012.8	4 636.7	5 647.6
GNI: Gross national income per capita (current US$)	2 863.0	4 617.0	5 572.4
Gross fixed capital formation (% of GDP)	20.4	24.6	27.2
Balance of payments, current account (million US$)	474	−1 623	−177
CPI: Consumer price index (2000=100)	175[a]	219	240
Agricultural production index (2004-2006=100)	98	121	116
Food production index (2004-2006=100)	98	122	118
Unemployment (% of labour force)[b]	7.4[c]	7.6	4.9[d]
Employment in industrial sector (% of employed)[ef]	17.2[g]	18.6	17.8
Employment in agricultural sector (% of employed)[ef]	31.5[g]	28.2	27.8
Labour force participation, adult female pop. (%)	55.3	53.7	54.4
Labour force participation, adult male pop. (%)	84.7	82.5	82.6
Tourist arrivals at national borders (000)[hi]	860	1 047	1 272
Energy production, primary (000 mt oil equivalent)	29 184	27 043	...
Mobile-cellular subscriptions (per 100 inhabitants)	46.5	102.2	110.7
Individuals using the Internet (%)	6.0[j]	29.0[k]	35.1[k]

Total trade		Major trading partners			2012
	(million US$)	(% of exports)		(% of imports)	
Exports	23 852.0	United States	44.7	United States	26.9
Imports	25 196.5	Chile	8.4	China	11.2
Balance	−1 344.5	Peru	8.4	Colombia	8.7

Social indicators

Population growth rate (average annual %)	2010-2015	1.6
Urban population growth rate (average annual %)	2010-2015	2.1
Rural population growth rate (average annual %)	2010-2015	−0.5
Urban population (%)	2013	68.6
Population aged 0-14 years (%)	2013	30.0
Population aged 60+ years (females and males, % of total)	2013	10.0/9.0
Sex ratio (males per 100 females)	2013	100.0
Life expectancy at birth (females and males, years)	2010-2015	79.3/73.6
Infant mortality rate (per 1 000 live births)	2010-2015	17.0
Fertility rate, total (live births per woman)	2010-2015	2.6
Contraceptive prevalence (ages 15-49, %)	2006-2012	72.7[l]
International migrant stock (000 and % of total population)[m]	mid-2013	359.3/2.3
Refugees and others of concern to UNHCR	mid-2013	135 940
Education: Government expenditure (% of GDP)	2006-2012	4.4
Education: Primary-secondary gross enrolment ratio (f/m per 100)	2006-2012	100.9/100.3
Education: Female third-level students (% of total)	2006-2012	52.9
Intentional homicides (females and males, per 100 000)	2008-2010	3.3/36.7
Seats held by women in national parliaments (%)	2014	41.6

Environmental indicators

Threatened species	2013	2 301
Forested area (% of land area)	2011	38.9
CO_2 emission estimates (000 metric tons and metric tons per capita)	2010	32 610/2.3
Energy consumption per capita (kilograms oil equivalent)	2010	766.0
Precipitation in the capital city, total mean (millimetres)		1 014[n]

a Series linked to former series. b Urban areas only. c 2007. d Break in series; data not strictly comparable. e Age group 10 years and over. f The indices are shown in terms of ISIC Rev.2. g Fourth quarter. h Arrivals of non-resident visitors at national borders. i Excludes nationals residing abroad. j ITU estimate. k Age group 5 years and over. l 2004. m Includes refugees. n Based on WMO Climatological Normals (CLINO) for the period 1961-1990.

Egypt

Region	Northern Africa
Currency	Egyptian Pound (EGP)
Surface area (square kilometres)	1 002 000
Population in 2012 (estimated, 000)	80 722
Population density in 2012 (per square kilometre)	80.6
Capital city and population in 2011 (000)	Cairo (11 169)
United Nations membership date	24 October 1945

Economic indicators	2005	2010	2012
GDP: Gross domestic product (million current US$)	94 456	214 630	254 671
GDP: Growth rate at constant 2005 prices (annual %)	4.5	5.2	2.2
GDP per capita (current US$)	1 316.0	2 749.0	3 154.9
GNI: Gross national income per capita (current US$)	1 301.9	2 734.5	3 138.2
Gross fixed capital formation (% of GDP)	16.9	19.2	16.0
Exchange rates (national currency per US$)[a]	5.73	5.79	6.31
Balance of payments, current account (million US$)	2 103	−4 504	−6 972
CPI: Consumer price index (2000=100)	134	232[b]	273
Agricultural production index (2004-2006=100)	99	109	119
Food production index (2004-2006=100)	99	110	120
Unemployment (% of labour force)	11.1	9.0	12.7
Employment in industrial sector (% of employed)	21.5[cde]	25.3	23.5[f]
Employment in agricultural sector (% of employed)	30.9[cde]	28.2	29.2[f]
Labour force participation, adult female pop. (%)	20.2	23.3	23.6
Labour force participation, adult male pop. (%)	75.5	74.1	74.6
Tourist arrivals at national borders (000)	8 244	14 051	11 196
Energy production, primary (000 mt oil equivalent)	80 493	92 681	...
Mobile-cellular subscriptions (per 100 inhabitants)	18.4	87.1	115.3
Individuals using the Internet (%)	12.8	31.4	44.1

Total trade		Major trading partners			2012
	(million US$)	(% of exports)			(% of imports)
Exports	29 417.0	Italy	7.9	China	9.4
Imports	69 865.6	India	6.9	United States	7.6
Balance	−40 448.6	United States	6.9	Germany	6.7

Social indicators		
Population growth rate (average annual %)	2010-2015	1.6
Urban population growth rate (average annual %)	2010-2015	2.0
Rural population growth rate (average annual %)	2010-2015	1.4
Urban population (%)	2013	43.8
Population aged 0-14 years (%)	2013	31.1
Population aged 60+ years (females and males, % of total)	2013	9.6/7.7
Sex ratio (males per 100 females)	2013	100.9
Life expectancy at birth (females and males, years)	2010-2015	73.5/68.7
Infant mortality rate (per 1 000 live births)	2010-2015	18.9
Fertility rate, total (live births per woman)	2010-2015	2.8
Contraceptive prevalence (ages 15-49, %)	2006-2012	60.3
International migrant stock (000 and % of total population)[g]	mid-2013	297.5/0.4
Refugees and others of concern to UNHCR	mid-2013	201 766
Education: Government expenditure (% of GDP)	2006-2012	3.8
Education: Primary-secondary gross enrolment ratio (f/m per 100)	2006-2012	92.5/96.3
Education: Female third-level students (% of total)	2006-2012	46.5
Intentional homicides (females and males, per 100 000)	2008-2010	</2.2

Environmental indicators		
Threatened species	2013	135
Forested area (% of land area)	2011	<
CO_2 emission estimates (000 metric tons and metric tons per capita)	2010	204 609/2.5
Energy consumption per capita (kilograms oil equivalent)	2010	911.0
Precipitation in the capital city, total mean (millimetres)		25[h]
Temperature in the capital city, mean °C (minimum and maximum)		15.8/27.7[h]

a Principal rate. b Series linked to former series. c The indices are shown in terms of ISIC Rev.3. d Age group 15 to 64 years. e Average of May and November. f 2011. g Includes refugees. h Based on monthly averages for the period 1971-2000.

El Salvador

Region	Central America
Currency	El Salvador Colon (SVC)
Surface area (square kilometres)	21 041 [a]
Population in 2012 (estimated, 000)	6 297
Population density in 2012 (per square kilometre)	299.3
Capital city and population in 2011 (000)	San Salvador (1 605)
United Nations membership date	24 October 1945

Economic indicators	2005	2010	2012
GDP: Gross domestic product (million current US$)	17 094	21 418	23 864
GDP: Growth rate at constant 2005 prices (annual %)	3.6	1.4	1.9
GDP per capita (current US$)	2 814.9	3 444.5	3 789.6
GNI: Gross national income per capita (current US$)	2 734.2	3 357.0	3 641.5
Gross fixed capital formation (% of GDP)	15.3	13.3	14.2
Exchange rates (national currency per US$) [b]	8.75	8.75	8.75
Balance of payments, current account (million US$)	−622	−570	−1 257
CPI: Consumer price index (2000=100) [c]	118	140 [d]	149
Industrial production index (2005=100) [e]	100	106	111
Agricultural production index (2004-2006=100)	99	111	115
Food production index (2004-2006=100)	99	109	117
Employment in industrial sector (% of employed) [e]	22.2 [fg]	21.4 [hi]	21.1 [hi]
Employment in agricultural sector (% of employed) [e]	20.0 [fg]	20.8 [hi]	21.0 [hi]
Labour force participation, adult female pop. (%)	44.7	47.2	47.6
Labour force participation, adult male pop. (%)	77.7	79.2	79.0
Tourist arrivals at national borders (000)	1 127	1 150	1 255
Energy production, primary (000 mt oil equivalent)	234	310	...
Mobile-cellular subscriptions (per 100 inhabitants)	39.9	124.3 [j]	138.1 [k]
Individuals using the Internet (%)	4.2 [fk]	15.9 [f]	25.5 [k]

Total trade		Major trading partners			2012
	(million US$)	(% of exports)			(% of imports)
Exports	5 339.1	United States	46.6	United States	37.9
Imports	10 269.6	Honduras	14.3	Guatemala	9.7
Balance	−4 930.5	Guatemala	13.4	Mexico	6.8

Social indicators		
Population growth rate (average annual %)	2010-2015	0.7
Urban population growth rate (average annual %)	2010-2015	1.4
Rural population growth rate (average annual %)	2010-2015	−0.8
Urban population (%)	2013	65.8
Population aged 0-14 years (%)	2013	30.0
Population aged 60+ years (females and males, % of total)	2013	10.6/8.9
Sex ratio (males per 100 females)	2013	90.1
Life expectancy at birth (females and males, years)	2010-2015	77.0/67.7
Infant mortality rate (per 1 000 live births)	2010-2015	17.3
Fertility rate, total (live births per woman)	2010-2015	2.2
Contraceptive prevalence (ages 15-49, %) [l]	2006-2012	72.5
International migrant stock (000 and % of total population) [m]	mid-2013	41.6/0.7
Refugees and others of concern to UNHCR	mid-2013	45
Education: Government expenditure (% of GDP)	2006-2012	3.4
Education: Primary-secondary gross enrolment ratio (f/m per 100)	2006-2012	87.8/90.3
Education: Female third-level students (% of total)	2006-2012	53.6
Intentional homicides (females and males, per 100 000)	2008-2010	13.2/100.9
Seats held by women in national parliaments (%)	2014	26.2

Environmental indicators		
Threatened species	2013	80
Forested area (% of land area)	2011	13.6
CO$_2$ emission estimates (000 metric tons and metric tons per capita)	2010	6 243/1.0
Energy consumption per capita (kilograms oil equivalent)	2010	352.0
Precipitation in the capital city, total mean (millimetres)		1 734 [n]
Temperature in the capital city, mean °C (minimum and maximum)		18.4/30.1 [n]

a The total surface is 21040.79 square kilometres, without taking into account the last ruling of The Hague. b Principal rate. c Urban areas. d Series linked to former series. e The indices are shown in terms of ISIC Rev.3. f Age group 10 years and over. g December. h Age group 16 years and over. i January to December. j Estimate. k ITU estimate. l Age group 15 to 44 years. m Includes refugees. n Based on monthly averages for the period 1953-1990.

Equatorial Guinea

Region	Middle Africa		
Currency	CFA Franc (XAF)		
Surface area (square kilometres)	28 051		
Population in 2012 (estimated, 000)	736		
Population density in 2012 (per square kilometre)	26.3		
Capital city and population in 2011 (000)	Malabo (137)		
United Nations membership date	12 November 1968		

Economic indicators	2005	2010	2012
GDP: Gross domestic product (million current US$)	7 206	12 386	14 491
GDP: Growth rate at constant 2005 prices (annual %)	8.9	1.3	5.7
GDP per capita (current US$)	11 936.6	17 792.0	19 680.3
GNI: Gross national income per capita (current US$)	6 061.7	11 338.5	12 696.1
Gross fixed capital formation (% of GDP)	21.7	49.0	44.7
Exchange rates (national currency per US$)[a]	556.04	490.91	497.16
CPI: Consumer price index (2000=100)[b]	145[c]	...	...
Agricultural production index (2004-2006=100)	100	111	116
Food production index (2004-2006=100)	101	113	117
Labour force participation, adult female pop. (%)	80.3	80.5	80.6
Labour force participation, adult male pop. (%)	92.5	92.3	92.3
Energy production, primary (000 mt oil equivalent)	24 609	25 964	...
Mobile-cellular subscriptions (per 100 inhabitants)	15.9	57.0	67.7
Individuals using the Internet (%)	1.2	6.0	13.9[d]

Social indicators		
Population growth rate (average annual %)	2010-2015	2.8
Urban population growth rate (average annual %)	2010-2015	3.2
Rural population growth rate (average annual %)	2010-2015	2.4
Urban population (%)	2013	39.8
Population aged 0-14 years (%)	2013	38.9
Population aged 60+ years (females and males, % of total)	2013	4.5/4.8
Sex ratio (males per 100 females)	2013	105.0
Life expectancy at birth (females and males, years)	2010-2015	54.5/51.5
Infant mortality rate (per 1 000 live births)	2010-2015	88.9
Fertility rate, total (live births per woman)	2010-2015	4.9
Contraceptive prevalence (ages 15-49, %)	2006-2012	10.1[e]
International migrant stock (000 and % of total population)[f]	mid-2013	10.1/1.3
Refugees and others of concern to UNHCR	mid-2013	0[g]
Education: Government expenditure (% of GDP)[h]	2006-2012	0.6[i]
Education: Primary-secondary gross enrolment ratio (f/m per 100)[h]	2006-2012	61.6/72.6[i]
Education: Female third-level students (% of total)	2006-2012	30.3[e]
Intentional homicides (females and males, per 100 000)[k]	2008-2010	10.8/30.1
Seats held by women in national parliaments (%)	2014	24.0

Environmental indicators		
Threatened species	2013	135
Forested area (% of land area)	2011	57.6
CO$_2$ emission estimates (000 metric tons and metric tons per capita)	2010	4 675/6.7
Energy consumption per capita (kilograms oil equivalent)	2010	2 392.0

a Official rate. b Malabo. c 2006. d ITU estimate. e 2000. f Data refer to foreign citizens. g Value is zero, not available or not applicable. h UNESCO estimate. i 2003. j 2002. k Estimates.

Eritrea

Region	Eastern Africa
Currency	Nakfa (ERN)
Surface area (square kilometres)	117 600
Population in 2012 (estimated, 000)	6 131
Population density in 2012 (per square kilometre)	52.1
Capital city and population in 2011 (000)	Asmara (712)
United Nations membership date	28 May 1993

Economic indicators	2005	2010	2012
GDP: Gross domestic product (million current US$)	1 098	2 117	3 108
GDP: Growth rate at constant 2005 prices (annual %)	2.6	2.2	7.5
GDP per capita (current US$)	226.3	368.8	506.9
GNI: Gross national income per capita (current US$)	224.4	365.3	502.2
Gross fixed capital formation (% of GDP)	20.3	9.3	9.5
Exchange rates (national currency per US$)[a]	15.38	15.38	15.38
Agricultural production index (2004-2006=100)	106	106	111
Food production index (2004-2006=100)	106	106	111
Labour force participation, adult female pop. (%)	78.1	79.6	79.9
Labour force participation, adult male pop. (%)	89.4	89.7	89.8
Tourist arrivals at national borders (000)[bc]	83	84	107[d]
Mobile-cellular subscriptions (per 100 inhabitants)	0.9	3.5	5.5
Individuals using the Internet (%)[e]	0.4[f]	0.6	0.8

Social indicators		
Population growth rate (average annual %)	2010-2015	3.2
Urban population growth rate (average annual %)	2010-2015	5.0
Rural population growth rate (average annual %)	2010-2015	2.3
Urban population (%)	2013	22.2
Population aged 0-14 years (%)	2013	43.2
Population aged 60+ years (females and males, % of total)	2013	4.4/3.1
Sex ratio (males per 100 females)	2013	99.6
Life expectancy at birth (females and males, years)	2010-2015	64.9/60.2
Infant mortality rate (per 1 000 live births)	2010-2015	41.8
Fertility rate, total (live births per woman)	2010-2015	4.7
Contraceptive prevalence (ages 15-49, %)	2006-2012	8.0[g]
International migrant stock (000 and % of total population)[h]	mid-2013	15.8/0.3
Refugees and others of concern to UNHCR	mid-2013	3 533
Education: Government expenditure (% of GDP)	2006-2012	2.1
Education: Primary-secondary gross enrolment ratio (f/m per 100)	2006-2012	32.2/39.1
Education: Female third-level students (% of total)	2006-2012	27.4
Intentional homicides (females and males, per 100 000)[h]	2008-2010	6.2/29.8
Seats held by women in national parliaments (%)	2014	22.0

Environmental indicators		
Threatened species	2013	113
Forested area (% of land area)	2011	15.1
CO_2 emission estimates (000 metric tons and metric tons per capita)	2010	513/0.1
Energy consumption per capita (kilograms oil equivalent)	2010	30.0
Precipitation in the capital city, total mean (millimetres)		533
Temperature in the capital city, mean °C (minimum and maximum)		8.9/23.2

a Official rate. b Arrivals of non-resident visitors at national borders. c Includes nationals residing abroad. d 2011. e ITU estimate. f 2007. g 2002. h Estimates.

Estonia

Region	Northern Europe
Currency	Euro (EUR)[a]
Surface area (square kilometres)	45 227
Population in 2012 (estimated, 000)	1 291
Population density in 2012 (per square kilometre)	28.5
Capital city and population in 2011 (000)	Tallinn (400)
United Nations membership date	17 September 1991

Economic indicators	2005	2010	2012
GDP: Gross domestic product (million current US$)	13 903	19 045	22 376
GDP: Growth rate at constant 2005 prices (annual %)	8.9	2.6	3.9
GDP per capita (current US$)	10 492.2	14 666.4	17 335.3
GNI: Gross national income per capita (current US$)	10 093.0	13 850.7	16 508.5
Gross fixed capital formation (% of GDP)	32.1	19.0	25.2
Exchange rates (national currency per US$)	13.22[bc]	11.71[bc]	0.76[de]
Balance of payments, current account (million US$)	−1 386	535	−405
CPI: Consumer price index (2000=100)	119	151	164
Industrial production index (2005=100)	100	104	125
Agricultural production index (2004-2006=100)	103	110	125
Food production index (2004-2006=100)	103	110	125
Unemployment (% of labour force)[f]	7.9	16.9	10.1
Employment in industrial sector (% of employed)[f]	33.8[g]	30.5[h]	31.1[h]
Employment in agricultural sector (% of employed)[f]	5.2[g]	4.2[h]	4.7[h]
Labour force participation, adult female pop. (%)	53.3	56.2	56.0
Labour force participation, adult male pop. (%)	65.4	67.6	68.7
Tourist arrivals at national borders (000)	1 917	2 372	2 744
Energy production, primary (000 mt oil equivalent)	3 184	3 963	...
Mobile-cellular subscriptions (per 100 inhabitants)	107.4	123.2[i]	154.6[j]
Individuals using the Internet (%)	61.5[k]	74.1[l]	79.0[k]

Total trade		Major trading partners			2012
	(million US$)	(% of exports)		(% of imports)	
Exports	18 157.5	Russian Federation	17.5	Russian Federation	11.8
Imports	19 750.3	Sweden	14.1	Finland	10.1
Balance	−1 592.8	Finland	12.8	Germany	8.5

Social indicators		
Population growth rate (average annual %)	2010-2015	−0.3
Urban population growth rate (average annual %)	2010-2015	<
Rural population growth rate (average annual %)	2010-2015	−0.3
Urban population (%)	2013	69.6
Population aged 0-14 years (%)	2013	15.8
Population aged 60+ years (females and males, % of total)	2013	29.0/18.6
Sex ratio (males per 100 females)	2013	86.5
Life expectancy at birth (females and males, years)	2010-2015	79.5/68.9
Infant mortality rate (per 1 000 live births)	2010-2015	4.2
Fertility rate, total (live births per woman)	2010-2015	1.6
Contraceptive prevalence (ages 15-49, %)[m]	2006-2012	70.3[n]
International migrant stock (000 and % of total population)	mid-2013	210.0/16.3
Refugees and others of concern to UNHCR	mid-2013	92 754
Education: Government expenditure (% of GDP)	2006-2012	5.7
Education: Primary-secondary gross enrolment ratio (f/m per 100)	2006-2012	104.1/104.4
Education: Female third-level students (% of total)	2006-2012	60.9
Intentional homicides (females and males, per 100 000)	2008-2010	3.4/14.3
Seats held by women in national parliaments (%)	2014	19.0

Environmental indicators		
Threatened species	2013	17
Forested area (% of land area)	2011	52.1
CO_2 emission estimates (000 metric tons and metric tons per capita)	2010	18 324/13.7
Energy consumption per capita (kilograms oil equivalent)	2010	3 838.0
Precipitation in the capital city, total mean (millimetres)		693[o]
Temperature in the capital city, mean °C (minimum and maximum)		2.1/9.1[o]

a Beginning 1 January 2011, the Estonian Kroon (EEK) was replaced by the euro (1 EUR=156466 EEK). b Official rate. c Estonian Kroon (EEK). d Market rate. e Euro. f Age group 15 to 74 years. g Excludes conscripts. h European Labour Force Survey (Eurostat). i Excludes 1,890,000 prepaid cards that are used to provide Travel SIM service. j Excludes 2,720,698 prepaid cards that are used to provide Travel SIM/WorldMobile service. k Age group 16 to 74 years. l Age group 16 to 74 years within the last 3 months. m Age group 20 to 49 years. n 1994. o Based on monthly averages for the period 1971-2000.

Ethiopia

Region	Eastern Africa
Currency	Birr (ETB)
Surface area (square kilometres)	1 104 300
Population in 2012 (estimated, 000)	91 729
Population density in 2012 (per square kilometre)	83.1
Capital city and population in 2011 (000)	Addis Ababa (2 979)
United Nations membership date	13 November 1945

Economic indicators	2005	2010	2012
GDP: Gross domestic product (million current US$)	12 164	26 311	41 605
GDP: Growth rate at constant 2005 prices (annual %)	11.8	12.6	8.5
GDP per capita (current US$)	159.7	302.1	453.6
GNI: Gross national income per capita (current US$)	159.9	301.5	452.6
Gross fixed capital formation (% of GDP)	26.0	27.0	34.6
Exchange rates (national currency per US$)[a]	8.68	16.55	18.18
Balance of payments, current account (million US$)	−1 568	−425	−2 985
CPI: Consumer price index (2000=100)[b]	138	313	518[c]
Agricultural production index (2004-2006=100)	102	137	143
Food production index (2004-2006=100)	103	137	144
Employment in industrial sector (% of employed)	6.6[defg]	...	...
Employment in agricultural sector (% of employed)	79.3[defg]	...	...
Labour force participation, adult female pop. (%)	78.4	78.2	78.2
Labour force participation, adult male pop. (%)	90.9	89.7	89.4
Tourist arrivals at national borders (000)[hi]	227	468	596
Energy production, primary (000 mt oil equivalent)	244	426	...
Mobile-cellular subscriptions (per 100 inhabitants)	0.6	8.3	23.7
Individuals using the Internet (%)	0.2	0.8[i]	1.5[i]

Total trade		Major trading partners			2012
	(million US$)	(% of exports)			(% of imports)
Exports	2 891.3	China	11.1	China	21.6
Imports	11 912.9	Germany	10.8	Saudi Arabia	14.1
Balance	−9 021.6	Somalia	9.0	India	8.3

Social indicators		
Population growth rate (average annual %)	2010-2015	2.6
Urban population growth rate (average annual %)	2010-2015	3.6
Rural population growth rate (average annual %)	2010-2015	1.8
Urban population (%)	2013	17.5
Population aged 0-14 years (%)	2013	42.7
Population aged 60+ years (females and males, % of total)	2013	5.4/4.9
Sex ratio (males per 100 females)	2013	100.1
Life expectancy at birth (females and males, years)	2010-2015	65.0/61.7
Infant mortality rate (per 1 000 live births)	2010-2015	49.7
Fertility rate, total (live births per woman)	2010-2015	4.6
Contraceptive prevalence (ages 15-49, %)	2006-2012	28.6
International migrant stock (000 and % of total population)[k]	mid-2013	718.2/0.8
Refugees and others of concern to UNHCR	mid-2013	410 446
Education: Government expenditure (% of GDP)	2006-2012	4.7
Education: Primary-secondary gross enrolment ratio (f/m per 100)	2006-2012	65.8/71.2
Education: Female third-level students (% of total)	2006-2012	31.5
Intentional homicides (females and males, per 100 000)[l]	2008-2010	9.2/41.9
Seats held by women in national parliaments (%)	2014	27.8

Environmental indicators		
Threatened species	2013	141
Forested area (% of land area)	2011	12.2
CO$_2$ emission estimates (000 metric tons and metric tons per capita)	2010	6 489/0.1
Energy consumption per capita (kilograms oil equivalent)	2010	26.0
Precipitation in the capital city, total mean (millimetres)		1 165[m]
Temperature in the capital city, mean °C (minimum and maximum)		9.3/23.2[m]

a Official rate. b Index base 2001=100. c Series linked to former series. d The indices are shown in terms of ISIC Rev.3. e Age group 10 years and over. f March. g Break in series; data not strictly comparable. h Arrivals through all ports of entry. i Includes nationals residing abroad. j ITU estimate. k Includes refugees. l Estimates. m Based on monthly averages for the period 1981-2010.

Faeroe Islands

Region	Northern Europe
Currency	Danish Krone (DKK)
Surface area (square kilometres)	1 393
Population in 2012 (estimated, 000)	50
Population density in 2012 (per square kilometre)	35.5
Capital city and population in 2011 (000)	Tórshavn (20)

Economic indicators	2005	2010	2012
Exchange rates (national currency per US$)[a]	6.32	5.61	5.66
Balance of payments, current account (million US$)	31	144	194[b]
CPI: Consumer price index (2000=100)	109	121	127
Agricultural production index (2004-2006=100)	100	102	103
Food production index (2004-2006=100)	100	102	103
Employment in industrial sector (% of employed)	22.2[cde]	...	...
Employment in agricultural sector (% of employed)	11.1[cde]	...	...
Energy production, primary (000 mt oil equivalent)	9	7	...
Mobile-cellular subscriptions (per 100 inhabitants)	87.1	122.1	124.3[f]
Individuals using the Internet (%)	67.9[f]	75.2	85.3[f]

Total trade	Major trading partners				2012
(million US$)[g]	(% of exports)[g]				(% of imports)[g]
Exports	761.7	United Kingdom	17.3	Denmark	30.4
Imports	783.4	Denmark	11.0	Norway	18.1
Balance	−21.7	France	10.8	Chile	6.6

Social indicators		
Population growth rate (average annual %)	2010-2015	−<
Urban population growth rate (average annual %)	2010-2015	1.0
Rural population growth rate (average annual %)	2010-2015	0.1
Urban population (%)	2013	41.5
Population aged 0-14 years (%)[hij]	2013	22.0[k]
Population aged 60+ years (females and males, % of total)[hij]	2013	20.5/18.1[k]
Sex ratio (males per 100 females)[hij]	2013	108.2[k]
Life expectancy at birth (females and males, years)[h]	2010-2015	82.3/76.8[k]
International migrant stock (000 and % of total population)	mid-2013	3.6/7.4

Environmental indicators		
Threatened species	2013	13
Forested area (% of land area)	2011	<
CO_2 emission estimates (000 metric tons and metric tons per capita)	2010	711/14.6
Energy consumption per capita (kilograms oil equivalent)	2010	4 942.0[l]
Precipitation in the capital city, total mean (millimetres)		1 284[m]
Temperature in the capital city, mean °C (minimum and maximum)		4.5/8.6[m]

a Market rate. b 2011. c The indices are shown in terms of ISIC Rev.2. d Age group 16 years and over. e September. f ITU estimate. g 2009. h Data compiled by the United Nations Demographic Yearbook system. i Data refer to the latest available census. j De jure estimate. k 2008. l UNSD estimate. m Based on monthly averages for the period 1961-1990.

Fiji

Region	Oceania-Melanesia
Currency	Fiji Dollar (FJD)
Surface area (square kilometres)	18 272
Population in 2012 (estimated, 000)	875
Population density in 2012 (per square kilometre)	47.9
Capital city and population in 2011 (000)	Suva (177)
United Nations membership date	13 October 1970

Economic indicators	2005	2010	2012
GDP: Gross domestic product (million current US$)	3 007	3 225	3 999
GDP: Growth rate at constant 2005 prices (annual %)	5.4	−0.2	1.5
GDP per capita (current US$)	3 655.5	3 747.8	4 571.9
GNI: Gross national income per capita (current US$)	3 579.3	3 571.0	4 506.7
Gross fixed capital formation (% of GDP)	18.1	12.6	16.5
Exchange rates (national currency per US$)[a]	1.74	1.82	1.79
Balance of payments, current account (million US$)	−212	−142	−56
CPI: Consumer price index (2000=100)	115	146	165
Industrial production index (2005=100)[b]	100	101	104[c]
Agricultural production index (2004-2006=100)	99	82	83
Food production index (2004-2006=100)	99	82	83
Labour force participation, adult female pop. (%)	38.1	37.4	37.5
Labour force participation, adult male pop. (%)	73.8	72.0	72.0
Tourist arrivals at national borders (000)[d]	545	632	661
Energy production, primary (000 mt oil equivalent)	29	36	...
Mobile-cellular subscriptions (per 100 inhabitants)	24.9[e]	81.1[f]	98.1[g]
Individuals using the Internet (%)	8.5	20.0[h]	33.7[h]

Total trade		Major trading partners			2012
	(million US$)	(% of exports)[i]			(% of imports)
Exports	1 220.6	Bunkers	17.7	Singapore	31.8
Imports	2 252.6	Australia	14.8	Australia	18.3
Balance	−1 032.0	United States	12.3	New Zealand	13.9

Social indicators

Population growth rate (average annual %)	2010-2015	0.7
Urban population growth rate (average annual %)	2010-2015	1.6
Rural population growth rate (average annual %)	2010-2015	−<
Urban population (%)	2013	53.0
Population aged 0-14 years (%)	2013	28.9
Population aged 60+ years (females and males, % of total)	2013	9.3/8.0
Sex ratio (males per 100 females)	2013	103.8
Life expectancy at birth (females and males, years)	2010-2015	72.9/66.9
Infant mortality rate (per 1 000 live births)	2010-2015	16.0
Fertility rate, total (live births per woman)	2010-2015	2.6
Contraceptive prevalence (ages 15-49, %)	2006-2012	40.9[j]
International migrant stock (000 and % of total population)	mid-2013	22.8/2.6
Refugees and others of concern to UNHCR	mid-2013	13
Education: Government expenditure (% of GDP)	2006-2012	4.1
Education: Primary-secondary gross enrolment ratio (f/m per 100)	2006-2012	99.0/95.2
Education: Female third-level students (% of total)[k]	2006-2012	53.1[l]
Intentional homicides (females and males, per 100 000)	2008-2010	</1.5

Environmental indicators

Threatened species	2013	278
Forested area (% of land area)	2011	55.7
CO_2 emission estimates (000 metric tons and metric tons per capita)	2010	1 290/1.5
Energy consumption per capita (kilograms oil equivalent)	2010	524.0
Precipitation in the capital city, total mean (millimetres)		3 040[m]
Temperature in the capital city, mean °C (minimum and maximum)		22.2/28.7[m]

a Official rate. **b** The indices are shown in terms of ISIC Rev.3. **c** 2011. **d** Excludes nationals residing abroad. **e** Data refer to March of the following year. **f** June 2011. **g** December. **h** ITU estimate. **i** See technical notes. **j** 1974. **k** UNESCO estimate. **l** 2005. **m** Based on monthly averages for the period 1961-1990.

Finland

Region	Northern Europe
Currency	Euro (EUR)
Surface area (square kilometres)	336 852 [a]
Population in 2012 (estimated, 000)	5 408 [b]
Population density in 2012 (per square kilometre)	16.1
Capital city and population in 2011 (000)	Helsinki (1 134)
United Nations membership date	14 December 1955

Economic indicators	2005	2010	2012
GDP: Gross domestic product (million current US$)	195 778	236 706	247 389
GDP: Growth rate at constant 2005 prices (annual %)	2.9	3.4	−0.8
GDP per capita (current US$)	37 316.9	44 098.4	45 741.0
GNI: Gross national income per capita (current US$)	37 488.7	44 754.7	45 684.5
Gross fixed capital formation (% of GDP)	20.1	18.9	19.6
Exchange rates (national currency per US$) [c]	0.85	0.75	0.76
Balance of payments, current account (million US$)	7 788	5 944	−3 699
CPI: Consumer price index (2000=100)	106 [d]	116	124
Industrial production index (2005=100)	100	100	100
Agricultural production index (2004-2006=100)	102	94	94
Food production index (2004-2006=100)	102	94	94
Unemployment (% of labour force) [e]	8.4	8.4	7.7
Employment in industrial sector (% of employed) [e]	25.6 [f]	23.2 [g]	22.7 [g]
Employment in agricultural sector (% of employed) [e]	4.8 [f]	4.4 [g]	4.1 [g]
Labour force participation, adult female pop. (%)	56.8	56.2	56.0
Labour force participation, adult male pop. (%)	65.4	64.6	64.3
Tourist arrivals at national borders (000)	3 140	3 670	4 226
Energy production, primary (000 mt oil equivalent)	5 339	5 155	...
Mobile-cellular subscriptions (per 100 inhabitants)	100.5	156.4	172.5
Individuals using the Internet (%) [h]	74.5	86.9	91.0

Total trade	Major trading partners				2012
	(million US$)	(% of exports)		(% of imports)	
Exports	72 974.5	Sweden	10.9	Russian Federation	17.6
Imports	76 089.0	Russian Federation	9.9	Germany	12.0
Balance	−3 114.5	Germany	8.8	Sweden	10.4

Social indicators		
Population growth rate (average annual %) [b]	2010-2015	0.3
Urban population growth rate (average annual %) [b]	2010-2015	0.5
Rural population growth rate (average annual %) [b]	2010-2015	−0.5
Urban population (%) [b]	2013	84.0
Population aged 0-14 years (%) [b]	2013	16.5
Population aged 60+ years (females and males, % of total) [b]	2013	28.8/23.8
Sex ratio (males per 100 females) [b]	2013	96.6
Life expectancy at birth (females and males, years) [b]	2010-2015	83.6/77.3
Infant mortality rate (per 1 000 live births) [b]	2010-2015	2.3
Fertility rate, total (live births per woman) [b]	2010-2015	1.9
Contraceptive prevalence (ages 15-49, %) [i]	2006-2012	77.4 [j]
International migrant stock (000 and % of total population) [b]	mid-2013	293.2/5.4
Refugees and others of concern to UNHCR	mid-2013	13 215 [k]
Education: Government expenditure (% of GDP)	2006-2012	6.8
Education: Primary-secondary gross enrolment ratio (f/m per 100)	2006-2012	104.8/102.6
Education: Female third-level students (% of total)	2006-2012	54.0
Intentional homicides (females and males, per 100 000)	2008-2010	1.3/3.3
Seats held by women in national parliaments (%)	2014	42.5

Environmental indicators		
Threatened species	2013	25
Forested area (% of land area)	2011	72.9
CO_2 emission estimates (000 metric tons and metric tons per capita)	2010	61 793/11.5
Energy consumption per capita (kilograms oil equivalent)	2010	4 908.0
Precipitation in the capital city, total mean (millimetres)		650 [l]
Temperature in the capital city, mean °C (minimum and maximum)		1.0/8.7 [l]

a Excludes Åland Islands. b Includes Åland Islands. c Market rate. d Series linked to former series. e Age group 15 to 74 years. f The indices are shown in terms of ISIC Rev.3. g European Labour Force Survey (Eurostat). h Age group 16 to 74 years. i Age group 25 to 49 years. j 1989-1990. k Refugee population refers to the end of 2012. l Based on monthly averages for the period 1971-2000.

France

Region	Western Europe
Currency	Euro (EUR)
Surface area (square kilometres)	551 500
Population in 2012 (estimated, 000)	63 937
Population density in 2012 (per square kilometre)	115.9
Capital city and population in 2011 (000)	Paris (10 620)
United Nations membership date	24 October 1945

Economic indicators	2005	2010	2012
GDP: Gross domestic product (million current US$)	2 136 555	2 565 039	2 611 221
GDP: Growth rate at constant 2005 prices (annual %)	1.8	1.7	0.0
GDP per capita (current US$)	33 764.6	39 361.6	39 617.3
GNI: Gross national income per capita (current US$)	34 292.7	40 161.5	40 297.3
Gross fixed capital formation (% of GDP)	19.4	19.5	19.8
Exchange rates (national currency per US$)[a]	0.85	0.75	0.76
Balance of payments, current account (million US$)	−10 260	−33 734	−57 246
CPI: Consumer price index (2000=100)	110	119	123
Industrial production index (2005=100)[b]	100	89	89
Agricultural production index (2004-2006=100)	100	97	98
Food production index (2004-2006=100)	100	97	98
Unemployment (% of labour force)[c]	8.9	9.3	9.8
Employment in industrial sector (% of employed)[d]	23.7[e]	22.2	21.7
Employment in agricultural sector (% of employed)[d]	3.6[e]	2.9	2.9
Labour force participation, adult female pop. (%)	49.9	50.9	50.9
Labour force participation, adult male pop. (%)	62.4	62.0	61.8
Tourist arrivals at national borders (000)	74 988	77 648	83 013
Energy production, primary (000 mt oil equivalent)[fg]	46 907	47 624	...
Mobile-cellular subscriptions (per 100 inhabitants)	78.8	92.0	98.1
Individuals using the Internet (%)	42.9[h]	77.3[i]	83.0[i]

Total trade		Major trading partners			2012
	(million US$)[g]		(% of exports)[g]		(% of imports)[g]
Exports	556 575.7	Germany	16.4	Germany	17.3
Imports	663 268.6	Italy	7.4	China	8.0
Balance	−106 692.9	Belgium	7.3	Belgium	7.6

Social indicators

Population growth rate (average annual %)	2010-2015	0.6
Urban population growth rate (average annual %)	2010-2015	1.1
Rural population growth rate (average annual %)	2010-2015	−3.3
Urban population (%)	2013	86.9
Population aged 0-14 years (%)	2013	18.2
Population aged 60+ years (females and males, % of total)	2013	26.5/21.6
Sex ratio (males per 100 females)	2013	93.9
Life expectancy at birth (females and males, years)	2010-2015	85.1/78.2
Infant mortality rate (per 1 000 live births)	2010-2015	3.2
Fertility rate, total (live births per woman)	2010-2015	2.0
Contraceptive prevalence (ages 15-49, %)	2006-2012	76.6[j]
International migrant stock (000 and % of total population)	mid-2013	7 439.1/11.6
Refugees and others of concern to UNHCR	mid-2013	276 730
Education: Government expenditure (% of GDP)	2006-2012	5.9
Education: Primary-secondary gross enrolment ratio (f/m per 100)	2006-2012	109.4/108.9
Education: Female third-level students (% of total)	2006-2012	54.8
Intentional homicides (females and males, per 100 000)	2008-2010	0.9/1.9
Seats held by women in national parliaments (%)	2014	26.2

Environmental indicators

Threatened species	2013	229
Forested area (% of land area)	2011	29.2
CO$_2$ emission estimates (000 metric tons and metric tons per capita)[g]	2010	360 977/5.8
Energy consumption per capita (kilograms oil equivalent)[fg]	2010	2 820.0
Precipitation in the capital city, total mean (millimetres)		650[k]
Temperature in the capital city, mean °C (minimum and maximum)		8.5/15.5[k]

a Market rate. b Excludes the Overseas Departments (French Guiana, Guadeloupe, Martinique, Mayotte and Réunion). c Age group 15 to 74 years. d European Labour Force Survey (Eurostat). e The indices are shown in terms of ISIC Rev.3. f Excludes Guadeloupe, French Guiana, Martinique, New Caledonia, French Polynesia, Réunion and St. Pierre Miquelon. g Includes Monaco. h Age group 11 years and over using the Internet within the last month. i Age group 16 to 74 years. j 2004-2005. k Based on monthly averages for the period 1971-2000.

French Guiana

Region	South America
Currency	Euro (EUR)
Surface area (square kilometres)	83 534
Population in 2012 (estimated, 000)	243
Population density in 2012 (per square kilometre)	2.9
Capital city and population in 2011 (000)	Cayenne (67)

Economic indicators	2005	2010	2012
Exchange rates (national currency per US$)[a]	0.85	0.75	0.76
CPI: Consumer price index (2000=100)	108	119	123
Agricultural production index (2004-2006=100)	95	90	92
Food production index (2004-2006=100)	95	90	92
Employment in industrial sector (% of employed)[bc]	...	14.1	14.9
Labour force participation, adult female pop. (%)	45.6	47.1	48.8
Labour force participation, adult male pop. (%)	61.5	60.0	60.6
Tourist arrivals at national borders (000)	95	83[d]	...
Energy production, primary (000 mt oil equivalent)[e]	53	64	...

Social indicators		
Population growth rate (average annual %)	2010-2015	2.5
Urban population growth rate (average annual %)	2010-2015	2.8
Rural population growth rate (average annual %)	2010-2015	1.8
Urban population (%)	2013	76.7
Population aged 0-14 years (%)	2013	32.3
Population aged 60+ years (females and males, % of total)	2013	7.9/7.9
Sex ratio (males per 100 females)	2013	100.1
Life expectancy at birth (females and males, years)	2010-2015	80.8/73.8
Infant mortality rate (per 1 000 live births)	2010-2015	12.2
Fertility rate, total (live births per woman)	2010-2015	3.1
International migrant stock (000 and % of total population)	mid-2013	104.3/41.9

Environmental indicators		
Threatened species	2013	66
Forested area (% of land area)	2011	98.3
CO_2 emission estimates (000 metric tons and metric tons per capita)	2010	700/3.0
Energy consumption per capita (kilograms oil equivalent)	2010	1 240.0[e]
Precipitation in the capital city, total mean (millimetres)[f]		3 674[g]
Temperature in the capital city, mean °C (minimum and maximum)[f]		22.5/30.1[g]

a Market rate. b March to June. c Excludes the institutional population. d 2009. e UNSD estimate. f Rochambeau. g Based on monthly averages for the period 1961-1990.

French Polynesia

Region	Oceania-Polynesia
Currency	CFP Franc (XPF)
Surface area (square kilometres)	4 000
Population in 2012 (estimated, 000)	274
Population density in 2012 (per square kilometre)	68.5
Capital city and population in 2011 (000)	Papeete (137)

Economic indicators	2005	2010	2012
GDP: Gross domestic product (million current US$)	5 703	6 963	7 150
GDP: Growth rate at constant 2005 prices (annual %)	1.4	2.2	2.4
GDP per capita (current US$)	22 374.0	25 975.9	26 113.3
GNI: Gross national income per capita (current US$)	22 374.0	25 975.9	26 113.3
Gross fixed capital formation (% of GDP)	24.0	22.3	22.3
Exchange rates (national currency per US$)[a]	100.84	90.81	89.98
Balance of payments, current account (million US$)	9	153	331[b]
CPI: Consumer price index (2000=100)	106	116	120
Agricultural production index (2004-2006=100)	104	99	108
Food production index (2004-2006=100)	104	99	108
Employment in industrial sector (% of employed)[c]	8.8	8.3	8.3[b]
Employment in agricultural sector (% of employed)[c]	4.3	3.4	3.4[b]
Labour force participation, adult female pop. (%)	47.2	47.0	47.1
Labour force participation, adult male pop. (%)	65.8	64.0	64.1
Tourist arrivals at national borders (000)[d]	208	154	169
Energy production, primary (000 mt oil equivalent)	15	24	...
Mobile-cellular subscriptions (per 100 inhabitants)	47.1	79.7	81.7[e]
Individuals using the Internet (%)	21.5	49.0	52.9[e]

Total trade		Major trading partners			2012
	(million US$)	(% of exports)			(% of imports)
Exports	139.0	Japan	27.8	France	24.1
Imports	1 706.3	China, Hong Kong SAR	27.6	China	9.8
Balance	−1 567.3	United States	17.0	Republic of Korea	9.7

Social indicators		
Population growth rate (average annual %)	2010-2015	1.1
Urban population growth rate (average annual %)	2010-2015	1.1
Rural population growth rate (average annual %)	2010-2015	1.0
Urban population (%)	2013	51.4
Population aged 0-14 years (%)	2013	22.6
Population aged 60+ years (females and males, % of total)	2013	11.1/10.5
Sex ratio (males per 100 females)	2013	104.5
Life expectancy at birth (females and males, years)	2010-2015	78.6/74.0
Infant mortality rate (per 1 000 live births)	2010-2015	6.9
Fertility rate, total (live births per woman)	2010-2015	2.1
International migrant stock (000 and % of total population)	mid-2013	34.8/12.6

Environmental indicators		
Threatened species	2013	173
Forested area (% of land area)	2011	43.7
CO_2 emission estimates (000 metric tons and metric tons per capita)	2010	883/3.3
Energy consumption per capita (kilograms oil equivalent)	2010	1 165.0
Precipitation in the capital city, total mean (millimetres)[f]		1 761[g]
Temperature in the capital city, mean °C (minimum and maximum)[f]		22.3/29.5[g]

a UN operational exchange rate. b 2011. c Administrative records and related sources. d Excludes nationals residing abroad. e ITU estimate. f Tahiti. g Based on monthly averages for the period 1961-1990.

Gabon

Region	Middle Africa
Currency	CFA Franc (XAF)
Surface area (square kilometres)	267 668
Population in 2012 (estimated, 000)	1 633
Population density in 2012 (per square kilometre)	6.1
Capital city and population in 2011 (000)	Libreville (686)
United Nations membership date	20 September 1960

Economic indicators	2005	2010	2012
GDP: Gross domestic product (million current US$)	9 459	18 771	24 076
GDP: Growth rate at constant 2005 prices (annual %)	5.6	5.6	6.2
GDP per capita (current US$)	6 857.0	12 062.1	14 747.1
GNI: Gross national income per capita (current US$)	6 099.3	10 436.6	12 904.6
Gross fixed capital formation (% of GDP)	19.8	24.0	25.0
Exchange rates (national currency per US$)[a]	556.04	490.91	497.16
Balance of payments, current account (million US$)	1 983	...	...
CPI: Consumer price index (2000=100)[bc]	105	123	124[d]
Agricultural production index (2004-2006=100)	100	117	121
Food production index (2004-2006=100)	100	115	119
Employment in industrial sector (% of employed)	11.8[efg]	...	...
Employment in agricultural sector (% of employed)	24.2[efg]	...	...
Labour force participation, adult female pop. (%)	54.4	55.5	56.0
Labour force participation, adult male pop. (%)	64.1	64.7	65.1
Tourist arrivals at national borders (000)[h]	269	...	...
Energy production, primary (000 mt oil equivalent)	13 822	13 093	...
Mobile-cellular subscriptions (per 100 inhabitants)	53.7[i]	106.9	187.4[i]
Individuals using the Internet (%)	4.9	7.2[j]	8.6[j]

Total trade		Major trading partners			2012
	(million US$)[k]	(% of exports)[k]		(% of imports)[k]	
Exports	5 356.0	United States	59.0	France	32.9
Imports	2 500.9	China	8.0	Belgium	15.7
Balance	2 855.1	Spain	5.3	United States	7.1

Social indicators		
Population growth rate (average annual %)	2010-2015	2.4
Urban population growth rate (average annual %)	2010-2015	2.3
Rural population growth rate (average annual %)	2010-2015	−0.4
Urban population (%)	2013	86.9
Population aged 0-14 years (%)	2013	38.5
Population aged 60+ years (females and males, % of total)	2013	8.0/6.6
Sex ratio (males per 100 females)	2013	101.0
Life expectancy at birth (females and males, years)	2010-2015	64.3/62.3
Infant mortality rate (per 1 000 live births)	2010-2015	43.3
Fertility rate, total (live births per woman)	2010-2015	4.1
Contraceptive prevalence (ages 15-49, %)	2006-2012	32.7[l]
International migrant stock (000 and % of total population)[m]	mid-2013	395.0/23.6
Refugees and others of concern to UNHCR	mid-2013	4 000
Education: Government expenditure (% of GDP)[n]	2006-2012	3.8[l]
Education: Primary-secondary gross enrolment ratio (f/m per 100)	2006-2012	95.1/98.0[o]
Education: Female third-level students (% of total)	2006-2012	35.7[o]
Intentional homicides (females and males, per 100 000)[p]	2008-2010	7.0/20.5
Seats held by women in national parliaments (%)	2014	15.0

Environmental indicators		
Threatened species	2013	210
Forested area (% of land area)	2011	85.4
CO_2 emission estimates (000 metric tons and metric tons per capita)	2010	2 572/1.7
Energy consumption per capita (kilograms oil equivalent)	2010	651.0
Precipitation in the capital city, total mean (millimetres)		2 842[q]
Temperature in the capital city, mean °C (minimum and maximum)		23.3/28.6[q]

a Official rate. b Libreville. c African population. d 2011. e Core Welfare Indicators Questionnaire (World Bank). f The indices are shown in terms of ISIC Rev.2. g Break in series; data not strictly comparable. h Arrivals of non-resident tourists at Libreville airport. i Includes inactive subscribers. j ITU estimate. k 2009. l 2000. m Data refer to foreign citizens. n UNESCO estimate. o 1999. p Estimates. q Based on monthly averages for the period 1961-1990.

Gambia

Region	Western Africa
Currency	Dalasi (GMD)
Surface area (square kilometres)	11 295
Population in 2012 (estimated, 000)	1 791
Population density in 2012 (per square kilometre)	158.6
Capital city and population in 2011 (000)	Banjul (506)
United Nations membership date	21 September 1965

Economic indicators	2005	2010	2012
GDP: Gross domestic product (million current US$)	624	952	917
GDP: Growth rate at constant 2005 prices (annual %)	−0.9	6.5	6.3
GDP per capita (current US$)	434.5	566.4	512.1
GNI: Gross national income per capita (current US$)	418.9	548.8	448.5
Gross fixed capital formation (% of GDP)	29.5	27.8	33.7
Exchange rates (national currency per US$)[a]	28.13	28.39	33.92
Balance of payments, current account (million US$)	−43	56	58
CPI: Consumer price index (2000=100)[b]	157	193	202[c]
Agricultural production index (2004-2006=100)	94	134	107
Food production index (2004-2006=100)	94	134	107
Labour force participation, adult female pop. (%)	71.7	72.2	72.2
Labour force participation, adult male pop. (%)	83.5	83.2	83.0
Tourist arrivals at national borders (000)[d]	108	91	157
Mobile-cellular subscriptions (per 100 inhabitants)	16.5	85.5	83.6
Individuals using the Internet (%)	3.8[e]	9.2	12.5[e]

Total trade		Major trading partners			2012
	(million US$)[c]	(% of exports)[c]		(% of imports)[c]	
Exports	94.7	Senegal	35.3	Côte d'Ivoire	21.1
Imports	343.7	Guinea	23.1	Brazil	9.7
Balance	−249.0	Mali	16.7	China	8.8

Social indicators

Population growth rate (average annual %)	2010-2015	3.2
Urban population growth rate (average annual %)	2010-2015	3.6
Rural population growth rate (average annual %)	2010-2015	1.4
Urban population (%)	2013	58.4
Population aged 0-14 years (%)	2013	45.9
Population aged 60+ years (females and males, % of total)	2013	3.5/3.9
Sex ratio (males per 100 females)	2013	97.9
Life expectancy at birth (females and males, years)	2010-2015	60.1/57.4
Infant mortality rate (per 1 000 live births)	2010-2015	55.3
Fertility rate, total (live births per woman)	2010-2015	5.8
Contraceptive prevalence (ages 15-49, %)	2006-2012	17.5[f]
International migrant stock (000 and % of total population)	mid-2013	162.9/8.8
Refugees and others of concern to UNHCR	mid-2013	9 609
Education: Government expenditure (% of GDP)	2006-2012	4.1
Education: Primary-secondary gross enrolment ratio (f/m per 100)[g]	2006-2012	72.7/73.0
Education: Female third-level students (% of total)	2006-2012	19.2[h]
Intentional homicides (females and males, per 100 000)[i]	2008-2010	6.3/15.4
Seats held by women in national parliaments (%)	2014	9.4

Environmental indicators

Threatened species	2013	52
Forested area (% of land area)	2011	47.6
CO₂ emission estimates (000 metric tons and metric tons per capita)	2010	473/0.3
Energy consumption per capita (kilograms oil equivalent)	2010	93.0[j]
Precipitation in the capital city, total mean (millimetres)		977
Temperature in the capital city, mean °C (minimum and maximum)		19.9/32.0

a Market rate. b Banjul and Kombo St. Mary only. c 2011. d Charter tourists only. e ITU estimate. f 2001. g UNESCO estimate. h 2004. i Estimates. j UNSD estimate.

Georgia

Region	Western Asia
Currency	Lari (GEL)
Surface area (square kilometres)	69 700
Population in 2012 (estimated, 000)	4 358[a]
Population density in 2012 (per square kilometre)	62.5
Capital city and population in 2011 (000)	Tbilisi (1 121)
United Nations membership date	31 July 1992

Economic indicators

	2005	2010	2012
GDP: Gross domestic product (million current US$)	6 411	11 638	15 830
GDP: Growth rate at constant 2005 prices (annual %)	9.6	6.3	6.1
GDP per capita (current US$)	1 432.5	2 651.9	3 632.1
GNI: Gross national income per capita (current US$)	1 453.6	2 570.0	3 607.8
Gross fixed capital formation (% of GDP)	28.1	19.3	24.9
Exchange rates (national currency per US$)[b]	1.79	1.77	1.66
Balance of payments, current account (million US$)	−695	−1 196	−1 850
CPI: Consumer price index (2000=100)[c]	132	189	...
Industrial production index (2005=100)[d]	100	137	192
Agricultural production index (2004-2006=100)	121	67	72
Food production index (2004-2006=100)	121	68	73
Employment in industrial sector (% of employed)	9.3[d]	...	...
Employment in agricultural sector (% of employed)	54.3[d]	...	...
Labour force participation, adult female pop. (%)	55.4	55.6	56.2
Labour force participation, adult male pop. (%)	73.3	73.9	74.7
Tourist arrivals at national borders (000)[e]	560	2 032	4 428
Energy production, primary (000 mt oil equivalent)	619	1 020	...
Mobile-cellular subscriptions (per 100 inhabitants)	26.2	91.5[fg]	109.2
Individuals using the Internet (%)	6.1[h]	26.9	45.5[h]

Total trade		Major trading partners			2012
	(million US$)	(% of exports)			(% of imports)
Exports	2 377.5	Azerbaijan	26.4	Turkey	17.8
Imports	7 839.6	Armenia	11.0	Azerbaijan	8.1
Balance	−5 462.1	United States	9.5	Ukraine	7.6

Social indicators

Population growth rate (average annual %)[a]	2010-2015	−0.4
Urban population growth rate (average annual %)[a]	2010-2015	−0.4
Rural population growth rate (average annual %)[a]	2010-2015	−0.9
Urban population (%)[a]	2013	53.1
Population aged 0-14 years (%)[a]	2013	17.9
Population aged 60+ years (females and males, % of total)[a]	2013	22.5/16.7
Sex ratio (males per 100 females)[a]	2013	89.2
Life expectancy at birth (females and males, years)[a]	2010-2015	77.7/70.5
Infant mortality rate (per 1 000 live births)[a]	2010-2015	19.4
Fertility rate, total (live births per woman)[a]	2010-2015	1.8
Contraceptive prevalence (ages 15-49, %)[i]	2006-2012	47.3[j]
International migrant stock (000 and % of total population)[a]	mid-2013	189.9/4.4
Refugees and others of concern to UNHCR	mid-2013	284 003
Education: Government expenditure (% of GDP)	2006-2012	2.0
Education: Primary-secondary gross enrolment ratio (f/m per 100)	2006-2012	97.6/100.9
Education: Female third-level students (% of total)	2006-2012	55.9
Intentional homicides (females and males, per 100 000)	2008-2010	1.2/7.7
Seats held by women in national parliaments (%)	2014	12.0

Environmental indicators

Threatened species	2013	51
Forested area (% of land area)	2011	39.4
CO$_2$ emission estimates (000 metric tons and metric tons per capita)	2010	6 236/1.4
Energy consumption per capita (kilograms oil equivalent)	2010	664.0
Precipitation in the capital city, total mean (millimetres)		496[k]
Temperature in the capital city, mean °C (minimum and maximum)		13.0/13.0[kl]

a Includes Abkhazia and South Ossetia. b Official rate. c 5 cities. d The indices are shown in terms of ISIC Rev.3. e Arrivals of non-resident visitors at national borders. f Methodology revised. g Active subscriptions in the last quarter. h ITU estimate. i Age group 15 to 44 years. j 2005. k Based on WMO Climatological Normals (CLINO) for the period 1961-1990. l Refers to average temperature.

Germany

Region	Western Europe
Currency	Euro (EUR)
Surface area (square kilometres)	357 137
Population in 2012 (estimated, 000)	82 800
Population density in 2012 (per square kilometre)	231.8
Capital city and population in 2011 (000)	Berlin (3 462)
United Nations membership date	18 September 1973

Economic indicators	2005	2010	2012
GDP: Gross domestic product (million current US$)	2 766 254	3 304 439	3 425 956
GDP: Growth rate at constant 2005 prices (annual %)	0.7	4.0	0.7
GDP per capita (current US$)	32 996.0	39 804.2	41 376.2
GNI: Gross national income per capita (current US$)	33 369.7	40 672.1	42 364.2
Gross fixed capital formation (% of GDP)	17.3	17.4	17.7
Exchange rates (national currency per US$)[a]	0.85	0.75	0.76
Balance of payments, current account (million US$)	140 216	207 725	240 743
CPI: Consumer price index (2000=100)	108	117	122
Industrial production index (2005=100)	100	104	111
Agricultural production index (2004-2006=100)	100	102	105
Food production index (2004-2006=100)	100	102	105
Unemployment (% of labour force)[b]	11.2	7.1	5.5
Employment in industrial sector (% of employed)[c]	29.8[d]	28.4	28.2
Employment in agricultural sector (% of employed)[c]	2.4[d]	1.6	1.5
Labour force participation, adult female pop. (%)	50.6	52.7	53.5
Labour force participation, adult male pop. (%)	66.6	66.3	66.4
Tourist arrivals at national borders (000)[e]	21 500	26 875	30 411
Energy production, primary (000 mt oil equivalent)	97 180	81 700	...
Mobile-cellular subscriptions (per 100 inhabitants)	96.0	127.0[f]	131.3[f]
Individuals using the Internet (%)[g]	68.7	82.0	84.0

Total trade		Major trading partners			2012
	(million US$)	(% of exports)			(% of imports)
Exports	1 416 184.3	France	9.5	Netherlands	9.5
Imports	1 173 287.6	United States	7.9	China	8.6
Balance	242 896.6	Netherlands	6.4	France	7.1

Social indicators

Population growth rate (average annual %)	2010-2015	−0.1
Urban population growth rate (average annual %)	2010-2015	−<
Rural population growth rate (average annual %)	2010-2015	−0.7
Urban population (%)	2013	74.2
Population aged 0-14 years (%)	2013	13.1
Population aged 60+ years (females and males, % of total)	2013	29.5/24.6
Sex ratio (males per 100 females)	2013	96.4
Life expectancy at birth (females and males, years)	2010-2015	83.1/78.2
Infant mortality rate (per 1 000 live births)	2010-2015	3.1
Fertility rate, total (live births per woman)	2010-2015	1.4
Contraceptive prevalence (ages 15-49, %)[h]	2006-2012	70.1[i]
International migrant stock (000 and % of total population)	mid-2013	9 845.2/11.9
Refugees and others of concern to UNHCR	mid-2013	279 878
Education: Government expenditure (% of GDP)	2006-2012	5.1
Education: Primary-secondary gross enrolment ratio (f/m per 100)	2006-2012	99.5/103.3
Education: Female third-level students (% of total)	2006-2012	50.6
Intentional homicides (females and males, per 100 000)	2008-2010	0.8/0.9
Seats held by women in national parliaments (%)	2014	36.5

Environmental indicators

Threatened species	2013	110
Forested area (% of land area)	2011	31.8
CO_2 emission estimates (000 metric tons and metric tons per capita)	2010	744 774/9.1
Energy consumption per capita (kilograms oil equivalent)	2010	3 260.0
Precipitation in the capital city, total mean (millimetres)		571[j]
Temperature in the capital city, mean °C (minimum and maximum)		5.9/13.4[j]

a Market rate. b Age group 15 to 74 years. c European Labour Force Survey (Eurostat). d The indices are shown in terms of ISIC Rev.3. e Arrivals of non-resident tourists in all types of accommodation establishments. f Excludes data-only SIM cards. g Age group 16 to 74 years. h Age group 20 to 39 years. i 1992. j Based on monthly averages for the period 1971-2000.

Ghana

Region	Western Africa
Currency	Cedi (GHS)
Surface area (square kilometres)	238 533
Population in 2012 (estimated, 000)	25 366
Population density in 2012 (per square kilometre)	106.3
Capital city and population in 2011 (000)	Accra (2 573)
United Nations membership date	8 March 1957

Economic indicators	2005	2010	2012
GDP: Gross domestic product (million current US$)	17 198	32 174	40 711
GDP: Growth rate at constant 2005 prices (annual %)	6.2	8.0	7.9
GDP per capita (current US$)	804.3	1 326.1	1 604.9
GNI: Gross national income per capita (current US$)	794.5	1 304.1	1 528.3
Gross fixed capital formation (% of GDP)	20.6	24.7	29.0
Exchange rates (national currency per US$)[a]	0.91	1.47	1.88
Balance of payments, current account (million US$)	−1 105	−2 747	−4 778
CPI: Consumer price index (2000=100)	251	511	607
Agricultural production index (2004-2006=100)	100	125	136
Food production index (2004-2006=100)	100	125	136
Employment in industrial sector (% of employed)	13.6[bcdef]	15.4[ghi]	...
Employment in agricultural sector (% of employed)	57.2[bcdef]	41.5[ghi]	...
Labour force participation, adult female pop. (%)	67.6	66.9	67.2
Labour force participation, adult male pop. (%)	71.7	70.9	71.2
Tourist arrivals at national borders (000)[j]	429	931	...
Energy production, primary (000 mt oil equivalent)	484	839	...
Mobile-cellular subscriptions (per 100 inhabitants)	13.3	71.5	100.3
Individuals using the Internet (%)	1.8	7.8[kl]	17.1[m]

Total trade		Major trading partners			2012
	(million US$)	(% of exports)			(% of imports)
Exports	18 761.2	South Africa	24.2	China	17.2
Imports	14 011.9	India	10.0	United States	11.2
Balance	4 749.3	United Arab Emirates	8.7	United Kingdom	10.0

Social indicators		
Population growth rate (average annual %)	2010-2015	2.1
Urban population growth rate (average annual %)	2010-2015	3.5
Rural population growth rate (average annual %)	2010-2015	0.9
Urban population (%)	2013	53.2
Population aged 0-14 years (%)	2013	38.5
Population aged 60+ years (females and males, % of total)	2013	5.8/4.9
Sex ratio (males per 100 females)	2013	98.3
Life expectancy at birth (females and males, years)	2010-2015	61.9/60.0
Infant mortality rate (per 1 000 live births)	2010-2015	51.1
Fertility rate, total (live births per woman)	2010-2015	3.9
Contraceptive prevalence (ages 15-49, %)	2006-2012	23.5
International migrant stock (000 and % of total population)	mid-2013	358.8/1.4
Refugees and others of concern to UNHCR	mid-2013	19 207
Education: Government expenditure (% of GDP)	2006-2012	8.1
Education: Primary-secondary gross enrolment ratio (f/m per 100)	2006-2012	80.2/87.0
Education: Female third-level students (% of total)	2006-2012	37.7
Intentional homicides (females and males, per 100 000)[n]	2008-2010	5.9/25.1
Seats held by women in national parliaments (%)	2014	10.9

Environmental indicators		
Threatened species	2013	215
Forested area (% of land area)	2011	21.2
CO_2 emission estimates (000 metric tons and metric tons per capita)	2010	8 991/0.4
Energy consumption per capita (kilograms oil equivalent)	2010	129.0
Precipitation in the capital city, total mean (millimetres)		807°
Temperature in the capital city, mean °C (minimum and maximum)		23.4/30.8°

a Principal rate. b 2006. c Living standards survey. d The indices are shown in terms of ISIC Rev.3. e Age group 15 to 64 years. f September of the preceding year to September of the current year. g Population census. h September. i Break in series; data not strictly comparable. j Includes nationals residing abroad. k Age group 12 years and over. l Break in comparability. m ITU estimate. n Estimates. o Based on monthly averages for the period 1961-1990.

Greece

Region	Southern Europe
Currency	Euro (EUR)
Surface area (square kilometres)	131 957
Population in 2012 (estimated, 000)	11 125
Population density in 2012 (per square kilometre)	84.3
Capital city and population in 2011 (000)	Athens (3 414)
United Nations membership date	25 October 1945

Economic indicators	2005	2010	2012
GDP: Gross domestic product (million current US$)	240 076	294 223	248 941
GDP: Growth rate at constant 2005 prices (annual %)	2.3	-4.9	-6.4
GDP per capita (current US$)	21 742.8	26 482.7	22 377.4
GNI: Gross national income per capita (current US$)	21 426.4	25 739.5	22 487.9
Gross fixed capital formation (% of GDP)	20.7	17.6	13.1
Exchange rates (national currency per US$)[a]	0.85	0.75	0.76
Balance of payments, current account (million US$)	-18 233	-30 274	-6 172
CPI: Consumer price index (2000=100)	118[b]	139	145
Industrial production index (2005=100)	100	85	75
Agricultural production index (2004-2006=100)	103	82	86
Food production index (2004-2006=100)	103	86	86
Unemployment (% of labour force)[c]	9.9	12.5	24.2
Employment in industrial sector (% of employed)[d]	22.4[e]	19.7	16.7
Employment in agricultural sector (% of employed)[d]	12.4[e]	12.5	13.0
Labour force participation, adult female pop. (%)	42.1	44.1	44.2
Labour force participation, adult male pop. (%)	64.7	64.4	62.6
Tourist arrivals at national borders (000)[fg]	14 765	15 007	15 518
Energy production, primary (000 mt oil equivalent)	9 251	8 440	...
Mobile-cellular subscriptions (per 100 inhabitants)	91.8	108.2	116.9
Individuals using the Internet (%)[h]	24.0	44.4	56.0

Total trade		Major trading partners			2012
	(million US$)		(% of exports)		(% of imports)
Exports	35 179.7	Turkey	10.8	Russian Federation	12.4
Imports	62 341.3	Italy	7.7	Germany	9.2
Balance	-27 161.6	Germany	6.4	Italy	7.8

Social indicators		
Population growth rate (average annual %)	2010-2015	<
Urban population growth rate (average annual %)	2010-2015	0.6
Rural population growth rate (average annual %)	2010-2015	-0.4
Urban population (%)	2013	61.9
Population aged 0-14 years (%)	2013	14.7
Population aged 60+ years (females and males, % of total)	2013	28.0/23.3
Sex ratio (males per 100 females)	2013	97.4
Life expectancy at birth (females and males, years)	2010-2015	83.0/78.3
Infant mortality rate (per 1 000 live births)	2010-2015	3.6
Fertility rate, total (live births per woman)	2010-2015	1.5
Contraceptive prevalence (ages 15-49, %)[i]	2006-2012	76.2[j]
International migrant stock (000 and % of total population)[k]	mid-2013	988.2/8.9
Refugees and others of concern to UNHCR	mid-2013	52 380[l]
Education: Government expenditure (% of GDP)	2006-2012	4.1[m]
Education: Primary-secondary gross enrolment ratio (f/m per 100)	2006-2012	105.6/108.1
Education: Female third-level students (% of total)	2006-2012	49.8
Intentional homicides (females and males, per 100 000)	2008-2010	</5.0
Seats held by women in national parliaments (%)	2014	21.0

Environmental indicators		
Threatened species	2013	281
Forested area (% of land area)	2011	30.5
CO_2 emission estimates (000 metric tons and metric tons per capita)	2010	86 646/7.6
Energy consumption per capita (kilograms oil equivalent)	2010	2 537.0
Precipitation in the capital city, total mean (millimetres)		414[n]
Temperature in the capital city, mean °C (minimum and maximum)		12.3/22.5[n]

a Market rate. b Series linked to former series. c Age group 15 to 74 years. d European Labour Force Survey (Eurostat). e The indices are shown in terms of ISIC Rev.3. f Up to 2007, information based on administrative data. g From 2008, information based on border surveys. h Age group 16 to 74 years. i Age group 16 to 45 years. j 2001. k Data refer to foreign citizens. l Refugee population refers to the end of 2012. m 2005. n Based on monthly averages for the period 1955-1997.

Greenland

Region	Northern America
Currency	Danish Krone (DKK)
Surface area (square kilometres)	2 166 086
Population in 2012 (estimated, 000)	57
Population density in 2012 (per square kilometre)	<
Capital city and population in 2011 (000)	Nuuk (16)

Economic indicators	2005	2010	2012
GDP: Gross domestic product (million current US$)	1 650	2 265	2 343
GDP: Growth rate at constant 2005 prices (annual %)	3.7	4.9	2.2
GDP per capita (current US$)	28 977.4	40 063.7	41 266.5
GNI: Gross national income per capita (current US$)	28 290.6	39 129.1	40 302.9
Gross fixed capital formation (% of GDP)	24.8	53.4	51.2
Exchange rates (national currency per US$)[a]	6.32	5.61	5.66
CPI: Consumer price index (2000=100)	113	132	140
Agricultural production index (2004-2006=100)	100	99	99
Food production index (2004-2006=100)	99	99	99
Energy production, primary (000 mt oil equivalent)	17	24	...
Mobile-cellular subscriptions (per 100 inhabitants)	81.3	100.1	103.8
Individuals using the Internet (%)	57.7	63.0	64.9[b]

Total trade		Major trading partners			2012
	(million US$)	(% of exports)			(% of imports)
Exports	476.9	Denmark	90.8	Denmark	59.3
Imports	856.0	Portugal	3.1	Sweden	21.5
Balance	−379.1	Switzerland	2.6	Norway	3.8

Social indicators		
Population growth rate (average annual %)	2010-2015	0.3
Urban population growth rate (average annual %)	2010-2015	0.3
Rural population growth rate (average annual %)	2010-2015	−1.9
Urban population (%)	2013	85.2
Population aged 0-14 years (%)[cde]	2013	21.7[f]
Population aged 60+ years (females and males, % of total)[cde]	2013	11.1/11.7[f]
Sex ratio (males per 100 females)[cde]	2013	112.8[f]
Life expectancy at birth (females and males, years)[c]	2010-2015	72.9/68.2[g]
Fertility rate, total (live births per woman)[c]	2010-2015	2.1[h]
International migrant stock (000 and % of total population)	mid-2013	5.7/10.0

Environmental indicators		
Threatened species	2013	16
Forested area (% of land area)	2011	0.0
CO$_2$ emission estimates (000 metric tons and metric tons per capita)	2010	634/11.1
Energy consumption per capita (kilograms oil equivalent)	2010	4 093.0
Precipitation in the capital city, total mean (millimetres)		754[i]
Temperature in the capital city, mean °C (minimum and maximum)		−4.0/1.3[i]

a Market rate. b ITU estimate. c Data compiled by the United Nations Demographic Yearbook system. d Data refer to the latest available census. e De jure estimate. f 2012. g 2007-2011. h 2011. i Based on monthly averages for the period 1961-1990.

Grenada

Region	Caribbean
Currency	E.C. Dollar (XCD)
Surface area (square kilometres)	344
Population in 2012 (estimated, 000)	105
Population density in 2012 (per square kilometre)	306.6
Capital city and population in 2011 (000)	St.George's (41)
United Nations membership date	17 September 1974

Economic indicators	2005	2010	2012
GDP: Gross domestic product (million current US$)	695	770	783
GDP: Growth rate at constant 2005 prices (annual %)	13.3	−0.4	−1.7
GDP per capita (current US$)	6 754.4	7 353.2	7 418.3
GNI: Gross national income per capita (current US$)	6 481.7	6 870.4	6 989.3
Gross fixed capital formation (% of GDP)	46.3	22.1	17.5
Exchange rates (national currency per US$)[a]	2.70	2.70	2.70
Balance of payments, current account (million US$)	−193	−203	−214
CPI: Consumer price index (2000=100)	112	136[b]	143
Agricultural production index (2004-2006=100)	77	90	97
Food production index (2004-2006=100)	77	90	97
Tourist arrivals at national borders (000)	99	110	116
Mobile-cellular subscriptions (per 100 inhabitants)	45.6	116.7	121.6[c]
Individuals using the Internet (%)[c]	20.5	33.5	42.1

Total trade	Major trading partners		2012
(million US$)[d]	(% of exports)		(% of imports)[d]
Imports 281.8	...	United States	31.9
	...	Trinidad and Tobago	25.2
	...	United Kingdom	4.2

Social indicators		
Population growth rate (average annual %)	2010-2015	0.4
Urban population growth rate (average annual %)	2010-2015	1.2
Rural population growth rate (average annual %)	2010-2015	−0.2
Urban population (%)	2013	39.8
Population aged 0-14 years (%)	2013	26.8
Population aged 60+ years (females and males, % of total)	2013	11.2/8.5
Sex ratio (males per 100 females)	2013	100.3
Life expectancy at birth (females and males, years)	2010-2015	75.2/70.2
Infant mortality rate (per 1 000 live births)	2010-2015	8.9
Fertility rate, total (live births per woman)	2010-2015	2.2
Contraceptive prevalence (ages 15-49, %)[e]	2006-2012	54.3[f]
International migrant stock (000 and % of total population)	mid-2013	11.4/10.7
Refugees and others of concern to UNHCR	mid-2013	0[g]
Education: Government expenditure (% of GDP)	2006-2012	3.9[h]
Education: Primary-secondary gross enrolment ratio (f/m per 100)	2006-2012	105.1/105.6
Education: Female third-level students (% of total)	2006-2012	57.1
Intentional homicides (females and males, per 100 000)	2008-2010	3.8/19.2
Seats held by women in national parliaments (%)	2014	33.3

Environmental indicators		
Threatened species	2013	44
Forested area (% of land area)	2011	50.0
CO$_2$ emission estimates (000 metric tons and metric tons per capita)	2010	260/2.5
Energy consumption per capita (kilograms oil equivalent)	2010	841.0

a Official rate. b Series linked to former series. c ITU estimate. d 2009. e Age group 15 to 44 years. f 1990. g Value is zero, not available or not applicable. h 2003.

Guadeloupe

Region	Caribbean
Currency	Euro (EUR)
Surface area (square kilometres)	1 705
Population in 2012 (estimated, 000)	464[a]
Population density in 2012 (per square kilometre)	271.9
Capital city and population in 2011 (000)	Basse-Terre (13)

Economic indicators	2005	2010	2012
Exchange rates (national currency per US$)[b]	0.85	0.75	0.76
CPI: Consumer price index (2000=100)	112	122	128
Agricultural production index (2004-2006=100)	103	89	110
Food production index (2004-2006=100)	103	89	110
Employment in industrial sector (% of employed)[cd]	...	13.8	13.5
Employment in agricultural sector (% of employed)	...	...	3.3[cd]
Labour force participation, adult female pop. (%)	48.6	51.4	50.1
Labour force participation, adult male pop. (%)	56.1	57.5	57.3
Tourist arrivals at national borders (000)[ef]	372[g]	392	418[h]
Energy production, primary (000 mt oil equivalent)[i]	22	24	...

Social indicators		
Population growth rate (average annual %)[a]	2010-2015	0.5
Urban population growth rate (average annual %)[a]	2010-2015	0.5
Rural population growth rate (average annual %)[a]	2010-2015	0.1
Urban population (%)[a]	2013	98.4
Population aged 0-14 years (%)[a]	2013	21.5
Population aged 60+ years (females and males, % of total)[a]	2013	19.8/17.0
Sex ratio (males per 100 females)[a]	2013	89.1
Life expectancy at birth (females and males, years)[a]	2010-2015	84.0/77.4
Infant mortality rate (per 1 000 live births)[a]	2010-2015	5.6
Fertility rate, total (live births per woman)[a]	2010-2015	2.1
Contraceptive prevalence (ages 15-49, %)	2006-2012	29.4[j]
International migrant stock (000 and % of total population)[a]	mid-2013	97.1/20.8

Environmental indicators		
Threatened species	2013	60
Forested area (% of land area)	2011	38.1
CO$_2$ emission estimates (000 metric tons and metric tons per capita)	2010	1 737/3.8
Energy consumption per capita (kilograms oil equivalent)	2010	1 225.0[l]
Precipitation in the capital city, total mean (millimetres)[k]		1 779[l]
Temperature in the capital city, mean °C (minimum and maximum)[k]		22.1/30.5[l]

a Includes Saint-Barthélemy and Saint-Martin (French part). b Market rate. c March to June. d Excludes the institutional population. e Air arrivals. f Excludes Saint-Barthélemy and Saint-Martin (French part). g Data based on a survey conducted at Guadeloupe airport. h 2011. i UNSD estimate. j 1976. k Le Raizet. l Based on monthly averages for the period 1961-1990.

Guam

	Region	Oceania-Micronesia
	Currency	U.S. Dollar (USD)
Surface area (square kilometres)		549
Population in 2012 (estimated, 000)		163
Population density in 2012 (per square kilometre)		296.6
Capital city and population in 2011 (000)		Hagåtña (169)

Economic indicators	2005	2010	2012
CPI: Consumer price index (2000=100)	116	154	164
Agricultural production index (2004-2006=100)	100	97	98
Food production index (2004-2006=100)	100	97	98
Unemployment (% of labour force)[a]	...	...	12.2
Employment in industrial sector (% of employed)	...	14.0[b]	...
Employment in agricultural sector (% of employed)	...	0.3[b]	...
Labour force participation, adult female pop. (%)	56.1	54.8	55.8
Labour force participation, adult male pop. (%)	69.7	70.1	69.5
Tourist arrivals at national borders (000)	1 228	1 196	1 283
Mobile-cellular subscriptions (per 100 inhabitants)	59.1[c]	...	...
Individuals using the Internet (%)	38.6	54.0[d]	61.5[d]

Social indicators		
Population growth rate (average annual %)	2010-2015	1.3
Urban population growth rate (average annual %)	2010-2015	1.2
Rural population growth rate (average annual %)	2010-2015	0.7
Urban population (%)	2013	93.3
Population aged 0-14 years (%)	2013	26.2
Population aged 60+ years (females and males, % of total)	2013	13.2/11.4
Sex ratio (males per 100 females)	2013	103.0
Life expectancy at birth (females and males, years)	2010-2015	81.5/76.1
Infant mortality rate (per 1 000 live births)	2010-2015	9.7
Fertility rate, total (live births per woman)	2010-2015	2.4
Contraceptive prevalence (ages 15-49, %)[e]	2006-2012	66.6[f]
International migrant stock (000 and % of total population)	mid-2013	80.8/48.9

Environmental indicators		
Threatened species	2013	46
Forested area (% of land area)	2011	47.9

a Age group 16 years and over. b Population census. c 2004. d ITU estimate. e Age group 18 to 44 years.
f 2002.

Guatemala

Region	Central America
Currency	Quetzal (GTQ)
Surface area (square kilometres)	108 889
Population in 2012 (estimated, 000)	15 083
Population density in 2012 (per square kilometre)	138.5
Capital city and population in 2011 (000)	Guatemala City (1 168)
United Nations membership date	21 November 1945

Economic indicators	2005	2010	2012
GDP: Gross domestic product (million current US$)	27 211	41 341	50 377
GDP: Growth rate at constant 2005 prices (annual %)	3.3	2.9	3.0
GDP per capita (current US$)	2 146.2	2 882.6	3 340.0
GNI: Gross national income per capita (current US$)	2 119.7	2 797.9	3 241.9
Gross fixed capital formation (% of GDP)	18.3	14.8	14.6
Exchange rates (national currency per US$)[a]	7.61	8.02	7.89
Balance of payments, current account (million US$)	−1 241	−626	−1 309
CPI: Consumer price index (2000=100)	144	193	213
Agricultural production index (2004-2006=100)	98	129	134
Food production index (2004-2006=100)	97	131	136
Employment in industrial sector (% of employed)[bc]	22.8[de]	21.8	19.5
Employment in agricultural sector (% of employed)[bc]	33.2[de]	33.5	32.3
Labour force participation, adult female pop. (%)	44.9	48.8	49.1
Labour force participation, adult male pop. (%)	87.4	88.2	88.2
Tourist arrivals at national borders (000)[f]	1 316	1 876	1 951
Energy production, primary (000 mt oil equivalent)	1 354	964	...
Mobile-cellular subscriptions (per 100 inhabitants)	35.5	125.6	137.3
Individuals using the Internet (%)	5.7	10.5[g]	16.0[g]

Total trade		Major trading partners			2012
	(million US$)		(% of exports)		(% of imports)
Exports	10 124.6	United States	41.0	United States	38.1
Imports	16 978.7	El Salvador	11.0	Mexico	11.3
Balance	−6 854.1	Honduras	7.9	China	7.5

Social indicators		
Population growth rate (average annual %)	2010-2015	2.5
Urban population growth rate (average annual %)	2010-2015	3.4
Rural population growth rate (average annual %)	2010-2015	1.6
Urban population (%)	2013	50.7
Population aged 0-14 years (%)	2013	40.4
Population aged 60+ years (females and males, % of total)	2013	6.9/6.3
Sex ratio (males per 100 females)	2013	95.2
Life expectancy at birth (females and males, years)	2010-2015	75.5/68.4
Infant mortality rate (per 1 000 live births)	2010-2015	23.5
Fertility rate, total (live births per woman)	2010-2015	3.8
Contraceptive prevalence (ages 15-49, %)	2006-2012	43.3[h]
International migrant stock (000 and % of total population)[i]	mid-2013	72.8/0.5
Refugees and others of concern to UNHCR	mid-2013	186
Education: Government expenditure (% of GDP)	2006-2012	3.0
Education: Primary-secondary gross enrolment ratio (f/m per 100)	2006-2012	90.8/95.5
Education: Female third-level students (% of total)	2006-2012	50.8
Intentional homicides (females and males, per 100 000)	2008-2010	10.0/84.5
Seats held by women in national parliaments (%)	2014	13.3

Environmental indicators		
Threatened species	2013	264
Forested area (% of land area)	2011	33.6
CO_2 emission estimates (000 metric tons and metric tons per capita)	2010	11 109/0.8
Energy consumption per capita (kilograms oil equivalent)	2010	255.0
Precipitation in the capital city, total mean (millimetres)		1 186
Temperature in the capital city, mean °C (minimum and maximum)		14.7/25.0

a Market rate. b The indices are shown in terms of ISIC Rev.3. c Break in series; data not strictly comparable. d 2006. e Age group 10 years and over. f Arrivals of non-resident visitors at national borders. g ITU estimate. h 2002. i Includes refugees.

Guinea

Region	Western Africa
Currency	Guinean Franc (GNF)
Surface area (square kilometres)	245 857
Population in 2012 (estimated, 000)	11 451
Population density in 2012 (per square kilometre)	46.6
Capital city and population in 2011 (000)	Conakry (1 786)
United Nations membership date	12 December 1958

Economic indicators	2005	2010	2012
GDP: Gross domestic product (million current US$)	2 935	5 233	6 093
GDP: Growth rate at constant 2005 prices (annual %)	3.0	1.9	3.9
GDP per capita (current US$)	306.5	481.1	532.1
GNI: Gross national income per capita (current US$)	301.4	474.1	520.3
Gross fixed capital formation (% of GDP)	27.6	30.0	41.9
Exchange rates (national currency per US$)[a]	4 500.00	6 083.95	7 089.53[b]
Balance of payments, current account (million US$)	−160	−327	−1 039
CPI: Consumer price index (2000=100)[c]	185	439	613
Agricultural production index (2004-2006=100)	101	113	122
Food production index (2004-2006=100)	101	113	122
Labour force participation, adult female pop. (%)	63.8	65.3	65.5
Labour force participation, adult male pop. (%)	78.3	78.3	78.3
Tourist arrivals at national borders (000)[d]	45	30[e]	...
Energy production, primary (000 mt oil equivalent)	43	42	...
Mobile-cellular subscriptions (per 100 inhabitants)	2.1	40.1	45.6[f]
Individuals using the Internet (%)	0.5	1.0[f]	1.5[f]

Total trade		Major trading partners			2012
	(million US$)[g]	(% of exports)[g]		(% of imports)[g]	
Exports	1 430.5	France	24.5	Netherlands	20.6
Imports	1 835.5	Switzerland	19.5	France	10.1
Balance	−405.0	Russian Federation	10.6	United Kingdom	7.9

Social indicators		
Population growth rate (average annual %)	2010-2015	2.5
Urban population growth rate (average annual %)	2010-2015	3.9
Rural population growth rate (average annual %)	2010-2015	1.8
Urban population (%)	2013	36.4
Population aged 0-14 years (%)	2013	42.3
Population aged 60+ years (females and males, % of total)	2013	5.4/4.8
Sex ratio (males per 100 females)	2013	100.3
Life expectancy at birth (females and males, years)	2010-2015	56.7/55.2
Infant mortality rate (per 1 000 live births)	2010-2015	73.6
Fertility rate, total (live births per woman)	2010-2015	5.0
Contraceptive prevalence (ages 15-49, %)	2006-2012	9.1[h]
International migrant stock (000 and % of total population)[i][j]	mid-2013	378.5/3.2
Refugees and others of concern to UNHCR	mid-2013	11 020
Education: Government expenditure (% of GDP)	2006-2012	2.5
Education: Primary-secondary gross enrolment ratio (f/m per 100)	2006-2012	56.7/73.4
Education: Female third-level students (% of total)	2006-2012	26.7
Intentional homicides (females and males, per 100 000)[k]	2008-2010	9.5/35.3
Seats held by women in national parliaments (%)	2014	21.9

Environmental indicators		
Threatened species	2013	152
Forested area (% of land area)	2011	26.5
CO_2 emission estimates (000 metric tons and metric tons per capita)	2010	1 235/0.1
Energy consumption per capita (kilograms oil equivalent)	2010	45.0[l]
Precipitation in the capital city, total mean (millimetres)		3 776
Temperature in the capital city, mean °C (minimum and maximum)		22.9/29.9

a Market rate. b 2011. c Conakry. d Air arrivals at Conakry airport. e 2007. f ITU estimate. g 2008. h 2005. i Data refer to foreign citizens. j Includes refugees. k Estimates. l UNSD estimate.

Guinea-Bissau

Region	Western Africa
Currency	CFA Franc (XOF)
Surface area (square kilometres)	36 125
Population in 2012 (estimated, 000)	1 664
Population density in 2012 (per square kilometre)	46.1
Capital city and population in 2011 (000)	Bissau (423)
United Nations membership date	17 September 1974

Economic indicators	2005	2010	2012
GDP: Gross domestic product (million current US$)	587	845	849
GDP: Growth rate at constant 2005 prices (annual %)	6.5	4.4	−2.8
GDP per capita (current US$)	412.8	532.6	510.4
GNI: Gross national income per capita (current US$)	404.6	532.0	506.8
Gross fixed capital formation (% of GDP)	6.1	6.6	7.6
Exchange rates (national currency per US$)[a]	556.04	490.91	497.16
Balance of payments, current account (million US$)	−10	−71	...
CPI: Consumer price index (2000=100)[bc]	104	122[d]	...
Agricultural production index (2004-2006=100)	99	126	137
Food production index (2004-2006=100)	99	126	138
Labour force participation, adult female pop. (%)	66.2	68.0	68.1
Labour force participation, adult male pop. (%)	78.5	78.4	78.5
Tourist arrivals at national borders (000)[e]	5	30[f]	...
Mobile-cellular subscriptions (per 100 inhabitants)	7.2	47.2[g]	69.5[g]
Individuals using the Internet (%)	1.9	2.5[g]	2.9[g]

Social indicators		
Population growth rate (average annual %)	2010-2015	2.4
Urban population growth rate (average annual %)	2010-2015	3.6
Rural population growth rate (average annual %)	2010-2015	0.9
Urban population (%)	2013	45.3
Population aged 0-14 years (%)	2013	41.5
Population aged 60+ years (females and males, % of total)	2013	5.6/5.0
Sex ratio (males per 100 females)	2013	98.9
Life expectancy at birth (females and males, years)	2010-2015	55.7/52.7
Infant mortality rate (per 1 000 live births)	2010-2015	93.9
Fertility rate, total (live births per woman)	2010-2015	5.0
Contraceptive prevalence (ages 15-49, %)	2006-2012	14.0
International migrant stock (000 and % of total population)[h]	mid-2013	18.0/1.1
Refugees and others of concern to UNHCR	mid-2013	7 907
Education: Government expenditure (% of GDP)	2006-2012	5.3[i]
Education: Primary-secondary gross enrolment ratio (f/m per 100)	2006-2012	40.6/62.4[j]
Intentional homicides (females and males, per 100 000)[k]	2008-2010	9.0/31.7
Seats held by women in national parliaments (%)	2014	11.0

Environmental indicators		
Threatened species	2013	61
Forested area (% of land area)	2011	71.6
CO_2 emission estimates (000 metric tons and metric tons per capita)	2010	238/0.2
Energy consumption per capita (kilograms oil equivalent)	2010	52.0[l]
Precipitation in the capital city, total mean (millimetres)		1 756[m]
Temperature in the capital city, mean °C (minimum and maximum)		19.7/32.1[m]

a Official rate. b Bissau. c Index base 2003=100. d Series linked to former series. e Air arrivals. f 2007. g ITU estimate. h Includes refugees. i 1999. j 2000. k Estimates. l UNSD estimate. m January to November only.

Guyana

Region	South America
Currency	Guyana Dollar (GYD)
Surface area (square kilometres)	214 969
Population in 2012 (estimated, 000)	795
Population density in 2012 (per square kilometre)	3.7
Capital city and population in 2011 (000)	Georgetown (127)
United Nations membership date	20 September 1966

Economic indicators	2005	2010	2012
GDP: Gross domestic product (million current US$)	1 315	2 259	2 851
GDP: Growth rate at constant 2005 prices (annual %)	−2.0	4.4	4.8
GDP per capita (current US$)	1 728.9	2 874.0	3 584.7
GNI: Gross national income per capita (current US$)	1 717.8	2 890.2	3 583.2
Gross fixed capital formation (% of GDP)	20.3	25.4	24.9
Exchange rates (national currency per US$)[a]	200.25	203.50	204.25
Balance of payments, current account (million US$)	−96	−155	−395
CPI: Consumer price index (2000=100)[b]	128	177[c]	186[d]
Agricultural production index (2004-2006=100)	94	106	113
Food production index (2004-2006=100)	94	106	113
Labour force participation, adult female pop. (%)	39.4	41.6	42.3
Labour force participation, adult male pop. (%)	81.8	81.4	80.9
Tourist arrivals at national borders (000)[e]	117	152	177
Mobile-cellular subscriptions (per 100 inhabitants)	37.7	74.3	72.2
Individuals using the Internet (%)	13.8[fg]	29.9	33.0[g]

Total trade		Major trading partners			2012
	(million US$)	(% of exports)		(% of imports)	
Exports	1 045.3	United States	29.0	United States	26.0
Imports	1 878.4	Venezuela	13.9	Trinidad and Tobago	14.9
Balance	−833.1	United Kingdom	11.4	Curaçao	10.5

Social indicators		
Population growth rate (average annual %)	2010-2015	0.5
Urban population growth rate (average annual %)	2010-2015	0.5
Rural population growth rate (average annual %)	2010-2015	0.1
Urban population (%)	2013	28.5
Population aged 0-14 years (%)	2013	36.1
Population aged 60+ years (females and males, % of total)	2013	6.7/4.1
Sex ratio (males per 100 females)	2013	103.3
Life expectancy at birth (females and males, years)	2010-2015	68.9/63.5
Infant mortality rate (per 1 000 live births)	2010-2015	28.5
Fertility rate, total (live births per woman)	2010-2015	2.6
Contraceptive prevalence (ages 15-49, %)	2006-2012	42.5
International migrant stock (000 and % of total population)	mid-2013	14.8/1.9
Refugees and others of concern to UNHCR	mid-2013	10
Education: Government expenditure (% of GDP)	2006-2012	3.2
Education: Primary-secondary gross enrolment ratio (f/m per 100)	2006-2012	96.4/84.7
Education: Female third-level students (% of total)	2006-2012	66.8
Intentional homicides (females and males, per 100 000)	2008-2010	7.5/23.5
Seats held by women in national parliaments (%)	2014	31.3

Environmental indicators		
Threatened species	2013	86
Forested area (% of land area)	2011	77.2
CO_2 emission estimates (000 metric tons and metric tons per capita)	2010	1 700/2.2
Energy consumption per capita (kilograms oil equivalent)	2010	745.0
Precipitation in the capital city, mean (millimetres)		2 263[h]
Temperature in the capital city, mean °C (minimum and maximum)		24.0/30.5[h]

a Principal rate. b Georgetown. c Series linked to former series. d 2011. e Arrivals to Timehri airport only.
f 2007. g ITU estimate. h Based on monthly averages for the period 1961-1990.

Haiti

Region	Caribbean
Currency	Gourde (HTG)
Surface area (square kilometres)	27 750
Population in 2012 (estimated, 000)	10 174
Population density in 2012 (per square kilometre)	366.6
Capital city and population in 2011 (000)	Port-au-Prince (2 207)
United Nations membership date	24 October 1945

Economic indicators	2005	2010	2012
GDP: Gross domestic product (million current US$)	3 807	6 079	7 187
GDP: Growth rate at constant 2005 prices (annual %)	1.8	−5.4	2.8
GDP per capita (current US$)	411.1	614.3	706.5
GNI: Gross national income per capita (current US$)	418.1	615.3	707.6
Gross fixed capital formation (% of GDP)	14.3	13.3	15.2
Exchange rates (national currency per US$)[a]	43.00	39.88	42.55
Balance of payments, current account (million US$)	7	−166	−349
CPI: Consumer price index (2000=100)	252[b]	375	432
Agricultural production index (2004-2006=100)	102	106	107
Food production index (2004-2006=100)	102	108	107
Labour force participation, adult female pop. (%)	58.4	60.1	60.6
Labour force participation, adult male pop. (%)	69.5	70.5	70.8
Tourist arrivals at national borders (000)[cd]	112	255	295[e]
Energy production, primary (000 mt oil equivalent)	23	15	...
Mobile-cellular subscriptions (per 100 inhabitants)	5.4[f]	40.0	59.4
Individuals using the Internet (%)[f]	6.4	8.4	9.8

Social indicators		
Population growth rate (average annual %)	2010-2015	1.4
Urban population growth rate (average annual %)	2010-2015	3.7
Rural population growth rate (average annual %)	2010-2015	−1.7
Urban population (%)	2013	56.1
Population aged 0-14 years (%)	2013	35.0
Population aged 60+ years (females and males, % of total)	2013	7.3/6.3
Sex ratio (males per 100 females)	2013	97.7
Life expectancy at birth (females and males, years)	2010-2015	64.9/61.1
Infant mortality rate (per 1 000 live births)	2010-2015	40.2
Fertility rate, total (live births per woman)	2010-2015	3.2
Contraceptive prevalence (ages 15-49, %)	2006-2012	32.0[g]
International migrant stock (000 and % of total population)	mid-2013	38.1/0.4
Refugees and others of concern to UNHCR	mid-2013	9
Intentional homicides (females and males, per 100 000)	2008-2010	1.4/8.2
Seats held by women in national parliaments (%)	2014	4.2

Environmental indicators		
Threatened species	2013	156
Forested area (% of land area)	2011	3.6
CO$_2$ emission estimates (000 metric tons and metric tons per capita)	2010	2 118/0.2
Energy consumption per capita (kilograms oil equivalent)	2010	67.0

a Principal rate. b Series linked to former series. c Air arrivals. d From 2007, includes nationals residing abroad. e Includes data for only 10 months; data for September and October are not available. f ITU estimate. g 2005-2006.

Honduras

Region	Central America
Currency	Lempira (HNL)
Surface area (square kilometres)	112 492
Population in 2012 (estimated, 000)	7 936
Population density in 2012 (per square kilometre)	70.6
Capital city and population in 2011 (000)	Tegucigalpa (1 088)
United Nations membership date	17 December 1945

Economic indicators

	2005	2010	2012
GDP: Gross domestic product (million current US$)	9 757	15 839	18 564
GDP: Growth rate at constant 2005 prices (annual %)	6.1	3.7	3.9
GDP per capita (current US$)	1 414.3	2 078.3	2 339.3
GNI: Gross national income per capita (current US$)	1 348.1	1 982.7	2 177.3
Gross fixed capital formation (% of GDP)	24.9	21.6	24.3
Exchange rates (national currency per US$)[a]	18.90	18.90	19.96
Balance of payments, current account (million US$)	−304	−682	−1 587
CPI: Consumer price index (2000=100)	150	208	233
Industrial production index (2005=100)[b]	100	113	125
Agricultural production index (2004-2006=100)	103	111	126
Food production index (2004-2006=100)	104	110	123
Unemployment (% of labour force)[c]	...	4.3	...
Employment in industrial sector (% of employed)[d]	20.9[ce]	19.5[c]	19.8[fgh]
Employment in agricultural sector (% of employed)[d]	39.2[ce]	36.0[c]	35.3[fgh]
Labour force participation, adult female pop. (%)	39.6	41.9	42.5
Labour force participation, adult male pop. (%)	83.7	82.9	82.9
Tourist arrivals at national borders (000)	673	863	895
Energy production, primary (000 mt oil equivalent)	148	255	...
Mobile-cellular subscriptions (per 100 inhabitants)	18.6	125.1	93.2[i]
Individuals using the Internet (%)	6.5[j]	11.1	18.1[k]

Total trade

	(million US$)
Exports	5 006.9
Imports	8 646.6
Balance	−3 639.7

Major trading partners 2012

(% of exports)		(% of imports)	
United States	46.5	United States	40.9
Germany	10.1	China	8.9
Belgium	5.7	Mexico	7.7

Social indicators

Population growth rate (average annual %)	2010-2015	2.0
Urban population growth rate (average annual %)	2010-2015	3.1
Rural population growth rate (average annual %)	2010-2015	0.8
Urban population (%)	2013	53.3
Population aged 0-14 years (%)	2013	35.2
Population aged 60+ years (females and males, % of total)	2013	6.8/6.2
Sex ratio (males per 100 females)	2013	100.1
Life expectancy at birth (females and males, years)	2010-2015	76.2/71.3
Infant mortality rate (per 1 000 live births)	2010-2015	22.3
Fertility rate, total (live births per woman)	2010-2015	3.0
Contraceptive prevalence (ages 15-49, %)	2006-2012	65.2[l]
International migrant stock (000 and % of total population)[m]	mid-2013	27.5/0.3
Refugees and others of concern to UNHCR	mid-2013	65
Education: Primary-secondary gross enrolment ratio (f/m per 100)	2006-2012	96.3/90.1
Education: Female third-level students (% of total)	2006-2012	53.0
Intentional homicides (females and males, per 100 000)	2008-2010	9.7/131.7
Seats held by women in national parliaments (%)	2014	25.8

Environmental indicators

Threatened species	2013	275
Forested area (% of land area)	2011	45.3
CO_2 emission estimates (000 metric tons and metric tons per capita)	2010	8 101/1.1
Energy consumption per capita (kilograms oil equivalent)	2010	343.0
Precipitation in the capital city, total mean (millimetres)		872[n]
Temperature in the capital city, mean °C (minimum and maximum)		16.7/27.9[n]

a Principal rate. **b** The indices are shown in terms of ISIC Rev.3. **c** Age group 10 years and over. **d** The indices are shown in terms of ISIC Rev.2. **e** September. **f** 2011. **g** May. **h** Break in series; data not strictly comparable. **i** Decrease due to the merger of the second and third operators of the mobile market. **j** Age group 5 years and over. **k** ITU estimate. **l** 2005-2006. **m** Includes refugees. **n** Based on WMO Climatological Normals (CLINO) for the period 1961-1990.

Hungary

Region	Eastern Europe
Currency	Forint (HUF)
Surface area (square kilometres)	93 026
Population in 2012 (estimated, 000)	9 976
Population density in 2012 (per square kilometre)	107.2
Capital city and population in 2011 (000)	Budapest (1 737)
United Nations membership date	14 December 1955

Economic indicators	2005	2010	2012
GDP: Gross domestic product (million current US$)	110 322	127 501	124 600
GDP: Growth rate at constant 2005 prices (annual %)	4.0	1.1	−1.7
GDP per capita (current US$)	10 927.3	12 731.4	12 489.8
GNI: Gross national income per capita (current US$)	10 337.5	12 129.3	11 818.9
Gross fixed capital formation (% of GDP)	22.8	18.6	17.4
Exchange rates (national currency per US$)[a]	213.58	208.65	220.93
Balance of payments, current account (million US$)	−8 238	261	1 119
CPI: Consumer price index (2000=100)	133	173	190
Industrial production index (2005=100)	100	108	112
Agricultural production index (2004-2006=100)	96	80	79
Food production index (2004-2006=100)	96	80	79
Unemployment (% of labour force)[b]	7.2	11.2	10.9
Employment in industrial sector (% of employed)[b]	32.4[cd]	30.7[e]	29.8[e]
Employment in agricultural sector (% of employed)[b]	5.0[cd]	4.5[e]	5.2[e]
Labour force participation, adult female pop. (%)	42.9	43.7	44.7
Labour force participation, adult male pop. (%)	58.3	58.3	59.9
Tourist arrivals at national borders (000)[f]	9 979	9 510	10 353
Energy production, primary (000 mt oil equivalent)	7 028	6 763	...
Mobile-cellular subscriptions (per 100 inhabitants)	92.4	120.3	116.4
Individuals using the Internet (%)[g]	39.0	65.0	72.0

Total trade		Major trading partners			2012
	(million US$)		(% of exports)		(% of imports)
Exports	103 006.0	Germany	25.0	Germany	24.7
Imports	94 266.2	Romania	6.0	Russian Federation	8.8
Balance	8 739.8	Slovakia	5.9	Austria	6.9

Social indicators		
Population growth rate (average annual %)	2010-2015	−0.2
Urban population growth rate (average annual %)	2010-2015	0.5
Rural population growth rate (average annual %)	2010-2015	−1.7
Urban population (%)	2013	70.4
Population aged 0-14 years (%)	2013	14.7
Population aged 60+ years (females and males, % of total)	2013	27.8/19.6
Sex ratio (males per 100 females)	2013	90.6
Life expectancy at birth (females and males, years)	2010-2015	78.5/70.4
Infant mortality rate (per 1 000 live births)	2010-2015	4.8
Fertility rate, total (live births per woman)	2010-2015	1.4
Contraceptive prevalence (ages 15-49, %)[h]	2006-2012	80.6[i]
International migrant stock (000 and % of total population)[j]	mid-2013	472.8/4.8
Refugees and others of concern to UNHCR	mid-2013	8 552[k]
Education: Government expenditure (% of GDP)	2006-2012	4.9
Education: Primary-secondary gross enrolment ratio (f/m per 100)	2006-2012	100.0/101.7
Education: Female third-level students (% of total)	2006-2012	55.9
Intentional homicides (females and males, per 100 000)	2008-2010	1.2/1.6
Seats held by women in national parliaments (%)	2014	9.4

Environmental indicators		
Threatened species	2013	66
Forested area (% of land area)	2011	22.5
CO$_2$ emission estimates (000 metric tons and metric tons per capita)	2010	50 541/5.1
Energy consumption per capita (kilograms oil equivalent)	2010	2 244.0
Precipitation in the capital city, total mean (millimetres)		516[l]
Temperature in the capital city, mean °C (minimum and maximum)		6.3/15.0[l]

a Official rate. b Age group 15 to 74 years. c The indices are shown in terms of ISIC Rev.3. d Excludes conscripts. e European Labour Force Survey (Eurostat). f New series. g Age group 16 to 74 years. h Age group 18 to 41 years. i 1992-1993. j Includes refugees. k Refugee population refers to the end of 2012. l Based on monthly averages for the period 1961-1990.

Iceland

Region	Northern Europe
Currency	Iceland Krona (ISK)
Surface area (square kilometres)	103 000
Population in 2012 (estimated, 000)	326
Population density in 2012 (per square kilometre)	3.2
Capital city and population in 2011 (000)	Reykjavík (206)
United Nations membership date	19 November 1946

Economic indicators	2005	2010	2012
GDP: Gross domestic product (million current US$)	16 286	12 565	13 579
GDP: Growth rate at constant 2005 prices (annual %)	7.2	−4.1	1.4
GDP per capita (current US$)	54 883.3	39 506.4	41 670.2
GNI: Gross national income per capita (current US$)	52 906.0	32 574.6	37 064.0
Gross fixed capital formation (% of GDP)	28.3	12.7	14.5
Exchange rates (national currency per US$)[a]	62.98	115.05	128.99
Balance of payments, current account (million US$)	−2 648	−1 012	−740
CPI: Consumer price index (2000=100)[b]	122	182	199
Agricultural production index (2004-2006=100)	99	110	115
Food production index (2004-2006=100)	99	110	115
Unemployment (% of labour force)[c]	2.6	7.6	6.0
Employment in industrial sector (% of employed)[c]	21.7[d]	18.3[e]	18.2[e]
Employment in agricultural sector (% of employed)[c]	6.5[d]	5.5[e]	5.5[e]
Labour force participation, adult female pop. (%)	70.8	70.4	70.6
Labour force participation, adult male pop. (%)	80.2	78.6	77.3
Tourist arrivals at national borders (000)	374	489	673
Energy production, primary (000 mt oil equivalent)	953	1 710	...
Mobile-cellular subscriptions (per 100 inhabitants)	95.4	106.5	105.4[f]
Individuals using the Internet (%)	87.0[c]	93.4[g]	96.2[g]

Total trade		Major trading partners			2012
	(million US$)	(% of exports)		(% of imports)	
Exports	5 063.4	Netherlands	30.0	Norway	16.6
Imports	4 771.9	Germany	12.9	United States	10.2
Balance	291.5	United Kingdom	9.8	Germany	9.2

Social indicators		
Population growth rate (average annual %)	2010-2015	1.1
Urban population growth rate (average annual %)	2010-2015	1.3
Rural population growth rate (average annual %)	2010-2015	−0.6
Urban population (%)	2013	94.0
Population aged 0-14 years (%)	2013	20.7
Population aged 60+ years (females and males, % of total)	2013	18.9/17.0
Sex ratio (males per 100 females)	2013	101.4
Life expectancy at birth (females and males, years)	2010-2015	83.8/80.2
Infant mortality rate (per 1 000 live births)	2010-2015	1.8
Fertility rate, total (live births per woman)	2010-2015	2.1
International migrant stock (000 and % of total population)	mid-2013	34.4/10.4
Refugees and others of concern to UNHCR	mid-2013	402
Education: Government expenditure (% of GDP)	2006-2012	7.6
Education: Primary-secondary gross enrolment ratio (f/m per 100)	2006-2012	104.1/103.4
Education: Female third-level students (% of total)	2006-2012	62.2
Intentional homicides (females and males, per 100 000)	2008-2010	0.0/0.0
Seats held by women in national parliaments (%)	2014	39.7

Environmental indicators		
Threatened species	2013	19
Forested area (% of land area)	2011	<
CO$_2$ emission estimates (000 metric tons and metric tons per capita)	2010	1 960/6.1
Energy consumption per capita (kilograms oil equivalent)	2010	7 238.0
Precipitation in the capital city, total mean (millimetres)		798[h]
Temperature in the capital city, mean °C (minimum and maximum)		1.9/7.0[h]

a Official rate. b Annual averages are based on the months February to December and January of the following year. c Age group 16 to 74 years. d The indices are shown in terms of ISIC Rev.3. e European Labour Force Survey (Eurostat). f ITU estimate. g Age group 16 to 74 years using the Internet within the last 3 months. h Based on WMO Climatological Normals (CLINO) for the period 1961-1990.

India

Region	Southern Asia
Currency	Indian Rupee (INR)
Surface area (square kilometres)	3 287 263
Population in 2012 (estimated, 000)	1 236 687
Population density in 2012 (per square kilometre)	376.2
Capital city and population in 2011 (000)	New Delhi (250)[a]
United Nations membership date	30 October 1945

Economic indicators	2005	2010	2012
GDP: Gross domestic product (million current US$)	837 499	1 704 795	1 875 213
GDP: Growth rate at constant 2005 prices (annual %)	9.3	10.5	3.2
GDP per capita (current US$)	743.0	1 414.0	1 516.3
GNI: Gross national income per capita (current US$)	737.8	1 399.2	1 501.2
Gross fixed capital formation (% of GDP)	31.5	33.8	32.1
Exchange rates (national currency per US$)[b]	45.06	44.81	54.78
Balance of payments, current account (million US$)	−10 284	−54 516	−91 471
CPI: Consumer price index (2000=100)[c]	122	183	217
Industrial production index (2005=100)[de]	100	152	159
Agricultural production index (2004-2006=100)	100	125	130
Food production index (2004-2006=100)	100	124	129
Unemployment (% of labour force)	4.4	3.5	...
Employment in industrial sector (% of employed)[fg]	19.0	22.4	24.7
Employment in agricultural sector (% of employed)[fg]	55.8	51.1	47.2
Labour force participation, adult female pop. (%)	36.9	28.6	28.8
Labour force participation, adult male pop. (%)	83.3	80.8	80.9
Tourist arrivals at national borders (000)[h]	3 919	5 776	6 578
Energy production, primary (000 mt oil equivalent)	314 739	420 079	...
Mobile-cellular subscriptions (per 100 inhabitants)	7.9	61.4[i]	68.7[ij]
Individuals using the Internet (%)[k]	2.4	7.5	12.6

Total trade		Major trading partners			2012
	(million US$)	(% of exports)			(% of imports)
Exports	289 564.8	United States	12.8	China	11.1
Imports	488 976.4	United Arab Emirates	12.4	United Arab Emirates	7.7
Balance	−199 411.6	China	5.1	Saudi Arabia	6.7

Social indicators		
Population growth rate (average annual %)	2010-2015	1.2
Urban population growth rate (average annual %)	2010-2015	2.5
Rural population growth rate (average annual %)	2010-2015	0.8
Urban population (%)	2013	32.0
Population aged 0-14 years (%)	2013	29.1
Population aged 60+ years (females and males, % of total)	2013	9.0/7.7
Sex ratio (males per 100 females)	2013	107.1
Life expectancy at birth (females and males, years)	2010-2015	68.1/64.6
Infant mortality rate (per 1 000 live births)	2010-2015	43.8
Fertility rate, total (live births per woman)	2010-2015	2.5
Contraceptive prevalence (ages 15-49, %)	2006-2012	54.8
International migrant stock (000 and % of total population)[l]	mid-2013	5 338.5/0.4
Refugees and others of concern to UNHCR	mid-2013	190 957
Education: Government expenditure (% of GDP)	2006-2012	3.2
Education: Primary-secondary gross enrolment ratio (f/m per 100)	2006-2012	86.5/87.9
Education: Female third-level students (% of total)	2006-2012	41.8
Intentional homicides (females and males, per 100 000)	2008-2010	1.5/3.9
Seats held by women in national parliaments (%)	2014	11.4

Environmental indicators		
Threatened species	2013	973
Forested area (% of land area)	2011	23.1
CO$_2$ emission estimates (000 metric tons and metric tons per capita)	2010	2 007 180/1.7
Energy consumption per capita (kilograms oil equivalent)	2010	440.0
Precipitation in the capital city, total mean (millimetres)		716[m]
Temperature in the capital city, mean °C (minimum and maximum)		19.0/31.3[m]

a The capital is New Delhi, included in the urban agglomeration of Delhi. **b** Market rate. **c** Industrial workers. **d** The indices are shown in terms of ISIC Rev.3. **e** Average of 12 months beginning 1 April of the year stated. **f** July of the preceding year to June of the current year. **g** Excludes Leh and Kargil of Jammu and Kashmir districts, some villages in Nagaland, Andaman and Nicobar Islands. **h** Excludes nationals residing abroad. **i** December. **j** Break in comparability. **k** ITU estimate. **l** Includes refugees. **m** Based on monthly averages for the period 1901-2000.

Indonesia

Region	South-Eastern Asia
Currency	Rupiah (IDR)
Surface area (square kilometres)	1 910 931
Population in 2012 (estimated, 000)	246 864
Population density in 2012 (per square kilometre)	129.2
Capital city and population in 2011 (000)	Jakarta (9 769)
United Nations membership date	28 September 1950

Economic indicators	2005	2010	2012
GDP: Gross domestic product (million current US$)	285 869	709 191	878 043
GDP: Growth rate at constant 2005 prices (annual %)	5.7	6.2	6.2
GDP per capita (current US$)	1 273.5	2 946.7	3 556.8
GNI: Gross national income per capita (current US$)	1 211.5	2 863.9	3 453.6
Gross fixed capital formation (% of GDP)	23.6	32.0	33.2
Exchange rates (national currency per US$)[a]	9 830.00	8 991.00	9 670.00
Balance of payments, current account (million US$)	278	5 144	−24 074
CPI: Consumer price index (2000=100)	156	227	250
Agricultural production index (2004-2006=100)	98	121	132
Food production index (2004-2006=100)	98	121	133
Unemployment (% of labour force)	10.8	7.3	6.2
Employment in industrial sector (% of employed)[b]	18.7[c]	19.3[d]	20.6[de]
Employment in agricultural sector (% of employed)[b]	44.0[c]	38.3[d]	35.9[de]
Labour force participation, adult female pop. (%)	50.0	51.2	51.3
Labour force participation, adult male pop. (%)	85.4	84.5	84.4
Tourist arrivals at national borders (000)	5 002	7 003	8 044
Energy production, primary (000 mt oil equivalent)	219 724	349 446	...
Mobile-cellular subscriptions (per 100 inhabitants)	20.6	88.1	115.2
Individuals using the Internet (%)	3.6	10.9	15.4

Total trade		Major trading partners			2012
	(million US$)	(% of exports)			(% of imports)
Exports	190 031.8	Japan	15.9	China	15.3
Imports	191 690.9	China	11.4	Singapore	13.6
Balance	−1 659.1	Singapore	9.0	Japan	11.9

Social indicators		
Population growth rate (average annual %)	2010-2015	1.2
Urban population growth rate (average annual %)	2010-2015	2.5
Rural population growth rate (average annual %)	2010-2015	−0.6
Urban population (%)	2013	52.3
Population aged 0-14 years (%)	2013	28.9
Population aged 60+ years (females and males, % of total)	2013	8.8/7.4
Sex ratio (males per 100 females)	2013	101.2
Life expectancy at birth (females and males, years)	2010-2015	72.8/68.7
Infant mortality rate (per 1 000 live births)	2010-2015	25.6
Fertility rate, total (live births per woman)	2010-2015	2.4
Contraceptive prevalence (ages 15-49, %)	2006-2012	61.4
International migrant stock (000 and % of total population)[fg]	mid-2013	295.4/0.1
Refugees and others of concern to UNHCR	mid-2013	10 340
Education: Government expenditure (% of GDP)	2006-2012	2.8
Education: Primary-secondary gross enrolment ratio (f/m per 100)	2006-2012	97.1/94.5
Education: Female third-level students (% of total)	2006-2012	46.1
Intentional homicides (females and males, per 100 000)[h]	2008-2010	2.3/13.9
Seats held by women in national parliaments (%)	2014	18.6

Environmental indicators		
Threatened species	2013	1 206
Forested area (% of land area)	2011	51.8
CO$_2$ emission estimates (000 metric tons and metric tons per capita)	2010	433 634/1.8
Energy consumption per capita (kilograms oil equivalent)	2010	543.0
Precipitation in the capital city, total mean (millimetres)		1 655[i]
Temperature in the capital city, mean °C (minimum and maximum)		25.0/31.8[j]

a Market rate. **b** August. **c** The indices are shown in terms of ISIC Rev.3. **d** The indices are shown in terms of ISIC Rev.2. **e** 2011. **f** Data refer to foreign citizens. **g** Includes refugees. **h** Estimates. **i** Based on monthly averages for the period 1930-1960. **j** Based on monthly averages for the period 1994-1999.

Iran (Islamic Republic of)

Region	Southern Asia
Currency	Iranian Rial (IRR)
Surface area (square kilometres)	1 628 750
Population in 2012 (estimated, 000)	76 424
Population density in 2012 (per square kilometre)	46.9
Capital city and population in 2011 (000)	Tehran (7 304)
United Nations membership date	24 October 1945

Economic indicators	2005	2010	2012
GDP: Gross domestic product (million current US$)	205 587	421 716	551 588
GDP: Growth rate at constant 2005 prices (annual %)	5.3	5.8	−1.9
GDP per capita (current US$)	2 930.6	5 663.5	7 217.4
GNI: Gross national income per capita (current US$)	2 885.5	5 620.8	7 156.1
Gross fixed capital formation (% of GDP)	25.8	26.5	23.4
Exchange rates (national currency per US$)[a]	9 091.00	10 353.00	12 260.00
CPI: Consumer price index (2000=100)	193	386	593
Agricultural production index (2004-2006=100)	103	107	112
Food production index (2004-2006=100)	103	107	112
Unemployment (% of labour force)[b]	10.3[c]	11.5[d]	...
Employment in industrial sector (% of employed)[be]	30.3[f]	32.2[c]	...
Employment in agricultural sector (% of employed)[be]	24.7[f]	21.2[c]	...
Labour force participation, adult female pop. (%)	19.4	16.0	16.4
Labour force participation, adult male pop. (%)	74.4	71.9	73.1
Tourist arrivals at national borders (000)[g]	1 889	2 938	3 834
Energy production, primary (000 mt oil equivalent)	318 568	367 945	...
Mobile-cellular subscriptions (per 100 inhabitants)	12.2[h]	73.1	76.9
Individuals using the Internet (%)	8.1[i]	14.7[j]	26.0[i]

Total trade		Major trading partners			2012
	(million US$)[k]	(% of exports)[kl]		(% of imports)[kl]	
Exports	130 544.0	Asia nes	47.0	United Arab Emirates	26.6
Imports	68 319.0	Europe nes	18.9	Areas nes	14.7
Balance	62 225.0	Areas nes	7.1	China	10.3

Social indicators		
Population growth rate (average annual %)	2010-2015	1.3
Urban population growth rate (average annual %)	2010-2015	1.3
Rural population growth rate (average annual %)	2010-2015	0.6
Urban population (%)	2013	69.4
Population aged 0-14 years (%)	2013	23.8
Population aged 60+ years (females and males, % of total)	2013	8.3/7.8
Sex ratio (males per 100 females)	2013	101.2
Life expectancy at birth (females and males, years)	2010-2015	75.9/72.1
Infant mortality rate (per 1 000 live births)	2010-2015	15.7
Fertility rate, total (live births per woman)	2010-2015	1.9
Contraceptive prevalence (ages 15-49, %)	2006-2012	73.3[m]
International migrant stock (000 and % of total population)[n]	mid-2013	2 649.5/3.4
Refugees and others of concern to UNHCR	mid-2013	862 808
Education: Government expenditure (% of GDP)	2006-2012	3.7
Education: Primary-secondary gross enrolment ratio (f/m per 100)	2006-2012	92.1/96.0
Education: Female third-level students (% of total)	2006-2012	49.8
Intentional homicides (females and males, per 100 000)	2008-2010	0.6/2.3
Seats held by women in national parliaments (%)	2014	3.1

Environmental indicators		
Threatened species	2013	112
Forested area (% of land area)	2011	6.8
CO_2 emission estimates (000 metric tons and metric tons per capita)	2010	571 144/7.7
Energy consumption per capita (kilograms oil equivalent)	2010	2 954.0
Precipitation in the capital city, total mean (millimetres)		230[o]
Temperature in the capital city, mean °C (minimum and maximum)		11.7/22.5[o]

a Official rate. **b** Age group 10 years and over. **c** 2008. **d** 2009. **e** The indices are shown in terms of ISIC Rev.3. **f** Break in series; data not strictly comparable. **g** Arrivals of non-resident visitors at national borders. **h** October. **i** ITU estimate. **j** Refers to total population. **k** 2011. **l** See technical notes. **m** 2002. **n** Includes refugees. **o** Based on monthly averages for the period 1961-1990.

Iraq

Region	Western Asia
Currency	Iraqi Dinar (IQD)
Surface area (square kilometres)	435 244
Population in 2012 (estimated, 000)	32 778
Population density in 2012 (per square kilometre)	75.3
Capital city and population in 2011 (000)	Baghdad (6 036)
United Nations membership date	21 December 1945

Economic indicators

	2005	2010	2012
GDP: Gross domestic product (million current US$)	36 268	122 041	149 370
GDP: Growth rate at constant 2005 prices (annual %)	4.4	5.9	8.4
GDP per capita (current US$)	1 324.8	3 941.6	4 557.0
GNI: Gross national income per capita (current US$)	1 351.8	3 993.0	4 674.7
Gross fixed capital formation (% of GDP)	19.1	18.4	20.3
Exchange rates (national currency per US$)[a]	1 487.00	1 170.00	1 166.00
Balance of payments, current account (million US$)	−3 335	6 488	29 541
CPI: Consumer price index (2000=100)	323	660[b]	739
Agricultural production index (2004-2006=100)	104	105	112
Food production index (2004-2006=100)	104	104	112
Employment in industrial sector (% of employed)[c]	17.7[d]	18.2[e]	...
Employment in agricultural sector (% of employed)[c]	29.7[d]	23.4[e]	...
Labour force participation, adult female pop. (%)	13.6	14.5	14.7
Labour force participation, adult male pop. (%)	69.1	69.5	69.7
Tourist arrivals at national borders (000)[f]	864[e]	1 518	...
Energy production, primary (000 mt oil equivalent)	99 648	126 674	...
Mobile-cellular subscriptions (per 100 inhabitants)	5.6	73.5	79.4[g]
Individuals using the Internet (%)	0.9[g]	2.5	7.1[g]

Social indicators

Population growth rate (average annual %)	2010-2015	2.9
Urban population growth rate (average annual %)	2010-2015	3.1
Rural population growth rate (average annual %)	2010-2015	3.2
Urban population (%)	2013	66.4
Population aged 0-14 years (%)	2013	40.1
Population aged 60+ years (females and males, % of total)	2013	5.6/4.5
Sex ratio (males per 100 females)	2013	102.2
Life expectancy at birth (females and males, years)	2010-2015	73.1/66.0
Infant mortality rate (per 1 000 live births)	2010-2015	28.1
Fertility rate, total (live births per woman)	2010-2015	4.1
Contraceptive prevalence (ages 15-49, %)	2006-2012	51.2
International migrant stock (000 and % of total population)[hi]	mid-2013	95.8/0.3
Refugees and others of concern to UNHCR	mid-2013	1 366 368
Education: Primary-secondary gross enrolment ratio (f/m per 100)	2006-2012	73.9/90.8
Education: Female third-level students (% of total)[j]	2006-2012	36.2[k]
Intentional homicides (females and males, per 100 000)[l]	2008-2010	0.8/3.3
Seats held by women in national parliaments (%)	2014	25.2

Environmental indicators

Threatened species	2013	62
Forested area (% of land area)	2011	1.9
CO_2 emission estimates (000 metric tons and metric tons per capita)	2010	114 573/3.6
Energy consumption per capita (kilograms oil equivalent)	2010	1 236.0
Precipitation in the capital city, total mean (millimetres)		123[m]
Temperature in the capital city, mean °C (minimum and maximum)		14.9/30.6[m]

a Principal rate. **b** Series linked to former series. **c** The indices are shown in terms of ISIC Rev.3. **d** 2006. **e** 2008. **f** Arrivals of non-resident visitors at national borders. **g** ITU estimate. **h** Data refer to foreign citizens. **i** Includes refugees. **j** UNESCO estimate. **k** 2005. **l** Estimates. **m** Based on monthly averages for the period 1976-2008.

Ireland

Region	Northern Europe
Currency	Euro (EUR)
Surface area (square kilometres)	69 825
Population in 2012 (estimated, 000)	4 576
Population density in 2012 (per square kilometre)	65.5
Capital city and population in 2011 (000)	Dublin (1 121)
United Nations membership date	14 December 1955

Economic indicators	2005	2010	2012
GDP: Gross domestic product (million current US$)	202 578	209 388	210 638
GDP: Growth rate at constant 2005 prices (annual %)	6.1	−1.1	0.2
GDP per capita (current US$)	48 720.0	46 868.4	46 032.1
GNI: Gross national income per capita (current US$)	42 046.9	38 920.8	37 803.9
Gross fixed capital formation (% of GDP)	26.8	12.2	10.6
Exchange rates (national currency per US$)[a]	0.85	0.75	0.76
Balance of payments, current account (million US$)	−7 150	2 319	9 245
CPI: Consumer price index (2000=100)	119	128	133[b]
Industrial production index (2005=100)	100	109	107
Agricultural production index (2004-2006=100)	99	101	97
Food production index (2004-2006=100)	99	101	97
Unemployment (% of labour force)[cd]	4.3	13.9	14.7
Employment in industrial sector (% of employed)	27.9[ef]	19.5[g]	18.3[g]
Employment in agricultural sector (% of employed)	5.9[ef]	4.5[g]	4.7[g]
Labour force participation, adult female pop. (%)	51.9	53.1	52.7
Labour force participation, adult male pop. (%)	72.5	69.0	67.9
Tourist arrivals at national borders (000)[h]	7 333	7 134[i]	7 550
Energy production, primary (000 mt oil equivalent)	1 541	1 763	...
Mobile-cellular subscriptions (per 100 inhabitants)	102.7	105.2[jk]	107.1[jk]
Individuals using the Internet (%)[l]	41.6	69.9	79.0

Total trade		Major trading partners			2012
	(million US$)	(% of exports)		(% of imports)	
Exports	118 295.5	United States	19.7	United Kingdom	33.5
Imports	63 100.4	United Kingdom	16.6	United States	13.1
Balance	55 195.1	Belgium	14.7	Germany	7.0

Social indicators		
Population growth rate (average annual %)	2010-2015	1.1
Urban population growth rate (average annual %)	2010-2015	1.6
Rural population growth rate (average annual %)	2010-2015	0.3
Urban population (%)	2013	62.8
Population aged 0-14 years (%)	2013	21.6
Population aged 60+ years (females and males, % of total)	2013	17.9/16.0
Sex ratio (males per 100 females)	2013	98.6
Life expectancy at birth (females and males, years)	2010-2015	82.7/78.4
Infant mortality rate (per 1 000 live births)	2010-2015	2.9
Fertility rate, total (live births per woman)	2010-2015	2.0
Contraceptive prevalence (ages 15-49, %)[m]	2006-2012	64.8[n]
International migrant stock (000 and % of total population)	mid-2013	735.5/15.9
Refugees and others of concern to UNHCR	mid-2013	10 323[o]
Education: Government expenditure (% of GDP)	2006-2012	6.5
Education: Primary-secondary gross enrolment ratio (f/m per 100)	2006-2012	110.0/109.0
Education: Female third-level students (% of total)	2006-2012	51.7
Intentional homicides (females and males, per 100 000)	2008-2010	</2.1
Seats held by women in national parliaments (%)	2014	15.7

Environmental indicators		
Threatened species	2013	34
Forested area (% of land area)	2011	10.9
CO$_2$ emission estimates (000 metric tons and metric tons per capita)	2010	39 967/8.9
Energy consumption per capita (kilograms oil equivalent)	2010	3 210.0
Precipitation in the capital city, total mean (millimetres)		758[p]
Temperature in the capital city, mean °C (minimum and maximum)		6.4/12.5[p]

a Market rate. **b** Series linked to former series. **c** Age group 15 to 74 years. **d** 2009: Break in series; data not strictly comparable. **e** The indices are shown in terms of ISIC Rev.3. **f** Second quarter. **g** European Labour Force Survey (Eurostat). **h** Includes tourists from Northern Ireland. **i** Methodology revised; data not strictly comparable. **j** December. **k** Excludes data only mobile broadband (HSDPA). **l** Age group 16 to 74 years. **m** Age group 18 to 49 years. **n** 2004-2005. **o** Refugee population refers to the end of 2012. **p** Based on monthly averages for the period 1981-2010.

Israel

Region	Western Asia
Currency	New Sheqel (NIS)
Surface area (square kilometres)	22 072
Population in 2012 (estimated, 000)	7 644
Population density in 2012 (per square kilometre)	346.3
Capital city and population in 2011 (000)	Jerusalem (791)
United Nations membership date	11 May 1949

Economic indicators	2005	2010	2012
GDP: Gross domestic product (million current US$)	133 701	217 690	241 069
GDP: Growth rate at constant 2005 prices (annual %)	4.9	5.0	3.2
GDP per capita (current US$)	20 246.5	29 336.8	31 537.4
GNI: Gross national income per capita (current US$)	20 033.8	28 649.7	30 549.3
Gross fixed capital formation (% of GDP)	16.0	16.9	19.1
Exchange rates (national currency per US$)[a]	4.60	3.55	3.73
Balance of payments, current account (million US$)	4 043	7 172	850
CPI: Consumer price index (2000=100)	109	124	130
Industrial production index (2005=100)	100	126	134
Agricultural production index (2004-2006=100)	100	104	111
Food production index (2004-2006=100)	100	105	112
Unemployment (% of labour force)[bc]	9.0	6.6	6.9
Employment in industrial sector (% of employed)[d]	21.4	20.4[efg]	...
Employment in agricultural sector (% of employed)[d]	2.0	1.7[eg]	...
Labour force participation, adult female pop. (%)	50.1	52.6	58.1
Labour force participation, adult male pop. (%)	60.7	62.3	69.5
Tourist arrivals at national borders (000)[h]	1 903	2 803	2 886
Energy production, primary (000 mt oil equivalent)	1 592	3 078	...
Mobile-cellular subscriptions (per 100 inhabitants)	117.5	122.8[i]	119.9[i]
Individuals using the Internet (%)	25.2	67.5[i]	73.4[i]

Total trade		Major trading partners			2012
	(million US$)	(% of exports)			(% of imports)[k]
Exports	63 140.6	United States	27.8	Areas nes	19.5
Imports	73 112.1	China, Hong Kong SAR	7.7	United States	12.9
Balance	−9 971.5	United Kingdom	5.7	China	7.3

Social indicators		
Population growth rate (average annual %)	2010-2015	1.3
Urban population growth rate (average annual %)	2010-2015	1.7
Rural population growth rate (average annual %)	2010-2015	0.9
Urban population (%)	2013	92.0
Population aged 0-14 years (%)	2013	27.7
Population aged 60+ years (females and males, % of total)	2013	16.6/13.8
Sex ratio (males per 100 females)	2013	98.1
Life expectancy at birth (females and males, years)	2010-2015	83.5/79.8
Infant mortality rate (per 1 000 live births)	2010-2015	3.3
Fertility rate, total (live births per woman)	2010-2015	2.9
Contraceptive prevalence (ages 15-49, %)[l]	2006-2012	68.0[m]
International migrant stock (000 and % of total population)[n]	mid-2013	2 046.9/26.5
Refugees and others of concern to UNHCR	mid-2013	56 549
Education: Government expenditure (% of GDP)	2006-2012	5.6
Education: Primary-secondary gross enrolment ratio (f/m per 100)	2006-2012	103.8/102.4
Education: Female third-level students (% of total)	2006-2012	55.6
Intentional homicides (females and males, per 100 000)	2008-2010	1.6/7.2
Seats held by women in national parliaments (%)	2014	22.5

Environmental indicators		
Threatened species	2013	143
Forested area (% of land area)	2011	7.1
CO$_2$ emission estimates (000 metric tons and metric tons per capita)	2010	70 598/9.5
Energy consumption per capita (kilograms oil equivalent)	2010	3 104.0
Precipitation in the capital city, total mean (millimetres)		537[o]
Temperature in the capital city, mean °C (minimum and maximum)		13.9/22.3[p]

a Market rate. b Nonstandard geographical coverage. c Excludes armed forces and/or conscripts. d The indices are shown in terms of ISIC Rev.3. e 2009. f Excludes mining and quarrying. g Break in series; data not strictly comparable. h Excludes nationals residing abroad. i ITU estimate. j Age group 20 years and over. k See technical notes. l Age group 18 to 39 years. m 1987-1988. n Includes refugees. o Based on monthly averages for the period 1981-2010. p Based on monthly averages for the period 1995-2009.

Italy

Region	Southern Europe
Currency	Euro (EUR)
Surface area (square kilometres)	301 339
Population in 2012 (estimated, 000)	60 885
Population density in 2012 (per square kilometre)	202.1
Capital city and population in 2011 (000)	Rome (3 298)
United Nations membership date	14 December 1955

Economic indicators	2005	2010	2012
GDP: Gross domestic product (million current US$)	1 786 275	2 055 355	2 013 392
GDP: Growth rate at constant 2005 prices (annual %)	0.9	1.7	−2.5
GDP per capita (current US$)	30 445.2	33 967.8	33 069.0
GNI: Gross national income per capita (current US$)	30 454.0	33 807.5	32 828.4
Gross fixed capital formation (% of GDP)	21.1	19.6	18.1
Exchange rates (national currency per US$)[a]	0.85	0.75	0.76
Balance of payments, current account (million US$)	−29 744	−72 633	−8 054
CPI: Consumer price index (2000=100)	112[b]	123[b]	131
Industrial production index (2005=100)	100	89	84
Agricultural production index (2004-2006=100)	100	95	87
Food production index (2004-2006=100)	100	95	87
Unemployment (% of labour force)[c]	7.7	8.4	10.7
Employment in industrial sector (% of employed)[d]	30.8[e]	28.8	27.8
Employment in agricultural sector (% of employed)[d]	4.2[e]	3.8	3.7
Labour force participation, adult female pop. (%)	37.7	38.0	39.4
Labour force participation, adult male pop. (%)	61.1	59.3	59.4
Tourist arrivals at national borders (000)[f]	36 513	43 626	46 360
Energy production, primary (000 mt oil equivalent)[g]	21 749	20 258	...
Mobile-cellular subscriptions (per 100 inhabitants)	121.9	154.7	159.5[h]
Individuals using the Internet (%)[i]	35.0	53.7	58.0

Total trade		Major trading partners			2012
	(million US$)[j]	(% of exports)[j]			(% of imports)[j]
Exports	501 528.9	Germany	12.5	Germany	14.5
Imports	489 104.1	France	11.1	France	8.3
Balance	12 424.8	United States	6.8	China	6.6

Social indicators		
Population growth rate (average annual %)	2010-2015	0.2
Urban population growth rate (average annual %)	2010-2015	0.5
Rural population growth rate (average annual %)	2010-2015	−0.4
Urban population (%)	2013	68.7
Population aged 0-14 years (%)	2013	14.1
Population aged 60+ years (females and males, % of total)	2013	29.7/24.5
Sex ratio (males per 100 females)	2013	94.5
Life expectancy at birth (females and males, years)	2010-2015	84.9/79.5
Infant mortality rate (per 1 000 live births)	2010-2015	2.8
Fertility rate, total (live births per woman)	2010-2015	1.5
Contraceptive prevalence (ages 15-49, %)[k]	2006-2012	62.7[l]
International migrant stock (000 and % of total population)	mid-2013	5 721.5/9.4
Refugees and others of concern to UNHCR	mid-2013	71 264[m]
Education: Government expenditure (% of GDP)	2006-2012	4.5
Education: Primary-secondary gross enrolment ratio (f/m per 100)	2006-2012	99.8/101.0
Education: Female third-level students (% of total)	2006-2012	57.6
Intentional homicides (females and males, per 100 000)	2008-2010	</1.6
Seats held by women in national parliaments (%)	2014	31.4

Environmental indicators		
Threatened species	2013	273
Forested area (% of land area)	2011	31.4
CO_2 emission estimates (000 metric tons and metric tons per capita)[j]	2010	405 975/6.7
Energy consumption per capita (kilograms oil equivalent)[g]	2010	2 691.0
Precipitation in the capital city, total mean (millimetres)		733[n]
Temperature in the capital city, mean °C (minimum and maximum)		10.6/20.3[n]

a Market rate. **b** Excludes tobacco. **c** Age group 15 to 74 years. **d** European Labour Force Survey (Eurostat). **e** The indices are shown in terms of ISIC Rev.3. **f** Excludes seasonal and border workers. **g** Includes San Marino and the Holy See. **h** Includes mobile virtual network operators. **i** Age group 16 to 74 years. **j** Includes San Marino. **k** Age group 20 to 49 years. **l** 1995-1996. **m** Refugee population refers to the end of 2012. **n** Based on monthly averages for the period 1961-1990.

Jamaica

Region	Caribbean
Currency	Jamaican Dollar (JMD)
Surface area (square kilometres)	10 991
Population in 2012 (estimated, 000)	2 769
Population density in 2012 (per square kilometre)	251.9
Capital city and population in 2011 (000)	Kingston (571)
United Nations membership date	18 September 1962

Economic indicators	2005	2010	2012
GDP: Gross domestic product (million current US$)	11 239	13 231	14 795
GDP: Growth rate at constant 2005 prices (annual %)	0.9	−1.5	−0.5
GDP per capita (current US$)	4 190.4	4 826.2	5 343.1
GNI: Gross national income per capita (current US$)	3 938.1	4 645.8	5 186.6
Gross fixed capital formation (% of GDP)	26.8	19.9	19.7
Exchange rates (national currency per US$)[a]	64.38	85.60	92.56
Balance of payments, current account (million US$)	−1 071	−934	−1 905
CPI: Consumer price index (2000=100)	166	296	319[b]
Agricultural production index (2004-2006=100)	96	97	104
Food production index (2004-2006=100)	96	97	104
Unemployment (% of labour force)[c]	11.3	12.4	13.9
Employment in industrial sector (% of employed)[c]	17.7[d]	15.9[ef]	15.5[ef]
Employment in agricultural sector (% of employed)[c]	18.1[d]	20.2[ef]	18.1[ef]
Labour force participation, adult female pop. (%)	57.5	55.7	56.1
Labour force participation, adult male pop. (%)	76.2	71.5	71.0
Tourist arrivals at national borders (000)[gh]	1 479	1 922	1 986
Energy production, primary (000 mt oil equivalent)	17	18	...
Mobile-cellular subscriptions (per 100 inhabitants)	73.9	116.1	96.5[i]
Individuals using the Internet (%)	12.8[j]	27.7[k]	46.5[j]

Total trade		Major trading partners			2012
	(million US$)	(% of exports)		(% of imports)	
Exports	1 711.8	United States	48.1	United States	35.7
Imports	6 580.4	Canada	7.1	Venezuela	15.4
Balance	−4 868.6	Slovenia	4.2	Trinidad and Tobago	10.6

Social indicators		
Population growth rate (average annual %)	2010-2015	0.5
Urban population growth rate (average annual %)	2010-2015	0.5
Rural population growth rate (average annual %)	2010-2015	0.2
Urban population (%)	2013	52.2
Population aged 0-14 years (%)	2013	27.2
Population aged 60+ years (females and males, % of total)	2013	11.7/10.8
Sex ratio (males per 100 females)	2013	97.0
Life expectancy at birth (females and males, years)	2010-2015	76.0/70.9
Infant mortality rate (per 1 000 live births)	2010-2015	20.9
Fertility rate, total (live births per woman)	2010-2015	2.3
Contraceptive prevalence (ages 15-49, %)	2006-2012	69.0[l]
International migrant stock (000 and % of total population)	mid-2013	34.9/1.3
Refugees and others of concern to UNHCR	mid-2013	20
Education: Government expenditure (% of GDP)	2006-2012	6.4
Education: Primary-secondary gross enrolment ratio (f/m per 100)	2006-2012	94.4/94.2[m]
Education: Female third-level students (% of total)	2006-2012	68.9
Intentional homicides (females and males, per 100 000)	2008-2010	10.3/95.2
Seats held by women in national parliaments (%)	2014	12.7

Environmental indicators		
Threatened species	2013	289
Forested area (% of land area)	2011	31.1
CO$_2$ emission estimates (000 metric tons and metric tons per capita)	2010	7 152/2.6
Energy consumption per capita (kilograms oil equivalent)	2010	807.0
Precipitation in the capital city, total mean (millimetres)		813[n]
Temperature in the capital city, mean °C (minimum and maximum)		22.9/31.4[n]

a Market rate. b 2011. c Age group 14 years and over. d The indices are shown in terms of ISIC Rev.2. e The indices are shown in terms of ISIC Rev.3. f Average of quarterly estimates. g Arrivals of non-resident tourists by air. h Includes nationals residing abroad. i Decrease due to the cancellation of subscriptions as two operators merged. j ITU estimate. k Age group 14 years and over using the Internet via any device. l 2002-2003. m 2004. n Based on monthly averages for the period 1951-1980.

Japan

Region	Eastern Asia
Currency	Yen (JPY)
Surface area (square kilometres)	377 930[a]
Population in 2012 (estimated, 000)	127 250
Population density in 2012 (per square kilometre)	336.7
Capital city and population in 2011 (000)	Tokyo (37 217)
United Nations membership date	18 December 1956

Economic indicators	2005	2010	2012
GDP: Gross domestic product (million current US$)	4 571 867	5 495 387	5 960 180
GDP: Growth rate at constant 2005 prices (annual %)	1.3	4.7	2.0
GDP per capita (current US$)	36 005.0	43 150.9	46 838.5
GNI: Gross national income per capita (current US$)	36 844.5	44 311.5	48 324.3
Gross fixed capital formation (% of GDP)	22.3	20.0	21.2
Exchange rates (national currency per US$)[b]	117.97	81.45	86.55
Balance of payments, current account (million US$)	165 783	203 916	60 859
CPI: Consumer price index (2000=100)	98[c]	97	97
Industrial production index (2005=100)	100	94	92
Agricultural production index (2004-2006=100)	101	100	102
Food production index (2004-2006=100)	101	100	102
Unemployment (% of labour force)	4.4	5.1	4.3
Employment in industrial sector (% of employed)[de]	27.9	25.3	...
Employment in agricultural sector (% of employed)[de]	4.4	3.7	...
Labour force participation, adult female pop. (%)	48.4	49.4	48.1
Labour force participation, adult male pop. (%)	73.3	71.6	70.4
Tourist arrivals at national borders (000)[fg]	6 728	8 611	8 358
Energy production, primary (000 mt oil equivalent)[h]	38 138	37 725	...
Mobile-cellular subscriptions (per 100 inhabitants)	76.3[i]	97.4[jk]	109.4[j]
Individuals using the Internet (%)[l]	66.9	78.2	79.1

Total trade		Major trading partners			2012
	(million US$)	(% of exports)			(% of imports)
Exports	798 567.6	China	18.1	China	21.3
Imports	885 843.3	United States	17.8	United States	8.8
Balance	−87 275.7	Republic of Korea	7.7	Australia	6.4

Social indicators		
Population growth rate (average annual %)	2010-2015	−0.1
Urban population growth rate (average annual %)	2010-2015	0.6
Rural population growth rate (average annual %)	2010-2015	−7.6
Urban population (%)	2013	92.5
Population aged 0-14 years (%)	2013	13.1
Population aged 60+ years (females and males, % of total)	2013	35.0/29.5
Sex ratio (males per 100 females)	2013	94.8
Life expectancy at birth (females and males, years)	2010-2015	86.9/80.0
Infant mortality rate (per 1 000 live births)	2010-2015	2.2
Fertility rate, total (live births per woman)	2010-2015	1.4
Contraceptive prevalence (ages 15-49, %)[m]	2006-2012	54.3[n]
International migrant stock (000 and % of total population)[o]	mid-2013	2 437.2/1.9
Refugees and others of concern to UNHCR	mid-2013	9 300[p]
Education: Government expenditure (% of GDP)	2006-2012	3.8
Education: Primary-secondary gross enrolment ratio (f/m per 100)	2006-2012	102.2/102.1
Education: Female third-level students (% of total)	2006-2012	46.0
Intentional homicides (females and males, per 100 000)	2008-2010	</<
Seats held by women in national parliaments (%)	2014	8.1

Environmental indicators		
Threatened species	2013	351
Forested area (% of land area)	2011	68.6
CO$_2$ emission estimates (000 metric tons and metric tons per capita)	2010	1 169 758/9.2
Energy consumption per capita (kilograms oil equivalent)[h]	2010	3 177.0
Precipitation in the capital city, total mean (millimetres)		1 529[q]
Temperature in the capital city, mean °C (minimum and maximum)		12.9/20.0[q]

a Data refer to 1 October 2007. b Market rate. c Series linked to former series. d Average of monthly estimates. e The indices are shown in terms of ISIC Rev.3. f Arrivals of non-resident visitors at national borders. g Excludes nationals residing abroad. h Includes Okinawa. i Includes Personal Handy-phone System. j Includes Personal Handy-phone System and data cards. k December. l Age group 6 years and over. m Age group 20 to 49 years. n 2005. o Data refer to foreign citizens. p UNHCR estimate. q Based on monthly averages for the period 1981-2010.

Jordan

Region	Western Asia
Currency	Jordanian Dinar (JOD)
Surface area (square kilometres)	89 328
Population in 2012 (estimated, 000)	7 009
Population density in 2012 (per square kilometre)	78.5
Capital city and population in 2011 (000)	Amman (1 179)
United Nations membership date	14 December 1955

Economic indicators	2005	2010	2012
GDP: Gross domestic product (million current US$)	12 589	26 425	30 937
GDP: Growth rate at constant 2005 prices (annual %)	8.1	2.3	2.7
GDP per capita (current US$)	2 402.7	4 094.1	4 413.7
GNI: Gross national income per capita (current US$)	2 466.9	4 080.0	4 386.2
Gross fixed capital formation (% of GDP)	30.6	23.5	26.9
Exchange rates (national currency per US$)[a]	0.71	0.71	0.71
Balance of payments, current account (million US$)	−2 272	−1 882	−5 694
CPI: Consumer price index (2000=100)	113	149	163
Industrial production index (2005=100)[b]	100	105	105
Agricultural production index (2004-2006=100)	98	129	128
Food production index (2004-2006=100)	97	129	128
Employment in industrial sector (% of employed)	20.7[b]	18.7	17.5
Employment in agricultural sector (% of employed)	3.4[b]	2.0	2.0
Labour force participation, adult female pop. (%)	12.3	15.6	15.3
Labour force participation, adult male pop. (%)	67.5	67.9	66.2
Tourist arrivals at national borders (000)	2 987	4 207	4 162
Energy production, primary (000 mt oil equivalent)	205	143	...
Mobile-cellular subscriptions (per 100 inhabitants)	58.7	107.0	139.1
Individuals using the Internet (%)	12.9	27.2[d]	41.0[e]

Total trade		Major trading partners			2012
	(million US$)		(% of exports)[f]		(% of imports)
Exports	7 877.1	Iraq	15.5	Saudi Arabia	23.5
Imports	20 691.4	United States	14.3	China	9.4
Balance	−12 814.3	Free zones	9.9	United States	6.7

Social indicators

Population growth rate (average annual %)	2010-2015	3.5
Urban population growth rate (average annual %)	2010-2015	2.2
Rural population growth rate (average annual %)	2010-2015	0.5
Urban population (%)	2013	83.2
Population aged 0-14 years (%)	2013	34.0
Population aged 60+ years (females and males, % of total)	2013	5.5/5.2
Sex ratio (males per 100 females)	2013	104.2
Life expectancy at birth (females and males, years)	2010-2015	75.5/72.2
Infant mortality rate (per 1 000 live births)	2010-2015	17.1
Fertility rate, total (live births per woman)	2010-2015	3.3
Contraceptive prevalence (ages 15-49, %)	2006-2012	59.3
International migrant stock (000 and % of total population)[gh]	mid-2013	2 925.8/40.2
Refugees and others of concern to UNHCR	mid-2013	616 042[i]
Education: Government expenditure (% of GDP)	2006-2012	4.9[j]
Education: Primary-secondary gross enrolment ratio (f/m per 100)	2006-2012	94.4/93.7
Education: Female third-level students (% of total)	2006-2012	52.7
Intentional homicides (females and males, per 100 000)	2008-2010	2.6/11.4
Seats held by women in national parliaments (%)	2014	12.0

Environmental indicators

Threatened species	2013	99
Forested area (% of land area)	2011	1.1
CO_2 emission estimates (000 metric tons and metric tons per capita)	2010	20 804/3.4
Energy consumption per capita (kilograms oil equivalent)	2010	1 155.0
Precipitation in the capital city, total mean (millimetres)		269
Temperature in the capital city, mean °C (minimum and maximum)		11.3/23.5

a Official rate. **b** The indices are shown in terms of ISIC Rev.3. **c** Includes nationals residing abroad. **d** Age group 5 years and over. **e** ITU estimate. **f** See technical notes. **g** Data refer to foreign citizens. **h** Includes refugees. **i** Refugee figure for Iraqis in Jordan is a Government estimate. UNHCR has registered and is assisting 24,900 Iraqis at mid-2013. **j** 1999.

Kazakhstan

Region	Central Asia
Currency	Tenge (KZT)
Surface area (square kilometres)	2 724 900
Population in 2012 (estimated, 000)	16 271
Population density in 2012 (per square kilometre)	6.0
Capital city and population in 2011 (000)	Astana (664)
United Nations membership date	2 March 1992

Economic indicators	2005	2010	2012
GDP: Gross domestic product (million current US$)	57 621	149 335	202 656
GDP: Growth rate at constant 2005 prices (annual %)	9.7	7.0	5.0
GDP per capita (current US$)	3 825.0	9 379.7	12 454.9
GNI: Gross national income per capita (current US$)	3 400.9	8 001.2	10 659.3
Gross fixed capital formation (% of GDP)	28.0	24.4	20.8
Exchange rates (national currency per US$)[a]	133.98	147.50	150.74
Balance of payments, current account (million US$)	−1 056	1 393	7 716
CPI: Consumer price index (2000=100)	140	198[b]	...
Agricultural production index (2004-2006=100)	100	107	112
Food production index (2004-2006=100)	100	108	113
Unemployment (% of labour force)	8.1	5.8	5.3
Employment in industrial sector (% of employed)	18.0[c]	18.7	19.4
Employment in agricultural sector (% of employed)	32.4[c]	28.3	25.5
Labour force participation, adult female pop. (%)	64.6	66.9	67.5
Labour force participation, adult male pop. (%)	75.2	76.6	77.5
Tourist arrivals at national borders (000)	3 143	3 196	4 807
Energy production, primary (000 mt oil equivalent)	124 792	165 407	...
Mobile-cellular subscriptions (per 100 inhabitants)	35.6	121.1	175.4
Individuals using the Internet (%)	3.0	31.6[d]	53.3[e]

Total trade		Major trading partners			2012
	(million US$)	(% of exports)			(% of imports)
Exports	92 281.5	China	17.9	Russian Federation	38.4
Imports	44 538.1	Italy	16.8	China	16.8
Balance	47 743.4	Netherlands	8.1	Ukraine	6.6

Social indicators		
Population growth rate (average annual %)	2010-2015	1.0
Urban population growth rate (average annual %)	2010-2015	0.9
Rural population growth rate (average annual %)	2010-2015	1.3
Urban population (%)	2013	53.4
Population aged 0-14 years (%)	2013	25.8
Population aged 60+ years (females and males, % of total)	2013	12.4/7.9
Sex ratio (males per 100 females)	2013	92.9
Life expectancy at birth (females and males, years)	2010-2015	72.3/60.9
Infant mortality rate (per 1 000 live births)	2010-2015	24.6
Fertility rate, total (live births per woman)	2010-2015	2.4
Contraceptive prevalence (ages 15-49, %)	2006-2012	50.7
International migrant stock (000 and % of total population)	mid-2013	3 476.2/21.1
Refugees and others of concern to UNHCR	mid-2013	11 294
Education: Government expenditure (% of GDP)	2006-2012	3.1
Education: Primary-secondary gross enrolment ratio (f/m per 100)	2006-2012	99.5/101.1
Education: Female third-level students (% of total)	2006-2012	58.5
Intentional homicides (females and males, per 100 000)	2008-2010	8.4/26.9
Seats held by women in national parliaments (%)	2014	25.2

Environmental indicators		
Threatened species	2013	76
Forested area (% of land area)	2011	1.2
CO$_2$ emission estimates (000 metric tons and metric tons per capita)	2010	248 525/15.5
Energy consumption per capita (kilograms oil equivalent)	2010	4 811.0
Precipitation in the capital city, total mean (millimetres)		318
Temperature in the capital city, mean °C (minimum and maximum)		−4.0/7.6

a Official rate. **b** 2008. **c** The indices are shown in terms of ISIC Rev.3. **d** Age group 16 to 74 years. **e** ITU estimate.

Kenya

Region	Eastern Africa
Currency	Kenya Shilling (KES)
Surface area (square kilometres)	591 958
Population in 2012 (estimated, 000)	43 178
Population density in 2012 (per square kilometre)	72.9
Capital city and population in 2011 (000)	Nairobi (3 363)
United Nations membership date	16 December 1963

Economic indicators

	2005	2010	2012
GDP: Gross domestic product (million current US$)	18 739	32 181	40 697
GDP: Growth rate at constant 2005 prices (annual %)	5.9	5.8	4.6
GDP per capita (current US$)	523.7	786.7	942.5
GNI: Gross national income per capita (current US$)	520.6	783.0	938.6
Gross fixed capital formation (% of GDP)	18.7	20.3	20.4
Exchange rates (national currency per US$)[a]	72.37	80.75	86.00
Balance of payments, current account (million US$)	−252	−2 369	−4 253
CPI: Consumer price index (2000=100)[b]	100[c]	134[d]	167
Agricultural production index (2004-2006=100)	103	124	145
Food production index (2004-2006=100)	103	125	148
Employment in industrial sector (% of employed)	6.7[ef]	...	...
Employment in agricultural sector (% of employed)	61.1[ef]	...	...
Labour force participation, adult female pop. (%)	60.2	61.5	62.0
Labour force participation, adult male pop. (%)	70.0	71.7	72.2
Tourist arrivals at national borders (000)	1 399	1 470	...
Energy production, primary (000 mt oil equivalent)	347	401	...
Mobile-cellular subscriptions (per 100 inhabitants)	13.0	61.6	71.9
Individuals using the Internet (%)	3.1	14.0	32.1[g]

Total trade	Major trading partners				2012
	(million US$)[h]	(% of exports)[h]			(% of imports)[h]
Exports	5 169.1	Uganda	12.7	China	12.6
Imports	12 092.9	United Kingdom	9.8	United Arab Emirates	12.1
Balance	−6 923.8	United Rep. Tanzania	8.1	India	10.8

Social indicators

Population growth rate (average annual %)	2010-2015	2.7
Urban population growth rate (average annual %)	2010-2015	4.4
Rural population growth rate (average annual %)	2010-2015	2.1
Urban population (%)	2013	24.8
Population aged 0-14 years (%)	2013	42.2
Population aged 60+ years (females and males, % of total)	2013	4.7/4.0
Sex ratio (males per 100 females)	2013	99.6
Life expectancy at birth (females and males, years)	2010-2015	63.5/59.7
Infant mortality rate (per 1 000 live births)	2010-2015	51.6
Fertility rate, total (live births per woman)	2010-2015	4.4
Contraceptive prevalence (ages 15-49, %)	2006-2012	45.5
International migrant stock (000 and % of total population)[i]	mid-2013	955.5/2.2
Refugees and others of concern to UNHCR	mid-2013	620 148
Education: Government expenditure (% of GDP)	2006-2012	6.7
Education: Primary-secondary gross enrolment ratio (f/m per 100)	2006-2012	86.2/90.4
Education: Female third-level students (% of total)	2006-2012	41.2
Intentional homicides (females and males, per 100 000)[j]	2008-2010	3.3/37.0
Seats held by women in national parliaments (%)	2014	19.1

Environmental indicators

Threatened species	2013	419
Forested area (% of land area)	2011	6.1
CO$_2$ emission estimates (000 metric tons and metric tons per capita)	2010	12 417/0.3
Energy consumption per capita (kilograms oil equivalent)	2010	95.0
Precipitation in the capital city, total mean (millimetres)		1 024
Temperature in the capital city, mean °C (minimum and maximum)		12.0/23.4

a Official rate. **b** Index base 2007=100. **c** 2007. **d** Series linked to former series. **e** Household income and expenditure survey. **f** The indices are shown in terms of ISIC Rev.2. **g** ITU estimate. **h** 2010. **i** Includes refugees. **j** Estimates.

Kiribati

Region	Oceania-Micronesia
Currency	Australian Dollar (AUD)
Surface area (square kilometres)	726 [a]
Population in 2012 (estimated, 000)	101
Population density in 2012 (per square kilometre)	138.8
Capital city and population in 2011 (000)	Bairiki (...) [b]
United Nations membership date	14 September 1999

Economic indicators	2005	2010	2012
GDP: Gross domestic product (million current US$)	106	151	176
GDP: Growth rate at constant 2005 prices (annual %)	−0.2	−0.5	3.0
GDP per capita (current US$)	1 174.5	1 539.9	1 745.2
GNI: Gross national income per capita (current US$)	1 406.7	1 770.9	2 076.9
Gross fixed capital formation (% of GDP)	48.2	42.2	43.1
Exchange rates (national currency per US$) [c]	1.36	0.98	0.96
CPI: Consumer price index (2000=100) [d]	110	125 [e]	...
Agricultural production index (2004-2006=100)	95	118	120
Food production index (2004-2006=100)	95	118	120
Tourist arrivals at national borders (000) [fg]	4	5	5
Mobile-cellular subscriptions (per 100 inhabitants)	0.7	10.6	15.6 [h]
Individuals using the Internet (%)	4.0 [h]	9.1	10.8 [h]

Total trade		Major trading partners			2012
	(million US$)	(% of exports) [i]			(% of imports)
Exports	5.8	Morocco	46.6	Australia	24.3
Imports	108.6	Asia nes	20.7	Japan	21.1
Balance	−102.8	China, Hong Kong SAR	10.3	Singapore	15.4

Social indicators

Population growth rate (average annual %)	2010-2015	1.5
Urban population growth rate (average annual %)	2010-2015	1.8
Rural population growth rate (average annual %)	2010-2015	1.3
Urban population (%)	2013	44.2
Population aged 0-14 years (%)	2013	31.9
Population aged 60+ years (females and males, % of total)	2013	7.4/5.7
Sex ratio (males per 100 females)	2013	98.9
Life expectancy at birth (females and males, years)	2010-2015	71.6/65.9
Infant mortality rate (per 1 000 live births)	2010-2015	34.3
Fertility rate, total (live births per woman)	2010-2015	3.0
Contraceptive prevalence (ages 15-49, %)	2006-2012	36.1 [j]
International migrant stock (000 and % of total population)	mid-2013	2.6/2.6
Education: Government expenditure (% of GDP)	2006-2012	11.9 [k]
Education: Primary-secondary gross enrolment ratio (f/m per 100)	2006-2012	106.3/99.4
Seats held by women in national parliaments (%)	2014	8.7

Environmental indicators

Threatened species	2013	101
Forested area (% of land area)	2011	15.0
CO$_2$ emission estimates (000 metric tons and metric tons per capita)	2010	62/0.6
Energy consumption per capita (kilograms oil equivalent)	2010	209.0 [l]

a Land area only. Excludes 84 square km of uninhabited islands. b Population estimates for Bairiki have not been made available. c Official rate. d Tarawa. e 2008. f Air arrivals. g Tarawa and Christmas Island. h ITU estimate. i See technical notes. j 2000. k 2001. l UNSD estimate.

Kuwait

Region	Western Asia
Currency	Kuwaiti Dinar (KWD)
Surface area (square kilometres)	17 818
Population in 2012 (estimated, 000)	3 251
Population density in 2012 (per square kilometre)	182.4
Capital city and population in 2011 (000)	Kuwait City (2 406)
United Nations membership date	14 May 1963

Economic indicators

	2005	2010	2012
GDP: Gross domestic product (million current US$)	80 798	119 918	183 219
GDP: Growth rate at constant 2005 prices (annual %)	10.6	−2.4	5.1
GDP per capita (current US$)	35 185.9	40 085.1	56 366.6
GNI: Gross national income per capita (current US$)	39 042.6	43 234.1	59 194.3
Gross fixed capital formation (% of GDP)	14.6	18.7	15.1
Exchange rates (national currency per US$)[a]	0.29	0.28	0.28
Balance of payments, current account (million US$)	30 071	36 958	79 209
CPI: Consumer price index (2000=100)	109	141	152
Agricultural production index (2004-2006=100)	97	134	168
Food production index (2004-2006=100)	97	135	168
Employment in industrial sector (% of employed)	20.6[bcd]	...	...
Employment in agricultural sector (% of employed)	2.7[bcd]	...	...
Labour force participation, adult female pop. (%)	44.4	42.8	43.4
Labour force participation, adult male pop. (%)	81.9	82.3	82.8
Tourist arrivals at national borders (000)[e]	3 474	5 208	5 729
Energy production, primary (000 mt oil equivalent)[f]	146 560	134 656	...
Mobile-cellular subscriptions (per 100 inhabitants)	61.1[g]	145.4	191.1[h]
Individuals using the Internet (%)	25.9	61.4[h]	79.2[h]

Total trade

	(million US$)[i]	Major trading partners	(% of exports)[i]		2012 (% of imports)[i]
Exports	102 695.8	...	China		14.8
Imports	25 142.0	...	United States		10.7
Balance	77 553.8	...	Japan		6.6

Social indicators

Population growth rate (average annual %)	2010-2015	3.6
Urban population growth rate (average annual %)	2010-2015	2.4
Rural population growth rate (average annual %)	2010-2015	1.7
Urban population (%)	2013	98.3
Population aged 0-14 years (%)	2013	24.8
Population aged 60+ years (females and males, % of total)	2013	3.9/3.8
Sex ratio (males per 100 females)	2013	148.7
Life expectancy at birth (females and males, years)	2010-2015	75.5/73.4
Infant mortality rate (per 1 000 live births)	2010-2015	8.6
Fertility rate, total (live births per woman)	2010-2015	2.6
Contraceptive prevalence (ages 15-49, %)	2006-2012	52.0[j]
International migrant stock (000 and % of total population)[kl]	mid-2013	2 028.1/60.2
Refugees and others of concern to UNHCR	mid-2013	94 676
Education: Government expenditure (% of GDP)[m]	2006-2012	3.8
Education: Primary-secondary gross enrolment ratio (f/m per 100)	2006-2012	102.9/103.1
Education: Female third-level students (% of total)[m]	2006-2012	64.3[n]
Intentional homicides (females and males, per 100 000)	2008-2010	0.6/1.6
Seats held by women in national parliaments (%)	2014	4.6

Environmental indicators

Threatened species	2013	42
Forested area (% of land area)	2011	<
CO_2 emission estimates (000 metric tons and metric tons per capita)	2010	93 619/34.2
Energy consumption per capita (kilograms oil equivalent)[f]	2010	11 998.0
Precipitation in the capital city, total mean (millimetres)		116[o]
Temperature in the capital city, mean °C (minimum and maximum)		19.9/34.3[o]

a Official rate. **b** Population census. **c** The indices are shown in terms of ISIC Rev.3. **d** Break in series; data not strictly comparable. **e** Arrivals of non-resident visitors at national borders. **f** Data for crude petroleum production include 50 per cent of the output of the Neutral Zone. **g** Incomplete coverage. **h** ITU estimate. **i** 2011. **j** 1999. **k** Data refer to foreign citizens. **l** Includes refugees. **m** UNESCO estimate. **n** 2004. **o** Based on monthly averages for the period 1994-2008.

Kyrgyzstan

Region	Central Asia
Currency	Som (KGS)
Surface area (square kilometres)	199 949
Population in 2012 (estimated, 000)	5 474
Population density in 2012 (per square kilometre)	27.4
Capital city and population in 2011 (000)	Bishkek (839)
United Nations membership date	2 March 1992

Economic indicators	2005	2010	2012
GDP: Gross domestic product (million current US$)	2 460	4 794	6 475
GDP: Growth rate at constant 2005 prices (annual %)	−0.2	−0.5	−0.9
GDP per capita (current US$)	487.9	898.8	1 182.8
GNI: Gross national income per capita (current US$)	471.9	834.8	1 081.3
Gross fixed capital formation (% of GDP)	16.2	28.1	28.2
Exchange rates (national currency per US$)[a]	41.30	47.10	47.40
Balance of payments, current account (million US$)	−37	−312	−1 431
CPI: Consumer price index (2000=100)	122	...	...
Agricultural production index (2004-2006=100)	98	105	106
Food production index (2004-2006=100)	98	106	108
Unemployment (% of labour force)	8.1	8.4[b]	...
Employment in industrial sector (% of employed)[cd]	17.6	20.6[e]	...
Employment in agricultural sector (% of employed)[cd]	38.5	34.0[e]	...
Labour force participation, adult female pop. (%)	54.1	55.2	55.7
Labour force participation, adult male pop. (%)	75.9	78.2	79.0
Tourist arrivals at national borders (000)[f]	...	855	2 406
Energy production, primary (000 mt oil equivalent)	1 426	1 157	...
Mobile-cellular subscriptions (per 100 inhabitants)	10.7	98.9	124.8
Individuals using the Internet (%)	10.5	18.4[g]	21.7[g]

Total trade		Major trading partners			2012
	(million US$)	(% of exports)		(% of imports)	
Exports	1 683.2	Switzerland	32.6	Russian Federation	33.2
Imports	5 373.2	Kazakhstan	24.1	China	22.5
Balance	−3 690.0	Russian Federation	13.0	Kazakhstan	9.7

Social indicators		
Population growth rate (average annual %)	2010-2015	1.4
Urban population growth rate (average annual %)	2010-2015	1.3
Rural population growth rate (average annual %)	2010-2015	0.9
Urban population (%)	2013	35.5
Population aged 0-14 years (%)	2013	30.4
Population aged 60+ years (females and males, % of total)	2013	7.5/5.4
Sex ratio (males per 100 females)	2013	97.3
Life expectancy at birth (females and males, years)	2010-2015	71.8/63.4
Infant mortality rate (per 1 000 live births)	2010-2015	33.1
Fertility rate, total (live births per woman)	2010-2015	3.1
Contraceptive prevalence (ages 15-49, %)	2006-2012	47.8[h]
International migrant stock (000 and % of total population)	mid-2013	227.0/4.1
Refugees and others of concern to UNHCR	mid-2013	197 769[i]
Education: Government expenditure (% of GDP)	2006-2012	6.8
Education: Primary-secondary gross enrolment ratio (f/m per 100)[j]	2006-2012	92.1/92.8
Education: Female third-level students (% of total)	2006-2012	55.3
Intentional homicides (females and males, per 100 000)	2008-2010	2.9/11.3
Seats held by women in national parliaments (%)	2014	23.3

Environmental indicators		
Threatened species	2013	40
Forested area (% of land area)	2011	5.1
CO$_2$ emission estimates (000 metric tons and metric tons per capita)	2010	6 394/1.2
Energy consumption per capita (kilograms oil equivalent)	2010	540.0
Precipitation in the capital city, total mean (millimetres)		442[k]
Temperature in the capital city, mean °C (minimum and maximum)		4.8/17.0[k]

a Official rate. **b** 2009. **c** November. **d** The indices are shown in terms of ISIC Rev.3. **e** 2008. **f** Arrivals of non-resident visitors at national borders. **g** ITU estimate. **h** 2005-2006. **i** Includes 172,000 people who are in an internally displaced person-like situation. **j** National estimate. **k** Based on monthly averages for the period 1961-1990.

Lao People's Democratic Republic

Region	South-Eastern Asia
Currency	Kip (LAK)
Surface area (square kilometres)	236 800
Population in 2012 (estimated, 000)	6 646
Population density in 2012 (per square kilometre)	28.1
Capital city and population in 2011 (000)	Vientiane (810)
United Nations membership date	14 December 1955

Economic indicators	2005	2010	2012
GDP: Gross domestic product (million current US$)	2 717	6 744	9 100
GDP: Growth rate at constant 2005 prices (annual %)	6.8	8.1	7.9
GDP per capita (current US$)	469.2	1 054.4	1 369.3
GNI: Gross national income per capita (current US$)	457.9	985.7	1 265.7
Gross fixed capital formation (% of GDP)	34.3	29.0	32.1
Exchange rates (national currency per US$)[a]	10 743.00	8 058.78	7 987.45
Balance of payments, current account (million US$)	−174	29	−415
CPI: Consumer price index (2000=100)	163[b]	208	233
Agricultural production index (2004-2006=100)	100	130	155
Food production index (2004-2006=100)	100	128	152
Labour force participation, adult female pop. (%)	77.5	76.4	76.3
Labour force participation, adult male pop. (%)	79.6	78.7	78.9
Tourist arrivals at national borders (000)	672	1 670	2 140
Energy production, primary (000 mt oil equivalent)	615	739[c]	...
Mobile-cellular subscriptions (per 100 inhabitants)	11.4	64.6	101.9[d]
Individuals using the Internet (%)	0.9	7.0	10.8[d]

Social indicators		
Population growth rate (average annual %)	2010-2015	1.9
Urban population growth rate (average annual %)	2010-2015	4.4
Rural population growth rate (average annual %)	2010-2015	−0.4
Urban population (%)	2013	36.5
Population aged 0-14 years (%)	2013	35.2
Population aged 60+ years (females and males, % of total)	2013	6.4/5.3
Sex ratio (males per 100 females)	2013	99.1
Life expectancy at birth (females and males, years)	2010-2015	69.4/66.7
Infant mortality rate (per 1 000 live births)	2010-2015	36.2
Fertility rate, total (live births per woman)	2010-2015	3.1
Contraceptive prevalence (ages 15-49, %)	2006-2012	38.4[e]
International migrant stock (000 and % of total population)[fg]	mid-2013	21.8/0.3
Refugees and others of concern to UNHCR	mid-2013	0[h]
Education: Government expenditure (% of GDP)	2006-2012	3.3
Education: Primary-secondary gross enrolment ratio (f/m per 100)	2006-2012	73.2/79.9
Education: Female third-level students (% of total)	2006-2012	41.8
Intentional homicides (females and males, per 100 000)[i]	2008-2010	3.0/6.3
Seats held by women in national parliaments (%)	2014	25.0

Environmental indicators		
Threatened species	2013	197
Forested area (% of land area)	2011	67.9
CO$_2$ emission estimates (000 metric tons and metric tons per capita)	2010	1 872/0.3
Energy consumption per capita (kilograms oil equivalent)	2010	110.0[c]
Precipitation in the capital city, total mean (millimetres)		1 661[j]
Temperature in the capital city, mean °C (minimum and maximum)		21.8/31.1[j]

a Market rate. b Series linked to former series. c UNSD estimate. d ITU estimate. e 2005. f Data refer to foreign citizens. g Includes refugees. h Value is zero, not available or not applicable. i Estimates. j Based on monthly averages for the period 1951-2000.

Latvia

Region	Northern Europe
Currency	Lats (LVL)
Surface area (square kilometres)	64 562
Population in 2012 (estimated, 000)	2 060
Population density in 2012 (per square kilometre)	31.9
Capital city and population in 2011 (000)	Riga (701)
United Nations membership date	17 September 1991

Economic indicators

	2005	2010	2012
GDP: Gross domestic product (million current US$)	15 938	24 099	28 379
GDP: Growth rate at constant 2005 prices (annual %)	10.1	−1.3	5.0
GDP per capita (current US$)	7 154.8	11 528.0	13 773.4
GNI: Gross national income per capita (current US$)	7 063.8	11 757.1	13 755.8
Gross fixed capital formation (% of GDP)	31.0	18.2	22.8
Exchange rates (national currency per US$)[a]	0.59	0.54	0.53
Balance of payments, current account (million US$)	−1 992	724	−702
CPI: Consumer price index (2000=100)	122	169	180
Industrial production index (2005=100)	100	98	113
Agricultural production index (2004-2006=100)	105	109	128
Food production index (2004-2006=100)	105	109	128
Unemployment (% of labour force)[bc]	8.9	18.7	15.1
Employment in industrial sector (% of employed)[b]	25.8[de]	24.0[f]	23.5[f]
Employment in agricultural sector (% of employed)[b]	12.1[de]	8.8[f]	8.4[f]
Labour force participation, adult female pop. (%)	50.9	53.8	54.5
Labour force participation, adult male pop. (%)	66.3	65.4	67.1
Tourist arrivals at national borders (000)[g]	1 116	1 373	1 435
Energy production, primary (000 mt oil equivalent)	294	358	...
Mobile-cellular subscriptions (per 100 inhabitants)	81.2	102.4[h]	103.4[h]
Individuals using the Internet (%)[i]	46.0	68.4	74.0

Total trade	Major trading partners				2012
(million US$)	(% of exports)		(% of imports)		
Exports	12 685.5	Lithuania	16.0	Lithuania	19.9
Imports	16 082.4	Estonia	13.0	Germany	11.5
Balance	−3 396.9	Russian Federation	11.4	Russian Federation	9.4

Social indicators

Population growth rate (average annual %)	2010-2015	−0.6
Urban population growth rate (average annual %)	2010-2015	−0.4
Rural population growth rate (average annual %)	2010-2015	−0.4
Urban population (%)	2013	67.7
Population aged 0-14 years (%)	2013	14.8
Population aged 60+ years (females and males, % of total)	2013	29.3/18.4
Sex ratio (males per 100 females)	2013	84.2
Life expectancy at birth (females and males, years)	2010-2015	77.5/66.6
Infant mortality rate (per 1 000 live births)	2010-2015	7.3
Fertility rate, total (live births per woman)	2010-2015	1.6
Contraceptive prevalence (ages 15-49, %)[j]	2006-2012	67.8[k]
International migrant stock (000 and % of total population)	mid-2013	282.9/13.8
Refugees and others of concern to UNHCR	mid-2013	281 066
Education: Government expenditure (% of GDP)	2006-2012	5.0
Education: Primary-secondary gross enrolment ratio (f/m per 100)	2006-2012	100.5/102.6
Education: Female third-level students (% of total)	2006-2012	61.1
Intentional homicides (females and males, per 100 000)	2008-2010	4.9/12.3
Seats held by women in national parliaments (%)	2014	25.0

Environmental indicators

Threatened species	2013	25
Forested area (% of land area)	2011	54.1
CO$_2$ emission estimates (000 metric tons and metric tons per capita)	2010	7 610/3.4
Energy consumption per capita (kilograms oil equivalent)	2010	1 429.0
Precipitation in the capital city, total mean (millimetres)		633
Temperature in the capital city, mean °C (minimum and maximum)		2.3/9.9

a Official rate. **b** Age group 15 to 74 years. **c** 2011: Break in series; data not strictly comparable. **d** The indices are shown in terms of ISIC Rev.3. **e** Excludes conscripts. **f** European Labour Force Survey (Eurostat). **g** Non-resident departures. **h** ITU estimate. **i** Age group 16 to 74 years. **j** Age group 18 to 49 years. **k** 1995.

Lebanon

Region	Western Asia
Currency	Lebanese Pound (LBP)
Surface area (square kilometres)	10 452
Population in 2012 (estimated, 000)	4 647
Population density in 2012 (per square kilometre)	444.6
Capital city and population in 2011 (000)	Beirut (2 022)
United Nations membership date	24 October 1945

Economic indicators	2005	2010	2012
GDP: Gross domestic product (million current US$)	21 861	37 124	42 490
GDP: Growth rate at constant 2005 prices (annual %)	1.0	6.9	1.5
GDP per capita (current US$)	5 483.2	8 551.9	9 143.4
GNI: Gross national income per capita (current US$)	5 614.1	8 521.9	9 054.4
Gross fixed capital formation (% of GDP)	22.1	34.2	29.6
Exchange rates (national currency per US$)[a]	1 507.50	1 507.50	1 507.50
Balance of payments, current account (million US$)	−2 748	−7 552	−1 663
CPI: Consumer price index (2000=100)	105[b]	105[c]	118[c]
Agricultural production index (2004-2006=100)	97	92	102
Food production index (2004-2006=100)	97	92	102
Labour force participation, adult female pop. (%)	20.3	22.0	22.8
Labour force participation, adult male pop. (%)	70.6	70.0	70.5
Tourist arrivals at national borders (000)[d]	1 140	2 168	1 366
Energy production, primary (000 mt oil equivalent)	90	72	...
Mobile-cellular subscriptions (per 100 inhabitants)	24.5[e]	67.8	93.2
Individuals using the Internet (%)	10.1[f]	43.7[eg]	61.3[e]

Total trade		Major trading partners			2012
	(million US$)	(% of exports)			(% of imports)
Exports	4 446.2	South Africa	19.4	United States	11.2
Imports	21 146.5	Switzerland	12.3	Italy	8.6
Balance	−16 700.3	Saudi Arabia	7.9	China	8.2

Social indicators		
Population growth rate (average annual %)	2010-2015	3.0
Urban population growth rate (average annual %)	2010-2015	0.9
Rural population growth rate (average annual %)	2010-2015	−0.2
Urban population (%)	2013	87.5
Population aged 0-14 years (%)	2013	20.8
Population aged 60+ years (females and males, % of total)	2013	12.3/12.0
Sex ratio (males per 100 females)	2013	103.3
Life expectancy at birth (females and males, years)	2010-2015	82.1/77.9
Infant mortality rate (per 1 000 live births)	2010-2015	8.4
Fertility rate, total (live births per woman)	2010-2015	1.5
Contraceptive prevalence (ages 15-49, %)	2006-2012	58.0[h]
International migrant stock (000 and % of total population)[i]	mid-2013	849.7/17.6
Refugees and others of concern to UNHCR	mid-2013	580 383
Education: Government expenditure (% of GDP)	2006-2012	1.7
Education: Primary-secondary gross enrolment ratio (f/m per 100)	2006-2012	86.6/90.9
Education: Female third-level students (% of total)	2006-2012	54.3
Intentional homicides (females and males, per 100 000)[j]	2008-2010	0.5/2.9
Seats held by women in national parliaments (%)	2014	3.1

Environmental indicators		
Threatened species	2013	59
Forested area (% of land area)	2011	13.4
CO$_2$ emission estimates (000 metric tons and metric tons per capita)	2010	20 387/4.8
Energy consumption per capita (kilograms oil equivalent)	2010	1 446.0
Precipitation in the capital city, total mean (millimetres)		826[k]

a Market rate. **b** Beirut. **c** Index base 2008=100. **d** Excludes nationals residing abroad, Syrian nationals, Palestinians and students. **e** ITU estimate. **f** Age group 6 years and over. **g** Age group 15 years and over. **h** 2004. **i** Includes refugees. **j** Estimates. **k** Based on monthly averages for the period 1981-1990.

Lesotho

Region	Southern Africa
Currency	Loti (LSL)
Surface area (square kilometres)	30 355
Population in 2012 (estimated, 000)	2 052
Population density in 2012 (per square kilometre)	67.6
Capital city and population in 2011 (000)	Maseru (239)
United Nations membership date	17 October 1966

Economic indicators	2005	2010	2012
GDP: Gross domestic product (million current US$)	1 368	2 204	2 443
GDP: Growth rate at constant 2005 prices (annual %)	2.7	7.9	4.0
GDP per capita (current US$)	710.5	1 097.0	1 190.9
GNI: Gross national income per capita (current US$)	967.6	1 305.3	1 444.3
Gross fixed capital formation (% of GDP)	21.1	27.2	30.8
Exchange rates (national currency per US$)[a]	6.32	6.63	8.50
Balance of payments, current account (million US$)	−27	−405	−587
CPI: Consumer price index (2000=100)	140	198[b]	220
Agricultural production index (2004-2006=100)	102	110	99
Food production index (2004-2006=100)	102	111	98
Labour force participation, adult female pop. (%)	61.8	58.7	58.8
Labour force participation, adult male pop. (%)	75.5	73.0	73.3
Tourist arrivals at national borders (000)	347[c]	414	422
Energy production, primary (000 mt oil equivalent)	40	60[d]	...
Mobile-cellular subscriptions (per 100 inhabitants)	12.1	45.5	59.2
Individuals using the Internet (%)[e]	2.6	3.9	4.6

Total trade		Major trading partners			2012
	(million US$)[f]	(% of exports)[f]		(% of imports)[f]	
Exports	628.1	South Africa	48.9	South Africa	95.2
Imports	1 356.1	United States	31.8	Japan	2.5
Balance	−728.0	Canada	15.1	Germany	1.1

Social indicators		
Population growth rate (average annual %)	2010-2015	1.1
Urban population growth rate (average annual %)	2010-2015	3.6
Rural population growth rate (average annual %)	2010-2015	<
Urban population (%)	2013	29.0
Population aged 0-14 years (%)	2013	36.4
Population aged 60+ years (females and males, % of total)	2013	7.6/5.1
Sex ratio (males per 100 females)	2013	97.4
Life expectancy at birth (females and males, years)	2010-2015	49.6/49.2
Infant mortality rate (per 1 000 live births)	2010-2015	60.1
Fertility rate, total (live births per woman)	2010-2015	3.1
Contraceptive prevalence (ages 15-49, %)	2006-2012	47.0
International migrant stock (000 and % of total population)[gh]	mid-2013	3.1/0.2
Refugees and others of concern to UNHCR	mid-2013	37
Education: Government expenditure (% of GDP)	2006-2012	13.0
Education: Primary-secondary gross enrolment ratio (f/m per 100)[i]	2006-2012	88.7/83.1
Education: Female third-level students (% of total)	2006-2012	59.4
Intentional homicides (females and males, per 100 000)[j]	2008-2010	9.9/36.6
Seats held by women in national parliaments (%)	2014	26.7

Environmental indicators		
Threatened species	2013	16
Forested area (% of land area)	2011	1.5
CO$_2$ emission estimates (000 metric tons and metric tons per capita)	2010	18/0.0
Energy consumption per capita (kilograms oil equivalent)	2010	39.0[d]

a Principal rate. b Series linked to former series. c 2006. d UNSD estimate. e ITU estimate. f 2009. g Data refer to foreign citizens. h Includes refugees. i UNESCO estimate. j Estimates.

Liberia

Region	Western Africa
Currency	Liberian Dollar (LRD)
Surface area (square kilometres)	111 369
Population in 2012 (estimated, 000)	4 190
Population density in 2012 (per square kilometre)	37.6
Capital city and population in 2011 (000)	Monrovia (750)
United Nations membership date	2 November 1945

Economic indicators	2005	2010	2012
GDP: Gross domestic product (million current US$)	608	1 074	1 492
GDP: Growth rate at constant 2005 prices (annual %)	5.3	7.3	11.3
GDP per capita (current US$)	186.0	271.2	355.9
GNI: Gross national income per capita (current US$)	135.3	233.6	223.9
Gross fixed capital formation (% of GDP)	16.4	12.6	12.6
Exchange rates (national currency per US$)[a]	56.50	71.50	72.50
Balance of payments, current account (million US$)	−184	−415	−756[b]
Agricultural production index (2004-2006=100)	105	100	104
Food production index (2004-2006=100)	104	120	126
Employment in industrial sector (% of employed)	2.5[cde]	9.2[f]	...
Employment in agricultural sector (% of employed)	47.6[cde]	48.9[f]	...
Labour force participation, adult female pop. (%)	58.5	58.1	58.2
Labour force participation, adult male pop. (%)	62.9	64.3	64.7
Mobile-cellular subscriptions (per 100 inhabitants)	5.0	39.3	56.4
Individuals using the Internet (%)	0.6[cg]	2.3	3.8[g]

Social indicators		
Population growth rate (average annual %)	2010-2015	2.6
Urban population growth rate (average annual %)	2010-2015	3.4
Rural population growth rate (average annual %)	2010-2015	1.9
Urban population (%)	2013	48.9
Population aged 0-14 years (%)	2013	42.9
Population aged 60+ years (females and males, % of total)	2013	5.1/4.4
Sex ratio (males per 100 females)	2013	101.4
Life expectancy at birth (females and males, years)	2010-2015	61.2/59.3
Infant mortality rate (per 1 000 live births)	2010-2015	61.2
Fertility rate, total (live births per woman)	2010-2015	4.8
Contraceptive prevalence (ages 15-49, %)	2006-2012	11.4
International migrant stock (000 and % of total population)	mid-2013	225.5/5.3
Refugees and others of concern to UNHCR	mid-2013	60 469
Education: Government expenditure (% of GDP)	2006-2012	2.8
Education: Primary-secondary gross enrolment ratio (f/m per 100)	2006-2012	72.4/81.4
Education: Female third-level students (% of total)	2006-2012	35.3[h]
Intentional homicides (females and males, per 100 000)[i]	2008-2010	3.3/16.9
Seats held by women in national parliaments (%)	2014	11.0

Environmental indicators		
Threatened species	2013	151
Forested area (% of land area)	2011	44.6
CO$_2$ emission estimates (000 metric tons and metric tons per capita)	2010	799/0.2
Energy consumption per capita (kilograms oil equivalent)	2010	64.0

a Principal rate. b 2011. c 2007. d Core Welfare Indicators Questionnaire (World Bank). e The indices are shown in terms of ISIC Rev.2. f Break in series; data not strictly comparable. g ITU estimate. h 2000. i Estimates.

Libya

Region	Northern Africa
Currency	Libyan Dinar (LYD)
Surface area (square kilometres)	1 759 540
Population in 2012 (estimated, 000)	6 155
Population density in 2012 (per square kilometre)	3.5
Capital city and population in 2011 (000)	Tripoli (1 127)
United Nations membership date	14 December 1955

Economic indicators	2005	2010	2012
GDP: Gross domestic product (million current US$)	45 451	80 942	95 802
GDP: Growth rate at constant 2005 prices (annual %)	10.3	4.3	104.5
GDP per capita (current US$)	8 124.4	13 399.7	15 565.8
GNI: Gross national income per capita (current US$)	8 072.5	13 319.1	15 472.2
Gross fixed capital formation (% of GDP)	27.8	40.2	33.3
Exchange rates (national currency per US$)[a]	1.35	1.25	1.26
Balance of payments, current account (million US$)	14 945	16 801	23 836
Agricultural production index (2004-2006=100)	101	110	113
Food production index (2004-2006=100)	101	110	113
Labour force participation, adult female pop. (%)	29.6	29.8	30.0
Labour force participation, adult male pop. (%)	75.0	76.1	76.4
Tourist arrivals at national borders (000)[b]	81	34[c]	...
Energy production, primary (000 mt oil equivalent)	98 005	95 256	...
Mobile-cellular subscriptions (per 100 inhabitants)	34.7	171.5[d]	148.2[d]
Individuals using the Internet (%)[d]	3.9	14.0	14.0[e]

Total trade		Major trading partners			2012
	(million US$)[f]	(% of exports)[f]		(% of imports)[fg]	
Exports	36 440.4	Italy	42.3	Turkey	10.6
Imports	17 674.4	France	15.5	Europe nes	10.0
Balance	18 766.0	China	9.4	China	9.8

Social indicators

Population growth rate (average annual %)	2010-2015	0.9
Urban population growth rate (average annual %)	2010-2015	1.0
Rural population growth rate (average annual %)	2010-2015	-≺
Urban population (%)	2013	78.1
Population aged 0-14 years (%)	2013	29.4
Population aged 60+ years (females and males, % of total)	2013	7.5/6.9
Sex ratio (males per 100 females)	2013	100.0
Life expectancy at birth (females and males, years)	2010-2015	77.2/73.4
Infant mortality rate (per 1 000 live births)	2010-2015	13.8
Fertility rate, total (live births per woman)	2010-2015	2.4
Contraceptive prevalence (ages 15-49, %)	2006-2012	45.2[h]
International migrant stock (000 and % of total population)[i]	mid-2013	756.0/12.2
Refugees and others of concern to UNHCR	mid-2013	83 201
Education: Government expenditure (% of GDP)	2006-2012	2.7[j]
Education: Primary-secondary gross enrolment ratio (f/m per 100)	2006-2012	112.5/106.0
Education: Female third-level students (% of total)[k]	2006-2012	51.4[j]
Intentional homicides (females and males, per 100 000)[m]	2008-2010	</5.2
Seats held by women in national parliaments (%)	2014	16.5

Environmental indicators

Threatened species	2013	49
Forested area (% of land area)	2011	<
CO_2 emission estimates (000 metric tons and metric tons per capita)	2010	58 987/9.3
Energy consumption per capita (kilograms oil equivalent)	2010	2 967.0
Precipitation in the capital city, total mean (millimetres)		334[n]
Temperature in the capital city, mean °C (minimum and maximum)		15.6/25.4[n]

a Official rate. **b** Arrivals of non-resident tourists in hotels and similar establishments. **c** 2008. **d** ITU estimate. **e** 2011. **f** 2010. **g** See technical notes. **h** 1995. **i** Data refer to foreign citizens. **j** 1999. **k** UNESCO estimate. **l** 2003. **m** Estimates. **n** Based on monthly averages for the period 1961-1990.

Liechtenstein

Region	Western Europe
Currency	Swiss Franc (CHF)
Surface area (square kilometres)	160
Population in 2012 (estimated, 000)	37
Population density in 2012 (per square kilometre)	229.1
Capital city and population in 2011 (000)	Vaduz (5)
United Nations membership date	18 September 1990

Economic indicators	2005	2010	2012
GDP: Gross domestic product (million current US$)	3 658	5 109	5 827
GDP: Growth rate at constant 2005 prices (annual %)	4.8	7.9	1.9
GDP per capita (current US$)	105 306.8	141 458.3	158 976.8
GNI: Gross national income per capita (current US$)	89 979.9	119 326.5	131 162.7
Gross fixed capital formation (% of GDP)	21.4	20.1	20.1
Exchange rates (national currency per US$)[a]	1.31[b]	0.95	0.91
Agricultural production index (2004-2006=100)	101	102	105
Food production index (2004-2006=100)	101	102	105
Tourist arrivals at national borders (000)[c]	50	50	54
Mobile-cellular subscriptions (per 100 inhabitants)	79.3	98.5[d]	103.9[d]
Individuals using the Internet (%)	63.4	80.0	89.4[d]

Social indicators		
Population growth rate (average annual %)	2010-2015	0.7
Urban population growth rate (average annual %)	2010-2015	0.5
Rural population growth rate (average annual %)	2010-2015	0.8
Urban population (%)	2013	14.3
Population aged 0-14 years (%)[efg]	2013	15.8[h]
Population aged 60+ years (females and males, % of total)[efg]	2013	21.4/19.2[h]
Sex ratio (males per 100 females)[efg]	2013	97.9[h]
Fertility rate, total (live births per woman)[e]	2010-2015	1.7[h]
International migrant stock (000 and % of total population)[i]	mid-2013	12.2/33.1
Refugees and others of concern to UNHCR	mid-2013	153
Education: Government expenditure (% of GDP)	2006-2012	2.1
Education: Primary-secondary gross enrolment ratio (f/m per 100)[j]	2006-2012	102.7/115.1
Education: Female third-level students (% of total)	2006-2012	32.8
Seats held by women in national parliaments (%)	2014	20.0

Environmental indicators		
Threatened species	2013	4
Forested area (% of land area)	2011	43.1

a UN operational exchange rate. b December 2005. c Arrivals of non-resident tourists in hotels and similar establishments. d ITU estimate. e Data compiled by the United Nations Demographic Yearbook system. f Data refer to the latest available census. g De jure estimate. h 2011. i Data refer to foreign citizens. j National estimate.

Lithuania

Region	Northern Europe
Currency	Litas (LTL)
Surface area (square kilometres)	65 300
Population in 2012 (estimated, 000)	3 028
Population density in 2012 (per square kilometre)	46.4
Capital city and population in 2011 (000)	Vilnius (546)
United Nations membership date	17 September 1991

Economic indicators

	2005	2010	2012
GDP: Gross domestic product (million current US$)	26 100	36 709	42 339
GDP: Growth rate at constant 2005 prices (annual %)	7.8	1.6	3.7
GDP per capita (current US$)	7 940.9	11 963.4	13 984.2
GNI: Gross national income per capita (current US$)	7 820.2	11 722.3	13 535.7
Gross fixed capital formation (% of GDP)	22.9	16.4	16.7
Exchange rates (national currency per US$)[a]	2.91	2.61	2.61
Balance of payments, current account (million US$)	−1 831	15	−100
CPI: Consumer price index (2000=100)	104[b]	134	144
Industrial production index (2005=100)	100	103	114
Agricultural production index (2004-2006=100)	106	99	121
Food production index (2004-2006=100)	106	99	121
Unemployment (% of labour force)[cd]	8.3	17.8	13.4
Employment in industrial sector (% of employed)	29.1[ef]	24.4[g]	24.8[g]
Employment in agricultural sector (% of employed)	14.0[ef]	9.0[g]	8.9[g]
Labour force participation, adult female pop. (%)	51.0	54.3	55.8
Labour force participation, adult male pop. (%)	63.3	64.2	66.3
Tourist arrivals at national borders (000)	2 000	1 507	1 900
Energy production, primary (000 mt oil equivalent)	1 252	359	...
Mobile-cellular subscriptions (per 100 inhabitants)	127.5[h]	147.2[h]	151.8
Individuals using the Internet (%)	36.2[i]	62.1[i]	68.0[j]

Total trade

	(million US$)	Major trading partners			2012
		(% of exports)		(% of imports)	
Exports	29 652.7	Russian Federation	18.9	Russian Federation	32.3
Imports	32 237.6	Latvia	10.9	Germany	9.8
Balance	−2 584.9	Estonia	7.8	Poland	9.7

Social indicators

Population growth rate (average annual %)	2010-2015	−0.5
Urban population growth rate (average annual %)	2010-2015	−0.3
Rural population growth rate (average annual %)	2010-2015	−0.8
Urban population (%)	2013	67.3
Population aged 0-14 years (%)	2013	15.2
Population aged 60+ years (females and males, % of total)	2013	25.3/15.4
Sex ratio (males per 100 females)	2013	85.3
Life expectancy at birth (females and males, years)	2010-2015	78.1/66.0
Infant mortality rate (per 1 000 live births)	2010-2015	5.4
Fertility rate, total (live births per woman)	2010-2015	1.5
Contraceptive prevalence (ages 15-49, %)[k]	2006-2012	50.7[l]
International migrant stock (000 and % of total population)	mid-2013	147.8/4.9
Refugees and others of concern to UNHCR	mid-2013	4 937
Education: Government expenditure (% of GDP)	2006-2012	5.4
Education: Primary-secondary gross enrolment ratio (f/m per 100)	2006-2012	103.4/102.2
Education: Female third-level students (% of total)	2006-2012	59.0
Intentional homicides (females and males, per 100 000)	2008-2010	3.6/12.1
Seats held by women in national parliaments (%)	2014	24.1

Environmental indicators

Threatened species	2013	23
Forested area (% of land area)	2011	34.6
CO_2 emission estimates (000 metric tons and metric tons per capita)	2010	13 549/4.1
Energy consumption per capita (kilograms oil equivalent)	2010	1 832.0
Precipitation in the capital city, total mean (millimetres)		683[m]
Temperature in the capital city, mean °C (minimum and maximum)		2.4/10.1[m]

a Official rate. b Series linked to former series. c Age group 15 to 74 years. d 2007: Break in series; data not strictly comparable. e The indices are shown in terms of ISIC Rev.3. f Excludes conscripts. g European Labour Force Survey (Eurostat). h Active mobile subscriptions. i Age group 16 to 74 years using the Internet within the last 12 months. j Age group 16 to 74 years. k Age group 18 to 49 years. l 1994-1995. m Based on monthly averages for the period 1961-1990.

Luxembourg

Region	Western Europe
Currency	Euro (EUR)
Surface area (square kilometres)	2 586
Population in 2012 (estimated, 000)	524
Population density in 2012 (per square kilometre)	202.5
Capital city and population in 2011 (000)	Luxembourg (94)
United Nations membership date	24 October 1945

Economic indicators	2005	2010	2012
GDP: Gross domestic product (million current US$)	37 643	52 053	55 143
GDP: Growth rate at constant 2005 prices (annual %)	5.3	3.1	−0.2
GDP per capita (current US$)	82 217.5	102 490.4	105 287.0
GNI: Gross national income per capita (current US$)	70 605.2	70 828.7	71 739.7
Gross fixed capital formation (% of GDP)	22.0	16.8	18.7
Exchange rates (national currency per US$)[a]	0.85	0.75	0.76
Balance of payments, current account (million US$)	4 406	4 090	3 608
CPI: Consumer price index (2000=100)	112[b]	125	133
Industrial production index (2005=100)	100	89	83
Agricultural production index (2004-2006=100)	99	93	90
Food production index (2004-2006=100)	99	93	90
Unemployment (% of labour force)[cd]	4.5	4.4	5.1
Employment in industrial sector (% of employed)[e]	17.2[f]	12.6	12.4
Employment in agricultural sector (% of employed)[e]	1.8[f]	1.0	1.3
Labour force participation, adult female pop. (%)	45.4	48.8	50.7
Labour force participation, adult male pop. (%)	64.7	65.4	64.9
Tourist arrivals at national borders (000)[g]	913	805	905
Energy production, primary (000 mt oil equivalent)	82	133	...
Mobile-cellular subscriptions (per 100 inhabitants)	111.6	143.3	145.5
Individuals using the Internet (%)[h]	70.0	90.6	92.0

Total trade		Major trading partners			2012
	(million US$)	(% of exports)		(% of imports)	
Exports	13 691.9	Germany	27.4	Belgium	24.5
Imports	24 011.0	France	14.7	Germany	22.8
Balance	−10 319.1	Belgium	12.9	France	12.8

Social indicators		
Population growth rate (average annual %)	2010-2015	1.4
Urban population growth rate (average annual %)	2010-2015	1.6
Rural population growth rate (average annual %)	2010-2015	−0.2
Urban population (%)	2013	85.9
Population aged 0-14 years (%)	2013	17.5
Population aged 60+ years (females and males, % of total)	2013	21.1/17.6
Sex ratio (males per 100 females)	2013	99.1
Life expectancy at birth (females and males, years)	2010-2015	83.0/77.9
Infant mortality rate (per 1 000 live births)	2010-2015	2.0
Fertility rate, total (live births per woman)	2010-2015	1.7
International migrant stock (000 and % of total population)	mid-2013	229.4/43.3
Refugees and others of concern to UNHCR	mid-2013	4 091[i]
Education: Government expenditure (% of GDP)	2006-2012	3.7[j]
Education: Primary-secondary gross enrolment ratio (f/m per 100)	2006-2012	100.3/97.7
Education: Female third-level students (% of total)	2006-2012	51.9
Intentional homicides (females and males, per 100 000)	2008-2010	0.8/2.0
Seats held by women in national parliaments (%)	2014	28.3

Environmental indicators		
Threatened species	2013	9
Forested area (% of land area)	2011	33.5
CO$_2$ emission estimates (000 metric tons and metric tons per capita)	2010	10 820/21.3
Energy consumption per capita (kilograms oil equivalent)	2010	8 556.0
Precipitation in the capital city, total mean (millimetres)		876[k]
Temperature in the capital city, mean °C (minimum and maximum)		4.7/12.3[k]

a Market rate. b Series linked to former series. c Age group 15 to 74 years. d 2007: Break in series; data not strictly comparable. e European Labour Force Survey (Eurostat). f The indices are shown in terms of ISIC Rev.3. g Arrivals of non-resident tourists in all types of accommodation establishments. h Age group 16 to 74 years. i Refugee population refers to the end of 2012. j 2001. k Based on WMO Climatological Normals (CLINO) for the period 1961-1990.

Madagascar

Region	Eastern Africa
Currency	Malagasy Ariary (MGA)
Surface area (square kilometres)	587 295
Population in 2012 (estimated, 000)	22 294
Population density in 2012 (per square kilometre)	38.0
Capital city and population in 2011 (000)	Antananarivo (1 987)
United Nations membership date	20 September 1960

Economic indicators	2005	2010	2012
GDP: Gross domestic product (million current US$)	5 039	8 745	9 968
GDP: Growth rate at constant 2005 prices (annual %)	4.6	0.4	2.7
GDP per capita (current US$)	275.5	414.9	447.1
GNI: Gross national income per capita (current US$)	295.1	410.5	438.7
Gross fixed capital formation (% of GDP)	22.2	20.7	17.3
Exchange rates (national currency per US$)[a]	2 159.82	2 146.12	2 270.56
Balance of payments, current account (million US$)	−554	...	...
CPI: Consumer price index (2000=100)	153	263	307
Agricultural production index (2004-2006=100)	103	124	123
Food production index (2004-2006=100)	103	124	123
Employment in industrial sector (% of employed)	3.7[bcd]	...	...
Employment in agricultural sector (% of employed)	80.4[bd]	...	...
Labour force participation, adult female pop. (%)	84.1	87.2	86.8
Labour force participation, adult male pop. (%)	89.1	91.0	90.6
Tourist arrivals at national borders (000)[e]	277	196	256
Energy production, primary (000 mt oil equivalent)	56	61	...
Mobile-cellular subscriptions (per 100 inhabitants)	2.9	37.2	39.1
Individuals using the Internet (%)[f]	0.6	1.7	2.1

Total trade		Major trading partners			2012
	(million US$)	(% of exports)			(% of imports)[g]
Exports	1 224.5	France	29.1	United Arab Emirates	14.6
Imports	2 659.0	China	8.4	China	14.3
Balance	−1 434.5	Germany	6.2	Europe nes	7.5

Social indicators		
Population growth rate (average annual %)	2010-2015	2.8
Urban population growth rate (average annual %)	2010-2015	4.7
Rural population growth rate (average annual %)	2010-2015	1.9
Urban population (%)	2013	33.8
Population aged 0-14 years (%)	2013	42.4
Population aged 60+ years (females and males, % of total)	2013	4.8/4.2
Sex ratio (males per 100 females)	2013	99.4
Life expectancy at birth (females and males, years)	2010-2015	66.0/63.0
Infant mortality rate (per 1 000 live births)	2010-2015	36.8
Fertility rate, total (live births per woman)	2010-2015	4.5
Contraceptive prevalence (ages 15-49, %)	2006-2012	39.9
International migrant stock (000 and % of total population)[h]	mid-2013	34.3/0.2
Refugees and others of concern to UNHCR	mid-2013	11
Education: Government expenditure (% of GDP)	2006-2012	2.7
Education: Primary-secondary gross enrolment ratio (f/m per 100)	2006-2012	85.3/87.4
Education: Female third-level students (% of total)	2006-2012	48.0
Intentional homicides (females and males, per 100 000)[i]	2008-2010	3.1/13.1
Seats held by women in national parliaments (%)	2014	23.1

Environmental indicators		
Threatened species	2013	873
Forested area (% of land area)	2011	21.5
CO_2 emission estimates (000 metric tons and metric tons per capita)	2010	2 012/0.1
Energy consumption per capita (kilograms oil equivalent)	2010	33.0
Precipitation in the capital city, total mean (millimetres)		1 365[j]
Temperature in the capital city, mean °C (minimum and maximum)		13.8/24.0[j]

a Official rate. b The indices are shown in terms of ISIC Rev.2. c Excludes mining and quarrying. d Break in series; data not strictly comparable. e Air arrivals of non-resident tourists. f ITU estimate. g See technical notes. h Data refer to foreign citizens. i Estimates. j Based on monthly averages for the period 1971-2000.

Malawi

Region	Eastern Africa
Currency	Malawi Kwacha (MWK)
Surface area (square kilometres)	118 484
Population in 2012 (estimated, 000)	15 906
Population density in 2012 (per square kilometre)	134.3
Capital city and population in 2011 (000)	Lilongwe (772)
United Nations membership date	1 December 1964

Economic indicators	2005	2010	2012
GDP: Gross domestic product (million current US$)	3 406	6 753	5 653
GDP: Growth rate at constant 2005 prices (annual %)	3.3	5.6	1.8
GDP per capita (current US$)	263.6	449.8	355.4
GNI: Gross national income per capita (current US$)	258.3	439.2	350.0
Gross fixed capital formation (% of GDP)	15.3	10.4	6.0
Exchange rates (national currency per US$)[a]	123.78	150.80	335.13
Balance of payments, current account (million US$)	−507	−786	−800
CPI: Consumer price index (2000=100)	199	309	403
Agricultural production index (2004-2006=100)	85	155	171
Food production index (2004-2006=100)	85	157	171
Labour force participation, adult female pop. (%)	79.2	85.1	84.7
Labour force participation, adult male pop. (%)	86.3	81.2	81.3
Tourist arrivals at national borders (000)[b]	438	746	767[c]
Energy production, primary (000 mt oil equivalent)	145	188[d]	...
Mobile-cellular subscriptions (per 100 inhabitants)	3.3	20.9	27.8
Individuals using the Internet (%)	0.4	2.3	4.4[e]

Total trade		Major trading partners			2012
	(million US$)[c]		(% of exports)[c]		(% of imports)[c]
Exports	1 425.3	Canada	8.8	South Africa	25.0
Imports	2 427.7	Zimbabwe	8.6	India	11.5
Balance	−1 002.4	South Africa	8.2	China	9.3

Social indicators		
Population growth rate (average annual %)	2010-2015	2.8
Urban population growth rate (average annual %)	2010-2015	4.2
Rural population growth rate (average annual %)	2010-2015	3.1
Urban population (%)	2013	16.0
Population aged 0-14 years (%)	2013	45.3
Population aged 60+ years (females and males, % of total)	2013	5.4/4.4
Sex ratio (males per 100 females)	2013	100.5
Life expectancy at birth (females and males, years)	2010-2015	55.2/54.9
Infant mortality rate (per 1 000 live births)	2010-2015	86.1
Fertility rate, total (live births per woman)	2010-2015	5.4
Contraceptive prevalence (ages 15-49, %)	2006-2012	46.1
International migrant stock (000 and % of total population)[f]	mid-2013	206.6/1.3
Refugees and others of concern to UNHCR	mid-2013	18 432
Education: Government expenditure (% of GDP)	2006-2012	5.4
Education: Primary-secondary gross enrolment ratio (f/m per 100)	2006-2012	92.6/91.5
Education: Female third-level students (% of total)	2006-2012	39.2
Intentional homicides (females and males, per 100 000)[g]	2008-2010	8.7/63.3
Seats held by women in national parliaments (%)	2014	22.3

Environmental indicators		
Threatened species	2013	170
Forested area (% of land area)	2011	34.0
CO_2 emission estimates (000 metric tons and metric tons per capita)	2010	1 238/0.1
Energy consumption per capita (kilograms oil equivalent)	2010	34.0
Precipitation in the capital city, total mean (millimetres)[h]		1 289[i]
Temperature in the capital city, mean °C (minimum and maximum)[h]		12.2/24.1[i]

a Official rate. b Departures. c 2011. d UNSD estimate. e ITU estimate. f Includes refugees. g Estimates.
h Mzuzu. i Based on WMO Climatological Normals (CLINO) for the period 1961-1990.

Malaysia

Region	South-Eastern Asia
Currency	Ringgit (MYR)
Surface area (square kilometres)	330 803
Population in 2012 (estimated, 000)	29 240[a]
Population density in 2012 (per square kilometre)	88.4
Capital city and population in 2011 (000)	Kuala Lumpur (1 556)[b]
United Nations membership date	17 September 1957

Economic indicators	2005	2010	2012
GDP: Gross domestic product (million current US$)	143 534	247 534	304 726
GDP: Growth rate at constant 2005 prices (annual %)	5.3	7.4	5.6
GDP per capita (current US$)	5 554.0	8 754.2	10 421.6
GNI: Gross national income per capita (current US$)	5 309.4	8 465.1	10 022.7
Gross fixed capital formation (% of GDP)	22.3	22.6	25.7
Exchange rates (national currency per US$)[c]	3.78	3.08	3.06
Balance of payments, current account (million US$)	19 980	26 998	18 638
CPI: Consumer price index (2000=100)	109[d]	124	130
Industrial production index (2005=100)[e]	100	107	113
Agricultural production index (2004-2006=100)	100	110	120
Food production index (2004-2006=100)	100	115	125
Unemployment (% of labour force)	3.3[f]	3.3	3.0
Employment in industrial sector (% of employed)[g]	29.7[e]	27.6[h]	28.4
Employment in agricultural sector (% of employed)[g]	14.6[e]	13.3[h]	12.6
Labour force participation, adult female pop. (%)	44.3	44.1	44.3
Labour force participation, adult male pop. (%)	77.6	75.0	75.3
Tourist arrivals at national borders (000)[i]	16 431	24 577	25 033
Energy production, primary (000 mt oil equivalent)	94 786	86 923[j]	...
Mobile-cellular subscriptions (per 100 inhabitants)	74.9	119.2	140.9
Individuals using the Internet (%)	48.6	56.3[k]	65.8[k]

Total trade		Major trading partners			2012
	(million US$)	(% of exports)			(% of imports)
Exports	227 449.5	Singapore	13.6	China	15.2
Imports	196 196.6	China	12.6	Singapore	13.2
Balance	31 252.9	Japan	11.9	Japan	10.3

Social indicators		
Population growth rate (average annual %)[a]	2010-2015	1.6
Urban population growth rate (average annual %)[a]	2010-2015	2.5
Rural population growth rate (average annual %)[a]	2010-2015	−1.0
Urban population (%)[a]	2013	74.2
Population aged 0-14 years (%)[a]	2013	26.1
Population aged 60+ years (females and males, % of total)[a]	2013	8.3/8.7
Sex ratio (males per 100 females)[a]	2013	94.3
Life expectancy at birth (females and males, years)[a]	2010-2015	77.3/72.7
Infant mortality rate (per 1 000 live births)[a]	2010-2015	4.1
Fertility rate, total (live births per woman)[a]	2010-2015	2.0
Contraceptive prevalence (ages 15-49, %)	2006-2012	49.0[l]
International migrant stock (000 and % of total population)[am]	mid-2013	2 469.2/8.3
Refugees and others of concern to UNHCR	mid-2013	225 685
Education: Government expenditure (% of GDP)	2006-2012	5.1
Education: Primary-secondary gross enrolment ratio (f/m per 100)	2006-2012	83.2/84.7[n]
Education: Female third-level students (% of total)	2006-2012	56.5
Intentional homicides (females and males, per 100 000)	2008-2010	1.0/3.3
Seats held by women in national parliaments (%)	2014	10.4

Environmental indicators		
Threatened species	2013	1 226
Forested area (% of land area)	2011	62.0
CO$_2$ emission estimates (000 metric tons and metric tons per capita)	2010	216 627/7.6
Energy consumption per capita (kilograms oil equivalent)	2010	2 486.0
Precipitation in the capital city, total mean (millimetres)		2 427[o]
Temperature in the capital city, mean °C (minimum and maximum)		23.2/32.4[o]

a Includes Sabah and Sarawak. b Kuala Lumpur is the financial capital and Putrajaya is the administrative capital. c Official rate. d Series linked to former series. e The indices are shown in terms of ISIC Rev.3. f 2006. g Age group 15 to 64 years. h Break in series; data not strictly comparable. i Includes Singapore residents crossing the frontier by road through Johore Causeway. j UNSD estimate. k Refers to total population. l 2004. m Includes refugees. n 2005. o Based on monthly averages for the period 1971-2000.

Maldives

Region	Southern Asia
Currency	Rufiyaa (MVR)
Surface area (square kilometres)	300
Population in 2012 (estimated, 000)	338
Population density in 2012 (per square kilometre)	1 128.1
Capital city and population in 2011 (000)	Male (132)
United Nations membership date	21 September 1965

Economic indicators	2005	2010	2012
GDP: Gross domestic product (million current US$)	1 091	2 335	2 606
GDP: Growth rate at constant 2005 prices (annual %)	−9.1	6.9	13.5
GDP per capita (current US$)	3 665.6	7 169.0	7 699.8
GNI: Gross national income per capita (current US$)	3 434.9	6 143.5	6 503.0
Gross fixed capital formation (% of GDP)	34.5	26.2	24.3
Exchange rates (national currency per US$)[a]	12.80	12.80	15.36
Balance of payments, current account (million US$)	−273	−196	−600
CPI: Consumer price index (2000=100)[b]	107[c]	146	184[c]
Agricultural production index (2004-2006=100)	89	81	88
Food production index (2004-2006=100)	89	81	88
Employment in industrial sector (% of employed)	24.3[defgh]	...	...
Employment in agricultural sector (% of employed)	11.5[defgh]	...	...
Labour force participation, adult female pop. (%)	50.2	55.1	55.9
Labour force participation, adult male pop. (%)	74.6	76.4	77.1
Tourist arrivals at national borders (000)[i]	395	792	958
Mobile-cellular subscriptions (per 100 inhabitants)	69.0	156.5	172.8
Individuals using the Internet (%)	6.9[jk]	26.5[l]	38.9[m]

Total trade		Major trading partners			2012
	(million US$)	(% of exports)		(% of imports)	
Exports	161.6	Thailand	27.4	United Arab Emirates	29.9
Imports	1 554.5	France	16.5	Singapore	18.1
Balance	−1 392.9	Italy	7.7	India	9.5

Social indicators

Population growth rate (average annual %)	2010-2015	1.9
Urban population growth rate (average annual %)	2010-2015	3.9
Rural population growth rate (average annual %)	2010-2015	−0.7
Urban population (%)	2013	43.5
Population aged 0-14 years (%)	2013	28.7
Population aged 60+ years (females and males, % of total)	2013	6.4/7.0
Sex ratio (males per 100 females)	2013	101.4
Life expectancy at birth (females and males, years)	2010-2015	78.8/76.7
Infant mortality rate (per 1 000 live births)	2010-2015	10.4
Fertility rate, total (live births per woman)	2010-2015	2.3
Contraceptive prevalence (ages 15-49, %)	2006-2012	34.7
International migrant stock (000 and % of total population)[n]	mid-2013	84.2/24.4
Education: Government expenditure (% of GDP)	2006-2012	6.8
Education: Primary-secondary gross enrolment ratio (f/m per 100)[o]	2006-2012	102.4/100.7[p]
Education: Female third-level students (% of total)	2006-2012	52.5
Intentional homicides (females and males, per 100 000)	2008-2010	</1.1
Seats held by women in national parliaments (%)	2014	6.8

Environmental indicators

Threatened species	2013	69
Forested area (% of land area)	2011	3.0
CO_2 emission estimates (000 metric tons and metric tons per capita)	2010	1 074/3.4
Energy consumption per capita (kilograms oil equivalent)	2010	1 132.0
Precipitation in the capital city, total mean (millimetres)		1 901[q]
Temperature in the capital city, mean °C (minimum and maximum)		25.8/30.6[q]

a Market rate. **b** Male. **c** Series linked to former series. **d** 2006. **e** Population census. **f** The indices are shown in terms of ISIC Rev.3. **g** Excludes conscripts. **h** Break in series; data not strictly comparable. **i** Air arrivals. **j** Country estimate. **k** Excludes mobile Internet users. **l** Age group 15 years and over. **m** ITU estimate. **n** Data refer to foreign citizens. **o** UNESCO estimate. **p** 2004. **q** Based on monthly averages for the period 1981-2000.

Mali

Region	Western Africa
Currency	CFA Franc (XOF)
Surface area (square kilometres)	1 240 192
Population in 2012 (estimated, 000)	14 854
Population density in 2012 (per square kilometre)	12.0
Capital city and population in 2011 (000)	Bamako (2 037)
United Nations membership date	28 September 1960

Economic indicators	2005	2010	2012
GDP: Gross domestic product (million current US$)	5 486	9 400	10 263
GDP: Growth rate at constant 2005 prices (annual %)	6.1	5.8	−1.2
GDP per capita (current US$)	459.4	672.1	690.9
GNI: Gross national income per capita (current US$)	441.6	642.2	657.8
Gross fixed capital formation (% of GDP)	15.4	21.2	16.2
Exchange rates (national currency per US$)[a]	556.04	490.91	497.16
Balance of payments, current account (million US$)	−438	−1 190	...
CPI: Consumer price index (2000=100)[b]	112	131[c]	142
Industrial production index (2005=100)[d]	100	74	84
Agricultural production index (2004-2006=100)	103	142	152
Food production index (2004-2006=100)	103	154	161
Employment in industrial sector (% of employed)	5.6[def]	...	...
Employment in agricultural sector (% of employed)	66.0[def]	...	...
Labour force participation, adult female pop. (%)	38.1	50.2	50.6
Labour force participation, adult male pop. (%)	70.0	81.4	81.4
Tourist arrivals at national borders (000)	...	169	134
Energy production, primary (000 mt oil equivalent)[g]	22	25	...
Mobile-cellular subscriptions (per 100 inhabitants)	5.8	48.4	89.6
Individuals using the Internet (%)	0.5	1.9[h]	2.2[h]

Total trade		Major trading partners			2012
	(million US$)	(% of exports)			(% of imports)
Exports	2 610.4	South Africa	51.8	Senegal	25.1
Imports	3 462.7	Switzerland	11.6	France	10.8
Balance	−852.3	China	7.8	China	10.6

Social indicators		
Population growth rate (average annual %)	2010-2015	3.0
Urban population growth rate (average annual %)	2010-2015	4.8
Rural population growth rate (average annual %)	2010-2015	1.9
Urban population (%)	2013	36.2
Population aged 0-14 years (%)	2013	47.4
Population aged 60+ years (females and males, % of total)	2013	4.7/3.7
Sex ratio (males per 100 females)	2013	101.6
Life expectancy at birth (females and males, years)	2010-2015	54.7/54.9
Infant mortality rate (per 1 000 live births)	2010-2015	86.7
Fertility rate, total (live births per woman)	2010-2015	6.9
Contraceptive prevalence (ages 15-49, %)	2006-2012	8.2
International migrant stock (000 and % of total population)[i]	mid-2013	195.6/1.3
Refugees and others of concern to UNHCR	mid-2013	368 702
Education: Government expenditure (% of GDP)	2006-2012	4.8
Education: Primary-secondary gross enrolment ratio (f/m per 100)	2006-2012	65.1/78.0
Education: Female third-level students (% of total)	2006-2012	28.9
Intentional homicides (females and males, per 100 000)[j]	2008-2010	1.4/14.7
Seats held by women in national parliaments (%)	2014	9.5

Environmental indicators		
Threatened species	2013	37
Forested area (% of land area)	2011	10.2
CO$_2$ emission estimates (000 metric tons and metric tons per capita)	2010	623/0.0
Energy consumption per capita (kilograms oil equivalent)	2010	15.0[g]
Precipitation in the capital city, total mean (millimetres)		991[k]
Temperature in the capital city, mean °C (minimum and maximum)		21.3/35.0[k]

a Official rate. b Bamako. c Series linked to former series. d The indices are shown in terms of ISIC Rev. 3. e 2006. f Break in series; data not strictly comparable. g UNSD estimate. h ITU estimate. i Includes refugees. j Estimates. k Based on monthly averages for the period 1950-2000.

Malta

Region	Southern Europe
Currency	Euro (EUR)[a]
Surface area (square kilometres)	316
Population in 2012 (estimated, 000)	428
Population density in 2012 (per square kilometre)	1 353.7
Capital city and population in 2011 (000)	Valletta (198)
United Nations membership date	1 December 1964

Economic indicators	2005	2010	2012
GDP: Gross domestic product (million current US$)	6 131	8 446	8 775
GDP: Growth rate at constant 2005 prices (annual %)	3.6	4.0	0.8
GDP per capita (current US$)	14 781.5	19 884.2	20 513.6
GNI: Gross national income per capita (current US$)	14 128.4	18 545.3	19 264.9
Gross fixed capital formation (% of GDP)	21.4	17.4	14.9
Exchange rates (national currency per US$)	0.36[bc]	0.75[de]	0.76[de]
Balance of payments, current account (million US$)	−524	−608	180
CPI: Consumer price index (2000=100)	113	127[f]	133
Industrial production index (2005=100)	100	103	107
Agricultural production index (2004-2006=100)	97	99	90
Food production index (2004-2006=100)	97	99	90
Unemployment (% of labour force)[g]	7.3	6.9	6.4
Employment in industrial sector (% of employed)[h]	29.5[i]	25.2	22.1
Employment in agricultural sector (% of employed)[h]	1.7[i]	1.3	1.0
Labour force participation, adult female pop. (%)	30.3	34.6	38.0
Labour force participation, adult male pop. (%)	68.6	67.2	66.5
Tourist arrivals at national borders (000)	1 171	1 339	1 444
Mobile-cellular subscriptions (per 100 inhabitants)	79.2	109.4	128.7
Individuals using the Internet (%)	41.2[i]	63.0[i]	70.0

Total trade		Major trading partners			2012
	(million US$)	(% of exports)[k]			(% of imports)
Exports	5 646.3	Bunkers	17.2	Italy	32.1
Imports	7 896.2	Germany	8.1	United Kingdom	6.0
Balance	−2 249.9	China, Hong Kong SAR	7.7	France	6.0

Social indicators		
Population growth rate (average annual %)	2010-2015	0.3
Urban population growth rate (average annual %)	2010-2015	0.5
Rural population growth rate (average annual %)	2010-2015	−2.8
Urban population (%)	2013	95.2
Population aged 0-14 years (%)	2013	14.7
Population aged 60+ years (females and males, % of total)	2013	25.2/21.8
Sex ratio (males per 100 females)	2013	99.9
Life expectancy at birth (females and males, years)	2010-2015	82.0/77.4
Infant mortality rate (per 1 000 live births)	2010-2015	4.8
Fertility rate, total (live births per woman)	2010-2015	1.4
Contraceptive prevalence (ages 15-49, %)[l]	2006-2012	85.8[m]
International migrant stock (000 and % of total population)	mid-2013	34.5/8.0
Refugees and others of concern to UNHCR	mid-2013	8 552[n]
Education: Government expenditure (% of GDP)	2006-2012	6.9
Education: Primary-secondary gross enrolment ratio (f/m per 100)	2006-2012	95.1/95.5
Education: Female third-level students (% of total)	2006-2012	56.0
Intentional homicides (females and males, per 100 000)	2008-2010	1.4/<
Seats held by women in national parliaments (%)	2014	14.3

Environmental indicators		
Threatened species	2013	30
Forested area (% of land area)	2011	0.9
CO$_2$ emission estimates (000 metric tons and metric tons per capita)	2010	2 587/6.2
Energy consumption per capita (kilograms oil equivalent)	2010	2 031.0
Precipitation in the capital city, total mean (millimetres)[o]		553[p]
Temperature in the capital city, mean °C (minimum and maximum)[o]		14.9/22.3[p]

a Beginning 1 January 2008, the Maltese Liri (MTL) was replaced by the euro (1 EUR=0.42924 MTL). b Official rate. c Maltese Liri (MTL). d Market rate. e Euro. f Series linked to former series. g Age group 15 to 74 years. h European Labour Force Survey (Eurostat). i The indices are shown in terms of ISIC Rev.3. j Age group 16 to 74 years. k See technical notes. l Age group 20 to 45 years. m 1993. n Refugee population refers to the end of 2012. o Luqa. p Based on monthly averages for the period 1961-1990.

Marshall Islands

Region	Oceania-Micronesia
Currency	U.S. Dollar (USD)
Surface area (square kilometres)	181
Population in 2012 (estimated, 000)	53
Population density in 2012 (per square kilometre)	290.4
Capital city and population in 2011 (000)	Majuro (31)
United Nations membership date	17 September 1991

Economic indicators	2005	2010	2012
GDP: Gross domestic product (million current US$)	139	177	198
GDP: Growth rate at constant 2005 prices (annual %)	2.0	5.6	1.9
GDP per capita (current US$)	2 676.7	3 384.4	3 773.0
GNI: Gross national income per capita (current US$)	3 468.9	4 102.0	4 747.5
Gross fixed capital formation (% of GDP)	56.8	56.8	56.8
CPI: Consumer price index (2000=100)[a]	107	135[b]	...
Agricultural production index (2004-2006=100)	97	175	185
Food production index (2004-2006=100)	97	175	185
Tourist arrivals at national borders (000)	9[c]	5[d]	5[d]
Mobile-cellular subscriptions (per 100 inhabitants)	1.3	...	...
Individuals using the Internet (%)	3.9	7.0[e]	10.0[e]

Social indicators		
Population growth rate (average annual %)	2010-2015	0.2
Urban population growth rate (average annual %)	2010-2015	2.0
Rural population growth rate (average annual %)	2010-2015	0.5
Urban population (%)	2013	72.5
Population aged 0-14 years (%)[fg]	2013	40.2
Population aged 60+ years (females and males, % of total)[fg]	2013	5.0/4.7
Sex ratio (males per 100 females)[fg]	2013	105.3
Life expectancy at birth (females and males, years)[f]	2010-2015	72.6/67.3[h]
Infant mortality rate (per 1 000 live births)[f]	2010-2015	26.3[h]
Fertility rate, total (live births per woman)[f]	2010-2015	4.1[h]
Contraceptive prevalence (ages 15-49, %)	2006-2012	44.6
International migrant stock (000 and % of total population)	mid-2013	1.7/3.2
Education: Government expenditure (% of GDP)	2006-2012	12.2[i]
Education: Primary-secondary gross enrolment ratio (f/m per 100)	2006-2012	106.5/105.1
Education: Female third-level students (% of total)	2006-2012	48.9
Seats held by women in national parliaments (%)	2014	3.0

Environmental indicators		
Threatened species	2013	94
Forested area (% of land area)	2011	70.2
CO$_2$ emission estimates (000 metric tons and metric tons per capita)	2010	103/1.9
Energy consumption per capita (kilograms oil equivalent)	2010	636.0[j]

a Majuro. b 2008. c Air and sea arrivals. d Air arrivals. e ITU estimate. f Data compiled by the Secretariat of the Pacific Community Demography Programme. g De facto estimate. h 2011. i 2003. j UNSD estimate.

Martinique

Region	Caribbean
Currency	Euro (EUR)
Surface area (square kilometres)	1 128
Population in 2012 (estimated, 000)	403
Population density in 2012 (per square kilometre)	357.0
Capital city and population in 2011 (000)	Fort-de-France (87)

Economic indicators	2005	2010	2012
Exchange rates (national currency per US$)[a]	0.85	0.75	0.76
CPI: Consumer price index (2000=100)	111	121	126
Agricultural production index (2004-2006=100)	99	81	102
Food production index (2004-2006=100)	99	81	102
Employment in industrial sector (% of employed)[bc]	...	11.9	11.8
Employment in agricultural sector (% of employed)[bc]	...	4.1	3.9
Labour force participation, adult female pop. (%)	46.2	48.9	50.0
Labour force participation, adult male pop. (%)	53.1	55.5	55.8
Tourist arrivals at national borders (000)	484	478	488
Energy production, primary (000 mt oil equivalent)	3	4[d]	...

Social indicators		
Population growth rate (average annual %)	2010-2015	0.2
Urban population growth rate (average annual %)	2010-2015	0.3
Rural population growth rate (average annual %)	2010-2015	0.4
Urban population (%)	2013	89.0
Population aged 0-14 years (%)	2013	18.4
Population aged 60+ years (females and males, % of total)	2013	23.1/20.9
Sex ratio (males per 100 females)	2013	85.2
Life expectancy at birth (females and males, years)	2010-2015	84.4/77.9
Infant mortality rate (per 1 000 live births)	2010-2015	6.2
Fertility rate, total (live births per woman)	2010-2015	1.8
Contraceptive prevalence (ages 15-49, %)	2006-2012	35.5[e]
International migrant stock (000 and % of total population)	mid-2013	60.7/15.0

Environmental indicators		
Threatened species	2013	37
Forested area (% of land area)	2011	45.8
CO_2 emission estimates (000 metric tons and metric tons per capita)	2010	2 279/5.6
Energy consumption per capita (kilograms oil equivalent)	2010	1 795.0[d]
Precipitation in the capital city, total mean (millimetres)[f]		2 030[g]
Temperature in the capital city, mean °C (minimum and maximum)[f]		22.8/29.7[g]

a Market rate. b March to June. c Excludes the institutional population. d UNSD estimate. e 1976. f Le Lamentin. g Based on WMO Climatological Normals (CLINO) for the period 1961-1990.

Mauritania

Region	Western Africa
Currency	Ouguiya (MRO)
Surface area (square kilometres)	1 030 700
Population in 2012 (estimated, 000)	3 796
Population density in 2012 (per square kilometre)	3.7
Capital city and population in 2011 (000)	Nouakchott (786)
United Nations membership date	27 October 1961

Economic indicators	2005	2010	2012
GDP: Gross domestic product (million current US$)	2 184	3 156	3 866
GDP: Growth rate at constant 2005 prices (annual %)	9.0	5.6	4.6
GDP per capita (current US$)	694.3	874.3	1 018.3
GNI: Gross national income per capita (current US$)	714.9	857.7	956.0
Gross fixed capital formation (% of GDP)	59.0	42.9	27.3
Exchange rates (national currency per US$)[a]	270.61	282.00	303.04
CPI: Consumer price index (2000=100)	139	185	205
Agricultural production index (2004-2006=100)	100	113	120
Food production index (2004-2006=100)	100	113	120
Labour force participation, adult female pop. (%)	25.9	28.3	28.6
Labour force participation, adult male pop. (%)	78.5	78.9	79.0
Energy production, primary (000 mt oil equivalent)	0	415	...
Mobile-cellular subscriptions (per 100 inhabitants)	24.5	80.2	111.1
Individuals using the Internet (%)	0.7	4.0[b]	5.4[b]

Total trade		Major trading partners			2012
	(million US$)		(% of exports)		(% of imports)
Exports	2 623.8	China	44.1	United Arab Emirates	23.5
Imports	2 970.6	Switzerland	10.7	Belgium	15.6
Balance	−346.8	Japan	8.9	France	11.2

Social indicators		
Population growth rate (average annual %)	2010-2015	2.5
Urban population growth rate (average annual %)	2010-2015	2.9
Rural population growth rate (average annual %)	2010-2015	1.8
Urban population (%)	2013	42.0
Population aged 0-14 years (%)	2013	40.1
Population aged 60+ years (females and males, % of total)	2013	5.6/4.4
Sex ratio (males per 100 females)	2013	101.4
Life expectancy at birth (females and males, years)	2010-2015	63.0/59.9
Infant mortality rate (per 1 000 live births)	2010-2015	71.7
Fertility rate, total (live births per woman)	2010-2015	4.7
Contraceptive prevalence (ages 15-49, %)	2006-2012	9.3
International migrant stock (000 and % of total population)[cd]	mid-2013	90.2/2.3
Refugees and others of concern to UNHCR	mid-2013	103 073
Education: Government expenditure (% of GDP)	2006-2012	3.7
Education: Primary-secondary gross enrolment ratio (f/m per 100)[e]	2006-2012	62.1/61.7
Education: Female third-level students (% of total)	2006-2012	29.3
Intentional homicides (females and males, per 100 000)[f]	2008-2010	11.4/18.0
Seats held by women in national parliaments (%)	2014	25.2

Environmental indicators		
Threatened species	2013	66
Forested area (% of land area)	2011	<
CO$_2$ emission estimates (000 metric tons and metric tons per capita)	2010	2 213/0.6
Energy consumption per capita (kilograms oil equivalent)	2010	196.0[g]

a Market rate. b ITU estimate. c Data refer to foreign citizens. d Includes refugees. e UNESCO estimate. f Estimates. g UNSD estimate.

Mauritius

Region	Eastern Africa	
Currency	Mauritius Rupee (MUR)	
Surface area (square kilometres)	1 969[a]	
Population in 2012 (estimated, 000)	1 240[b]	
Population density in 2012 (per square kilometre)	629.5	
Capital city and population in 2011 (000)	Port Louis (151)	
United Nations membership date	24 April 1968	

Economic indicators

	2005	2010	2012
GDP: Gross domestic product (million current US$)	6 489	9 718	11 452
GDP: Growth rate at constant 2005 prices (annual %)	1.8	4.1	3.2
GDP per capita (current US$)	5 350.4	7 896.9	9 238.4
GNI: Gross national income per capita (current US$)	5 310.8	7 991.9	9 336.9
Gross fixed capital formation (% of GDP)	21.5	24.9	22.8
Exchange rates (national currency per US$)[c]	30.67	30.39	30.52
Balance of payments, current account (million US$)	−324	−1 006	−1 175
CPI: Consumer price index (2000=100)	128	176	194
Industrial production index (2005=100)[d]	100	112	117[e]
Agricultural production index (2004-2006=100)	98	99	96
Food production index (2004-2006=100)	98	99	96
Unemployment (% of labour force)[fg]	9.5	7.7	8.0
Employment in industrial sector (% of employed)	32.4[d]	28.2[dfh]	27.6[fhi]
Employment in agricultural sector (% of employed)	10.0[d]	8.7[dfh]	7.8[fhi]
Labour force participation, adult female pop. (%)	41.1	43.3	43.5
Labour force participation, adult male pop. (%)	76.8	74.6	74.3
Tourist arrivals at national borders (000)	761	935	965
Energy production, primary (000 mt oil equivalent)	10	9	...
Mobile-cellular subscriptions (per 100 inhabitants)	52.3	91.7	113.1
Individuals using the Internet (%)	15.2[j]	28.3[k]	41.4[j]

Total trade

	(million US$)	Major trading partners	(% of exports)		2012 (% of imports)
Exports	2 257.7	United Kingdom	18.8	India	22.6
Imports	5 772.0	France	16.0	China	16.1
Balance	−3 514.3	United States	10.1	France	8.3

Social indicators

Population growth rate (average annual %)[b]	2010-2015	0.4
Urban population growth rate (average annual %)[b]	2010-2015	0.6
Rural population growth rate (average annual %)[b]	2010-2015	0.5
Urban population (%)[b]	2013	41.8
Population aged 0-14 years (%)[b]	2013	19.7
Population aged 60+ years (females and males, % of total)[b]	2013	15.1/12.2
Sex ratio (males per 100 females)[b]	2013	97.4
Life expectancy at birth (females and males, years)[b]	2010-2015	77.0/70.2
Infant mortality rate (per 1 000 live births)[b]	2010-2015	11.5
Fertility rate, total (live births per woman)[b]	2010-2015	1.5
Contraceptive prevalence (ages 15-49, %)	2006-2012	75.8[l]
International migrant stock (000 and % of total population)[b]	mid-2013	45.0/3.6
Refugees and others of concern to UNHCR	mid-2013	0[m]
Education: Government expenditure (% of GDP)	2006-2012	3.5
Education: Primary-secondary gross enrolment ratio (f/m per 100)	2006-2012	102.1/100.5
Education: Female third-level students (% of total)	2006-2012	56.6
Intentional homicides (females and males, per 100 000)	2008-2010	4.8/9.7
Seats held by women in national parliaments (%)	2014	18.8

Environmental indicators

Threatened species	2013	237
Forested area (% of land area)	2011	17.3
CO_2 emission estimates (000 metric tons and metric tons per capita)	2010	4 115/3.2
Energy consumption per capita (kilograms oil equivalent)	2010	967.0
Precipitation in the capital city, total mean (millimetres)		711[n]
Temperature in the capital city, mean °C (minimum and maximum)		21.6/29.4[n]

a Excludes the islands of Saint Brandon and Agalega. b Includes Agalega, Rodrigues and Saint Brandon. c Market rate. d The indices are shown in terms of ISIC Rev.3. e 2011. f Age group 16 years and over. g 2007: Break in series; data not strictly comparable. h Average of quarterly estimates. i Break in series; data not strictly comparable. j ITU estimate. k Age group 5 years and over. l 2002. m Value is zero, not available or not applicable. n Based on monthly averages for the period 1971-2000.

Mexico

Region	Central America
Currency	Mexican Peso (MXN)
Surface area (square kilometres)	1 964 375
Population in 2012 (estimated, 000)	120 847
Population density in 2012 (per square kilometre)	61.5
Capital city and population in 2011 (000)	Mexico City (20 446)
United Nations membership date	7 November 1945

Economic indicators	2005	2010	2012
GDP: Gross domestic product (million current US$)	866 346	1 051 128	1 183 655
GDP: Growth rate at constant 2005 prices (annual %)	3.0	5.1	3.9
GDP per capita (current US$)	7 823.8	8 916.5	9 794.6
GNI: Gross national income per capita (current US$)	7 678.0	8 814.2	9 651.7
Gross fixed capital formation (% of GDP)	21.3	21.1	22.5
Exchange rates (national currency per US$)[a]	10.78	12.36	13.01
Balance of payments, current account (million US$)	−8 614	−3 285	−14 642
CPI: Consumer price index (2000=100)	127	158	170
Industrial production index (2005=100)	100	101	107
Agricultural production index (2004-2006=100)	98	108	114
Food production index (2004-2006=100)	98	108	114
Unemployment (% of labour force)[b]	3.9[c]	...	...
Employment in industrial sector (% of employed)[d]	25.5[be]	25.5[b]	24.1[efg]
Employment in agricultural sector (% of employed)[d]	14.9[be]	13.1[b]	13.4[efg]
Labour force participation, adult female pop. (%)	41.1	43.8	45.0
Labour force participation, adult male pop. (%)	80.8	80.5	80.0
Tourist arrivals at national borders (000)[h]	21 915	23 290	23 403
Energy production, primary (000 mt oil equivalent)	233 572	202 374	...
Mobile-cellular subscriptions (per 100 inhabitants)	44.3	80.6	86.8[i]
Individuals using the Internet (%)[j]	17.2[k]	31.1	38.4

Total trade		Major trading partners			2012
	(million US$)	(% of exports)		(% of imports)	
Exports	370 642.6	United States	77.8	United States	50.1
Imports	370 751.4	Canada	2.9	China	15.4
Balance	−108.8	Spain	1.9	Japan	4.8

Social indicators		
Population growth rate (average annual %)	2010-2015	1.2
Urban population growth rate (average annual %)	2010-2015	1.5
Rural population growth rate (average annual %)	2010-2015	−0.2
Urban population (%)	2013	78.7
Population aged 0-14 years (%)	2013	28.5
Population aged 60+ years (females and males, % of total)	2013	10.2/8.7
Sex ratio (males per 100 females)	2013	94.0
Life expectancy at birth (females and males, years)	2010-2015	79.7/74.9
Infant mortality rate (per 1 000 live births)	2010-2015	14.2
Fertility rate, total (live births per woman)	2010-2015	2.2
Contraceptive prevalence (ages 15-49, %)	2006-2012	70.9
International migrant stock (000 and % of total population)[l]	mid-2013	1 103.5/0.9
Refugees and others of concern to UNHCR	mid-2013	2 584
Education: Government expenditure (% of GDP)	2006-2012	5.3
Education: Primary-secondary gross enrolment ratio (f/m per 100)	2006-2012	95.8/92.7
Education: Female third-level students (% of total)	2006-2012	49.8
Intentional homicides (females and males, per 100 000)	2008-2010	2.5/23.1
Seats held by women in national parliaments (%)	2014	37.4

Environmental indicators		
Threatened species	2013	1 074
Forested area (% of land area)	2011	33.3
CO_2 emission estimates (000 metric tons and metric tons per capita)	2010	443 311.3/3.9
Energy consumption per capita (kilograms oil equivalent)	2010	1 442.0
Precipitation in the capital city, total mean (millimetres)		816[m]
Temperature in the capital city, mean °C (minimum and maximum)		9.6/23.4[m]

a Principal rate. b Age group 14 years and over. c 2004. d The indices are shown in terms of ISIC Rev.2.
e Second quarter. f 2011. g Break in series; data not strictly comparable. h Includes nationals residing
abroad. i Preliminary. j Refers to total population. k ITU estimate. l Includes refugees. m Based on monthly
averages for the period 1951-1980.

Micronesia (Federated States of)

Region	Oceania-Micronesia
Currency	U.S. Dollar (USD)
Surface area (square kilometres)	702
Population in 2012 (estimated, 000)	103
Population density in 2012 (per square kilometre)	147.3
Capital city and population in 2011 (000)	Palikir (7)
United Nations membership date	17 September 1991

Economic indicators	2005	2010	2012
GDP: Gross domestic product (million current US$)	250	294	327
GDP: Growth rate at constant 2005 prices (annual %)	2.1	2.5	1.4
GDP per capita (current US$)	2 352.2	2 838.3	3 164.6
GNI: Gross national income per capita (current US$)	2 468.0	2 969.5	3 316.5
Gross fixed capital formation (% of GDP)	31.2	31.4	31.5
Agricultural production index (2004-2006=100)	101	98	99
Food production index (2004-2006=100)	101	98	99
Tourist arrivals at national borders (000)[ab]	19	26[c]	...
Mobile-cellular subscriptions (per 100 inhabitants)	12.9	24.8	24.6[d]
Individuals using the Internet (%)	11.9	20.0[d]	26.0[d]

Social indicators		
Population growth rate (average annual %)	2010-2015	0.2
Urban population growth rate (average annual %)	2010-2015	1.0
Rural population growth rate (average annual %)	2010-2015	0.4
Urban population (%)	2013	22.8
Population aged 0-14 years (%)	2013	35.1
Population aged 60+ years (females and males, % of total)	2013	7.5/6.5
Sex ratio (males per 100 females)	2013	104.8
Life expectancy at birth (females and males, years)	2010-2015	69.9/68.0
Infant mortality rate (per 1 000 live births)	2010-2015	32.7
Fertility rate, total (live births per woman)	2010-2015	3.3
International migrant stock (000 and % of total population)	mid-2013	2.6/2.5
Refugees and others of concern to UNHCR	mid-2013	0[e]
Education: Government expenditure (% of GDP)[f]	2006-2012	6.7[g]
Education: Primary-secondary gross enrolment ratio (f/m per 100)	2006-2012	98.6/96.5[h]
Intentional homicides (females and males, per 100 000)[i]	2008-2010	0.6/1.6
Seats held by women in national parliaments (%)	2014	0.0

Environmental indicators		
Threatened species	2013	163
Forested area (% of land area)	2011	91.7
CO$_2$ emission estimates (000 metric tons and metric tons per capita)	2010	103/0.9
Energy consumption per capita (kilograms oil equivalent)	2010	280.0[j]

a Arrivals in the States of Kosrae, Chuuk, Pohnpei and Yap. b Excludes citizens of the Federated States of Micronesia. c 2008. d ITU estimate. e Value is zero, not available or not applicable. f UNESCO estimate. g 2000. h 2005. i Estimates. j UNSD estimate.

Monaco

Region	Western Europe		
Currency	Euro (EUR)		
Surface area (square kilometres)	2		
Population in 2012 (estimated, 000)	38		
Population density in 2012 (per square kilometre)	18 789.5		
Capital city and population in 2011 (000)	Monaco (35)		
United Nations membership date	28 May 1993		

Economic indicators	2005	2010	2012
GDP: Gross domestic product (million current US$)	4 203	5 362	5 707
GDP: Growth rate at constant 2005 prices (annual %)	1.8	2.1	0.0
GDP per capita (current US$)	124 319.0	145 538.1	151 877.9
GNI: Gross national income per capita (current US$)	124 319.0	145 538.1	151 877.9
Gross fixed capital formation (% of GDP)	19.4	19.5	19.8
Exchange rates (national currency per US$)[a]	0.85	0.75	0.76
Tourist arrivals at national borders (000)[b]	286	279	292
Mobile-cellular subscriptions (per 100 inhabitants)	48.8	66.1	93.7
Individuals using the Internet (%)	55.5	75.0	87.0[c]

Social indicators		
Population growth rate (average annual %)	2010-2015	0.8
Urban population growth rate (average annual %)	2010-2015	<
Rural population growth rate (average annual %)	2010-2015	0.0
Urban population (%)	2013	100.0
Population aged 0-14 years (%)[def]	2013	12.8[g]
Population aged 60+ years (females and males, % of total)[def]	2013	33.3/29.3[g]
Sex ratio (males per 100 females)[def]	2013	94.7[g]
International migrant stock (000 and % of total population)	mid-2013	24.3/64.2
Refugees and others of concern to UNHCR	mid-2013	37[h]
Education: Government expenditure (% of GDP)	2006-2012	1.6
Seats held by women in national parliaments (%)	2014	20.8

Environmental indicators		
Threatened species	2013	14

a Market rate. b Arrivals of non-resident tourists in hotels and similar establishments. c ITU estimate.
d Data compiled by the United Nations Demographic Yearbook system. e Data refer to the latest available census. f Census, de jure, complete tabulation. g 2008. h Refugee population refers to the end of 2012.

Mongolia

Region	Eastern Asia
Currency	Togrog (MNT)
Surface area (square kilometres)	1 564 116
Population in 2012 (estimated, 000)	2 796
Population density in 2012 (per square kilometre)	1.8
Capital city and population in 2011 (000)	Ulaanbaatar (1 184)
United Nations membership date	27 October 1961

Economic indicators	2005	2010	2012
GDP: Gross domestic product (million current US$)	2 523	6 201	10 271
GDP: Growth rate at constant 2005 prices (annual %)	7.3	6.4	12.3
GDP per capita (current US$)	998.8	2 285.7	3 673.0
GNI: Gross national income per capita (current US$)	978.6	2 079.2	3 430.2
Gross fixed capital formation (% of GDP)	28.0	32.5	51.7
Exchange rates (national currency per US$)[a]	1 221.00	1 256.47	1 392.10
Balance of payments, current account (million US$)	84	−886	−3 362
CPI: Consumer price index (2000=100)[b]	110[c]	166	181[d]
Industrial production index (2005=100)[e]	100	114	108
Agricultural production index (2004-2006=100)	97	115	133
Food production index (2004-2006=100)	97	115	135
Employment in industrial sector (% of employed)	16.8[efgh]	16.2	17.3[d]
Employment in agricultural sector (% of employed)	39.9[efgh]	33.0	32.6[d]
Labour force participation, adult female pop. (%)	55.4	55.1	56.1
Labour force participation, adult male pop. (%)	65.2	67.6	68.8
Tourist arrivals at national borders (000)[i]	338	456	476
Energy production, primary (000 mt oil equivalent)	3 226	14 929	...
Mobile-cellular subscriptions (per 100 inhabitants)	21.9	90.3	117.6
Individuals using the Internet (%)	...	10.2[j]	16.4

Social indicators		
Population growth rate (average annual %)	2010-2015	1.5
Urban population growth rate (average annual %)	2010-2015	2.8
Rural population growth rate (average annual %)	2010-2015	−1.4
Urban population (%)	2013	70.4
Population aged 0-14 years (%)	2013	27.3
Population aged 60+ years (females and males, % of total)	2013	6.6/5.2
Sex ratio (males per 100 females)	2013	98.2
Life expectancy at birth (females and males, years)	2010-2015	71.5/63.6
Infant mortality rate (per 1 000 live births)	2010-2015	25.8
Fertility rate, total (live births per woman)	2010-2015	2.4
Contraceptive prevalence (ages 15-49, %)	2006-2012	55.2
International migrant stock (000 and % of total population)[k]	mid-2013	17.2/0.6
Refugees and others of concern to UNHCR	mid-2013	229
Education: Government expenditure (% of GDP)	2006-2012	5.5
Education: Primary-secondary gross enrolment ratio (f/m per 100)	2006-2012	109.6/109.2
Education: Female third-level students (% of total)	2006-2012	58.7
Intentional homicides (females and males, per 100 000)	2008-2010	4.1/11.1
Seats held by women in national parliaments (%)	2014	14.9

Environmental indicators		
Threatened species	2013	36
Forested area (% of land area)	2011	7.0
CO$_2$ emission estimates (000 metric tons and metric tons per capita)	2010	11 501/4.2
Energy consumption per capita (kilograms oil equivalent)	2010	1 138.0
Precipitation in the capital city, total mean (millimetres)		270[l]
Temperature in the capital city, mean °C (minimum and maximum)		−6.4/5.9[l]

a Market rate. **b** Index base 2006=100. **c** 2007. **d** 2011. **e** The indices are shown in terms of ISIC Rev.3. **f** Official estimates. **g** Age group 16 years and over. **h** December. **i** Excludes diplomats and foreign residents in Mongolia. **j** Refers to total population. **k** Data refer to foreign citizens. **l** Based on monthly averages for the period 1971-2001.

Montenegro

Region	Southern Europe
Currency	Euro (EUR)
Surface area (square kilometres)	13 812
Population in 2012 (estimated, 000)	621
Population density in 2012 (per square kilometre)	45.0
Capital city and population in 2011 (000)	Podgorica (156)
United Nations membership date	28 June 2006

Economic indicators	2005	2010	2012
GDP: Gross domestic product (million current US$)	2 257	4 111	4 046
GDP: Growth rate at constant 2005 prices (annual %)	4.2	2.5	−2.6
GDP per capita (current US$)	3 665.2	6 629.5	6 514.2
GNI: Gross national income per capita (current US$)	3 700.6	6 583.1	6 741.6
Gross fixed capital formation (% of GDP)	18.0	21.1	18.5
Exchange rates (national currency per US$) [a]	0.85	0.75	0.76
Balance of payments, current account (million US$)	−1 464[b]	−952	−769
CPI: Consumer price index (2000=100) [c]	100	122	...
Industrial production index (2005=100) [d]	100	79	66
Agricultural production index (2004-2006=100)	100[e]	91	90
Food production index (2004-2006=100)	100[e]	91	90
Unemployment (% of labour force)	17.2[f]	19.7	20.3
Employment in industrial sector (% of employed)	19.2[dghi]	20.0[d]	18.1
Employment in agricultural sector (% of employed)	8.6[dghi]	6.2[d]	5.7
Labour force participation, adult female pop. (%) [j]	45.7	43.9	44.3
Labour force participation, adult male pop. (%) [j]	64.2	60.4	60.8
Tourist arrivals at national borders (000) [k]	272	1 088	1 264
Energy production, primary (000 mt oil equivalent)	447	663	...
Mobile-cellular subscriptions (per 100 inhabitants)	86.7	185.3[l]	177.9[l]
Individuals using the Internet (%)	27.1[l]	37.5[l]	56.8[m]

Total trade		Major trading partners			2012
	(million US$)	(% of exports)			(% of imports)
Exports	468.8	Croatia	22.9	Serbia	29.3
Imports	2 336.4	Serbia	22.8	Greece	8.7
Balance	−1 867.6	Slovenia	7.9	China	7.2

Social indicators		
Population growth rate (average annual %)	2010-2015	0.1
Urban population growth rate (average annual %)	2010-2015	0.4
Rural population growth rate (average annual %)	2010-2015	−0.5
Urban population (%)	2013	63.7
Population aged 0-14 years (%)	2013	18.7
Population aged 60+ years (females and males, % of total)	2013	21.1/16.9
Sex ratio (males per 100 females)	2013	97.7
Life expectancy at birth (females and males, years)	2010-2015	77.1/72.4
Infant mortality rate (per 1 000 live births)	2010-2015	9.6
Fertility rate, total (live births per woman)	2010-2015	1.7
Contraceptive prevalence (ages 15-49, %)	2006-2012	39.4[n]
International migrant stock (000 and % of total population)	mid-2013	50.7/8.2
Refugees and others of concern to UNHCR	mid-2013	19 873
Education: Primary-secondary gross enrolment ratio (f/m per 100)	2006-2012	94.8/94.1
Education: Female third-level students (% of total)	2006-2012	54.3
Intentional homicides (females and males, per 100 000)	2008-2010	1.1/2.6
Seats held by women in national parliaments (%)	2014	14.8

Environmental indicators		
Threatened species	2013	84
Forested area (% of land area)	2011	40.4
CO$_2$ emission estimates (000 metric tons and metric tons per capita)	2010	2 579/4.1
Energy consumption per capita (kilograms oil equivalent)	2010	1 482.0
Precipitation in the capital city, total mean (millimetres)		1 661[o]
Temperature in the capital city, mean °C (minimum and maximum)		10.7/20.5[o]

a Market rate. b 2007. c Index base 2005=100. d The indices are shown in terms of ISIC Rev.3. e 2006. f 2008. g Age group 15 to 64 years. h October. i Break in series; data not strictly comparable. j Refers to Serbia and Montenegro. k Arrivals of non-resident tourists in all types of accommodation establishments. l ITU estimate. m Age group 16 to 74 years. n 2005-2006. o Based on monthly averages for the period 1961-1990.

Morocco

Region	Northern Africa
Currency	Morocco Dirham (MAD)
Surface area (square kilometres)	446 550
Population in 2012 (estimated, 000)	32 521
Population density in 2012 (per square kilometre)	72.8
Capital city and population in 2011 (000)	Rabat (1 843)
United Nations membership date	12 November 1956

Economic indicators	2005	2010	2012
GDP: Gross domestic product (million current US$)	59 524	90 771	95 992
GDP: Growth rate at constant 2005 prices (annual %)	3.0	3.6	2.7
GDP per capita (current US$)	1 975.9	2 868.6	2 951.7
GNI: Gross national income per capita (current US$)	1 950.5	2 790.7	2 850.9
Gross fixed capital formation (% of GDP)	27.5	30.7	31.4
Exchange rates (national currency per US$)[a]	9.25	8.36	8.43
Balance of payments, current account (million US$)	1 041	−3 925	−9 571
CPI: Consumer price index (2000=100)	107	108[bc]	111[c]
Agricultural production index (2004-2006=100)	93	126	124
Food production index (2004-2006=100)	93	127	124
Unemployment (% of labour force)	11.2	9.0	...
Employment in industrial sector (% of employed)[d]	19.5	22.1	21.4
Employment in agricultural sector (% of employed)[d]	45.4	40.2	39.2
Labour force participation, adult female pop. (%)	42.9	43.0	43.0
Labour force participation, adult male pop. (%)	59.7	58.9	57.4
Tourist arrivals at national borders (000)[e]	5 843	9 288	9 375
Energy production, primary (000 mt oil equivalent)	189	429	...
Mobile-cellular subscriptions (per 100 inhabitants)	40.8	100.1	119.7
Individuals using the Internet (%)	15.1[f]	52.0[g]	55.0[g]

Total trade		Major trading partners			2012
	(million US$)	(% of exports)			(% of imports)
Exports	21 417.2	France	21.6	Spain	13.2
Imports	44 789.8	Spain	16.5	France	12.4
Balance	−23 372.6	Brazil	5.9	China	6.6

Social indicators		
Population growth rate (average annual %)	2010-2015	1.4
Urban population growth rate (average annual %)	2010-2015	1.6
Rural population growth rate (average annual %)	2010-2015	0.1
Urban population (%)	2013	57.8
Population aged 0-14 years (%)	2013	27.9
Population aged 60+ years (females and males, % of total)	2013	8.6/7.1
Sex ratio (males per 100 females)	2013	97.5
Life expectancy at birth (females and males, years)	2010-2015	72.6/69.0
Infant mortality rate (per 1 000 live births)	2010-2015	26.3
Fertility rate, total (live births per woman)	2010-2015	2.8
Contraceptive prevalence (ages 15-49, %)	2006-2012	63.0[h]
International migrant stock (000 and % of total population)[i]	mid-2013	50.8/0.2
Refugees and others of concern to UNHCR	mid-2013	4 580
Education: Government expenditure (% of GDP)	2006-2012	5.4
Education: Primary-secondary gross enrolment ratio (f/m per 100)	2006-2012	87.4/95.7
Education: Female third-level students (% of total)	2006-2012	47.2
Intentional homicides (females and males, per 100 000)[j]	2008-2010	</1.4
Seats held by women in national parliaments (%)	2014	17.0

Environmental indicators		
Threatened species	2013	163
Forested area (% of land area)	2011	11.5
CO_2 emission estimates (000 metric tons and metric tons per capita)	2010	50 567/1.6
Energy consumption per capita (kilograms oil equivalent)	2010	464.0
Precipitation in the capital city, total mean (millimetres)[k]		300
Temperature in the capital city, mean °C (minimum and maximum)[k]		14.6/22.0

a Official rate. **b** Series replacing former series. **c** Index base 2006=100. **d** The indices are shown in terms of ISIC Rev.3. **e** Includes nationals residing abroad. **f** Age group 12 to 65 years using the Internet at least once during the last month. **g** Age group 6 to 74 years living within electrified areas. **h** 2003-2004. **i** Data refer to foreign citizens. **j** Estimates. **k** Casablanca.

Mozambique

Region	Eastern Africa
Currency	Metical (MZN)
Surface area (square kilometres)	801 590
Population in 2012 (estimated, 000)	25 203
Population density in 2012 (per square kilometre)	31.4
Capital city and population in 2011 (000)	Maputo (1 150)
United Nations membership date	16 September 1975

Economic indicators	2005	2010	2012
GDP: Gross domestic product (million current US$)	6 579	9 274	14 605
GDP: Growth rate at constant 2005 prices (annual %)	8.4	7.1	7.5
GDP per capita (current US$)	313.1	387.0	579.5
GNI: Gross national income per capita (current US$)	296.6	384.4	557.6
Gross fixed capital formation (% of GDP)	18.7	16.5	17.5
Exchange rates (national currency per US$)[a]	24.18	32.58	29.75
Balance of payments, current account (million US$)	−761	−1 450	−6 297
CPI: Consumer price index (2000=100)	173	287	319[bc]
Agricultural production index (2004-2006=100)	96	148	159
Food production index (2004-2006=100)	95	153	162
Labour force participation, adult female pop. (%)	27.9	25.9	26.3
Labour force participation, adult male pop. (%)	78.2	75.7	75.8
Tourist arrivals at national borders (000)[d]	578	1 718	2 113
Energy production, primary (000 mt oil equivalent)	3 245	4 471	...
Mobile-cellular subscriptions (per 100 inhabitants)	7.2	30.9	33.1[e]
Individuals using the Internet (%)	0.9[f]	4.2	4.9[f]

Total trade		Major trading partners			2012
(million US$)		(% of exports)		(% of imports)	
Exports	3 469.9	Netherlands	26.6	South Africa	31.4
Imports	6 177.2	South Africa	19.2	Netherlands	9.3
Balance	−2 707.3	China	18.4	United Arab Emirates	7.4

Social indicators		
Population growth rate (average annual %)	2010-2015	2.5
Urban population growth rate (average annual %)	2010-2015	3.1
Rural population growth rate (average annual %)	2010-2015	1.9
Urban population (%)	2013	31.7
Population aged 0-14 years (%)	2013	45.4
Population aged 60+ years (females and males, % of total)	2013	5.6/4.5
Sex ratio (males per 100 females)	2013	95.7
Life expectancy at birth (females and males, years)	2010-2015	51.1/49.2
Infant mortality rate (per 1 000 live births)	2010-2015	74.3
Fertility rate, total (live births per woman)	2010-2015	5.2
Contraceptive prevalence (ages 15-49, %)	2006-2012	11.6
International migrant stock (000 and % of total population)[gh]	mid-2013	218.8/0.9
Refugees and others of concern to UNHCR	mid-2013	13 172
Education: Government expenditure (% of GDP)	2006-2012	5.0
Education: Primary-secondary gross enrolment ratio (f/m per 100)	2006-2012	73.0/80.9
Education: Female third-level students (% of total)	2006-2012	38.7
Intentional homicides (females and males, per 100 000)[i]	2008-2010	8.4/53.7
Seats held by women in national parliaments (%)	2014	39.2

Environmental indicators		
Threatened species	2013	230
Forested area (% of land area)	2011	49.4
CO_2 emission estimates (000 metric tons and metric tons per capita)	2010	2 880/0.1
Energy consumption per capita (kilograms oil equivalent)	2010	80.0
Precipitation in the capital city, total mean (millimetres)		814[j]
Temperature in the capital city, mean °C (minimum and maximum)		18.6/27.2[j]

a Principal rate. **b** 2011. **c** Series linked to former series. **d** 2008: Methodology revised; data not strictly comparable. **e** Incomplete coverage. **f** ITU estimate. **g** Data refer to foreign citizens. **h** Includes refugees. **i** Estimates. **j** Based on monthly averages for the period 1961-1990.

Myanmar

Region	South-Eastern Asia
Currency	Kyat (MMK)
Surface area (square kilometres)	676 578
Population in 2012 (estimated, 000)	52 797
Population density in 2012 (per square kilometre)	78.0
Capital city and population in 2011 (000)	Nay Pyi Taw (1 060)
United Nations membership date	19 April 1948

Economic indicators	2005	2010	2012
GDP: Gross domestic product (million current US$)	11 931	41 518	59 444
GDP: Growth rate at constant 2005 prices (annual %)	13.6	10.2	6.3
GDP per capita (current US$)	237.8	799.5	1 125.9
GNI: Gross national income per capita (current US$)	237.8	799.5	1 125.9
Gross fixed capital formation (% of GDP)	12.7	22.9	34.8
Exchange rates (national currency per US$)[a]	1 061.00	851.00	854.50
Balance of payments, current account (million US$)	582	1 574	−1 424[b]
CPI: Consumer price index (2000=100)	297	156[c]	164[bc]
Agricultural production index (2004-2006=100)	99	135	140
Food production index (2004-2006=100)	99	135	139
Labour force participation, adult female pop. (%)	87.4	86.2	85.7
Labour force participation, adult male pop. (%)	83.3	83.0	82.9
Tourist arrivals at national borders (000)[d]	232	311	593
Energy production, primary (000 mt oil equivalent)	13 075	13 536	...
Mobile-cellular subscriptions (per 100 inhabitants)	0.3	1.2[e]	11.2[e]
Individuals using the Internet (%)	0.1	0.3	1.1[e]

Total trade		Major trading partners			2012
	(million US$)[f]	(% of exports)[f]			(% of imports)[f]
Exports	7 625.2	Thailand	41.7	China	27.1
Imports	4 164.3	China, Hong Kong SAR	21.1	Singapore	27.0
Balance	3 460.9	India	12.6	Thailand	11.4

Social indicators		
Population growth rate (average annual %)	2010-2015	0.8
Urban population growth rate (average annual %)	2010-2015	2.5
Rural population growth rate (average annual %)	2010-2015	−0.1
Urban population (%)	2013	33.8
Population aged 0-14 years (%)	2013	24.9
Population aged 60+ years (females and males, % of total)	2013	9.2/7.6
Sex ratio (males per 100 females)	2013	94.3
Life expectancy at birth (females and males, years)	2010-2015	67.1/63.0
Infant mortality rate (per 1 000 live births)	2010-2015	48.9
Fertility rate, total (live births per woman)	2010-2015	2.0
Contraceptive prevalence (ages 15-49, %)	2006-2012	46.0
International migrant stock (000 and % of total population)[g]	mid-2013	103.1/0.2
Refugees and others of concern to UNHCR	mid-2013	1 440 075
Education: Government expenditure (% of GDP)	2006-2012	0.8
Education: Primary-secondary gross enrolment ratio (f/m per 100)	2006-2012	78.8/78.0
Education: Female third-level students (% of total)	2006-2012	57.5
Intentional homicides (females and males, per 100 000)[h]	2008-2010	3.1/17.4
Seats held by women in national parliaments (%)	2014	5.6

Environmental indicators		
Threatened species	2013	282
Forested area (% of land area)	2011	48.2
CO$_2$ emission estimates (000 metric tons and metric tons per capita)	2010	8 988/0.2
Energy consumption per capita (kilograms oil equivalent)	2010	84.0
Precipitation in the capital city, total mean (millimetres)[i]		2 681[j]
Temperature in the capital city, mean °C (minimum and maximum)[i]		22.6/32.3[j]

a UN operational exchange rate. b 2011. c Index base 2006=100. d Includes tourist arrivals through border entry points to Yangon. e ITU estimate. f 2010. g Data refer to foreign citizens. h Estimates. i Yangon. j Based on monthly averages for the period 1961-1990.

Namibia

Region	Southern Africa
Currency	Namibia Dollar (NAD)
Surface area (square kilometres)	824 268
Population in 2012 (estimated, 000)	2 259
Population density in 2012 (per square kilometre)	2.7
Capital city and population in 2011 (000)	Windhoek (380)
United Nations membership date	23 April 1990

Economic indicators	2005	2010	2012
GDP: Gross domestic product (million current US$)	7 261	11 033	12 807
GDP: Growth rate at constant 2005 prices (annual %)	2.5	6.0	5.0
GDP per capita (current US$)	3 582.3	5 063.4	5 668.4
GNI: Gross national income per capita (current US$)	3 526.8	4 910.4	5 655.7
Gross fixed capital formation (% of GDP)	18.6	22.8	21.1
Exchange rates (national currency per US$)[a]	6.32	6.63	8.50
Balance of payments, current account (million US$)	333	105	−148[b]
CPI: Consumer price index (2000=100)[c]	114	160	179
Agricultural production index (2004-2006=100)	104	90	91
Food production index (2004-2006=100)	104	91	92
Employment in industrial sector (% of employed)	14.8[def]	17.7[eghi]	13.8[lj]
Employment in agricultural sector (% of employed)	29.9[def]	16.3[eghi]	27.4[lj]
Labour force participation, adult female pop. (%)	74.5	75.1	75.2
Labour force participation, adult male pop. (%)	81.2	82.1	82.2
Tourist arrivals at national borders (000)	778	984	1 027[b]
Energy production, primary (000 mt oil equivalent)	133	109	...
Mobile-cellular subscriptions (per 100 inhabitants)	21.6	85.5	103.0
Individuals using the Internet (%)	4.0[k]	11.6	12.9[k]

Total trade		Major trading partners			2012
	(million US$)	(% of exports)		(% of imports)	
Exports	5 377.0	South Africa	17.4	South Africa	69.7
Imports	7 132.0	United Kingdom	11.7	Switzerland	6.0
Balance	−1 755.0	Angola	9.3	China	4.0

Social indicators		
Population growth rate (average annual %)	2010-2015	1.9
Urban population growth rate (average annual %)	2010-2015	3.1
Rural population growth rate (average annual %)	2010-2015	0.7
Urban population (%)	2013	39.5
Population aged 0-14 years (%)	2013	36.0
Population aged 60+ years (females and males, % of total)	2013	6.2/4.7
Sex ratio (males per 100 females)	2013	94.4
Life expectancy at birth (females and males, years)	2010-2015	67.0/61.6
Infant mortality rate (per 1 000 live births)	2010-2015	33.5
Fertility rate, total (live births per woman)	2010-2015	3.1
Contraceptive prevalence (ages 15-49, %)	2006-2012	55.1
International migrant stock (000 and % of total population)	mid-2013	51.5/2.2
Refugees and others of concern to UNHCR	mid-2013	2 989
Education: Government expenditure (% of GDP)	2006-2012	8.4
Education: Primary-secondary gross enrolment ratio (f/m per 100)	2006-2012	93.3/90.6
Education: Female third-level students (% of total)	2006-2012	56.8
Intentional homicides (females and males, per 100 000)[l]	2008-2010	7.2/47.9
Seats held by women in national parliaments (%)	2014	25.6

Environmental indicators		
Threatened species	2013	100
Forested area (% of land area)	2011	8.8
CO_2 emission estimates (000 metric tons and metric tons per capita)	2010	3 173/1.4
Energy consumption per capita (kilograms oil equivalent)	2010	583.0
Precipitation in the capital city, total mean (millimetres)		368[m]
Temperature in the capital city, mean °C (minimum and maximum)		13.0/26.6[m]

a Official rate. **b** 2011. **c** Index base 2002=100. **d** 2004. **e** The indices are shown in terms of ISIC Rev.3. **f** Age group 15 to 69 years. **g** 2008. **h** Excludes regular military living in barracks. **i** Break in series; data not strictly comparable. **j** October. **k** ITU estimate. **l** Estimates. **m** Based on monthly averages for the period 1961-1990.

Nauru

Region	Oceania-Micronesia
Currency	Australian Dollar (AUD)
Surface area (square kilometres)	21
Population in 2012 (estimated, 000)	10
Population density in 2012 (per square kilometre)	477.7
Capital city and population in 2011 (000)	Nauru (10)
United Nations membership date	14 September 1999

Economic indicators	2005	2010	2012
GDP: Gross domestic product (million current US$)	26	62	121
GDP: Growth rate at constant 2005 prices (annual %)	−12.1	20.1	20.2
GDP per capita (current US$)	2 599.4	6 233.9	12 021.8
GNI: Gross national income per capita (current US$)	3 030.4	6 492.0	12 577.4
Gross fixed capital formation (% of GDP)	48.2	42.2	43.1
Exchange rates (national currency per US$)[a]	1.37	0.99	0.96
Agricultural production index (2004-2006=100)	101	104	103
Food production index (2004-2006=100)	101	104	103
Mobile-cellular subscriptions (per 100 inhabitants)	...	60.5	65.6
Individuals using the Internet (%)	...	...	54.0[bc]

Social indicators		
Population growth rate (average annual %)	2010-2015	0.2
Urban population growth rate (average annual %)	2010-2015	0.6
Rural population growth rate (average annual %)	2010-2015	0.0
Urban population (%)	2013	100.0
Population aged 0-14 years (%)[de]	2013	38.9
Population aged 60+ years (females and males, % of total)[de]	2013	3.6/3.2
Sex ratio (males per 100 females)[de]	2013	101.9
Life expectancy at birth (females and males, years)[d]	2010-2015	63.2/57.5[f]
Infant mortality rate (per 1 000 live births)[d]	2010-2015	33.0[f]
Fertility rate, total (live births per woman)[d]	2010-2015	4.3[g]
Contraceptive prevalence (ages 15-49, %)	2006-2012	35.6
International migrant stock (000 and % of total population)[h]	mid-2013	2.1/20.6
Refugees and others of concern to UNHCR	mid-2013	534
Education: Primary-secondary gross enrolment ratio (f/m per 100)[i]	2006-2012	82.8/74.0
Seats held by women in national parliaments (%)	2014	5.3

Environmental indicators		
Threatened species	2013	80
CO$_2$ emission estimates (000 metric tons and metric tons per capita)	2010	84/8.4
Energy consumption per capita (kilograms oil equivalent)	2010	2 720.0[j]

a UN operational exchange rate. b 2011. c Age group 15 years and over. d Data compiled by the Secretariat of the Pacific Community Demography Programme. e De facto estimate. f 2007-2011. g 2009-2011. h Data refer to foreign citizens. i National estimate. j UNSD estimate.

Nepal

Region	Southern Asia
Currency	Nepalese Rupee (NPR)
Surface area (square kilometres)	147 181
Population in 2012 (estimated, 000)	27 474
Population density in 2012 (per square kilometre)	186.7
Capital city and population in 2011 (000)	Kathmandu (1 015)
United Nations membership date	14 December 1955

Economic indicators	2005	2010	2012
GDP: Gross domestic product (million current US$)	8 259	16 305	18 029
GDP: Growth rate at constant 2005 prices (annual %)	3.1	4.8	4.9
GDP per capita (current US$)	326.5	607.3	656.2
GNI: Gross national income per capita (current US$)	327.4	612.0	662.5
Gross fixed capital formation (% of GDP)	19.9	22.2	20.0
Exchange rates (national currency per US$)[a]	74.05	71.95	87.77
Balance of payments, current account (million US$)	153	−128	577
CPI: Consumer price index (2000=100)	123	193[b]	230
Agricultural production index (2004-2006=100)	100	114	132
Food production index (2004-2006=100)	100	114	132
Labour force participation, adult female pop. (%)	55.5	56.5	54.3
Labour force participation, adult male pop. (%)	67.7	66.3	63.2
Tourist arrivals at national borders (000)[c]	375	603	803
Energy production, primary (000 mt oil equivalent)	225	287	...
Mobile-cellular subscriptions (per 100 inhabitants)	0.8	30.7	52.8[d]
Individuals using the Internet (%)	0.8	7.9[e]	11.2[d]

Total trade		Major trading partners			2012
	(million US$)[f]	(% of exports)[f]		(% of imports)[f]	
Exports	907.6	India	67.7	India	63.4
Imports	5 915.9	United States	7.7	China	11.7
Balance	−5 008.3	Germany	4.5	United Arab Emirates	5.6

Social indicators		
Population growth rate (average annual %)	2010-2015	1.2
Urban population growth rate (average annual %)	2010-2015	3.6
Rural population growth rate (average annual %)	2010-2015	1.3
Urban population (%)	2013	17.7
Population aged 0-14 years (%)	2013	34.7
Population aged 60+ years (females and males, % of total)	2013	7.8/7.9
Sex ratio (males per 100 females)	2013	93.8
Life expectancy at birth (females and males, years)	2010-2015	69.3/67.1
Infant mortality rate (per 1 000 live births)	2010-2015	35.5
Fertility rate, total (live births per woman)	2010-2015	2.3
Contraceptive prevalence (ages 15-49, %)	2006-2012	49.7
International migrant stock (000 and % of total population)[g]	mid-2013	971.3/3.5
Refugees and others of concern to UNHCR	mid-2013	51 870
Education: Government expenditure (% of GDP)	2006-2012	4.7
Education: Primary-secondary gross enrolment ratio (f/m per 100)	2006-2012	100.2/94.6
Education: Female third-level students (% of total)	2006-2012	41.7
Intentional homicides (females and males, per 100 000)[h]	2008-2010	2.2/14.9
Seats held by women in national parliaments (%)	2014	29.9

Environmental indicators		
Threatened species	2013	95
Forested area (% of land area)	2011	25.4
CO$_2$ emission estimates (000 metric tons and metric tons per capita)	2010	3 752/0.1
Energy consumption per capita (kilograms oil equivalent)	2010	49.0
Precipitation in the capital city, total mean (millimetres)		1 425
Temperature in the capital city, mean °C (minimum and maximum)		11.7/24.8

a Official rate. **b** Series linked to former series. **c** Includes arrivals from India. **d** ITU estimate. **e** December. **f** 2011. **g** Includes refugees. **h** Estimates.

Netherlands

Region	Western Europe
Currency	Euro (EUR)
Surface area (square kilometres)	37 354
Population in 2012 (estimated, 000)	16 714
Population density in 2012 (per square kilometre)	447.5
Capital city and population in 2011 (000)	Amsterdam (1 056)[a]
United Nations membership date	10 December 1945

Economic indicators

	2005	2010	2012
GDP: Gross domestic product (million current US$)	638 471	777 158	770 067
GDP: Growth rate at constant 2005 prices (annual %)	2.0	1.5	−1.3
GDP per capita (current US$)	39 164.6	46 773.8	46 073.1
GNI: Gross national income per capita (current US$)	39 353.6	46 056.2	46 507.8
Gross fixed capital formation (% of GDP)	18.9	17.4	17.0
Exchange rates (national currency per US$)[b]	0.85	0.75	0.76
Balance of payments, current account (million US$)	46 618	57 760	72 733
CPI: Consumer price index (2000=100)	113	122	128
Industrial production index (2005=100)	100	107	106
Agricultural production index (2004-2006=100)	100	111	112
Food production index (2004-2006=100)	100	111	112
Unemployment (% of labour force)[c]	4.7	4.5[d]	5.3
Employment in industrial sector (% of employed)[e]	19.6[f]	15.9[d]	15.3[g]
Employment in agricultural sector (% of employed)[e]	3.2[f]	2.8[d]	2.5[g]
Labour force participation, adult female pop. (%)	80.5	79.9	79.9
Labour force participation, adult male pop. (%)	89.0	87.6	87.3
Tourist arrivals at national borders (000)[h]	10 012	10 883	11 680
Energy production, primary (000 mt oil equivalent)[i]	65 446	72 992	...
Mobile-cellular subscriptions (per 100 inhabitants)	97.1	115.5[j]	117.5[k]
Individuals using the Internet (%)	81.0[l]	90.7[l]	93.0[m]

Total trade

	Major trading partners				2012
	(million US$)	(% of exports)		(% of imports)	
Exports	552 461.8	Germany	24.7	Germany	15.9
Imports	500 605.3	Belgium	11.3	Belgium	9.7
Balance	51 856.5	France	8.4	China	8.2

Social indicators

Population growth rate (average annual %)	2010-2015	0.3
Urban population growth rate (average annual %)	2010-2015	0.7
Rural population growth rate (average annual %)	2010-2015	−2.1
Urban population (%)	2013	84.0
Population aged 0-14 years (%)	2013	17.1
Population aged 60+ years (females and males, % of total)	2013	25.0/21.8
Sex ratio (males per 100 females)	2013	98.3
Life expectancy at birth (females and males, years)	2010-2015	82.8/78.9
Infant mortality rate (per 1 000 live births)	2010-2015	3.6
Fertility rate, total (live births per woman)	2010-2015	1.8
Contraceptive prevalence (ages 15-49, %)[n]	2006-2012	69.0
International migrant stock (000 and % of total population)	mid-2013	1 964.9/11.7
Refugees and others of concern to UNHCR	mid-2013	84 334[op]
Education: Government expenditure (% of GDP)	2006-2012	6.0
Education: Primary-secondary gross enrolment ratio (f/m per 100)	2006-2012	117.4/118.7
Education: Female third-level students (% of total)	2006-2012	51.8
Intentional homicides (females and males, per 100 000)	2008-2010	0.5/1.4
Seats held by women in national parliaments (%)	2014	38.7

Environmental indicators

Threatened species	2013	30
Forested area (% of land area)	2011	10.8
CO$_2$ emission estimates (000 metric tons and metric tons per capita)	2010	181 929/11.0
Energy consumption per capita (kilograms oil equivalent)[i]	2010	3 946.0
Precipitation in the capital city, total mean (millimetres)		780[q]
Temperature in the capital city, mean °C (minimum and maximum)		6.1/13.4[q]

a Amsterdam is the capital and The Hague is the seat of government. b Market rate. c Age group 15 to 74 years. d Break in series; data not strictly comparable. e European Labour Force Survey (Eurostat). f The indices are shown in terms of ISIC Rev.3. g 2011. h Arrivals of non-resident tourists in all types of accommodation establishments. i Excludes Suriname and the Netherlands Antilles. j July. k Third quarter. l Age group 16 to 74 years using the Internet within the last 12 months. m Age group 16 to 74 years. n Age group 18 to 45 years. o Refugee population refers to the end of 2012. p Asylum-seeker population refers to the end of 2011. q Based on monthly averages for the period 1971-2000.

Netherlands Antilles[a]

Region	Caribbean
Currency	Netherlands Antilles Guilder (ANG)
Population in 2012 (estimated, 000)	218
Capital city and population in 2011 (000)	Willemstad (115)

Economic indicators	2005	2010	2012
GDP: Gross domestic product (million current US$)	3 277	3 757	4 009
GDP: Growth rate at constant 2005 prices (annual %)	1.1	−0.3	0.3
GDP per capita (current US$)	18 086.5	18 090.4	18 360.1
GNI: Gross national income per capita (current US$)	18 003.9	17 900.8	18 167.6
Gross fixed capital formation (% of GDP)	29.9	37.4	34.9
Exchange rates (national currency per US$)[b]	1.79	...	...
Balance of payments, current account (million US$)	−106	−340[c]	...
CPI: Consumer price index (2000=100)[d]	110	130	137
Agricultural production index (2004-2006=100)	101	122	...
Food production index (2004-2006=100)	101	122	...
Employment in industrial sector (% of employed)[def]	15.3	17.6[g]	...
Employment in agricultural sector (% of employed)[def]	0.9	1.1[g]	...
Labour force participation, adult female pop. (%)	56.8	58.2	58.7
Labour force participation, adult male pop. (%)	72.5	71.3	70.9
Mobile-cellular subscriptions (per 100 inhabitants)	108.9[h]	...	...

Total trade		Major trading partners			2012
	(million US$)[g]		(% of exports)[gi]		(% of imports)[gi]
Exports	146.2	Netherlands	34.2	United States	39.4
Imports	1 437.0	United States	23.0	Netherlands	23.1
Balance	−1 290.8	Areas nes	12.9	Areas nes	3.9

Social indicators		
Urban population growth rate (average annual %)	2010-2015	0.9
Rural population growth rate (average annual %)	2010-2015	−2.2
Urban population (%)	2013	93.8
International migrant stock (000 and % of total population)	mid-2013	76.5/...
Education: Female third-level students (% of total)	2006-2012	59.7[j]

Environmental indicators		
Threatened species	2013	45
Forested area (% of land area)	2011	1.5[k]
CO$_2$ emission estimates (000 metric tons and metric tons per capita)	2010	4 723/23.5
Energy consumption per capita (kilograms oil equivalent)	2010	7 001.0
Precipitation in the capital city, total mean (millimetres)[d]		552[l]

a The Netherlands Antilles was dissolved on 10 October 2010. Unless otherwise indicated, the data refer to Curaçao, Sint Maarten (Dutch part), Bonaire, Saba and Sint Eustatius. b Official rate. c 2009. d Curaçao. e October. f The indices are shown in terms of ISIC Rev.3. g 2008. h 2004. i See technical notes. j 2002. k 2010. l Based on monthly averages for the period 1961-1990.

New Caledonia

Region	Oceania-Melanesia
Currency	CFP Franc (XPF)
Surface area (square kilometres)	18 575
Population in 2012 (estimated, 000)	253
Population density in 2012 (per square kilometre)	13.6
Capital city and population in 2011 (000)	Nouméa (157)

Economic indicators	2005	2010	2012
GDP: Gross domestic product (million current US$)	6 236	9 006	9 840
GDP: Growth rate at constant 2005 prices (annual %)	3.6	3.7	2.9
GDP per capita (current US$)	27 266.1	36 554.7	38 869.4
GNI: Gross national income per capita (current US$)	27 266.1	36 554.7	38 869.4
Gross fixed capital formation (% of GDP)	28.5	42.8	37.3
Exchange rates (national currency per US$) [a]	100.84	90.81	89.98
Balance of payments, current account (million US$)	−112	−1 426	−1 654 [b]
CPI: Consumer price index (2000=100) [c]	108	119	124
Agricultural production index (2004-2006=100)	100	97	98
Food production index (2004-2006=100)	101	97	98
Employment in industrial sector (% of employed) [def]	21.3	22.4 [g]	...
Employment in agricultural sector (% of employed) [def]	3.1	2.7 [g]	...
Labour force participation, adult female pop. (%)	47.7	45.8	45.7
Labour force participation, adult male pop. (%)	69.9	67.3	67.2
Tourist arrivals at national borders (000) [h]	101	99	112
Energy production, primary (000 mt oil equivalent)	31	27	...
Mobile-cellular subscriptions (per 100 inhabitants)	58.1	88.0	89.3 [i]
Individuals using the Internet (%)	32.4	42.0 [i]	58.0 [i]

Total trade		Major trading partners			2012
	(million US$)		(% of exports)		(% of imports)
Exports	1 292.9	France	18.4	France	22.2
Imports	3 245.0	Japan	15.7	Singapore	18.6
Balance	−1 952.1	Republic of Korea	12.1	Australia	10.9

Social indicators		
Population growth rate (average annual %)	2010-2015	1.3
Urban population growth rate (average annual %)	2010-2015	1.2
Rural population growth rate (average annual %)	2010-2015	1.9
Urban population (%)	2013	61.4
Population aged 0-14 years (%)	2013	22.7
Population aged 60+ years (females and males, % of total)	2013	14.5/13.7
Sex ratio (males per 100 females)	2013	102.4
Life expectancy at birth (females and males, years)	2010-2015	79.3/73.6
Infant mortality rate (per 1 000 live births)	2010-2015	13.1
Fertility rate, total (live births per woman)	2010-2015	2.1
International migrant stock (000 and % of total population)	mid-2013	63.0/24.6

Environmental indicators		
Threatened species	2013	490
Forested area (% of land area)	2011	45.9
CO_2 emission estimates (000 metric tons and metric tons per capita)	2010	3 917/15.6
Energy consumption per capita (kilograms oil equivalent)	2010	4 715.0
Precipitation in the capital city, total mean (millimetres)		1 072 [j]
Temperature in the capital city, mean °C (minimum and maximum)		20.2/26.0 [j]

a UN operational exchange rate. b 2011. c Nouméa. d Population census. e Age group 14 years and over.
f The indices are shown in terms of ISIC Rev.3. g 2008. h Includes nationals residing abroad. i ITU estimate.
j Based on monthly averages for the period 1961-1990.

New Zealand

Region	Oceania
Currency	New Zealand Dollar (NZD)
Surface area (square kilometres)	270 467
Population in 2012 (estimated, 000)	4 460
Population density in 2012 (per square kilometre)	16.5
Capital city and population in 2011 (000)	Wellington (410)
United Nations membership date	24 October 1945

Economic indicators	2005	2010	2012
GDP: Gross domestic product (million current US$)	113 813	143 470	171 256
GDP: Growth rate at constant 2005 prices (annual %)	3.4	0.2	2.9
GDP per capita (current US$)	27 530.1	32 844.8	38 399.4
GNI: Gross national income per capita (current US$)	25 705.0	31 190.4	36 430.3
Gross fixed capital formation (% of GDP)	23.9	18.6	18.8
Exchange rates (national currency per US$)[a]	1.47	1.30	1.22
Balance of payments, current account (million US$)	−8 044	−3 367	−6 963
CPI: Consumer price index (2000=100)	113	130	137
Industrial production index (2005=100)[b]	100	97	100
Agricultural production index (2004-2006=100)	99	104	113
Food production index (2004-2006=100)	99	105	114
Unemployment (% of labour force)	3.8	6.5	6.9
Employment in industrial sector (% of employed)[c]	22.0[de]	20.9[fg]	...
Employment in agricultural sector (% of employed)[c]	7.1[de]	6.6[fg]	...
Labour force participation, adult female pop. (%)	60.3	61.5	62.1
Labour force participation, adult male pop. (%)	74.8	74.2	73.9
Tourist arrivals at national borders (000)	2 353	2 435	2 473
Energy production, primary (000 mt oil equivalent)	10 051	12 846	...
Mobile-cellular subscriptions (per 100 inhabitants)	85.4	107.8[h]	110.3[h]
Individuals using the Internet (%)	62.7[i]	83.0[j]	89.5[i]

Total trade		Major trading partners			2012
	(million US$)	(% of exports)			(% of imports)
Exports	37 304.7	Australia	21.5	China	16.3
Imports	38 242.7	China	14.9	Australia	15.2
Balance	−938.0	United States	9.2	United States	9.3

Social indicators		
Population growth rate (average annual %)	2010-2015	1.0
Urban population growth rate (average annual %)	2010-2015	1.1
Rural population growth rate (average annual %)	2010-2015	0.7
Urban population (%)	2013	86.3
Population aged 0-14 years (%)	2013	20.2
Population aged 60+ years (females and males, % of total)	2013	20.2/18.4
Sex ratio (males per 100 females)	2013	96.5
Life expectancy at birth (females and males, years)	2010-2015	82.9/79.1
Infant mortality rate (per 1 000 live births)	2010-2015	4.3
Fertility rate, total (live births per woman)	2010-2015	2.1
Contraceptive prevalence (ages 15-49, %)[k]	2006-2012	75.0[l]
International migrant stock (000 and % of total population)	mid-2013	1 132.8/25.1
Refugees and others of concern to UNHCR	mid-2013	1 753[m]
Education: Government expenditure (% of GDP)	2006-2012	7.3
Education: Primary-secondary gross enrolment ratio (f/m per 100)	2006-2012	112.7/109.3
Education: Female third-level students (% of total)	2006-2012	57.9
Intentional homicides (females and males, per 100 000)	2008-2010	1.1/1.6
Seats held by women in national parliaments (%)	2014	33.9

Environmental indicators		
Threatened species	2013	181
Forested area (% of land area)	2011	31.4
CO$_2$ emission estimates (000 metric tons and metric tons per capita)	2010	31 525/7.2
Energy consumption per capita (kilograms oil equivalent)	2010	3 221.0
Precipitation in the capital city, total mean (millimetres)		957[n]
Temperature in the capital city, mean °C (minimum and maximum)		10.8/16.7[n]

a Market rate. **b** Average of four quarters ending 31 March of the year stated. **c** Average of quarterly estimates. **d** The indices are shown in terms of ISIC Rev.3. **e** Excludes Chathams, Antarctic Territory and other minor offshore islands. **f** 2009. **g** Break in series; data not strictly comparable. **h** Includes subscriptions active in the last 90 days only. **i** ITU estimate. **j** Population 15 years and over. **k** Age group 20 to 49 years. **l** 1995. **m** Refugee population refers to the end of 2012. **n** Based on monthly averages for the period 1981-2010.

Nicaragua

Region	Central America
Currency	Córdoba (NIO)
Surface area (square kilometres)	130 373
Population in 2012 (estimated, 000)	5 992
Population density in 2012 (per square kilometre)	46.0
Capital city and population in 2011 (000)	Managua (970)
United Nations membership date	24 October 1945

Economic indicators	2005	2010	2012
GDP: Gross domestic product (million current US$)	6 321	8 587	10 508
GDP: Growth rate at constant 2005 prices (annual %)	4.3	3.6	5.2
GDP per capita (current US$)	1 158.8	1 474.8	1 753.7
GNI: Gross national income per capita (current US$)	1 126.9	1 433.2	1 705.1
Gross fixed capital formation (% of GDP)	23.0	20.6	25.5
Exchange rates (national currency per US$)[a]	17.15	21.88	24.13
Balance of payments, current account (million US$)	−784	−857	−1 362
CPI: Consumer price index (2000=100)[b]	147	234[c]	271
Agricultural production index (2004-2006=100)	104	118	133
Food production index (2004-2006=100)	102	119	132
Employment in industrial sector (% of employed)[de]	19.7[f]	16.5	...
Employment in agricultural sector (% of employed)[de]	28.9[f]	32.2	...
Labour force participation, adult female pop. (%)	43.5	46.2	47.0
Labour force participation, adult male pop. (%)	80.5	80.0	80.1
Tourist arrivals at national borders (000)[g]	712	1 011	1 180
Energy production, primary (000 mt oil equivalent)	61	83	...
Mobile-cellular subscriptions (per 100 inhabitants)	20.6	68.5	89.8[h]
Individuals using the Internet (%)	2.6	10.0[h]	13.5[h]

Total trade	Major trading partners			2012
(million US$)	(% of exports)		(% of imports)	
Exports	2 690.0	United States	29.9	United States	18.0
Imports	5 917.1	Venezuela	16.5	Venezuela	13.6
Balance	−3 227.1	Canada	11.8	China	9.5

Social indicators		
Population growth rate (average annual %)	2010-2015	1.4
Urban population growth rate (average annual %)	2010-2015	1.9
Rural population growth rate (average annual %)	2010-2015	0.7
Urban population (%)	2013	58.1
Population aged 0-14 years (%)	2013	32.8
Population aged 60+ years (females and males, % of total)	2013	7.2/6.4
Sex ratio (males per 100 females)	2013	97.8
Life expectancy at birth (females and males, years)	2010-2015	77.7/71.6
Infant mortality rate (per 1 000 live births)	2010-2015	16.6
Fertility rate, total (live births per woman)	2010-2015	2.5
Contraceptive prevalence (ages 15-49, %)	2006-2012	72.4
International migrant stock (000 and % of total population)[i]	mid-2013	41.5/0.7
Refugees and others of concern to UNHCR	mid-2013	175
Education: Government expenditure (% of GDP)	2006-2012	4.6
Education: Primary-secondary gross enrolment ratio (f/m per 100)	2006-2012	95.5/94.0
Education: Female third-level students (% of total)[j]	2006-2012	52.1[k]
Intentional homicides (females and males, per 100 000)	2008-2010	1.8/20.7
Seats held by women in national parliaments (%)	2014	40.2

Environmental indicators		
Threatened species	2013	134
Forested area (% of land area)	2011	25.3
CO$_2$ emission estimates (000 metric tons and metric tons per capita)	2010	4 543/0.8
Energy consumption per capita (kilograms oil equivalent)	2010	254.0
Precipitation in the capital city, total mean (millimetres)[l]		1 989[m]
Temperature in the capital city, mean °C (minimum and maximum)[l]		26.9/26.9[mn]

a Principal rate. b Index base 1999=100. c Series linked to former series. d Age group 10 years and over. e The indices are shown in terms of ISIC Rev.2. f November. g Includes nationals residing abroad. h ITU estimate. i Includes refugees. j UNESCO estimate. k 2003. l Chinandega. m Based on WMO Climatological Normals (CLINO) for the period 1971-1990. n Refers to average temperature.

Niger

Region	Western Africa
Currency	CFA Franc (XOF)
Surface area (square kilometres)	1 267 000
Population in 2012 (estimated, 000)	17 157
Population density in 2012 (per square kilometre)	13.5
Capital city and population in 2011 (000)	Niamey (1 297)
United Nations membership date	20 September 1960

Economic indicators	2005	2010	2012
GDP: Gross domestic product (million current US$)	3 369	5 719	6 773
GDP: Growth rate at constant 2005 prices (annual %)	7.4	8.4	10.8
GDP per capita (current US$)	255.5	359.8	394.8
GNI: Gross national income per capita (current US$)	254.8	357.0	392.1
Gross fixed capital formation (% of GDP)	21.6	38.9	33.8
Exchange rates (national currency per US$)[a]	556.04	490.91	497.16
Balance of payments, current account (million US$)	−312	−1 136	...
CPI: Consumer price index (2000=100)[bc]	114	128[d]	133
Agricultural production index (2004-2006=100)	102	145	138
Food production index (2004-2006=100)	102	145	138
Employment in industrial sector (% of employed)	11.1[efg]	...	...
Employment in agricultural sector (% of employed)	56.9[efg]	...	...
Labour force participation, adult female pop. (%)	39.2	39.8	39.9
Labour force participation, adult male pop. (%)	90.7	90.1	89.8
Tourist arrivals at national borders (000)	58	74	82[h]
Energy production, primary (000 mt oil equivalent)	100	131	...
Mobile-cellular subscriptions (per 100 inhabitants)	2.5	23.7	32.4
Individuals using the Internet (%)[i]	0.2	0.8	1.4

Total trade		Major trading partners			2012
	(million US$)	(% of exports)			(% of imports)
Exports	1 306.7	France	39.2	China	21.2
Imports	1 684.8	Nigeria	9.1	France	11.8
Balance	−378.1	Mali	8.7	United States	6.7

Social indicators		
Population growth rate (average annual %)	2010-2015	3.9
Urban population growth rate (average annual %)	2010-2015	4.9
Rural population growth rate (average annual %)	2010-2015	3.2
Urban population (%)	2013	18.3
Population aged 0-14 years (%)	2013	50.1
Population aged 60+ years (females and males, % of total)	2013	4.4/4.1
Sex ratio (males per 100 females)	2013	101.6
Life expectancy at birth (females and males, years)	2010-2015	58.4/58.0
Infant mortality rate (per 1 000 live births)	2010-2015	53.6
Fertility rate, total (live births per woman)	2010-2015	7.6
Contraceptive prevalence (ages 15-49, %)	2006-2012	11.2
International migrant stock (000 and % of total population)[j]	mid-2013	132.3/0.7
Refugees and others of concern to UNHCR	mid-2013	55 188
Education: Government expenditure (% of GDP)	2006-2012	4.5
Education: Primary-secondary gross enrolment ratio (f/m per 100)	2006-2012	40.7/50.8
Education: Female third-level students (% of total)	2006-2012	27.8
Intentional homicides (females and males, per 100 000)[k]	2008-2010	1.3/6.3
Seats held by women in national parliaments (%)	2014	13.3

Environmental indicators		
Threatened species	2013	31
Forested area (% of land area)	2011	0.9
CO_2 emission estimates (000 metric tons and metric tons per capita)	2010	1 411/0.1
Energy consumption per capita (kilograms oil equivalent)	2010	31.0
Precipitation in the capital city, total mean (millimetres)		541[l]
Temperature in the capital city, mean °C (minimum and maximum)		22.4/36.2[l]

a Official rate. **b** Niamey. **c** African population. **d** Series linked to former series. **e** Core Welfare Indicators Questionnaire (World Bank). **f** The indices are shown in terms of ISIC Rev.2. **g** April to July. **h** 2011. **i** ITU estimate. **j** Includes refugees. **k** Estimates. **l** Based on monthly averages for the period 1961-1990.

Nigeria

Region	Western Africa
Currency	Naira (NGN)
Surface area (square kilometres)	923 768
Population in 2012 (estimated, 000)	168 834
Population density in 2012 (per square kilometre)	182.8
Capital city and population in 2011 (000)	Abuja (2 153)
United Nations membership date	7 October 1960

Economic indicators	2005	2010	2012
GDP: Gross domestic product (million current US$)	112 248	229 508	262 545
GDP: Growth rate at constant 2005 prices (annual %)	6.5	7.8	6.5
GDP per capita (current US$)	804.2	1 437.1	1 555.1
GNI: Gross national income per capita (current US$)	772.6	1 314.9	1 426.0
Gross fixed capital formation (% of GDP)	5.5	11.6	11.3
Exchange rates (national currency per US$)[a]	129.00	150.66	155.27
Balance of payments, current account (million US$)	36 529	14 459	20 353
CPI: Consumer price index (2000=100)[b]	207	338[c]	420
Agricultural production index (2004-2006=100)	100	102	108
Food production index (2004-2006=100)	100	102	108
Employment in industrial sector (% of employed)	11.5[defgh]	...	...
Employment in agricultural sector (% of employed)	44.6[defgh]	...	...
Labour force participation, adult female pop. (%)	47.6	47.9	48.1
Labour force participation, adult male pop. (%)	62.1	63.2	63.5
Tourist arrivals at national borders (000)	1 010	1 555	715[i]
Energy production, primary (000 mt oil equivalent)	150 680	166 061	...
Mobile-cellular subscriptions (per 100 inhabitants)	13.3	55.1	67.7
Individuals using the Internet (%)	3.6	24.0[j]	32.9[j]

Total trade		Major trading partners			2012
	(million US$)	(% of exports)			(% of imports)
Exports	143 151.2	United States	16.9	China	21.5
Imports	35 872.5	India	11.1	United States	13.6
Balance	107 278.7	Brazil	7.5	India	8.1

Social indicators

Population growth rate (average annual %)	2010-2015	2.8
Urban population growth rate (average annual %)	2010-2015	3.8
Rural population growth rate (average annual %)	2010-2015	1.3
Urban population (%)	2013	50.9
Population aged 0-14 years (%)	2013	44.4
Population aged 60+ years (females and males, % of total)	2013	4.7/4.2
Sex ratio (males per 100 females)	2013	103.7
Life expectancy at birth (females and males, years)	2010-2015	52.6/52.0
Infant mortality rate (per 1 000 live births)	2010-2015	76.3
Fertility rate, total (live births per woman)	2010-2015	6.0
Contraceptive prevalence (ages 15-49, %)	2006-2012	14.1
International migrant stock (000 and % of total population)[kl]	mid-2013	1 233.6/0.7
Refugees and others of concern to UNHCR	mid-2013	3 051
Education: Primary-secondary gross enrolment ratio (f/m per 100)	2006-2012	61.3/67.6
Education: Female third-level students (% of total)	2006-2012	40.7[m]
Intentional homicides (females and males, per 100 000)[n]	2008-2010	6.1/18.2
Seats held by women in national parliaments (%)	2014	6.7

Environmental indicators

Threatened species	2013	309
Forested area (% of land area)	2011	9.5
CO_2 emission estimates (000 metric tons and metric tons per capita)	2010	78 846/0.5
Energy consumption per capita (kilograms oil equivalent)	2010	117.0
Precipitation in the capital city, total mean (millimetres)		1 221
Temperature in the capital city, mean °C (minimum and maximum)		20.2/33.0

a Principal rate. **b** Rural and urban areas. **c** Series linked to former series. **d** 2004. **e** Living standards survey. **f** The indices are shown in terms of ISIC Rev.2. **g** September of the preceding year to August of the current year. **h** Break in series; data not strictly comparable. **i** 2011. **j** ITU estimate. **k** Data refer to foreign citizens. **l** Includes refugees. **m** 2005. **n** Estimates.

Niue

Region	Oceania-Polynesia
Currency	New Zealand Dollar (NZD)
Surface area (square kilometres)	260
Population in 2012 (estimated, 000)	1
Population density in 2012 (per square kilometre)	5.3
Capital city and population in 2011 (000)	Alofi (1)

Economic indicators	2005	2010	2012
Exchange rates (national currency per US$)[a]	1.46	1.31	1.22
CPI: Consumer price index (2000=100)	119	158[b]	...
Agricultural production index (2004-2006=100)	101	93	91
Food production index (2004-2006=100)	101	93	91
Tourist arrivals at national borders (000)[c]	3	6	6[d]
Mobile-cellular subscriptions (per 100 inhabitants)	37.6[e]	...	...
Individuals using the Internet (%)	51.7	77.0[f]	82.2[f]

Social indicators		
Population growth rate (average annual %)	2010-2015	−2.9
Urban population growth rate (average annual %)	2010-2015	−1.6
Rural population growth rate (average annual %)	2010-2015	−3.5
Urban population (%)	2013	38.8
Population aged 0-14 years (%)[gh]	2013	24.7
Population aged 60+ years (females and males, % of total)[gh]	2013	19.9/15.1
Sex ratio (males per 100 females)[gh]	2013	100.0
Life expectancy at birth (females and males, years)[g]	2010-2015	72.8/66.1[i]
Infant mortality rate (per 1 000 live births)[g]	2010-2015	10.2[i]
Fertility rate, total (live births per woman)[g]	2010-2015	2.2[i]
International migrant stock (000 and % of total population)	mid-2013	0.6/41.1
Education: Primary-secondary gross enrolment ratio (f/m per 100)[j]	2006-2012	124.3/96.1[k]

Environmental indicators		
Threatened species	2013	50
Forested area (% of land area)	2011	71.2
CO_2 emission estimates (000 metric tons and metric tons per capita)	2010	7/4.2
Energy consumption per capita (kilograms oil equivalent)	2010	1 118.0[l]

a UN operational exchange rate. **b** 2009. **c** Includes Niueans residing usually in New Zealand. **d** 2011. **e** 2004. **f** ITU estimate. **g** Data compiled by the Secretariat of the Pacific Community Demography Programme. **h** De facto estimate. **i** 2006-2011. **j** National estimate. **k** 2005. **l** UNSD estimate.

Northern Mariana Islands

Region	Oceania-Micronesia
Currency	U.S. Dollar (USD)
Surface area (square metres)	457
Population in 2012 (estimated, 000)	53
Population density in 2012 (per square kilometre)	116.6
Capital city and population in 2011 (000)	Garapan (4)[a]

Economic indicators	2005	2010	2012
CPI: Consumer price index (2000=100)[b]	100	122[c]	...
Tourist arrivals at national borders (000)[d]	498	375	336[e]
Mobile-cellular subscriptions (per 100 inhabitants)	29.9[f]	...	...

Social indicators		
Population growth rate (average annual %)	2010-2015	0.4
Urban population growth rate (average annual %)	2010-2015	1.9
Rural population growth rate (average annual %)	2010-2015	0.4
Urban population (%)	2013	91.7
Population aged 0-14 years (%)[gh]	2013	24.7
Population aged 60+ years (females and males, % of total)[gh]	2013	7.8/7.4
Sex ratio (males per 100 females)[gh]	2013	105.9
Life expectancy at birth (females and males, years)[g]	2010-2015	77.1/73.5[i]
Infant mortality rate (per 1 000 live births)[g]	2010-2015	4.9[j]
Fertility rate, total (live births per woman)[g]	2010-2015	2.2[k]
Contraceptive prevalence (ages 15-49, %)	2006-2012	20.5[l]
International migrant stock (000 and % of total population)	mid-2013	24.2/44.9

Environmental indicators		
Threatened species	2013	97
Forested area (% of land area)	2011	65.5

a 2000. b Saipan. c 2009. d Air arrivals. e 2011. f 2004. g Data compiled by the Secretariat of the Pacific Community Demography Programme. h De facto estimate. i 1999-2001. j 2006-2008. k 2010. l 1970.

Norway

Region	Northern Europe
Currency	Norwegian Krone (NOK)
Surface area (square kilometres)	323 787 [a]
Population in 2012 (estimated, 000)	4 994 [b]
Population density in 2012 (per square kilometre)	15.4
Capital city and population in 2011 (000)	Oslo (915)
United Nations membership date	27 November 1945

Economic indicators	2005	2010	2012
GDP: Gross domestic product (million current US$)	304 060	420 946	499 667
GDP: Growth rate at constant 2005 prices (annual %)	2.6	0.5	3.1
GDP per capita (current US$)	65 751.4	86 061.0	100 056.0
GNI: Gross national income per capita (current US$)	66 482.2	87 074.2	102 067.2
Gross fixed capital formation (% of GDP)	19.2	18.9	20.6
Exchange rates (national currency per US$) [c]	6.77	5.86	5.57
Balance of payments, current account (million US$)	49 967	50 258	72 609
CPI: Consumer price index (2000=100)	109	122	125
Industrial production index (2005=100)	100	88	85
Agricultural production index (2004-2006=100)	99	102	101
Food production index (2004-2006=100)	99	102	101
Unemployment (% of labour force) [d]	4.4	3.5	3.1
Employment in industrial sector (% of employed) [e]	20.8 [f]	19.7 [g]	20.2 [g]
Employment in agricultural sector (% of employed) [e]	3.3 [f]	2.5 [g]	2.2 [g]
Labour force participation, adult female pop. (%)	60.3	61.4	61.5
Labour force participation, adult male pop. (%)	70.5	70.0	69.5
Tourist arrivals at national borders (000) [h]	3 824	4 767	4 963 [i]
Energy production, primary (000 mt oil equivalent) [b]	230 931	216 583	...
Mobile-cellular subscriptions (per 100 inhabitants)	102.8	114.7	115.6 [i]
Individuals using the Internet (%) [d]	82.0	93.4	95.0

Total trade		Major trading partners			2012
	(million US$) [b]	(% of exports) [b]			(% of imports) [b]
Exports	160 999.5	United Kingdom	26.5	Sweden	13.5
Imports	87 321.0	Netherlands	12.2	Germany	12.4
Balance	73 678.5	Germany	12.0	China	9.2

Social indicators		
Population growth rate (average annual %) [b]	2010-2015	1.0
Urban population growth rate (average annual %) [b]	2010-2015	1.0
Rural population growth rate (average annual %) [b]	2010-2015	−0.7
Urban population (%) [b]	2013	79.9
Population aged 0-14 years (%) [b]	2013	18.7
Population aged 60+ years (females and males, % of total) [b]	2013	23.2/20.0
Sex ratio (males per 100 females) [b]	2013	100.3
Life expectancy at birth (females and males, years) [b]	2010-2015	83.5/79.3
Infant mortality rate (per 1 000 live births) [b]	2010-2015	2.6
Fertility rate, total (live births per woman) [b]	2010-2015	1.9
Contraceptive prevalence (ages 15-49, %) [k]	2006-2012	88.4 [l]
International migrant stock (000 and % of total population) [b]	mid-2013	694.5/13.8
Refugees and others of concern to UNHCR	mid-2013	53 315 [m]
Education: Government expenditure (% of GDP)	2006-2012	6.9
Education: Primary-secondary gross enrolment ratio (f/m per 100)	2006-2012	105.5/106.0
Education: Female third-level students (% of total)	2006-2012	60.3
Intentional homicides (females and males, per 100 000)	2008-2010	0.5/0.7
Seats held by women in national parliaments (%)	2014	39.6

Environmental indicators		
Threatened species	2013	44
Forested area (% of land area)	2011	33.3
CO$_2$ emission estimates (000 metric tons and metric tons per capita)	2010	57 140/11.7
Energy consumption per capita (kilograms oil equivalent) [b]	2010	6 195.0
Precipitation in the capital city, total mean (millimetres)		763 [n]
Temperature in the capital city, mean °C (minimum and maximum)		2.4/9.6 [n]

a Excludes Svalbard and Jan Mayen Islands. b Includes Svalbard and Jan Mayen Islands. c Official rate. d Age group 16 to 74 years. e European Labour Force Survey (Eurostat). f The indices are shown in terms of ISIC Rev.3. g Age group 15 to 74 years. h 1998-2011: Arrivals of non-resident tourists at national borders. i 2011. j Second quarter. k Age group 20 to 44 years. l 2005. m Refugee population refers to the end of 2012. n Based on monthly averages for the period 1961-1990.

Oman

Region	Western Asia
Currency	Oman Rial (OMR)
Surface area (square kilometres)	309 500
Population in 2012 (estimated, 000)	3 314
Population density in 2012 (per square kilometre)	10.7
Capital city and population in 2011 (000)	Masqat (743)
United Nations membership date	7 October 1971

Economic indicators	2005	2010	2012
GDP: Gross domestic product (million current US$)	30 905	58 813	78 111
GDP: Growth rate at constant 2005 prices (annual %)	4.0	5.6	5.0
GDP per capita (current US$)	12 252.6	20 983.9	23 569.9
GNI: Gross national income per capita (current US$)	11 847.3	19 999.4	22 492.4
Gross fixed capital formation (% of GDP)	23.2	27.9	29.6
Exchange rates (national currency per US$)[a]	0.38	0.38	0.38
Balance of payments, current account (million US$)	5 178	5 871	8 312
CPI: Consumer price index (2000=100)	102	134	143
Agricultural production index (2004-2006=100)	112	122	112
Food production index (2004-2006=100)	112	122	112
Employment in industrial sector (% of employed)	...	36.9[bcde]	...
Employment in agricultural sector (% of employed)	...	5.2[bcde]	...
Labour force participation, adult female pop. (%)	25.5	27.8	28.6
Labour force participation, adult male pop. (%)	76.5	79.8	81.8
Tourist arrivals at national borders (000)[f]	1 114	1 048	...
Energy production, primary (000 mt oil equivalent)	58 045	71 019	...
Mobile-cellular subscriptions (per 100 inhabitants)	54.9	165.5	181.7
Individuals using the Internet (%)	6.7	35.8[g]	60.0[h]

Total trade		Major trading partners			2012
	(million US$)[i]		(% of exports)[ij]		(% of imports)[i]
Exports	47 091.9	China	30.3	United Arab Emirates	27.4
Imports	23 619.4	Areas nes	12.3	Japan	12.6
Balance	23 472.5	India	9.8	United States	5.9

Social indicators		
Population growth rate (average annual %)	2010-2015	7.9
Urban population growth rate (average annual %)	2010-2015	2.2
Rural population growth rate (average annual %)	2010-2015	0.9
Urban population (%)	2013	74.0
Population aged 0-14 years (%)	2013	23.5
Population aged 60+ years (females and males, % of total)	2013	5.0/3.4
Sex ratio (males per 100 females)	2013	174.6
Life expectancy at birth (females and males, years)	2010-2015	78.9/74.7
Infant mortality rate (per 1 000 live births)	2010-2015	7.3
Fertility rate, total (live births per woman)	2010-2015	2.9
Contraceptive prevalence (ages 15-49, %)	2006-2012	31.7[k]
International migrant stock (000 and % of total population)[l]	mid-2013	1 112.0/30.6
Refugees and others of concern to UNHCR	mid-2013	164
Education: Government expenditure (% of GDP)	2006-2012	4.3
Education: Primary-secondary gross enrolment ratio (f/m per 100)	2006-2012	103.4/98.9
Education: Female third-level students (% of total)	2006-2012	50.4
Intentional homicides (females and males, per 100 000)[m]	2008-2010	1.3/2.8
Seats held by women in national parliaments (%)	2014	1.2

Environmental indicators		
Threatened species	2013	91
Forested area (% of land area)	2011	<
CO_2 emission estimates (000 metric tons and metric tons per capita)	2010	57 155/20.6
Energy consumption per capita (kilograms oil equivalent)	2010	8 132.0
Precipitation in the capital city, total mean (millimetres)		90[n]
Temperature in the capital city, mean °C (minimum and maximum)		23.9/33.0[n]

a Official rate. b Population census. c The indices are shown in terms of ISIC Rev.3. d December. e Break in series; data not strictly comparable. f Arrivals of non-resident tourists in hotels and similar establishments. g Age group 5 years and over. h ITU estimate. i 2011. j See technical notes. k 2000. l Data refer to foreign citizens. m Estimates. n Based on monthly averages for the period 1986-2009.

Pakistan

Region	Southern Asia
Currency	Pakistani Rupee (PKR)
Surface area (square kilometres)	796 095
Population in 2012 (estimated, 000)	179 160
Population density in 2012 (per square kilometre)	225.1
Capital city and population in 2011 (000)	Islamabad (919)
United Nations membership date	30 September 1947

Economic indicators	2005	2010	2012
GDP: Gross domestic product (million current US$)	117 708	174 508	215 117
GDP: Growth rate at constant 2005 prices (annual %)	7.7	1.6	4.0
GDP per capita (current US$)	745.1	1 007.9	1 200.7
GNI: Gross national income per capita (current US$)	759.5	1 046.2	1 262.6
Gross fixed capital formation (% of GDP)	15.1	14.2	13.3
Exchange rates (national currency per US$)[a]	59.83	85.71	97.14
Balance of payments, current account (million US$)	−3 606	−1 354	−2 025
CPI: Consumer price index (2000=100)	129	234	274
Agricultural production index (2004-2006=100)	100	110	119
Food production index (2004-2006=100)	101	113	122
Employment in industrial sector (% of employed)[bc]	20.3[d]	20.1[ef]	...
Employment in agricultural sector (% of employed)[bc]	43.0[d]	44.7[ef]	...
Labour force participation, adult female pop. (%)	19.3	23.9	24.4
Labour force participation, adult male pop. (%)	84.1	82.8	82.9
Tourist arrivals at national borders (000)	798	907	966
Energy production, primary (000 mt oil equivalent)	39 619	40 567	...
Mobile-cellular subscriptions (per 100 inhabitants)	8.1	57.1	66.8
Individuals using the Internet (%)	6.3	8.0[g]	10.0[g]

Total trade		Major trading partners			2012
	(million US$)	(% of exports)		(% of imports)	
Exports	24 613.7	United States	14.9	United Arab Emirates	16.5
Imports	43 813.3	United Arab Emirates	11.7	China	15.3
Balance	−19 199.6	China	10.6	Saudi Arabia	9.8

Social indicators

Population growth rate (average annual %)	2010-2015	1.7
Urban population growth rate (average annual %)	2010-2015	2.7
Rural population growth rate (average annual %)	2010-2015	1.2
Urban population (%)	2013	36.9
Population aged 0-14 years (%)	2013	33.8
Population aged 60+ years (females and males, % of total)	2013	6.5/6.5
Sex ratio (males per 100 females)	2013	105.7
Life expectancy at birth (females and males, years)	2010-2015	67.4/65.6
Infant mortality rate (per 1 000 live births)	2010-2015	65.1
Fertility rate, total (live births per woman)	2010-2015	3.2
Contraceptive prevalence (ages 15-49, %)	2006-2012	27.0
International migrant stock (000 and % of total population)[h]	mid-2013	4 080.8/2.2
Refugees and others of concern to UNHCR	mid-2013	2 648 083
Education: Government expenditure (% of GDP)	2006-2012	2.2
Education: Primary-secondary gross enrolment ratio (f/m per 100)	2006-2012	53.4/65.3
Education: Female third-level students (% of total)	2006-2012	47.6
Intentional homicides (females and males, per 100 000)[i]	2008-2010	2.9/4.3
Seats held by women in national parliaments (%)	2014	20.7

Environmental indicators

Threatened species	2013	119
Forested area (% of land area)	2011	2.1
CO_2 emission estimates (000 metric tons and metric tons per capita)	2010	161 264/0.9
Energy consumption per capita (kilograms oil equivalent)	2010	345.0
Precipitation in the capital city, total mean (millimetres)		1 142
Temperature in the capital city, mean °C (minimum and maximum)		14.1/28.6

a Market rate. b Age group 10 years and over. c The indices are shown in terms of ISIC Rev.2. d July. e 2008. f January. g ITU estimate. h Includes refugees. i Estimates.

Palau

Region	Oceania-Micronesia
Currency	U.S. Dollar (USD)
Surface area (square kilometres)	459
Population in 2012 (estimated, 000)	21
Population density in 2012 (per square kilometre)	45.2
Capital city and population in 2011 (000)	Melekeok (1)
United Nations membership date	15 December 1994

Economic indicators	2005	2010	2012
GDP: Gross domestic product (million current US$)	188	205	213
GDP: Growth rate at constant 2005 prices (annual %)	6.2	−3.4	−2.5
GDP per capita (current US$)	9 446.3	10 028.3	10 271.2
GNI: Gross national income per capita (current US$)	8 180.0	8 584.7	8 853.4
Gross fixed capital formation (% of GDP)	35.7	22.2	25.5
Tourist arrivals at national borders (000)[a]	81	86	119
Energy production, primary (000 mt oil equivalent)[b]	2	2	...
Mobile-cellular subscriptions (per 100 inhabitants)	30.4	70.9	82.6
Individuals using the Internet (%)	27.0[c]	...	...

Total trade		Major trading partners			2012
	(million US$)	(% of exports)			(% of imports)
Exports	9.0	Japan	82.2	United States	37.1
Imports	141.9	United States	3.3	Guam	32.4
Balance	−132.9	Guam	3.3	Japan	9.7

Social indicators		
Population growth rate (average annual %)	2010-2015	0.8
Urban population growth rate (average annual %)	2010-2015	1.7
Rural population growth rate (average annual %)	2010-2015	−4.3
Urban population (%)	2013	85.8
Population aged 0-14 years (%)[de]	2013	19.9
Population aged 60+ years (females and males, % of total)[de]	2013	11.7/9.4
Sex ratio (males per 100 females)[de]	2013	111.9
Life expectancy at birth (females and males, years)[d]	2010-2015	72.1/66.3[f]
Infant mortality rate (per 1 000 live births)[d]	2010-2015	12.2[g]
Fertility rate, total (live births per woman)[d]	2010-2015	1.7[g]
Contraceptive prevalence (ages 15-49, %)[h]	2006-2012	32.8[i]
International migrant stock (000 and % of total population)	mid-2013	5.6/26.7
Refugees and others of concern to UNHCR	mid-2013	2
Education: Government expenditure (% of GDP)[i]	2006-2012	7.3[k]
Education: Primary-secondary gross enrolment ratio (f/m per 100)[l]	2006-2012	100.4/100.7[c]
Education: Female third-level students (% of total)[j]	2006-2012	63.4[k]
Seats held by women in national parliaments (%)	2014	0.0

Environmental indicators		
Threatened species	2013	176
Forested area (% of land area)	2011	87.6
CO_2 emission estimates (000 metric tons and metric tons per capita)	2010	216/10.5
Energy consumption per capita (kilograms oil equivalent)	2010	3 595.0[b]

a Air arrivals (Palau International Airport). **b** UNSD estimate. **c** 2004. **d** Data compiled by the Secretariat of the Pacific Community Demography Programme. **e** De facto estimate. **f** 2001-2005. **g** 2010. **h** Age group 15 to 44 years. **i** 2003. **j** UNESCO estimate. **k** 2002. **l** National estimate.

Panama

Region	Central America
Currency	Balboa (PAB)
Surface area (square kilometres)	75 417
Population in 2012 (estimated, 000)	3 802
Population density in 2012 (per square kilometre)	50.4
Capital city and population in 2011 (000)	Panama City (1 426)
United Nations membership date	13 November 1945

Economic indicators	2005	2010	2012
GDP: Gross domestic product (million current US$)	15 465	27 053	36 253
GDP: Growth rate at constant 2005 prices (annual %)	7.2	7.4	10.7
GDP per capita (current US$)	4 594.5	7 355.1	9 534.4
GNI: Gross national income per capita (current US$)	4 167.7	6 749.7	8 754.5
Gross fixed capital formation (% of GDP)	16.8	24.5	27.6
Balance of payments, current account (million US$)	−1 022	−2 765	−3 267
CPI: Consumer price index (2000=100) [a][b]	103	127	142
Agricultural production index (2004-2006=100)	99	108	113
Food production index (2004-2006=100)	99	108	113
Employment in industrial sector (% of employed) [c]	17.0[d]	18.7[e]	18.2
Employment in agricultural sector (% of employed) [c]	19.3[d]	17.4[e]	16.7
Labour force participation, adult female pop. (%)	47.9	48.8	49.0
Labour force participation, adult male pop. (%)	81.2	82.0	81.9
Tourist arrivals at national borders (000)	702	1 324	1 606
Energy production, primary (000 mt oil equivalent)	320	361	...
Mobile-cellular subscriptions (per 100 inhabitants)	54.0	189.0	186.7
Individuals using the Internet (%)	11.5	40.1	45.2[f]

Total trade		Major trading partners			2012
	(million US$)	(% of exports)			(% of imports)[g]
Exports	821.9	United States	20.2	United States	23.6
Imports	12 623.4	Canada	14.6	Panama	20.3[h]
Balance	−11 801.5	Costa Rica	6.6	Free zones	10.8

Social indicators		
Population growth rate (average annual %)	2010-2015	1.6
Urban population growth rate (average annual %)	2010-2015	2.2
Rural population growth rate (average annual %)	2010-2015	−1.0
Urban population (%)	2013	76.5
Population aged 0-14 years (%)	2013	28.3
Population aged 60+ years (females and males, % of total)	2013	10.9/9.8
Sex ratio (males per 100 females)	2013	102.0
Life expectancy at birth (females and males, years)	2010-2015	80.4/74.7
Infant mortality rate (per 1 000 live births)	2010-2015	14.6
Fertility rate, total (live births per woman)	2010-2015	2.5
Contraceptive prevalence (ages 15-49, %)	2006-2012	52.2
International migrant stock (000 and % of total population)	mid-2013	158.4/4.1
Refugees and others of concern to UNHCR	mid-2013	18 181
Education: Government expenditure (% of GDP)	2006-2012	3.5
Education: Primary-secondary gross enrolment ratio (f/m per 100)	2006-2012	92.7/92.1
Education: Female third-level students (% of total)	2006-2012	60.0
Intentional homicides (females and males, per 100 000)	2008-2010	4.1/42.8
Seats held by women in national parliaments (%)	2014	8.5

Environmental indicators		
Threatened species	2013	359
Forested area (% of land area)	2011	43.6
CO$_2$ emission estimates (000 metric tons and metric tons per capita)	2010	9 625/2.8
Energy consumption per capita (kilograms oil equivalent)	2010	895.0
Precipitation in the capital city, total mean (millimetres)		1 907[i]
Temperature in the capital city, mean °C (minimum and maximum)		20.0/33.8[i]

a Urban areas. b Index base 2003=100. c August. d The indices are shown in terms of ISIC Rev.2. e The indices are shown in terms of ISIC Rev.3. f ITU estimate. g See technical notes. h Data refer to returned goods or goods resulting from outward processing, i.e. minor processing or, in general, operations which do not change the country of origin. When these goods come back they are recorded as re-imports and the country of origin is the country itself. i Based on monthly averages for the period 1971-2000.

Papua New Guinea

Region	Oceania-Melanesia
Currency	Kina (PGK)
Surface area (square kilometres)	462 840
Population in 2012 (estimated, 000)	7 167
Population density in 2012 (per square kilometre)	15.5
Capital city and population in 2011 (000)	Port Moresby (343)
United Nations membership date	10 October 1975

Economic indicators	2005	2010	2012
GDP: Gross domestic product (million current US$)	4 866	9 707	15 677
GDP: Growth rate at constant 2005 prices (annual %)	3.9	7.6	9.2
GDP per capita (current US$)	798.3	1 415.2	2 187.4
GNI: Gross national income per capita (current US$)	710.0	1 291.7	2 013.8
Gross fixed capital formation (% of GDP)	16.5	21.2	22.2
Exchange rates (national currency per US$)[a]	3.10	2.64	2.10
Balance of payments, current account (million US$)	539	−633	...
CPI: Consumer price index (2000=100)	146	189	...
Agricultural production index (2004-2006=100)	100	112	117
Food production index (2004-2006=100)	99	112	117
Labour force participation, adult female pop. (%)	71.3	70.6	70.5
Labour force participation, adult male pop. (%)	74.4	74.1	74.0
Tourist arrivals at national borders (000)	69	146	165[b]
Energy production, primary (000 mt oil equivalent)	2 805	683	...
Mobile-cellular subscriptions (per 100 inhabitants)	1.2	27.8	37.8[c]
Individuals using the Internet (%)	1.7	1.3[d]	2.3[c]

Total trade		Major trading partners			2012
	(million US$)		(% of exports)		(% of imports)
Exports	4 517.7	Australia	35.9	Australia	34.4
Imports	8 340.7	Japan	11.7	Singapore	14.3
Balance	−3 823.0	Germany	7.0	China	6.9

Social indicators		
Population growth rate (average annual %)	2010-2015	2.1
Urban population growth rate (average annual %)	2010-2015	2.7
Rural population growth rate (average annual %)	2010-2015	2.1
Urban population (%)	2013	12.6
Population aged 0-14 years (%)	2013	38.0
Population aged 60+ years (females and males, % of total)	2013	5.5/4.3
Sex ratio (males per 100 females)	2013	104.1
Life expectancy at birth (females and males, years)	2010-2015	64.5/60.3
Infant mortality rate (per 1 000 live births)	2010-2015	47.6
Fertility rate, total (live births per woman)	2010-2015	3.8
Contraceptive prevalence (ages 15-49, %)	2006-2012	35.7
International migrant stock (000 and % of total population)[ef]	mid-2013	25.4/0.4
Refugees and others of concern to UNHCR	mid-2013	9 787
Education: Primary-secondary gross enrolment ratio (f/m per 100)	2006-2012	45.1/53.9[g]
Education: Female third-level students (% of total)[h]	2006-2012	35.2[i]
Intentional homicides (females and males, per 100 000)[j]	2008-2010	3.8/22.0
Seats held by women in national parliaments (%)	2014	2.7

Environmental indicators		
Threatened species	2013	468
Forested area (% of land area)	2011	63.1
CO_2 emission estimates (000 metric tons and metric tons per capita)	2010	3 133/0.4
Energy consumption per capita (kilograms oil equivalent)	2010	173.0
Precipitation in the capital city, total mean (millimetres)		899[k]
Temperature in the capital city, mean °C (minimum and maximum)		23.3/31.3[k]

a Official rate. b 2011. c ITU estimate. d Age group 10 years and over. e Data refer to foreign citizens. f Includes refugees. g 1998. h UNESCO estimate. i 1999. j Estimates. k Based on monthly averages for the period 1973-2007.

Paraguay

Region	South America
Currency	Guaraní (PYG)
Surface area (square kilometres)	406 752
Population in 2012 (estimated, 000)	6 687
Population density in 2012 (per square kilometre)	16.4
Capital city and population in 2011 (000)	Asunción (2 139)
United Nations membership date	24 October 1945

Economic indicators	2005	2010	2012
GDP: Gross domestic product (million current US$)	8 735	20 048	25 935
GDP: Growth rate at constant 2005 prices (annual %)	2.1	13.1	−1.2
GDP per capita (current US$)	1 479.4	3 103.5	3 878.2
GNI: Gross national income per capita (current US$)	1 468.0	3 041.0	3 798.7
Gross fixed capital formation (% of GDP)	16.6	15.9	16.1
Exchange rates (national currency per US$)[a]	6 120.00	4 573.75	4 288.80
Balance of payments, current account (million US$)	−68	−66	116
CPI: Consumer price index (2000=100)[b]	150	212	237
Agricultural production index (2004-2006=100)	97	137	144
Food production index (2004-2006=100)	98	142	149
Unemployment (% of labour force)[cd]	...	7.3	8.1
Employment in industrial sector (% of employed)[ce]	15.7[f]	18.8	16.1[g]
Employment in agricultural sector (% of employed)[ce]	32.4[f]	26.8	27.2[g]
Labour force participation, adult female pop. (%)	54.6	54.8	55.4
Labour force participation, adult male pop. (%)	85.7	84.7	84.8
Tourist arrivals at national borders (000)[h]	341	465	579
Energy production, primary (000 mt oil equivalent)	4 403	4 668	...
Mobile-cellular subscriptions (per 100 inhabitants)	32.0	91.7	101.7
Individuals using the Internet (%)	7.9[i]	19.8[i]	27.1[j]

Total trade		Major trading partners			2012
	(million US$)	(% of exports)			(% of imports)
Exports	7 271.3	Brazil	39.2	China	27.6
Imports	11 555.1	Russian Federation	9.7	Brazil	23.5
Balance	−4 283.8	Argentina	8.3	Argentina	16.4

Social indicators

Population growth rate (average annual %)	2010-2015	1.7
Urban population growth rate (average annual %)	2010-2015	2.6
Rural population growth rate (average annual %)	2010-2015	0.3
Urban population (%)	2013	63.0
Population aged 0-14 years (%)	2013	32.4
Population aged 60+ years (females and males, % of total)	2013	8.5/7.9
Sex ratio (males per 100 females)	2013	101.6
Life expectancy at birth (females and males, years)	2010-2015	74.5/70.0
Infant mortality rate (per 1 000 live births)	2010-2015	30.4
Fertility rate, total (live births per woman)	2010-2015	2.9
Contraceptive prevalence (ages 15-49, %)[k]	2006-2012	79.4
International migrant stock (000 and % of total population)	mid-2013	185.8/2.7
Refugees and others of concern to UNHCR	mid-2013	143
Education: Government expenditure (% of GDP)	2006-2012	3.8
Education: Primary-secondary gross enrolment ratio (f/m per 100)	2006-2012	82.7/83.1
Education: Female third-level students (% of total)	2006-2012	57.8
Intentional homicides (females and males, per 100 000)	2008-2010	1.6/22.1
Seats held by women in national parliaments (%)	2014	15.0

Environmental indicators

Threatened species	2013	58
Forested area (% of land area)	2011	43.8
CO_2 emission estimates (000 metric tons and metric tons per capita)	2010	5 071/0.8
Energy consumption per capita (kilograms oil equivalent)	2010	392.0
Precipitation in the capital city, total mean (millimetres)		1 401[l]
Temperature in the capital city, mean °C (minimum and maximum)		18.2/28.4[l]

a Market rate. b Asunción. c Age group 10 years and over. d Urban areas only. e The indices are shown in terms of ISIC Rev.2. f October to December. g Excludes the departments of Boquerón and Alto Paraguay. h Excludes nationals residing abroad and crew members. i Age group 10 years and over using the Internet within the last 3 months. j ITU estimate. k Age group 15 to 44 years. l Based on monthly averages for the period 1971-2000.

Peru

Region	South America
Currency	Nuevo Sol (PEN)
Surface area (square kilometres)	1 285 216
Population in 2012 (estimated, 000)	29 988
Population density in 2012 (per square kilometre)	23.3
Capital city and population in 2011 (000)	Lima (9 130)
United Nations membership date	31 October 1945

Economic indicators

	2005	2010	2012
GDP: Gross domestic product (million current US$)	79 389	157 438	204 681
GDP: Growth rate at constant 2005 prices (annual %)	6.8	8.8	6.3
GDP per capita (current US$)	2 863.6	5 380.1	6 825.5
GNI: Gross national income per capita (current US$)	2 704.4	4 874.8	6 229.3
Gross fixed capital formation (% of GDP)	18.3	26.3	27.9
Exchange rates (national currency per US$)[a]	3.43	2.81	2.55
Balance of payments, current account (million US$)	1 148	−3 782	−6 842
CPI: Consumer price index (2000=100)[bc]	110	126[d]	135
Industrial production index (2005=100)[e]	100	131	139
Agricultural production index (2004-2006=100)	99	128	140
Food production index (2004-2006=100)	100	130	141
Unemployment (% of labour force)[fg]	9.6	7.9	6.8
Employment in industrial sector (% of employed)[h]	14.6[i]	17.7	17.4[j]
Employment in agricultural sector (% of employed)[h]	32.9[i]	25.7	25.8[j]
Labour force participation, adult female pop. (%)	57.6	67.6	68.0
Labour force participation, adult male pop. (%)	79.2	84.4	84.4
Tourist arrivals at national borders (000)[kl]	1 571	2 299	2 846
Energy production, primary (000 mt oil equivalent)	8 787	17 214	...
Mobile-cellular subscriptions (per 100 inhabitants)	20.3	101.9	98.8[m]
Individuals using the Internet (%)	17.1	34.8[n]	38.2[n]

Total trade		Major trading partners			2012
	(million US$)	(% of exports)			(% of imports)
Exports	45 946.2	China	17.1	United States	19.0
Imports	42 274.3	United States	14.2	China	18.5
Balance	3 671.9	Switzerland	11.0	Brazil	6.1

Social indicators

Population growth rate (average annual %)	2010-2015	1.3
Urban population growth rate (average annual %)	2010-2015	1.6
Rural population growth rate (average annual %)	2010-2015	−0.4
Urban population (%)	2013	77.9
Population aged 0-14 years (%)	2013	28.8
Population aged 60+ years (females and males, % of total)	2013	10.0/8.7
Sex ratio (males per 100 females)	2013	100.5
Life expectancy at birth (females and males, years)	2010-2015	77.4/72.0
Infant mortality rate (per 1 000 live births)	2010-2015	16.7
Fertility rate, total (live births per woman)	2010-2015	2.4
Contraceptive prevalence (ages 15-49, %)	2006-2012	74.4
International migrant stock (000 and % of total population)	mid-2013	104.9/0.4
Refugees and others of concern to UNHCR	mid-2013	1 801
Education: Government expenditure (% of GDP)	2006-2012	2.6
Education: Primary-secondary gross enrolment ratio (f/m per 100)	2006-2012	97.9/99.0
Education: Female third-level students (% of total)	2006-2012	51.6
Intentional homicides (females and males, per 100 000)	2008-2010	1.3/4.4
Seats held by women in national parliaments (%)	2014	22.3

Environmental indicators

Threatened species	2013	636
Forested area (% of land area)	2011	53.0
CO_2 emission estimates (000 metric tons and metric tons per capita)	2010	57 532/2.0
Energy consumption per capita (kilograms oil equivalent)	2010	652.0
Precipitation in the capital city, total mean (millimetres)		13
Temperature in the capital city, mean °C (minimum and maximum)		16.7/22.1

a Market rate. b Lima. c Metropolitan areas. d Series linked to former series. e The indices are shown in terms of ISIC Rev.3. f Age group 14 years and over. g Main city or metropolitan area. h The indices are shown in terms of ISIC Rev.2. i Third quarter. j 2011. k Includes nationals residing abroad. l Preliminary data. m Preliminary. n Age group 6 years and over.

Philippines

Region	South-Eastern Asia
Currency	Philippine Peso (PHP)
Surface area (square kilometres)	300 000
Population in 2012 (estimated, 000)	96 707
Population density in 2012 (per square kilometre)	322.4
Capital city and population in 2011 (000)	Manila (11 862)
United Nations membership date	24 October 1945

Economic indicators	2005	2010	2012
GDP: Gross domestic product (million current US$)	103 072	199 591	250 182
GDP: Growth rate at constant 2005 prices (annual %)	4.8	7.6	6.8
GDP per capita (current US$)	1 201.0	2 135.9	2 587.0
GNI: Gross national income per capita (current US$)	1 512.5	2 574.6	3 087.5
Gross fixed capital formation (% of GDP)	19.9	20.5	19.4
Exchange rates (national currency per US$)[a]	53.07	43.88	41.19
Balance of payments, current account (million US$)	1 980	8 922	7 126
CPI: Consumer price index (2000=100)	130	166	179
Agricultural production index (2004-2006=100)	100	113	119
Food production index (2004-2006=100)	100	113	119
Unemployment (% of labour force)	8.0[b]	7.4	7.0
Employment in industrial sector (% of employed)	15.6[cde]	15.0[c]	15.4[fg]
Employment in agricultural sector (% of employed)	36.0[cde]	33.2[c]	32.2[fg]
Labour force participation, adult female pop. (%)	49.8	50.3	51.0
Labour force participation, adult male pop. (%)	80.0	79.3	79.7
Tourist arrivals at national borders (000)[h]	2 623	3 520	4 273
Energy production, primary (000 mt oil equivalent)	6 560	9 101	...
Mobile-cellular subscriptions (per 100 inhabitants)	40.7	89.2	106.8[i]
Individuals using the Internet (%)	5.4[i]	25.0	36.2[i]

Total trade		Major trading partners			2012
	(million US$)	(% of exports)		(% of imports)	
Exports	51 995.2	Japan	19.0	United States	11.6
Imports	65 349.8	United States	14.2	China	10.9
Balance	−13 354.6	China	11.8	Japan	10.7

Social indicators		
Population growth rate (average annual %)	2010-2015	1.7
Urban population growth rate (average annual %)	2010-2015	2.2
Rural population growth rate (average annual %)	2010-2015	1.2
Urban population (%)	2013	49.3
Population aged 0-14 years (%)	2013	34.1
Population aged 60+ years (females and males, % of total)	2013	7.2/5.6
Sex ratio (males per 100 females)	2013	100.4
Life expectancy at birth (females and males, years)	2010-2015	72.2/65.3
Infant mortality rate (per 1 000 live births)	2010-2015	21.0
Fertility rate, total (live births per woman)	2010-2015	3.1
Contraceptive prevalence (ages 15-49, %)	2006-2012	48.9
International migrant stock (000 and % of total population)[jk]	mid-2013	213.2/0.2
Refugees and others of concern to UNHCR	mid-2013	57 940
Education: Government expenditure (% of GDP)	2006-2012	2.7
Education: Primary-secondary gross enrolment ratio (f/m per 100)	2006-2012	98.3/97.1
Education: Female third-level students (% of total)	2006-2012	54.3
Intentional homicides (females and males, per 100 000)	2008-2010	3.1/34.8
Seats held by women in national parliaments (%)	2014	27.3

Environmental indicators		
Threatened species	2013	737
Forested area (% of land area)	2011	25.9
CO_2 emission estimates (000 metric tons and metric tons per capita)	2010	81 524/0.9
Energy consumption per capita (kilograms oil equivalent)	2010	265.0
Precipitation in the capital city, total mean (millimetres)		2 201[l]
Temperature in the capital city, mean °C (minimum and maximum)		25.2/31.2[l]

a Market rate. b 2006. c The indices are shown in terms of ISIC Rev.3. d October. e Excludes regular military living in barracks. f Average of quarterly estimates. g Break in series; data not strictly comparable. h Includes nationals residing abroad. i ITU estimate. j Data refer to foreign citizens. k Includes refugees. l Based on monthly averages for the period 1971-2000.

Poland

Region	Eastern Europe
Currency	Zloty (PLN)
Surface area (square kilometres)	311 888
Population in 2012 (estimated, 000)	38 211
Population density in 2012 (per square kilometre)	122.5
Capital city and population in 2011 (000)	Warsaw (1 723)
United Nations membership date	24 October 1945

Economic indicators	2005	2010	2012
GDP: Gross domestic product (million current US$)	303 912	469 799	489 852
GDP: Growth rate at constant 2005 prices (annual %)	3.6	3.9	1.9
GDP per capita (current US$)	7 954.5	12 298.8	12 819.7
GNI: Gross national income per capita (current US$)	7 798.8	11 828.7	12 281.1
Gross fixed capital formation (% of GDP)	18.3	19.9	19.2
Exchange rates (national currency per US$)[a]	3.26	2.96	3.10
Balance of payments, current account (million US$)	−7 242	−24 030	−18 263
CPI: Consumer price index (2000=100)	115	131	142
Industrial production index (2005=100)	100	134	145
Agricultural production index (2004-2006=100)	99	101	107
Food production index (2004-2006=100)	99	101	107
Unemployment (% of labour force)[b]	17.8	9.6[c]	10.1
Employment in industrial sector (% of employed)	29.2[de]	30.2[f]	30.4[cf]
Employment in agricultural sector (% of employed)	17.4[de]	12.8[f]	12.6[cf]
Labour force participation, adult female pop. (%)	47.5	48.3	48.9
Labour force participation, adult male pop. (%)	62.5	64.3	64.8
Tourist arrivals at national borders (000)	15 200	12 470	14 840
Energy production, primary (000 mt oil equivalent)	74 494	61 046	...
Mobile-cellular subscriptions (per 100 inhabitants)	76.4	122.7	132.7[g]
Individuals using the Internet (%)[h]	38.8	62.3	65.0

Total trade		Major trading partners			2012
	(million US$)	(% of exports)			(% of imports)
Exports	179 603.6	Germany	24.9	Germany	20.9
Imports	191 430.1	United Kingdom	6.8	Russian Federation	14.6
Balance	−11 826.5	Czech Republic	6.2	China	9.0

Social indicators		
Population growth rate (average annual %)	2010-2015	<
Urban population growth rate (average annual %)	2010-2015	−<
Rural population growth rate (average annual %)	2010-2015	0.2
Urban population (%)	2013	60.7
Population aged 0-14 years (%)	2013	15.0
Population aged 60+ years (females and males, % of total)	2013	24.1/17.9
Sex ratio (males per 100 females)	2013	93.3
Life expectancy at birth (females and males, years)	2010-2015	80.5/72.2
Infant mortality rate (per 1 000 live births)	2010-2015	5.5
Fertility rate, total (live births per woman)	2010-2015	1.4
Contraceptive prevalence (ages 15-49, %)[i]	2006-2012	72.7[j]
International migrant stock (000 and % of total population)	mid-2013	663.8/1.7
Refugees and others of concern to UNHCR	mid-2013	30 273[k]
Education: Government expenditure (% of GDP)	2006-2012	5.2
Education: Primary-secondary gross enrolment ratio (f/m per 100)	2006-2012	97.7/98.6
Education: Female third-level students (% of total)	2006-2012	59.9
Intentional homicides (females and males, per 100 000)	2008-2010	0.8/2.2
Seats held by women in national parliaments (%)	2014	24.3

Environmental indicators		
Threatened species	2013	54
Forested area (% of land area)	2011	30.8
CO$_2$ emission estimates (000 metric tons and metric tons per capita)	2010	316 995/8.3
Energy consumption per capita (kilograms oil equivalent)	2010	2 445.0
Precipitation in the capital city, total mean (millimetres)		520[l]
Temperature in the capital city, mean °C (minimum and maximum)		4.0/12.3[l]

a Official rate. b Age group 15 to 74 years. c Break in series; data not strictly comparable. d The indices are shown in terms of ISIC Rev.3. e Excludes conscripts and regular military living in barracks. f European Labour Force Survey (Eurostat). g ITU estimate. h Age group 16 to 74 years. i Age group 20 to 49 years. j 1991. k Refugee population refers to the end of 2012. l Based on monthly averages for the period 1971-2000.

Portugal

Region	Southern Europe
Currency	Euro (EUR)
Surface area (square kilometres)	92 212
Population in 2012 (estimated, 000)	10 604
Population density in 2012 (per square kilometre)	115.0
Capital city and population in 2011 (000)	Lisbon (2 843)
United Nations membership date	14 December 1955

Economic indicators	2005	2010	2012
GDP: Gross domestic product (million current US$)	191 848	228 939	212 139
GDP: Growth rate at constant 2005 prices (annual %)	0.8	1.9	−3.2
GDP per capita (current US$)	18 252.2	21 618.9	20 006.0
GNI: Gross national income per capita (current US$)	17 981.5	20 877.9	19 518.2
Gross fixed capital formation (% of GDP)	23.1	19.7	16.0
Exchange rates (national currency per US$)[a]	0.85	0.75	0.76
Balance of payments, current account (million US$)	−19 821	−24 215	−4 359
CPI: Consumer price index (2000=100)[b]	117	127	135
Industrial production index (2005=100)	100	92	86
Agricultural production index (2004-2006=100)	97	104	99
Food production index (2004-2006=100)	97	104	100
Unemployment (% of labour force)[cd]	7.6	10.8	15.7
Employment in industrial sector (% of employed)[e]	30.6[f]	27.7	25.6
Employment in agricultural sector (% of employed)[e]	11.8[f]	10.9	10.5
Labour force participation, adult female pop. (%)	55.4	56.3	55.4
Labour force participation, adult male pop. (%)	69.3	67.9	67.2
Tourist arrivals at national borders (000)[g]	5 769	6 756	7 503
Energy production, primary (000 mt oil equivalent)[h]	599	2 532	...
Mobile-cellular subscriptions (per 100 inhabitants)	108.6	114.4[i]	115.1[i]
Individuals using the Internet (%)[j]	35.0	53.3	64.0

Total trade		Major trading partners			2012
	(million US$)	(% of exports)			(% of imports)
Exports	58 379.0	Spain	22.5	Spain	27.2
Imports	72 292.6	Germany	12.3	Germany	10.7
Balance	−13 913.6	France	11.8	France	6.0

Social indicators

Population growth rate (average annual %)	2010-2015	<
Urban population growth rate (average annual %)	2010-2015	0.9
Rural population growth rate (average annual %)	2010-2015	−1.4
Urban population (%)	2013	62.1
Population aged 0-14 years (%)	2013	14.8
Population aged 60+ years (females and males, % of total)	2013	27.3/22.0
Sex ratio (males per 100 females)	2013	94.0
Life expectancy at birth (females and males, years)	2010-2015	82.8/76.8
Infant mortality rate (per 1 000 live births)	2010-2015	2.8
Fertility rate, total (live births per woman)	2010-2015	1.3
Contraceptive prevalence (ages 15-49, %)	2006-2012	86.8[k]
International migrant stock (000 and % of total population)	mid-2013	893.9/8.4
Refugees and others of concern to UNHCR	mid-2013	1 276[l]
Education: Government expenditure (% of GDP)	2006-2012	5.6
Education: Primary-secondary gross enrolment ratio (f/m per 100)	2006-2012	110.8/111.0
Education: Female third-level students (% of total)	2006-2012	53.3
Intentional homicides (females and males, per 100 000)	2008-2010	1.0/2.5
Seats held by women in national parliaments (%)	2014	31.3

Environmental indicators

Threatened species	2013	249
Forested area (% of land area)	2011	37.8
CO$_2$ emission estimates (000 metric tons and metric tons per capita)	2010	52 318/4.9
Energy consumption per capita (kilograms oil equivalent)[h]	2010	1 774.0
Precipitation in the capital city, total mean (millimetres)		751[m]
Temperature in the capital city, mean °C (minimum and maximum)		12.8/20.8[m]

a Market rate. b Excludes rent. c Age group 15 to 74 years. d 2011: Break in series; data not strictly comparable. e European Labour Force Survey (Eurostat). f The indices are shown in terms of ISIC Rev.3. g Arrivals of non-resident tourists in all types of accommodation establishments. h Includes the Azores and Madeira. i Includes machine to machine (M2M) subscriptions. j Age group 16 to 74 years. k 2005-2006. l Refugee population refers to the end of 2012. m Based on monthly averages for the period 1961-1990.

Puerto Rico

Region	Caribbean
Currency	U.S. Dollar (USD)
Surface area (square kilometres)	8 870
Population in 2012 (estimated, 000)	3 694
Population density in 2012 (per square kilometre)	416.5
Capital city and population in 2011 (000)	San Juan (2 475)

Economic indicators	2005	2010	2012
GDP: Gross domestic product (million current US$)	87 276	100 196	103 516
GDP: Growth rate at constant 2005 prices (annual %)	−1.4	−0.3	−0.8
GDP per capita (current US$)	23 204.7	27 009.4	28 020.9
GNI: Gross national income per capita (current US$)	15 382.1	17 674.6	18 634.3
Gross fixed capital formation (% of GDP)	13.6	9.6	9.6
CPI: Consumer price index (2000=100)	111	131	137
Agricultural production index (2004-2006=100)	97	105	110
Food production index (2004-2006=100)	97	107	112
Unemployment (% of labour force)[ab]	11.3	16.4	14.5
Employment in industrial sector (% of employed)[bc]	19.0	13.7	14.0
Employment in agricultural sector (% of employed)[bc]	2.1	1.6	1.6
Labour force participation, adult female pop. (%)	38.1	35.1	34.1
Labour force participation, adult male pop. (%)	61.0	53.7	51.7
Tourist arrivals at national borders (000)[d]	3 686	3 186	3 069
Energy production, primary (000 mt oil equivalent)	12	14	...
Mobile-cellular subscriptions (per 100 inhabitants)	52.7	78.3	81.8[e]
Individuals using the Internet (%)	23.4[f]	45.3[g]	51.4[f]

Social indicators		
Population growth rate (average annual %)	2010-2015	−0.2
Urban population growth rate (average annual %)	2010-2015	0.1
Rural population growth rate (average annual %)	2010-2015	−9.6
Urban population (%)	2013	99.1
Population aged 0-14 years (%)	2013	19.5
Population aged 60+ years (females and males, % of total)	2013	20.8/17.0
Sex ratio (males per 100 females)	2013	92.6
Life expectancy at birth (females and males, years)	2010-2015	82.5/75.0
Infant mortality rate (per 1 000 live births)	2010-2015	6.3
Fertility rate, total (live births per woman)	2010-2015	1.6
Contraceptive prevalence (ages 15-49, %)[h]	2006-2012	84.1[i]
International migrant stock (000 and % of total population)	mid-2013	319.4/8.7
Education: Primary-secondary gross enrolment ratio (f/m per 100)	2006-2012	84.2/81.1
Education: Female third-level students (% of total)	2006-2012	58.8

Environmental indicators		
Threatened species	2013	115
Forested area (% of land area)	2011	63.2
Energy consumption per capita (kilograms oil equivalent)	2010	195.0
Precipitation in the capital city, total mean (millimetres)		1 431[j]
Temperature in the capital city, mean °C (minimum and maximum)		24.1/30.3[j]

a Official estimates. b Age group 16 years and over. c The indices are shown in terms of ISIC Rev.2. d Air arrivals of non-resident tourists. e October. f ITU estimate. g Population 12 years and over. h Age group 18 to 44 years. i 2002. j Based on monthly averages for the period 1981-2010.

Qatar

Region	Western Asia
Currency	Qatari Rial (QAR)
Surface area (square kilometres)	11 607
Population in 2012 (estimated, 000)	2 051
Population density in 2012 (per square kilometre)	176.7
Capital city and population in 2011 (000)	Doha (567)
United Nations membership date	21 September 1971

Economic indicators	2005	2010	2012
GDP: Gross domestic product (million current US$)	44 531	125 122	192 403
GDP: Growth rate at constant 2005 prices (annual %)	7.5	16.7	6.2
GDP per capita (current US$)	54 228.8	71 510.2	93 831.4
GNI: Gross national income per capita (current US$)	47 268.4	64 112.6	86 569.6
Gross fixed capital formation (% of GDP)	32.0	31.4	28.3
Exchange rates (national currency per US$)[a]	3.64	3.64	3.64
Balance of payments, current account (million US$)	...	...	61 585
CPI: Consumer price index (2000=100)[b]	119	162	165[c]
Industrial production index (2005=100)[d]	100	190	226
Agricultural production index (2004-2006=100)	95	120	133
Food production index (2004-2006=100)	95	120	133
Employment in industrial sector (% of employed)	41.6[def]	58.4[dg]	51.9
Employment in agricultural sector (% of employed)	3.0[def]	1.6[dg]	1.4
Labour force participation, adult female pop. (%)	44.7	50.5	50.8
Labour force participation, adult male pop. (%)	94.1	95.6	95.6
Tourist arrivals at national borders (000)[hij]	913	1 519	2 461
Energy production, primary (000 mt oil equivalent)	97 843	184 273	...
Mobile-cellular subscriptions (per 100 inhabitants)	87.3[k]	124.3[l]	134.1[m]
Individuals using the Internet (%)	24.7	81.6[no]	88.1[no]

Total trade		Major trading partners			2012
	(million US$)	(% of exports)			(% of imports)[p]
Exports	133 717.0	Japan	27.6	Areas nes	18.1
Imports	30 787.0	Republic of Korea	18.5	United States	9.0
Balance	102 930.0	India	10.9	China	8.0

Social indicators		
Population growth rate (average annual %)	2010-2015	5.9
Urban population growth rate (average annual %)	2010-2015	3.0
Rural population growth rate (average annual %)	2010-2015	–8.6
Urban population (%)	2013	99.1
Population aged 0-14 years (%)	2013	13.6
Population aged 60+ years (females and males, % of total)	2013	2.8/1.6
Sex ratio (males per 100 females)	2013	326.1
Life expectancy at birth (females and males, years)	2010-2015	79.4/77.7
Infant mortality rate (per 1 000 live births)	2010-2015	6.5
Fertility rate, total (live births per woman)	2010-2015	2.1
Contraceptive prevalence (ages 15-49, %)	2006-2012	43.2[q]
International migrant stock (000 and % of total population)[r]	mid-2013	1 601.0/73.8
Refugees and others of concern to UNHCR	mid-2013	1 347
Education: Government expenditure (% of GDP)	2006-2012	2.5
Education: Primary-secondary gross enrolment ratio (f/m per 100)	2006-2012	102.5/111.2[s]
Education: Female third-level students (% of total)	2006-2012	65.1
Intentional homicides (females and males, per 100 000)	2008-2010	0.6/0.6
Seats held by women in national parliaments (%)	2014	0.0

Environmental indicators		
Threatened species	2013	35
CO$_2$ emission estimates (000 metric tons and metric tons per capita)	2010	70 473/40.1
Energy consumption per capita (kilograms oil equivalent)	2010	19 588.0
Precipitation in the capital city, total mean (millimetres)		75[t]
Temperature in the capital city, mean °C (minimum and maximum)		21.6/32.7[t]

a Official rate. b Index base 2002=100. c 2011. d The indices are shown in terms of ISIC Rev.3. e 2006. f Break in series; data not strictly comparable. g 2009. h Arrivals of non-resident tourists in hotels and similar establishments. i Arrivals in hotels only. j 1995-2009: Includes domestic tourism. k Active and inactive subscriptions. l Active subscriptions. m Estimate. n Age group 15 years and over living in households (excludes population living in working camps). o Break in comparability. p See technical notes. q 1998. r Data refer to foreign citizens. s 2005. t Based on monthly averages for the period 1962-1992.

Republic of Korea

Region	Eastern Asia
Currency	South Korean Won (KRW)
Surface area (square kilometres)	100 148
Population in 2012 (estimated, 000)	49 003
Population density in 2012 (per square kilometre)	489.3
Capital city and population in 2011 (000)	Seoul (9 736)
United Nations membership date	17 September 1991

Economic indicators	2005	2010	2012
GDP: Gross domestic product (million current US$)	844 866	1 014 890	1 129 598
GDP: Growth rate at constant 2005 prices (annual %)	4.0	6.3	2.0
GDP per capita (current US$)	17 963.2	20 945.5	23 051.8
GNI: Gross national income per capita (current US$)	17 946.3	20 971.9	23 180.2
Gross fixed capital formation (% of GDP)	28.9	28.1	26.7
Exchange rates (national currency per US$)[a]	1 011.60	1 134.80	1 070.60
Balance of payments, current account (million US$)	18 607	29 394	43 335
CPI: Consumer price index (2000=100)[b]	100[c]	116	123
Industrial production index (2005=100)	100	139	149
Agricultural production index (2004-2006=100)	100	102	103
Food production index (2004-2006=100)	100	102	103
Unemployment (% of labour force)	3.7	3.7	3.2
Employment in industrial sector (% of employed)[d]	26.8	17.0	...
Employment in agricultural sector (% of employed)[d]	7.9	6.6	...
Labour force participation, adult female pop. (%)	50.0	49.3	49.9
Labour force participation, adult male pop. (%)	73.4	71.7	72.0
Tourist arrivals at national borders (000)[ef]	6 023	8 798	11 140
Energy production, primary (000 mt oil equivalent)	14 848	15 718	...
Mobile-cellular subscriptions (per 100 inhabitants)	81.5	105.4	110.4
Individuals using the Internet (%)[g]	73.5	83.7	84.1

Total trade		Major trading partners			2012
	(million US$)	(% of exports)			(% of imports)
Exports	547 854.4	China	24.5	China	15.5
Imports	519 575.6	United States	10.7	Japan	12.4
Balance	28 278.8	Japan	7.1	United States	8.4

Social indicators		
Population growth rate (average annual %)	2010-2015	0.5
Urban population growth rate (average annual %)	2010-2015	0.7
Rural population growth rate (average annual %)	2010-2015	−1.3
Urban population (%)	2013	83.8
Population aged 0-14 years (%)	2013	14.9
Population aged 60+ years (females and males, % of total)	2013	19.3/14.9
Sex ratio (males per 100 females)	2013	98.9
Life expectancy at birth (females and males, years)	2010-2015	84.6/77.9
Infant mortality rate (per 1 000 live births)	2010-2015	3.4
Fertility rate, total (live births per woman)	2010-2015	1.3
Contraceptive prevalence (ages 15-49, %)[h]	2006-2012	80.0
International migrant stock (000 and % of total population)[i]	mid-2013	1 232.2/2.5
Refugees and others of concern to UNHCR	mid-2013	2 506
Education: Government expenditure (% of GDP)	2006-2012	5.1
Education: Primary-secondary gross enrolment ratio (f/m per 100)	2006-2012	99.1/100.4
Education: Female third-level students (% of total)	2006-2012	39.6
Intentional homicides (females and males, per 100 000)	2008-2010	2.3/2.2
Seats held by women in national parliaments (%)	2014	15.7

Environmental indicators		
Threatened species	2013	69
Forested area (% of land area)	2011	64.0
CO$_2$ emission estimates (000 metric tons and metric tons per capita)	2010	567 103/11.8
Energy consumption per capita (kilograms oil equivalent)	2010	3 809.0
Precipitation in the capital city, total mean (millimetres)		1 344[j]
Temperature in the capital city, mean °C (minimum and maximum)		8.2/16.9[j]

a Market rate. b Index base 2005=100. c Series replacing former series. d The indices are shown in terms of ISIC Rev.3. e Arrivals of non-resident visitors at national borders. f Includes nationals residing abroad and crew members. g Age group 3 years and over. h Age group 15 to 44 years. i Data refer to foreign citizens. j Based on monthly averages for the period 1971-2000.

Republic of Moldova

Region	Eastern Europe
Currency	Moldovan Leu (MDL)
Surface area (square kilometres)	33 846
Population in 2012 (estimated, 000)	3 514 [a]
Population density in 2012 (per square kilometre)	103.8
Capital city and population in 2011 (000)	Chisinau (677)
United Nations membership date	2 March 1992

Economic indicators	2005	2010	2012
GDP: Gross domestic product (million current US$)	2 988	5 812	7 253
GDP: Growth rate at constant 2005 prices (annual %)	7.5	7.1	−0.8
GDP per capita (current US$)	793.3	1 626.5	2 063.9
GNI: Gross national income per capita (current US$)	900.5	1 762.3	2 233.8
Gross fixed capital formation (% of GDP)	24.6	22.6	23.4
Exchange rates (national currency per US$) [b]	12.83	12.15	12.06
Balance of payments, current account (million US$)	−226	−451	−495
CPI: Consumer price index (2000=100) [c]	100 [d]	153	172
Agricultural production index (2004-2006=100)	100	93	77
Food production index (2004-2006=100)	100	93	77
Unemployment (% of labour force)	7.3	7.4	5.6
Employment in industrial sector (% of employed) [e]	16.0	18.7	19.3
Employment in agricultural sector (% of employed) [e]	40.7	27.5	26.4
Labour force participation, adult female pop. (%)	46.9	37.6	37.0
Labour force participation, adult male pop. (%)	50.6	44.9	43.3
Tourist arrivals at national borders (000) [f]	23	8	11
Energy production, primary (000 mt oil equivalent)	13	18	...
Mobile-cellular subscriptions (per 100 inhabitants)	28.9	88.6	115.9
Individuals using the Internet (%)	14.6	32.3 [g]	43.4 [g]

Total trade		Major trading partners			2012
	(million US$)	(% of exports)		(% of imports)	
Exports	2 161.9	Russian Federation	30.3	Russian Federation	15.7
Imports	5 212.9	Romania	16.5	Romania	11.9
Balance	−3 051.0	Italy	9.4	Ukraine	11.4

Social indicators		
Population growth rate (average annual %) [a]	2010-2015	−0.8
Urban population growth rate (average annual %) [a]	2010-2015	0.8
Rural population growth rate (average annual %) [a]	2010-2015	−2.1
Urban population (%) [a]	2013	49.1
Population aged 0-14 years (%) [a]	2013	16.6
Population aged 60+ years (females and males, % of total) [a]	2013	19.6/14.6
Sex ratio (males per 100 females) [a]	2013	90.1
Life expectancy at birth (females and males, years) [a]	2010-2015	72.8/64.9
Infant mortality rate (per 1 000 live births) [a]	2010-2015	14.0
Fertility rate, total (live births per woman) [a]	2010-2015	1.5
Contraceptive prevalence (ages 15-49, %)	2006-2012	67.8 [h]
International migrant stock (000 and % of total population) [a]	mid-2013	391.5/11.2
Refugees and others of concern to UNHCR	mid-2013	2 277
Education: Government expenditure (% of GDP)	2006-2012	8.4
Education: Primary-secondary gross enrolment ratio (f/m per 100) [i]	2006-2012	80.4/79.7
Education: Female third-level students (% of total)	2006-2012	56.0
Intentional homicides (females and males, per 100 000)	2008-2010	4.1/9.5
Seats held by women in national parliaments (%)	2014	18.8

Environmental indicators		
Threatened species	2013	30
Forested area (% of land area)	2011	11.9
CO$_2$ emission estimates (000 metric tons and metric tons per capita)	2010	4 851/1.4
Energy consumption per capita (kilograms oil equivalent)	2010	575.0
Precipitation in the capital city, total mean (millimetres)		547 [j]
Temperature in the capital city, mean °C (minimum and maximum)		5.6/14.3 [j]

a Includes Transnistria. b Official rate. c Index base 2005=100. d Series replacing former series. e Excludes the Transnistria region and Bender. f Excludes the left bank of the river Nistru and the municipality of Bender. g ITU estimate. h 2005. i National estimate. j Based on monthly averages for the period 1961-1990.

Réunion

Region	Eastern Africa		
Currency	Euro (EUR)		
Surface area (square kilometres)	2 513		
Population in 2012 (estimated, 000)	865		
Population density in 2012 (per square kilometre)	344.3		
Capital city and population in 2011 (000)	Saint-Denis (145)		

Economic indicators	2005	2010	2012
Exchange rates (national currency per US$)[a]	0.85	0.75	0.76
CPI: Consumer price index (2000=100)	110	121	125
Agricultural production index (2004-2006=100)	99	105	108
Food production index (2004-2006=100)	99	105	108
Employment in industrial sector (% of employed)[bc]	...	14.1	13.1
Employment in agricultural sector (% of employed)[bc]	...	4.2	3.9
Labour force participation, adult female pop. (%)	51.1	51.9	51.8
Labour force participation, adult male pop. (%)	64.9	64.4	64.2
Tourist arrivals at national borders (000)	409	420	447
Energy production, primary (000 mt oil equivalent)	53	70	...

Social indicators		
Population growth rate (average annual %)	2010-2015	1.2
Urban population growth rate (average annual %)	2010-2015	1.3
Rural population growth rate (average annual %)	2010-2015	−2.7
Urban population (%)	2013	94.7
Population aged 0-14 years (%)	2013	25.1
Population aged 60+ years (females and males, % of total)	2013	13.6/11.4
Sex ratio (males per 100 females)	2013	96.2
Life expectancy at birth (females and males, years)	2010-2015	82.9/76.0
Infant mortality rate (per 1 000 live births)	2010-2015	4.2
Fertility rate, total (live births per woman)	2010-2015	2.2
Contraceptive prevalence (ages 15-49, %)[d]	2006-2012	66.6[e]
International migrant stock (000 and % of total population)	mid-2013	136.5/15.6

Environmental indicators		
Threatened species	2013	123
Forested area (% of land area)	2011	35.4
CO_2 emission estimates (000 metric tons and metric tons per capita)	2010	4 364/5.2
Energy consumption per capita (kilograms oil equivalent)	2010	1 579.0

a Market rate. b March to June. c Excludes the institutional population. d Age group 20 to 44 years. e 1997.

Romania

Region	Eastern Europe
Currency	Romanian Leu (RON)
Surface area (square kilometres)	238 391
Population in 2012 (estimated, 000)	21 755
Population density in 2012 (per square kilometre)	91.3
Capital city and population in 2011 (000)	Bucharest (1 937)
United Nations membership date	14 December 1955

Economic indicators	2005	2010	2012
GDP: Gross domestic product (million current US$)	99 173	164 792	169 396
GDP: Growth rate at constant 2005 prices (annual %)	4.2	−1.1	0.7
GDP per capita (current US$)	4 484.8	7 538.0	7 786.6
GNI: Gross national income per capita (current US$)	4 353.0	7 445.7	7 720.2
Gross fixed capital formation (% of GDP)	23.7	24.7	26.7
Exchange rates (national currency per US$)[a]	3.11	3.20	3.36
Balance of payments, current account (million US$)	−8 504	−7 258	−7 487
CPI: Consumer price index (2000=100)[b]	232	313	342
Industrial production index (2005=100)	100	123	136
Agricultural production index (2004-2006=100)	95	91	79
Food production index (2004-2006=100)	95	91	79
Unemployment (% of labour force)[c]	7.2	7.3	7.0
Employment in industrial sector (% of employed)	30.3[d]	28.7[e]	28.6[e]
Employment in agricultural sector (% of employed)	32.1[d]	30.1[e]	29.0[e]
Labour force participation, adult female pop. (%)	48.0	48.2	48.5
Labour force participation, adult male pop. (%)	62.5	64.5	64.7
Tourist arrivals at national borders (000)[f]	5 839	7 498	7 937
Energy production, primary (000 mt oil equivalent)	24 645	22 602	...
Mobile-cellular subscriptions (per 100 inhabitants)	61.3	113.4	106.1[g]
Individuals using the Internet (%)[h]	21.5	39.9	50.0

Total trade		Major trading partners			2012
	(million US$)	(% of exports)			(% of imports)
Exports	57 904.3	Germany	18.6	Germany	17.4
Imports	70 259.7	Italy	12.1	Italy	10.9
Balance	−12 355.4	France	7.0	Hungary	9.0

Social indicators		
Population growth rate (average annual %)	2010-2015	−0.3
Urban population growth rate (average annual %)	2010-2015	−0.2
Rural population growth rate (average annual %)	2010-2015	−0.3
Urban population (%)	2013	52.8
Population aged 0-14 years (%)	2013	15.1
Population aged 60+ years (females and males, % of total)	2013	23.8/18.1
Sex ratio (males per 100 females)	2013	95.0
Life expectancy at birth (females and males, years)	2010-2015	77.4/70.2
Infant mortality rate (per 1 000 live births)	2010-2015	10.5
Fertility rate, total (live births per woman)	2010-2015	1.4
Contraceptive prevalence (ages 15-49, %)[i]	2006-2012	70.3[j]
International migrant stock (000 and % of total population)	mid-2013	198.8/0.9
Refugees and others of concern to UNHCR	mid-2013	1 617[k]
Education: Government expenditure (% of GDP)	2006-2012	4.2
Education: Primary-secondary gross enrolment ratio (f/m per 100)	2006-2012	95.2/96.8
Education: Female third-level students (% of total)	2006-2012	56.0
Intentional homicides (females and males, per 100 000)	2008-2010	1.3/2.1
Seats held by women in national parliaments (%)	2014	13.5

Environmental indicators		
Threatened species	2013	86
Forested area (% of land area)	2011	28.7
CO$_2$ emission estimates (000 metric tons and metric tons per capita)	2010	78 681/3.7
Energy consumption per capita (kilograms oil equivalent)	2010	1 366.0
Precipitation in the capital city, total mean (millimetres)		595[l]
Temperature in the capital city, mean °C (minimum and maximum)		5.7/16.5[l]

a Principal rate. b Annual average is the weighted mean of monthly data. c Age group 15 to 74 years. d The indices are shown in terms of ISIC Rev.3. e European Labour Force Survey (Eurostat). f Arrivals of non-resident visitors at national borders. g July. h Age group 16 to 74 years. i Age group 15 to 44 years. j 2004. k Refugee population refers to the end of 2012. l Based on WMO Climatological Normals (CLINO) for the period 1961-1990.

Russian Federation

Region	Eastern Europe
Currency	Russian Rouble (RUB)
Surface area (square kilometres)	17 098 246
Population in 2012 (estimated, 000)	143 170
Population density in 2012 (per square kilometre)	8.4
Capital city and population in 2011 (000)	Moscow (11 621)
United Nations membership date	24 October 1945

Economic indicators	2005	2010	2012
GDP: Gross domestic product (million current US$)	764 016	1 524 917	2 029 812
GDP: Growth rate at constant 2005 prices (annual %)	6.4	4.5	3.4
GDP per capita (current US$)	5 308.1	10 617.9	14 177.7
GNI: Gross national income per capita (current US$)	5 157.2	10 279.0	13 711.1
Gross fixed capital formation (% of GDP)	18.0	21.6	22.0
Exchange rates (national currency per US$)[a]	28.78	30.48	30.37
Balance of payments, current account (million US$)	84 389	67 452	72 016
CPI: Consumer price index (2000=100)	200	325	...
Industrial production index (2005=100)[b]	100	112	120
Agricultural production index (2004-2006=100)	100	94	108
Food production index (2004-2006=100)	100	94	108
Unemployment (% of labour force)[c]	7.2[d]	7.5	5.5
Employment in industrial sector (% of employed)[bc]	29.8	27.9[de]	...
Employment in agricultural sector (% of employed)[bc]	10.2	9.7[de]	...
Labour force participation, adult female pop. (%)	56.2	56.4	57.0
Labour force participation, adult male pop. (%)	68.7	70.8	71.4
Tourist arrivals at national borders (000)[f]	22 201	22 281	28 177
Energy production, primary (000 mt oil equivalent)	1 231 227	1 320 374	...
Mobile-cellular subscriptions (per 100 inhabitants)	83.4	166.3	183.5
Individuals using the Internet (%)	15.2	43.0[g]	53.3[h]

Total trade		Major trading partners			2012
	(million US$)	(% of exports)[i]			(% of imports)
Exports	524 766.4	Netherlands	14.5	China	16.4
Imports	316 192.9	Areas nes	11.9	Germany	12.1
Balance	208 573.5	China	6.8	Ukraine	5.7

Social indicators		
Population growth rate (average annual %)	2010-2015	−0.2
Urban population growth rate (average annual %)	2010-2015	0.1
Rural population growth rate (average annual %)	2010-2015	−0.8
Urban population (%)	2013	74.2
Population aged 0-14 years (%)	2013	15.8
Population aged 60+ years (females and males, % of total)	2013	23.1/14.3
Sex ratio (males per 100 females)	2013	85.6
Life expectancy at birth (females and males, years)	2010-2015	74.3/61.7
Infant mortality rate (per 1 000 live births)	2010-2015	9.7
Fertility rate, total (live births per woman)	2010-2015	1.5
Contraceptive prevalence (ages 15-49, %)[j]	2006-2012	79.5
International migrant stock (000 and % of total population)	mid-2013	11 048.1/7.7
Refugees and others of concern to UNHCR	mid-2013	190 593
Education: Government expenditure (% of GDP)	2006-2012	4.1
Education: Primary-secondary gross enrolment ratio (f/m per 100)	2006-2012	88.5/89.9
Education: Female third-level students (% of total)	2006-2012	56.6
Intentional homicides (females and males, per 100 000)	2008-2010	8.7/29.1
Seats held by women in national parliaments (%)	2014	13.6

Environmental indicators		
Threatened species	2013	124
Forested area (% of land area)	2011	49.4
CO_2 emission estimates (000 metric tons and metric tons per capita)	2010	1 739 352/12.2
Energy consumption per capita (kilograms oil equivalent)	2010	4 732.0
Precipitation in the capital city, total mean (millimetres)		691
Temperature in the capital city, mean °C (minimum and maximum)		1.2/8.9

a Official rate. b The indices are shown in terms of ISIC Rev.3. c Age group 15 to 72 years. d Break in series; data not strictly comparable. e 2009. f Arrivals of non-resident visitors at national borders. g Age group 16 to 74 years. h ITU estimate. i See technical notes. j Age group less than 50 years.

Rwanda

Region	Eastern Africa
Currency	Rwanda Franc (RWF)
Surface area (square kilometres)	26 338
Population in 2012 (estimated, 000)	11 458
Population density in 2012 (per square kilometre)	435.0
Capital city and population in 2011 (000)	Kigali (1 004)
United Nations membership date	18 September 1962

Economic indicators	2005	2010	2012
GDP: Gross domestic product (million current US$)	2 581	5 625	7 103
GDP: Growth rate at constant 2005 prices (annual %)	9.4	7.2	8.0
GDP per capita (current US$)	273.8	519.0	619.9
GNI: Gross national income per capita (current US$)	270.9	514.8	613.5
Gross fixed capital formation (% of GDP)	15.8	21.0	22.9
Exchange rates (national currency per US$)[a]	553.72	594.45	631.41
Balance of payments, current account (million US$)	−65	−414	−821
CPI: Consumer price index (2000=100)[b]	138	214	240
Agricultural production index (2004-2006=100)	100	145	166
Food production index (2004-2006=100)	101	146	168
Employment in industrial sector (% of employed)	3.8[cd]	...	...
Employment in agricultural sector (% of employed)	78.8[cd]	...	...
Labour force participation, adult female pop. (%)	85.7	86.7	86.5
Labour force participation, adult male pop. (%)	83.9	85.6	85.5
Tourist arrivals at national borders (000)	494[e]	504	815
Energy production, primary (000 mt oil equivalent)	6	10	...
Mobile-cellular subscriptions (per 100 inhabitants)	2.4	33.4	50.5
Individuals using the Internet (%)	0.6[f]	8.0	8.0[f]

Total trade	Major trading partners			2012
(million US$)	(% of exports)			(% of imports)
Exports	505.7	United Rep. Tanzania	32.6	Uganda	14.4
Imports	1 624.2	Dem. Rep. of Congo	21.6	China	13.3
Balance	−1 118.5	Kenya	18.7	India	8.3

Social indicators		
Population growth rate (average annual %)	2010-2015	2.7
Urban population growth rate (average annual %)	2010-2015	4.5
Rural population growth rate (average annual %)	2010-2015	2.5
Urban population (%)	2013	19.7
Population aged 0-14 years (%)	2013	42.9
Population aged 60+ years (females and males, % of total)	2013	4.4/3.7
Sex ratio (males per 100 females)	2013	95.4
Life expectancy at birth (females and males, years)	2010-2015	65.3/61.9
Infant mortality rate (per 1 000 live births)	2010-2015	49.8
Fertility rate, total (live births per woman)	2010-2015	4.6
Contraceptive prevalence (ages 15-49, %)	2006-2012	51.6
International migrant stock (000 and % of total population)[g]	mid-2013	452.4/3.8
Refugees and others of concern to UNHCR	mid-2013	77 342
Education: Government expenditure (% of GDP)	2006-2012	4.2
Education: Primary-secondary gross enrolment ratio (f/m per 100)	2006-2012	85.4/83.4
Education: Female third-level students (% of total)	2006-2012	44.9
Intentional homicides (females and males, per 100 000)[h]	2008-2010	6.3/28.2
Seats held by women in national parliaments (%)	2014	63.8

Environmental indicators		
Threatened species	2013	58
Forested area (% of land area)	2011	18.0
CO$_2$ emission estimates (000 metric tons and metric tons per capita)	2010	594/0.1
Energy consumption per capita (kilograms oil equivalent)	2010	19.0[i]
Precipitation in the capital city, total mean (millimetres)		951[j]
Temperature in the capital city, mean °C (minimum and maximum)		15.7/26.9[j]

a Official rate. b Kigali. c The indices are shown in terms of ISIC Rev.3. d Break in series; data not strictly comparable. e 2006. f ITU estimate. g Includes refugees. h Estimates. i UNSD estimate. j Based on monthly averages for the period 1961-1990.

Saint Kitts and Nevis

Region	Caribbean
Currency	E.C. Dollar (XCD)
Surface area (square kilometres)	261
Population in 2012 (estimated, 000)	54
Population density in 2012 (per square kilometre)	205.3
Capital city and population in 2011 (000)	Basseterre (13)
United Nations membership date	23 September 1983

Economic indicators	2005	2010	2012
GDP: Gross domestic product (million current US$)	546	717	765
GDP: Growth rate at constant 2005 prices (annual %)	9.9	−2.4	0.0
GDP per capita (current US$)	11 108.7	13 695.5	14 267.5
GNI: Gross national income per capita (current US$)	10 393.6	13 138.0	13 776.7
Gross fixed capital formation (% of GDP)	42.0	33.0	26.5
Exchange rates (national currency per US$)[a]	2.70	2.70	2.70
Balance of payments, current account (million US$)	−65	−139	−71
CPI: Consumer price index (2000=100)[b]	111	136	145[cd]
Agricultural production index (2004-2006=100)	91	34	38
Food production index (2004-2006=100)	91	34	38
Tourist arrivals at national borders (000)[e]	141	98	104
Mobile-cellular subscriptions (per 100 inhabitants)	103.7[f]	152.7	156.4[g]
Individuals using the Internet (%)[g]	34.0	76.0	79.4

Total trade		Major trading partners			2012
	(million US$)[c]		(% of exports)[c]		(% of imports)[c]
Exports	44.9	United States	81.7	United States	67.3
Imports	246.7	Antigua and Barbuda	3.1	Trinidad and Tobago	6.3
Balance	−201.8	Trinidad and Tobago	2.7	United Kingdom	4.1

Social indicators		
Population growth rate (average annual %)	2010-2015	1.1
Urban population growth rate (average annual %)	2010-2015	1.4
Rural population growth rate (average annual %)	2010-2015	1.1
Urban population (%)	2013	32.1
Life expectancy at birth (females and males, years)[h]	2010-2015	70.7/68.2[i]
Contraceptive prevalence (ages 15-49, %)[j]	2006-2012	40.6[k]
International migrant stock (000 and % of total population)	mid-2013	5.7/10.5
Refugees and others of concern to UNHCR	mid-2013	1
Education: Government expenditure (% of GDP)	2006-2012	4.2
Education: Primary-secondary gross enrolment ratio (f/m per 100)	2006-2012	85.3/83.0
Education: Female third-level students (% of total)	2006-2012	67.3
Seats held by women in national parliaments (%)	2014	6.7

Environmental indicators		
Threatened species	2013	42
Forested area (% of land area)	2011	42.3
CO$_2$ emission estimates (000 metric tons and metric tons per capita)	2010	249/4.7
Energy consumption per capita (kilograms oil equivalent)	2010	1 573.0[l]

a Official rate. **b** Index base 2001=100. **c** 2011. **d** Series linked to former series. **e** Air arrivals of non-resident tourists. **f** December. **g** ITU estimate. **h** Data compiled by the United Nations Demographic Yearbook system. **i** 1998. **j** Age group 15 to 44 years. **k** 1984. **l** UNSD estimate.

Saint Lucia

Region	Caribbean
Currency	E.C. Dollar (XCD)
Surface area (square kilometres)	539 [ab]
Population in 2012 (estimated, 000)	181
Population density in 2012 (per square kilometre)	335.6
Capital city and population in 2011 (000)	Castries (21)
United Nations membership date	18 September 1979

Economic indicators	2005	2010	2012
GDP: Gross domestic product (million current US$)	937	1 252	1 318
GDP: Growth rate at constant 2005 prices (annual %)	−1.2	0.2	−3.0
GDP per capita (current US$)	5 661.9	7 059.6	7 288.9
GNI: Gross national income per capita (current US$)	5 208.0	6 826.8	7 204.0
Gross fixed capital formation (% of GDP)	28.8	27.8	26.2
Exchange rates (national currency per US$) [c]	2.70	2.70	2.70
Balance of payments, current account (million US$)	−129	−203	−184
CPI: Consumer price index (2000=100)	112	128	137
Agricultural production index (2004-2006=100)	89	91	99
Food production index (2004-2006=100)	89	91	99
Employment in industrial sector (% of employed)	16.1 [def]	...	...
Employment in agricultural sector (% of employed)	14.8 [de]	...	...
Labour force participation, adult female pop. (%)	63.1	62.4	62.6
Labour force participation, adult male pop. (%)	77.6	75.9	76.0
Tourist arrivals at national borders (000) [g]	318	306	307
Mobile-cellular subscriptions (per 100 inhabitants)	63.9	113.7	127.7 [h]
Individuals using the Internet (%)	21.6	43.3	48.6 [h]

Total trade		Major trading partners			2012
	(million US$) [i]	(% of exports) [i]		(% of imports) [i]	
Exports	164.0	United States	34.0	United States	42.6
Imports	655.7	Trinidad and Tobago	23.2	Trinidad and Tobago	23.8
Balance	−491.7	United Kingdom	15.1	Japan	4.3

Social indicators		
Population growth rate (average annual %)	2010-2015	0.8
Urban population growth rate (average annual %)	2010-2015	−3.1
Rural population growth rate (average annual %)	2010-2015	1.8
Urban population (%)	2013	16.1
Population aged 0-14 years (%)	2013	24.0
Population aged 60+ years (females and males, % of total)	2013	12.8/11.4
Sex ratio (males per 100 females)	2013	96.5
Life expectancy at birth (females and males, years)	2010-2015	77.4/72.1
Infant mortality rate (per 1 000 live births)	2010-2015	10.5
Fertility rate, total (live births per woman)	2010-2015	1.9
Contraceptive prevalence (ages 15-49, %) [j]	2006-2012	47.3 [k]
International migrant stock (000 and % of total population)	mid-2013	12.2/6.7
Refugees and others of concern to UNHCR	mid-2013	2
Education: Government expenditure (% of GDP)	2006-2012	4.3
Education: Primary-secondary gross enrolment ratio (f/m per 100)	2006-2012	87.9/90.1
Education: Female third-level students (% of total)	2006-2012	68.4
Intentional homicides (females and males, per 100 000)	2008-2010	2.8/41.0
Seats held by women in national parliaments (%)	2014	16.7

Environmental indicators		
Threatened species	2013	51
Forested area (% of land area)	2011	77.1
CO_2 emission estimates (000 metric tons and metric tons per capita)	2010	403/2.3
Energy consumption per capita (kilograms oil equivalent)	2010	775.0
Precipitation in the capital city, total mean (millimetres) [l]		1 399 [m]
Temperature in the capital city, mean °C (minimum and maximum) [l]		24.5/30.0

a Refers to habitable area. b Excludes St. Lucia's Forest Reserve. c Official rate. d 2004. e The indices are shown in terms of ISIC Rev.3. f Excludes mining and quarrying. g Excludes nationals residing abroad. h ITU estimate. i 2008. j Age group 15 to 44 years. k 1988. l Vieux Fort. m Based on monthly averages for the period 1973-2004.

Saint Vincent and the Grenadines

Region	Caribbean
Currency	E.C. Dollar (XCD)
Surface area (square kilometres)	389
Population in 2012 (estimated, 000)	109
Population density in 2012 (per square kilometre)	281.2
Capital city and population in 2011 (000)	Kingstown (31)
United Nations membership date	16 September 1980

Economic indicators	2005	2010	2012
GDP: Gross domestic product (million current US$)	551	681	694
GDP: Growth rate at constant 2005 prices (annual %)	2.5	−3.3	1.6
GDP per capita (current US$)	5 064.2	6 233.0	6 348.8
GNI: Gross national income per capita (current US$)	4 792.0	6 120.7	6 313.9
Gross fixed capital formation (% of GDP)	25.1	25.2	23.6
Exchange rates (national currency per US$)[a]	2.70	2.70	2.70
Balance of payments, current account (million US$)	−102	−208	−216
CPI: Consumer price index (2000=100)	109	135	154
Agricultural production index (2004-2006=100)	104	120	118
Food production index (2004-2006=100)	104	120	118
Labour force participation, adult female pop. (%)	53.3	55.5	55.7
Labour force participation, adult male pop. (%)	79.1	78.5	78.2
Tourist arrivals at national borders (000)[b]	96	72	74
Energy production, primary (000 mt oil equivalent)	2	2[c]	...
Mobile-cellular subscriptions (per 100 inhabitants)	64.9	120.5	123.9
Individuals using the Internet (%)	9.2[d]	38.5[e]	47.5[e]

Total trade	Major trading partners				2012
(million US$)		(% of exports)		(% of imports)	
Exports	43.0	Saint Lucia	25.6	United States	35.6
Imports	403.2	Trinidad and Tobago	15.8	Trinidad and Tobago	26.8
Balance	−360.2	Barbados	14.4	Venezuela	5.6

Social indicators		
Population growth rate (average annual %)	2010-2015	<
Urban population growth rate (average annual %)	2010-2015	0.8
Rural population growth rate (average annual %)	2010-2015	−0.8
Urban population (%)	2013	50.1
Population aged 0-14 years (%)	2013	25.3
Population aged 60+ years (females and males, % of total)	2013	11.0/9.5
Sex ratio (males per 100 females)	2013	101.9
Life expectancy at birth (females and males, years)	2010-2015	74.7/70.3
Infant mortality rate (per 1 000 live births)	2010-2015	17.0
Fertility rate, total (live births per woman)	2010-2015	2.0
Contraceptive prevalence (ages 15-49, %)[f]	2006-2012	58.3[g]
International migrant stock (000 and % of total population)	mid-2013	10.3/9.4
Refugees and others of concern to UNHCR	mid-2013	0[h]
Education: Government expenditure (% of GDP)	2006-2012	5.1
Education: Primary-secondary gross enrolment ratio (f/m per 100)	2006-2012	101.4/105.4
Intentional homicides (females and males, per 100 000)	2008-2010	5.6/30.8
Seats held by women in national parliaments (%)	2014	13.0

Environmental indicators		
Threatened species	2013	46
Forested area (% of land area)	2011	68.7
CO_2 emission estimates (000 metric tons and metric tons per capita)	2010	209/1.9
Energy consumption per capita (kilograms oil equivalent)	2010	650.0[c]

a Official rate. b Air arrivals of non-resident tourists. c UNSD estimate. d Estimate. e ITU estimate. f Age group 15 to 44 years. g 1988. h Value is zero, not available or not applicable.

Samoa

Region	Oceania-Polynesia
Currency	Tala (WST)
Surface area (square kilometres)	2 842
Population in 2012 (estimated, 000)	189
Population density in 2012 (per square kilometre)	66.5
Capital city and population in 2011 (000)	Apia (37)
United Nations membership date	15 December 1976

Economic indicators	2005	2010	2012
GDP: Gross domestic product (million current US$)	434	597	681
GDP: Growth rate at constant 2005 prices (annual %)	5.1	2.1	0.8
GDP per capita (current US$)	2 413.5	3 209.2	3 607.5
GNI: Gross national income per capita (current US$)	2 272.9	3 120.1	3 436.5
Gross fixed capital formation (% of GDP)[a]	10.4	9.0	9.1
Exchange rates (national currency per US$)[b]	2.76	2.34	2.28
Balance of payments, current account (million US$)	−47	−43	−35
CPI: Consumer price index (2000=100)[c]	133	174	188[d]
Agricultural production index (2004-2006=100)	102	109	106
Food production index (2004-2006=100)	102	109	106
Labour force participation, adult female pop. (%)	28.3	24.1	23.4
Labour force participation, adult male pop. (%)	69.2	60.5	58.4
Tourist arrivals at national borders (000)	102	122	126
Energy production, primary (000 mt oil equivalent)	4	5[e]	...
Mobile-cellular subscriptions (per 100 inhabitants)	13.3	...	...
Individuals using the Internet (%)	3.4	7.0[f]	12.9[f]

Total trade		Major trading partners			2012
	(million US$)	(% of exports)[g]			(% of imports)
Exports	76.1	Australia	50.7	New Zealand	24.2
Imports	345.5	Areas nes	23.1	Singapore	23.2
Balance	−269.4	New Zealand	9.7	United States	12.5

Social indicators

Population growth rate (average annual %)	2010-2015	0.8
Urban population growth rate (average annual %)	2010-2015	−0.5
Rural population growth rate (average annual %)	2010-2015	0.7
Urban population (%)	2013	19.4
Population aged 0-14 years (%)	2013	37.8
Population aged 60+ years (females and males, % of total)	2013	8.5/6.6
Sex ratio (males per 100 females)	2013	106.4
Life expectancy at birth (females and males, years)	2010-2015	76.4/70.0
Infant mortality rate (per 1 000 live births)	2010-2015	19.7
Fertility rate, total (live births per woman)	2010-2015	4.2
Contraceptive prevalence (ages 15-49, %)	2006-2012	28.7
International migrant stock (000 and % of total population)	mid-2013	5.6/3.0
Education: Government expenditure (% of GDP)	2006-2012	5.8
Education: Primary-secondary gross enrolment ratio (f/m per 100)	2006-2012	97.6/93.0
Education: Female third-level students (% of total)	2006-2012	44.3[h]
Intentional homicides (females and males, per 100 000)[i]	2008-2010	</1.8
Seats held by women in national parliaments (%)	2014	4.1

Environmental indicators

Threatened species	2013	90
Forested area (% of land area)	2011	60.4
CO_2 emission estimates (000 metric tons and metric tons per capita)	2010	161/0.9
Energy consumption per capita (kilograms oil equivalent)	2010	324.0[e]
Precipitation in the capital city, total mean (millimetres)		2 965[j]
Temperature in the capital city, mean °C (minimum and maximum)		23.5/30.2[j]

a Refers to gross public capital formation. **b** Official rate. **c** Excludes rent. **d** Series linked to former series. **e** UNSD estimate. **f** ITU estimate. **g** See technical notes. **h** 2000. **i** Estimates. **j** Based on monthly averages for the period 1971-2000.

San Marino

Region	Southern Europe
Currency	Euro (EUR)
Surface area (square kilometres)	61
Population in 2012 (estimated, 000)	31
Population density in 2012 (per square kilometre)	512.3
Capital city and population in 2011 (000)	San Marino (4)
United Nations membership date	2 March 1992

Economic indicators	2005	2010	2012
GDP: Gross domestic product (million current US$)	2 044	1 966	1 853
GDP: Growth rate at constant 2005 prices (annual %)	2.3	−7.5	−4.0
GDP per capita (current US$)	68 640.1	63 712.0	59 302.6
GNI: Gross national income per capita (current US$)	60 199.8	55 723.1	51 732.4
Gross fixed capital formation (% of GDP)	35.3	25.8	27.5
Exchange rates (national currency per US$)[a]	0.85	0.75	0.76
CPI: Consumer price index (2000=100)[b]	103	118	125
Unemployment (% of labour force)[cd]	...	...	5.2
Employment in industrial sector (% of employed)[cefg]	39.3	36.9[h]	...
Employment in agricultural sector (% of employed)[ceg]	0.5	0.3[h]	...
Tourist arrivals at national borders (000)[ij]	50	120	139
Mobile-cellular subscriptions (per 100 inhabitants)	56.6	97.0	112.7
Individuals using the Internet (%)	50.3	54.2[k]	50.9[l]

Social indicators		
Population growth rate (average annual %)	2010-2015	0.6
Urban population growth rate (average annual %)	2010-2015	0.7
Rural population growth rate (average annual %)	2010-2015	0.2
Urban population (%)	2013	94.2
Population aged 0-14 years (%)[mno]	2013	15.2[p]
Population aged 60+ years (females and males, % of total)[mno]	2013	23.2/19.7[p]
Sex ratio (males per 100 females)[mno]	2013	96.2[p]
Life expectancy at birth (females and males, years)[m]	2010-2015	84.6/78.0[q]
International migrant stock (000 and % of total population)[r]	mid-2013	4.9/15.4
Education: Primary-secondary gross enrolment ratio (f/m per 100)[s]	2006-2012	93.9/93.6
Education: Female third-level students (% of total)	2006-2012	56.4
Intentional homicides (females and males, per 100 000)	2008-2010	0.0/0.0
Seats held by women in national parliaments (%)	2014	18.3

Environmental indicators		
Forested area (% of land area)	2011	0.0

a Market rate. b Index base 2003=100. c Official estimates. d Age group 14 years and over. e December. f Refers to manufacturing and construction only. g The indices are shown in terms of ISIC Rev.3. h 2008. i Arrivals of non-resident tourists in hotels and similar establishments. j Includes Italian tourists. k 2009. l ITU estimate. m Data compiled by the United Nations Demographic Yearbook system. n Data refer to the latest available census. o De facto estimate. p 2004. q 2000. r Data refer to foreign citizens. s National estimate.

Sao Tome and Principe

Region	Middle Africa
Currency	Dobra (STD)
Surface area (square kilometres)	964
Population in 2012 (estimated, 000)	188
Population density in 2012 (per square kilometre)	195.1
Capital city and population in 2011 (000)	São Tomé (64)
United Nations membership date	16 September 1975

Economic indicators	2005	2010	2012
GDP: Gross domestic product (million current US$)	125	217	261
GDP: Growth rate at constant 2005 prices (annual %)	1.6	4.6	6.5
GDP per capita (current US$)	807.0	1 216.3	1 386.3
GNI: Gross national income per capita (current US$)	792.9	1 220.2	1 396.9
Gross fixed capital formation (% of GDP)	26.5	24.9	24.1
Exchange rates (national currency per US$)[a]	11 929.70	18 335.60	18 569.00
Balance of payments, current account (million US$)	−36	−88	−100
CPI: Consumer price index (2000=100)[b]	561	1 432	...
Agricultural production index (2004-2006=100)	99	118	122
Food production index (2004-2006=100)	99	118	122
Labour force participation, adult female pop. (%)	41.2	44.0	44.9
Labour force participation, adult male pop. (%)	74.9	76.7	77.5
Tourist arrivals at national borders (000)	16	8	12[c]
Mobile-cellular subscriptions (per 100 inhabitants)	7.8	62.1	71.0[d]
Individuals using the Internet (%)	13.8[d]	18.8	21.6[d]

Total trade		Major trading partners			2012
	(million US$)	(% of exports)			(% of imports)
Exports	6.0	Netherlands	43.3	Portugal	52.0
Imports	141.3	France	10.0	Angola	22.4
Balance	−135.3	Spain	10.0	Belgium	3.5

Social indicators		
Population growth rate (average annual %)	2010-2015	2.6
Urban population growth rate (average annual %)	2010-2015	3.0
Rural population growth rate (average annual %)	2010-2015	0.1
Urban population (%)	2013	64.1
Population aged 0-14 years (%)	2013	41.6
Population aged 60+ years (females and males, % of total)	2013	5.2/4.2
Sex ratio (males per 100 females)	2013	97.6
Life expectancy at birth (females and males, years)	2010-2015	68.2/64.2
Infant mortality rate (per 1 000 live births)	2010-2015	43.5
Fertility rate, total (live births per woman)	2010-2015	4.1
Contraceptive prevalence (ages 15-49, %)	2006-2012	38.4
International migrant stock (000 and % of total population)[e]	mid-2013	6.3/3.3
Refugees and others of concern to UNHCR	mid-2013	0[f]
Education: Government expenditure (% of GDP)	2006-2012	9.5
Education: Primary-secondary gross enrolment ratio (f/m per 100)	2006-2012	100.0/98.5
Education: Female third-level students (% of total)	2006-2012	45.7
Intentional homicides (females and males, per 100 000)[g]	2008-2010	0.7/3.4
Seats held by women in national parliaments (%)	2014	18.2

Environmental indicators		
Threatened species	2013	78
Forested area (% of land area)	2011	28.1
CO$_2$ emission estimates (000 metric tons and metric tons per capita)	2010	99/0.6
Energy consumption per capita (kilograms oil equivalent)	2010	203.0

a Official rate. **b** Index base 1996=100. **c** 2011. **d** ITU estimate. **e** Data refer to foreign citizens. **f** Value is zero, not available or not applicable. **g** Estimates.

Saudi Arabia

Region	Western Asia
Currency	Saudi Riyal (SAR)
Surface area (square kilometres)	2 206 714
Population in 2012 (estimated, 000)	28 288
Population density in 2012 (per square kilometre)	12.8
Capital city and population in 2011 (000)	Riyadh (5 451)
United Nations membership date	24 October 1945

Economic indicators	2005	2010	2012
GDP: Gross domestic product (million current US$)	328 461	526 811	711 050
GDP: Growth rate at constant 2005 prices (annual %)	7.3	7.4	5.1
GDP per capita (current US$)	13 303.4	19 326.6	25 136.2
GNI: Gross national income per capita (current US$)	13 320.9	19 585.0	25 524.7
Gross fixed capital formation (% of GDP)	19.3	24.5	22.2
Exchange rates (national currency per US$)[a]	3.74	3.75	3.75
Balance of payments, current account (million US$)	90 060	66 751	164 764
CPI: Consumer price index (2000=100)[b]	100	130	142
Industrial production index (2005=100)[c]	100	112	132
Agricultural production index (2004-2006=100)	100	105	108
Food production index (2004-2006=100)	100	105	108
Unemployment (% of labour force)	6.1[d]	5.6[d]	5.6[e]
Employment in industrial sector (% of employed)[c]	20.3[f]	20.4[g]	24.7
Employment in agricultural sector (% of employed)[c]	4.0[f]	4.1[g]	4.7
Labour force participation, adult female pop. (%)	17.6	17.7	18.2
Labour force participation, adult male pop. (%)	74.1	75.1	75.5
Tourist arrivals at national borders (000)	8 037	10 850	14 276
Energy production, primary (000 mt oil equivalent)[h]	584 410	543 496	...
Mobile-cellular subscriptions (per 100 inhabitants)	58.9	187.9	184.7
Individuals using the Internet (%)	12.7	41.0	54.0[i]

Total trade		Major trading partners			2012
	(million US$)	(% of exports)[j]		(% of imports)	
Exports	388 401.1	Asia nes	60.5	United States	13.0
Imports	155 593.0	N & C Ame nes	14.9	China	12.6
Balance	232 808.1	Europe nes	12.2	Germany	7.0

Social indicators		
Population growth rate (average annual %)	2010-2015	1.9
Urban population growth rate (average annual %)	2010-2015	2.4
Rural population growth rate (average annual %)	2010-2015	1.0
Urban population (%)	2013	82.7
Population aged 0-14 years (%)	2013	29.0
Population aged 60+ years (females and males, % of total)	2013	5.4/4.5
Sex ratio (males per 100 females)	2013	135.1
Life expectancy at birth (females and males, years)	2010-2015	77.5/73.8
Infant mortality rate (per 1 000 live births)	2010-2015	11.2
Fertility rate, total (live births per woman)	2010-2015	2.7
Contraceptive prevalence (ages 15-49, %)	2006-2012	23.8
International migrant stock (000 and % of total population)[kl]	mid-2013	9 060.4/31.4
Refugees and others of concern to UNHCR	mid-2013	70 663
Education: Government expenditure (% of GDP)	2006-2012	5.1
Education: Primary-secondary gross enrolment ratio (f/m per 100)[m]	2006-2012	109.0/107.1
Education: Female third-level students (% of total)	2006-2012	49.3
Intentional homicides (females and males, per 100 000)[n]	2008-2010	1.8/3.5
Seats held by women in national parliaments (%)	2014	19.9

Environmental indicators		
Threatened species	2013	115
Forested area (% of land area)	2011	<
CO$_2$ emission estimates (000 metric tons and metric tons per capita)	2010	464 101/16.9
Energy consumption per capita (kilograms oil equivalent)[h]	2010	6 355.0
Precipitation in the capital city, total mean (millimetres)		111[o]
Temperature in the capital city, mean °C (minimum and maximum)		17.7/33.3[o]

a Official rate. **b** All cities. **c** The indices are shown in terms of ISIC Rev.3. **d** Official estimates. **e** Break in series; data not strictly comparable. **f** 2006. **g** 2009. **h** Data for crude petroleum production include 50 per cent of the output of the Neutral Zone. **i** ITU estimate. **j** See technical notes. **k** Data refer to foreign citizens. **l** Includes refugees. **m** UNESCO estimate. **n** Estimates. **o** Based on monthly averages for the period 1982-2011.

Senegal

Region	Western Africa
Currency	CFA Franc (XOF)
Surface area (square kilometres)	196 712 [a]
Population in 2012 (estimated, 000)	13 726
Population density in 2012 (per square kilometre)	69.8
Capital city and population in 2011 (000)	Dakar (3 035)
United Nations membership date	28 September 1960

Economic indicators	2005	2010	2012
GDP: Gross domestic product (million current US$)	8 708	12 886	13 962
GDP: Growth rate at constant 2005 prices (annual %)	5.6	4.3	3.8
GDP per capita (current US$)	772.6	995.0	1 017.2
GNI: Gross national income per capita (current US$)	767.8	985.4	1 002.4
Gross fixed capital formation (% of GDP)	23.3	22.4	24.7
Exchange rates (national currency per US$) [b]	556.04	490.91	497.16
Balance of payments, current account (million US$)	−676	−589	...
CPI: Consumer price index (2000=100) [c]	108	122 [d]	128
Industrial production index (2005=100) [e]	100	104	110
Agricultural production index (2004-2006=100)	110	150	132
Food production index (2004-2006=100)	110	152	133
Employment in industrial sector (% of employed)	14.8 [efg]	...	...
Employment in agricultural sector (% of employed)	33.7 [efg]	...	...
Labour force participation, adult female pop. (%)	64.7	65.7	65.9
Labour force participation, adult male pop. (%)	87.9	87.9	88.0
Tourist arrivals at national borders (000)	769	900 [h]	1 001 [i]
Energy production, primary (000 mt oil equivalent)	13	17	...
Mobile-cellular subscriptions (per 100 inhabitants)	15.9	67.1	87.5
Individuals using the Internet (%)	4.8	16.0 [j]	19.2 [k]

Total trade		Major trading partners			2012
	(million US$)	(% of exports)			(% of imports)
Exports	2 531.7	Mali	15.6	France	14.7
Imports	6 434.2	Switzerland	13.2	Nigeria	11.8
Balance	−3 902.5	India	11.5	India	6.6

Social indicators		
Population growth rate (average annual %)	2010-2015	2.9
Urban population growth rate (average annual %)	2010-2015	3.3
Rural population growth rate (average annual %)	2010-2015	2.1
Urban population (%)	2013	43.1
Population aged 0-14 years (%)	2013	43.5
Population aged 60+ years (females and males, % of total)	2013	5.0/4.0
Sex ratio (males per 100 females)	2013	96.3
Life expectancy at birth (females and males, years)	2010-2015	64.7/61.8
Infant mortality rate (per 1 000 live births)	2010-2015	49.3
Fertility rate, total (live births per woman)	2010-2015	5.0
Contraceptive prevalence (ages 15-49, %)	2006-2012	13.1
International migrant stock (000 and % of total population) [l]	mid-2013	209.4/1.5
Refugees and others of concern to UNHCR	mid-2013	16 575
Education: Government expenditure (% of GDP)	2006-2012	5.6
Education: Primary-secondary gross enrolment ratio (f/m per 100) [m]	2006-2012	62.8/62.1
Education: Female third-level students (% of total) [n]	2006-2012	37.3
Intentional homicides (females and males, per 100 000) [o]	2008-2010	4.8/12.7
Seats held by women in national parliaments (%)	2014	43.3

Environmental indicators		
Threatened species	2013	103
Forested area (% of land area)	2011	43.8
CO_2 emission estimates (000 metric tons and metric tons per capita)	2010	7 053/0.6
Energy consumption per capita (kilograms oil equivalent)	2010	141.0
Precipitation in the capital city, total mean (millimetres)		514
Temperature in the capital city, mean °C (minimum and maximum)		21.7/27.6

a Surface area is based on the 2002 population and housing census. b Official rate. c Dakar. d Series linked to former series. e The indices are shown in terms of ISIC Rev.3. f 2006. g Break in series; data not strictly comparable. h Estimated data. i 2011. j Age group 12 years and over. k ITU estimate. l Includes refugees. m National estimate. n UNESCO estimate. o Estimates.

Serbia

Region	Southern Europe
Currency	Serbian Dinar (RSD)
Surface area (square kilometres)	88 361
Population in 2012 (estimated, 000)	9 553 [a]
Population density in 2012 (per square kilometre)	108.1
Capital city and population in 2011 (000)	Belgrade (1 135)
United Nations membership date	1 November 2000

Economic indicators

	2005	2010	2012
GDP: Gross domestic product (million current US$)	25 231	37 076	38 491
GDP: Growth rate at constant 2005 prices (annual %)	5.4	1.0	−1.8
GDP per capita (current US$)	3 391.0	5 084.9	5 314.8
GNI: Gross national income per capita (current US$)	3 354.2	4 971.8	5 196.6
Gross fixed capital formation (% of GDP)	19.0	17.8	17.9
Exchange rates (national currency per US$) [b]	...	80.40	85.45
Balance of payments, current account (million US$)	−6 890 [c]	−2 550	−4 002
CPI: Consumer price index (2000=100)	330	137 [d]	153 [de]
Industrial production index (2005=100)	100	97	98
Agricultural production index (2004-2006=100)	...	102	83
Food production index (2004-2006=100)	...	102	83
Unemployment (% of labour force)	13.6 [f]	19.2	23.9
Employment in industrial sector (% of employed)	27.6 [gh]	26.0 [ij]	26.5 [i]
Employment in agricultural sector (% of employed)	23.3 [gh]	22.2 [ij]	21.0 [i]
Labour force participation, adult female pop. (%) [k]	45.7	43.9	44.3
Labour force participation, adult male pop. (%) [k]	64.2	60.4	60.8
Tourist arrivals at national borders (000) [l]	453	683	810
Energy production, primary (000 mt oil equivalent) [m]	9 405	9 543	...
Mobile-cellular subscriptions (per 100 inhabitants)	67.9 [n]	122.1 [n]	92.8 [op]
Individuals using the Internet (%)	26.3 [q]	40.9	48.1 [r]

Total trade		Major trading partners			2012
	(million US$)	(% of exports)		(% of imports)	
Exports	11 353.1	Germany	11.6	Russian Federation	10.9
Imports	19 013.2	Italy	10.6	Germany	10.9
Balance	−7 660.1	Bosnia-Herzegovina	9.5	Italy	9.7

Social indicators

Population growth rate (average annual %) [a]	2010-2015	−0.5
Urban population growth rate (average annual %) [a]	2010-2015	0.5
Rural population growth rate (average annual %) [a]	2010-2015	−0.9
Urban population (%) [a]	2013	57.1
Population aged 0-14 years (%) [a]	2013	16.2
Population aged 60+ years (females and males, % of total) [a]	2013	23.2/18.8
Sex ratio (males per 100 females) [a]	2013	95.6
Life expectancy at birth (females and males, years) [a]	2010-2015	76.8/71.2
Infant mortality rate (per 1 000 live births) [a]	2010-2015	10.9
Fertility rate, total (live births per woman) [a]	2010-2015	1.4
Contraceptive prevalence (ages 15-49, %)	2006-2012	60.8
International migrant stock (000 and % of total population) [a]	mid-2013	532.5/5.6
Refugees and others of concern to UNHCR [a]	mid-2013	293 982
Education: Government expenditure (% of GDP)	2006-2012	4.8
Education: Primary-secondary gross enrolment ratio (f/m per 100) [s]	2006-2012	92.7/91.6
Education: Female third-level students (% of total)	2006-2012	55.8
Intentional homicides (females and males, per 100 000)	2008-2010	1.0/2.5
Seats held by women in national parliaments (%)	2014	33.6

Environmental indicators

Threatened species	2013	57
Forested area (% of land area)	2011	31.6
CO_2 emission estimates (000 metric tons and metric tons per capita)	2010	45 925/4.7
Energy consumption per capita (kilograms oil equivalent) [m]	2010	1 426.0
Precipitation in the capital city, total mean (millimetres)		683 [t]
Temperature in the capital city, mean °C (minimum and maximum)		7.8/16.7 [t]

a Includes Kosovo. **b** UN operational exchange rate. **c** 2007. **d** Index base 2006=100. **e** 2011. **f** 2008. **g** The indices are shown in terms of ISIC Rev.3. **h** October. **i** Average of semi-annual estimates. **j** Break in series; data not strictly comparable. **k** Refers to Serbia and Montenegro. **l** Arrivals of non-resident tourists in all types of accommodation establishments. **m** Excludes Kosovo. **n** Includes inactive prepaid subscriptions. **o** Break in comparability. **p** Includes prepaid subscriptions used in the last 90 days only. **q** Age group 16 to 74 years. **r** ITU estimate. **s** National estimate. **t** Based on monthly averages for the period 1961-1990.

Seychelles

Region	Eastern Africa
Currency	Seychelles Rupee (SCR)
Surface area (square kilometres)	456
Population in 2012 (estimated, 000)	92
Population density in 2012 (per square kilometre)	202.5
Capital city and population in 2011 (000)	Victoria (27)
United Nations membership date	21 September 1976

Economic indicators	2005	2010	2012
GDP: Gross domestic product (million current US$)	919	973	1 031
GDP: Growth rate at constant 2005 prices (annual %)	9.0	5.6	2.8
GDP per capita (current US$)	10 553.1	10 671.8	11 164.3
GNI: Gross national income per capita (current US$)	10 093.0	9 664.0	10 197.6
Gross fixed capital formation (% of GDP)	35.7	36.6	38.8
Exchange rates (national currency per US$)[a]	5.50	12.15	13.00
Balance of payments, current account (million US$)	−174	−214	−279
CPI: Consumer price index (2000=100)	115	215	236
Agricultural production index (2004-2006=100)	98	91	107
Food production index (2004-2006=100)	98	94	111
Tourist arrivals at national borders (000)	129	175	208
Mobile-cellular subscriptions (per 100 inhabitants)	70.4	135.9[b]	158.6[c]
Individuals using the Internet (%)	25.4	41.0[d]	47.1[d]

Total trade		Major trading partners			2012
	(million US$)[e]	(% of exports)[ef]		(% of imports)[e]	
Exports	326.6	Areas nes	27.3	United Arab Emirates	16.7
Imports	986.4	Saudi Arabia	26.9	Saudi Arabia	14.5
Balance	−659.8	France	16.2	Singapore	8.2

Social indicators		
Population growth rate (average annual %)	2010-2015	0.6
Urban population growth rate (average annual %)	2010-2015	1.1
Rural population growth rate (average annual %)	2010-2015	−0.5
Urban population (%)	2013	54.4
Population aged 0-14 years (%)	2013	22.1
Population aged 60+ years (females and males, % of total)	2013	12.5/9.2
Sex ratio (males per 100 females)	2013	103.7
Life expectancy at birth (females and males, years)	2010-2015	78.0/68.9
Infant mortality rate (per 1 000 live births)	2010-2015	8.2
Fertility rate, total (live births per woman)	2010-2015	2.2
International migrant stock (000 and % of total population)	mid-2013	12.1/13.0
Education: Government expenditure (% of GDP)	2006-2012	3.6
Education: Primary-secondary gross enrolment ratio (f/m per 100)	2006-2012	108.0/100.9
Education: Female third-level students (% of total)	2006-2012	74.8
Seats held by women in national parliaments (%)	2014	43.8

Environmental indicators		
Threatened species	2013	272
Forested area (% of land area)	2011	88.5
CO_2 emission estimates (000 metric tons and metric tons per capita)	2010	703/8.1
Energy consumption per capita (kilograms oil equivalent)	2010	2 672.0
Precipitation in the capital city, total mean (millimetres)		2 172[g]
Temperature in the capital city, mean °C (minimum and maximum)		24.4/29.8[g]

a Official rate. b January 2011. c December. d ITU estimate. e 2008. f See technical notes. g Based on WMO Climatological Normals (CLINO) for the period 1971-1990.

Sierra Leone

Region	Western Africa		
Currency	Leone (SLL)		
Surface area (square kilometres)	72 300		
Population in 2012 (estimated, 000)	5 979		
Population density in 2012 (per square kilometre)	82.7		
Capital city and population in 2011 (000)	Freetown (941)		
United Nations membership date	27 September 1961		

Economic indicators	2005	2010	2012
GDP: Gross domestic product (million current US$)	1 651	2 578	4 337
GDP: Growth rate at constant 2005 prices (annual %)	4.5	5.3	32.5
GDP per capita (current US$)	322.4	448.2	725.3
GNI: Gross national income per capita (current US$)	324.6	453.2	751.9
Gross fixed capital formation (% of GDP)	10.9	30.7	21.6
Exchange rates (national currency per US$)[a]	2 932.52	4 198.01	4 334.11
Balance of payments, current account (million US$)	−105	−585	−1 102
CPI: Consumer price index (2000=100)[b]	132	239[c]	313
Agricultural production index (2004-2006=100)	93	149	161
Food production index (2004-2006=100)	93	149	161
Employment in industrial sector (% of employed)	6.5[defghi]	...	...
Employment in agricultural sector (% of employed)	68.5[defghi]	...	...
Labour force participation, adult female pop. (%)	65.5	65.7	65.7
Labour force participation, adult male pop. (%)	67.0	68.6	68.9
Tourist arrivals at national borders (000)[j]	40	39	60
Energy production, primary (000 mt oil equivalent)	2	11[k]	...
Mobile-cellular subscriptions (per 100 inhabitants)	14.2[lm]	34.1[no]	36.1[m]
Individuals using the Internet (%)	0.2	0.6[m]	1.3[m]

Social indicators		
Population growth rate (average annual %)	2010-2015	1.9
Urban population growth rate (average annual %)	2010-2015	3.0
Rural population growth rate (average annual %)	2010-2015	1.5
Urban population (%)	2013	40.0
Population aged 0-14 years (%)	2013	41.6
Population aged 60+ years (females and males, % of total)	2013	4.5/4.3
Sex ratio (males per 100 females)	2013	98.6
Life expectancy at birth (females and males, years)	2010-2015	45.6/45.1
Infant mortality rate (per 1 000 live births)	2010-2015	116.7
Fertility rate, total (live births per woman)	2010-2015	4.8
Contraceptive prevalence (ages 15-49, %)	2006-2012	8.2
International migrant stock (000 and % of total population)[p]	mid-2013	96.4/1.6
Refugees and others of concern to UNHCR	mid-2013	4 218
Education: Government expenditure (% of GDP)	2006-2012	2.9
Education: Primary-secondary gross enrolment ratio (f/m per 100)[q]	2006-2012	47.2/67.3[r]
Education: Female third-level students (% of total)[q]	2006-2012	28.8[s]
Intentional homicides (females and males, per 100 000)[t]	2008-2010	6.3/24.0
Seats held by women in national parliaments (%)	2014	12.1

Environmental indicators		
Threatened species	2013	146
Forested area (% of land area)	2011	37.8
CO_2 emission estimates (000 metric tons and metric tons per capita)	2010	689/0.1
Energy consumption per capita (kilograms oil equivalent)	2010	35.0
Precipitation in the capital city, total mean (millimetres)		2 946[u]
Temperature in the capital city, mean °C (minimum and maximum)		23.8/29.9[u]

a Market rate. b Index base 2003=100. c Series linked to former series. d 2004. e Population census. f The indices are shown in terms of ISIC Rev.3. g Age group 10 years and over. h December. i Break in series; data not strictly comparable. j Air arrivals. k UNSD estimate. l 2007. m ITU estimate. n February 2011. o Includes multiple subscriptions by single individuals. p Includes refugees. q UNESCO estimate. r 2001. s 2002. t Estimates. u Based on monthly averages for the period 1961-1990.

Singapore

Region	South-Eastern Asia
Currency	Singapore Dollar (SGD)
Surface area (square kilometres)	716
Population in 2012 (estimated, 000)	5 303
Population density in 2012 (per square kilometre)	7 408.9
Capital city and population in 2011 (000)	Singapore (5 188)
United Nations membership date	21 September 1965

Economic indicators	2005	2010	2012
GDP: Gross domestic product (million current US$)	125 429	231 697	276 520
GDP: Growth rate at constant 2005 prices (annual %)	7.4	14.8	1.3
GDP per capita (current US$)	27 900.8	45 619.0	52 141.5
GNI: Gross national income per capita (current US$)	26 027.9	45 397.7	51 550.1
Gross fixed capital formation (% of GDP)	21.1	23.5	24.1
Exchange rates (national currency per US$)[a]	1.66	1.29	1.22
Balance of payments, current account (million US$)	26 869	62 026	51 437
CPI: Consumer price index (2000=100)	103	117	129
Agricultural production index (2004-2006=100)	90	92	105
Food production index (2004-2006=100)	90	92	105
Unemployment (% of labour force)	2.8[b]	2.1	1.8
Employment in industrial sector (% of employed)[cdef]	21.7	21.8[gh]	...
Employment in agricultural sector (% of employed)[cdfi]	1.1	1.1[gh]	...
Labour force participation, adult female pop. (%)	53.5	57.3	59.0
Labour force participation, adult male pop. (%)	76.7	77.5	77.5
Tourist arrivals at national borders (000)	7 079	9 161	11 098
Mobile-cellular subscriptions (per 100 inhabitants)	102.8	145.2	153.4[j]
Individuals using the Internet (%)	61.0[k]	71.0[l]	74.2[m]

Total trade		Major trading partners			2012
	(million US$)	(% of exports)			(% of imports)
Exports	408 393.0	Malaysia	12.3	Malaysia	10.6
Imports	379 722.9	China, Hong Kong SAR	11.0	China	10.3
Balance	28 670.1	China	10.8	United States	10.2

Social indicators

Population growth rate (average annual %)	2010-2015	2.0
Urban population growth rate (average annual %)	2010-2015	1.1
Rural population growth rate (average annual %)	2010-2015	0.0
Urban population (%)	2013	100.0
Population aged 0-14 years (%)	2013	16.1
Population aged 60+ years (females and males, % of total)	2013	16.7/14.9
Sex ratio (males per 100 females)	2013	97.4
Life expectancy at birth (females and males, years)	2010-2015	84.6/79.7
Infant mortality rate (per 1 000 live births)	2010-2015	1.8
Fertility rate, total (live births per woman)	2010-2015	1.3
Contraceptive prevalence (ages 15-49, %)[n]	2006-2012	62.0[o]
International migrant stock (000 and % of total population)	mid-2013	2 323.3/42.9
Refugees and others of concern to UNHCR	mid-2013	3
Education: Government expenditure (% of GDP)	2006-2012	3.2
Education: Female third-level students (% of total)	2006-2012	49.6
Intentional homicides (females and males, per 100 000)	2008-2010	0.5/1.0
Seats held by women in national parliaments (%)	2014	25.3

Environmental indicators

Threatened species	2013	287
Forested area (% of land area)	2011	3.3
CO_2 emission estimates (000 metric tons and metric tons per capita)	2010	13 509/2.6
Energy consumption per capita (kilograms oil equivalent)	2010	4 049.0
Precipitation in the capital city, total mean (millimetres)		2 150[p]
Temperature in the capital city, mean °C (minimum and maximum)		23.9/30.9[p]

a Market rate. b 2006. c June. d Data refer to permanent residents. e Refers to manufacturing and construction only. f The indices are shown in terms of ISIC Rev.3. g 2009. h Break in series; data not strictly comparable. i Includes mining and quarrying, electricity, gas and water supply and activities not classifiable by economic activity. j December. k Age group 15 years and over. l Age group 7 years and over. m ITU estimate. n Age group 15 to 44 years. o 1997. p Based on monthly averages for the period 1961-1990.

Slovakia

Region	Eastern Europe
Currency	Euro (EUR)[a]
Surface area (square kilometres)	49 036[b]
Population in 2012 (estimated, 000)	5 446
Population density in 2012 (per square kilometre)	111.1
Capital city and population in 2011 (000)	Bratislava (434)
United Nations membership date	19 January 1993

Economic indicators

	2005	2010	2012
GDP: Gross domestic product (million current US$)	47 896	87 276	91 349
GDP: Growth rate at constant 2005 prices (annual %)	6.7	4.4	1.8
GDP per capita (current US$)	8 883.6	16 062.7	16 774.3
GNI: Gross national income per capita (current US$)	8 632.5	15 845.5	16 422.0
Gross fixed capital formation (% of GDP)	26.6	21.0	20.1
Exchange rates (national currency per US$)	31.95[cd]	0.75[ef]	0.76[ef]
Balance of payments, current account (million US$)	−4 005	−3 240	2 039
CPI: Consumer price index (2000=100)	133	153	165
Industrial production index (2005=100)	100	127	145
Agricultural production index (2004-2006=100)	102	83	82
Food production index (2004-2006=100)	102	83	82
Unemployment (% of labour force)[g]	16.3	14.4	14.0[h]
Employment in industrial sector (% of employed)	38.8[ijk]	37.1[l]	37.5[hl]
Employment in agricultural sector (% of employed)	4.7[ijk]	3.2[l]	3.2[hl]
Labour force participation, adult female pop. (%)	51.2	50.8	51.0
Labour force participation, adult male pop. (%)	68.4	67.9	68.7
Tourist arrivals at national borders (000)	6 184	5 415	6 235
Energy production, primary (000 mt oil equivalent)	2 832	2 696	...
Mobile-cellular subscriptions (per 100 inhabitants)	83.8[m]	108.5	111.2
Individuals using the Internet (%)[n]	55.2	75.7[o]	80.0

Total trade

	(million US$)
Exports	79 867.0
Imports	76 859.4
Balance	3 007.6

Major trading partners
2012

(% of exports)		(% of imports)[p]	
Germany	21.4	Germany	17.1
Czech Republic	14.0	Europe nes	12.8
Poland	8.1	Russian Federation	9.9

Social indicators

Population growth rate (average annual %)	2010-2015	0.1
Urban population growth rate (average annual %)	2010-2015	0.1
Rural population growth rate (average annual %)	2010-2015	0.3
Urban population (%)	2013	54.6
Population aged 0-14 years (%)	2013	15.1
Population aged 60+ years (females and males, % of total)	2013	22.2/16.0
Sex ratio (males per 100 females)	2013	94.7
Life expectancy at birth (females and males, years)	2010-2015	79.2/71.5
Infant mortality rate (per 1 000 live births)	2010-2015	5.4
Fertility rate, total (live births per woman)	2010-2015	1.4
Contraceptive prevalence (ages 15-49, %)[q]	2006-2012	79.8[r]
International migrant stock (000 and % of total population)[s]	mid-2013	149.6/2.8
Refugees and others of concern to UNHCR	mid-2013	2 507[t]
Education: Government expenditure (% of GDP)	2006-2012	4.2
Education: Primary-secondary gross enrolment ratio (f/m per 100)	2006-2012	95.9/95.6
Education: Female third-level students (% of total)	2006-2012	59.6
Intentional homicides (females and males, per 100 000)	2008-2010	0.9/2.3
Seats held by women in national parliaments (%)	2014	18.7

Environmental indicators

Threatened species	2013	46
Forested area (% of land area)	2011	40.2
CO$_2$ emission estimates (000 metric tons and metric tons per capita)	2010	36 065/6.6
Energy consumption per capita (kilograms oil equivalent)	2010	2 694.0
Precipitation in the capital city, total mean (millimetres)		557[u]
Temperature in the capital city, mean °C (minimum and maximum)		5.7/15.2[u]

a Beginning 1 January 2009, the Slovak Koruna (SKK) was replaced by the euro (1 EUR=30.126 SKK). b Excludes inland water. c Official rate. d Slovak Koruna (SKK). e Market rate. f Euro. g Age group 15 to 74 years. h Break in series; data not strictly comparable. i The indices are shown in terms of ISIC Rev.3. j Excludes conscripts. k Excludes persons on child-care leave. l European Labour Force Survey (Eurostat). m No distinction made between active or inactive subscribers. n Age group 16 to 74 years. o Within the last 3 months. p See technical notes. q Age group 15 to 44 years. r 1997. s Includes refugees. t Refugee population refers to the end of 2012. u Based on monthly averages for the period 1971-2000.

Slovenia

Region	Southern Europe
Currency	Euro (EUR)[a]
Surface area (square kilometres)	20 273
Population in 2012 (estimated, 000)	2 068
Population density in 2012 (per square kilometre)	102.0
Capital city and population in 2011 (000)	Ljubljana (273)
United Nations membership date	22 May 1992

Economic indicators	2005	2010	2012
GDP: Gross domestic product (million current US$)	35 718	46 997	45 380
GDP: Growth rate at constant 2005 prices (annual %)	4.0	1.3	−2.5
GDP per capita (current US$)	17 855.8	22 878.0	21 946.7
GNI: Gross national income per capita (current US$)	17 717.8	22 583.4	21 705.9
Gross fixed capital formation (% of GDP)	25.4	19.7	17.8
Exchange rates (national currency per US$)	202.43[bc]	0.75[de]	0.76[de]
Balance of payments, current account (million US$)	−681	−59	1 486
CPI: Consumer price index (2000=100)	131	150	157
Industrial production index (2005=100)	100	103	103
Agricultural production index (2004-2006=100)	99	92	84
Food production index (2004-2006=100)	99	92	84
Unemployment (% of labour force)[f]	6.5	7.2	8.8
Employment in industrial sector (% of employed)	37.2[ghi]	32.5[j]	30.8[j]
Employment in agricultural sector (% of employed)	8.8[ghi]	8.8[j]	8.3[j]
Labour force participation, adult female pop. (%)	52.8	53.1	52.3
Labour force participation, adult male pop. (%)	66.0	65.6	63.5
Tourist arrivals at national borders (000)[k]	1 555	1 869	2 156
Energy production, primary (000 mt oil equivalent)	1 991	2 076	...
Mobile-cellular subscriptions (per 100 inhabitants)	87.9[l]	104.6	110.1
Individuals using the Internet (%)	46.8[m]	70.0[n]	70.0[n]

Total trade		Major trading partners			2012
	(million US$)	(% of exports)		(% of imports)	
Exports	27 080.0	Germany	21.2	Italy	17.3
Imports	28 382.6	Italy	11.3	Germany	16.2
Balance	−1 302.6	Austria	8.2	Austria	8.1

Social indicators		
Population growth rate (average annual %)	2010-2015	0.2
Urban population growth rate (average annual %)	2010-2015	0.2
Rural population growth rate (average annual %)	2010-2015	0.3
Urban population (%)	2013	49.8
Population aged 0-14 years (%)	2013	14.3
Population aged 60+ years (females and males, % of total)	2013	26.9/20.7
Sex ratio (males per 100 females)	2013	98.8
Life expectancy at birth (females and males, years)	2010-2015	82.7/76.2
Infant mortality rate (per 1 000 live births)	2010-2015	2.8
Fertility rate, total (live births per woman)	2010-2015	1.5
Contraceptive prevalence (ages 15-49, %)[o]	2006-2012	78.9[p]
International migrant stock (000 and % of total population)	mid-2013	233.3/11.3
Refugees and others of concern to UNHCR	mid-2013	241
Education: Government expenditure (% of GDP)	2006-2012	5.7
Education: Primary-secondary gross enrolment ratio (f/m per 100)	2006-2012	97.8/98.5
Education: Female third-level students (% of total)	2006-2012	60.6
Intentional homicides (females and males, per 100 000)	2008-2010	0.7/0.6
Seats held by women in national parliaments (%)	2014	33.3

Environmental indicators		
Threatened species	2013	123
Forested area (% of land area)	2011	62.3
CO_2 emission estimates (000 metric tons and metric tons per capita)	2010	15 316/7.6
Energy consumption per capita (kilograms oil equivalent)	2010	2 734.0
Precipitation in the capital city, total mean (millimetres)		1 368[q]
Temperature in the capital city, mean °C (minimum and maximum)		5.9/15.1[q]

a Beginning 1 January 2007, the Slovenian tolar (SIT) was replaced by the euro (1 EUR=239.64 SIT). b Official rate. c Slovenian tolar (SIT). d Market rate. e Euro. f Age group 15 to 74 years. g The indices are shown in terms of ISIC Rev.3. h Second quarter. i Excludes conscripts and regular military living in barracks. j European Labour Force Survey (Eurostat). k Arrivals of non-resident tourists in all types of accommodation establishments. l Revised methodology. m Using the Internet within the last 3 months. n Age group 16 to 74 years. o Age group 15 to 44 years. p 1994-1995. q Based on monthly averages for the period 1971-2000.

Solomon Islands

Region	Oceania-Melanesia
Currency	Solomon Is. Dollar (SBD)
Surface area (square kilometres)	28 896
Population in 2012 (estimated, 000)	550
Population density in 2012 (per square kilometre)	19.0
Capital city and population in 2011 (000)	Honiara (68)
United Nations membership date	19 September 1978

Economic indicators	2005	2010	2012
GDP: Gross domestic product (million current US$)	429	682	1 010
GDP: Growth rate at constant 2005 prices (annual %)	12.8	7.0	4.8
GDP per capita (current US$)	915.1	1 295.1	1 837.0
GNI: Gross national income per capita (current US$)	918.7	1 058.6	1 542.8
Gross fixed capital formation (% of GDP)	16.0	35.9	21.5
Exchange rates (national currency per US$)[a]	7.58	8.06	7.34
Balance of payments, current account (million US$)	−90	−210	2
CPI: Consumer price index (2000=100)[b]	149	226	249
Agricultural production index (2004-2006=100)	103	121	120
Food production index (2004-2006=100)	103	121	120
Labour force participation, adult female pop. (%)	53.7	53.4	53.4
Labour force participation, adult male pop. (%)	79.1	79.3	79.1
Tourist arrivals at national borders (000)	9[c]	21	24
Mobile-cellular subscriptions (per 100 inhabitants)	1.3	21.5	53.3
Individuals using the Internet (%)	0.8	5.0[d]	7.0[d]

Total trade		Major trading partners			2012
	(million US$)	(% of exports)			(% of imports)
Exports	491.7	China	40.4	Australia	31.8
Imports	493.4	Australia	24.0	Singapore	28.2
Balance	−1.7	United Kingdom	8.2	China	8.5

Social indicators		
Population growth rate (average annual %)	2010-2015	2.1
Urban population growth rate (average annual %)	2010-2015	4.7
Rural population growth rate (average annual %)	2010-2015	1.9
Urban population (%)	2013	21.4
Population aged 0-14 years (%)	2013	40.2
Population aged 60+ years (females and males, % of total)	2013	5.1/5.1
Sex ratio (males per 100 females)	2013	103.1
Life expectancy at birth (females and males, years)	2010-2015	69.0/66.2
Infant mortality rate (per 1 000 live births)	2010-2015	38.0
Fertility rate, total (live births per woman)	2010-2015	4.1
Contraceptive prevalence (ages 15-49, %)	2006-2012	34.6
International migrant stock (000 and % of total population)	mid-2013	7.9/1.4
Refugees and others of concern to UNHCR	mid-2013	3
Education: Government expenditure (% of GDP)	2006-2012	7.3
Education: Primary-secondary gross enrolment ratio (f/m per 100)	2006-2012	93.5/95.9
Intentional homicides (females and males, per 100 000)[e]	2008-2010	</1.3
Seats held by women in national parliaments (%)	2014	2.0

Environmental indicators		
Threatened species	2013	234
Forested area (% of land area)	2011	78.9
CO$_2$ emission estimates (000 metric tons and metric tons per capita)	2010	202/0.4
Energy consumption per capita (kilograms oil equivalent)	2010	121.0[f]
Precipitation in the capital city, total mean (millimetres)[g]		3 290[h]
Temperature in the capital city, mean °C (minimum and maximum)[g]		23.2/30.1[h]

a Official rate. **b** Honiara. **c** Excludes first quarter. **d** ITU estimate. **e** Estimates. **f** UNSD estimate. **g** Auki. **h** Based on WMO Climatological Normals (CLINO) for the period 1962-1990.

Somalia

Region	Eastern Africa
Currency	Somalia Shilling (SOS)
Surface area (square kilometres)	637 657
Population in 2012 (estimated, 000)	10 195
Population density in 2012 (per square kilometre)	16.0
Capital city and population in 2011 (000)	Mogadishu (1 554)
United Nations membership date	20 September 1960

Economic indicators	2005	2010	2012
GDP: Gross domestic product (million current US$)	2 316	1 071	1 306
GDP: Growth rate at constant 2005 prices (annual %)	3.0	2.6	2.6
GDP per capita (current US$)	273.5	111.2	128.1
GNI: Gross national income per capita (current US$)	262.5	106.7	122.9
Gross fixed capital formation (% of GDP)	20.3	19.9	20.0
Exchange rates (national currency per US$)[a]	15 141.00	31 900.00[b]	24 300.00[c]
Agricultural production index (2004-2006=100)	100	107	115
Food production index (2004-2006=100)	100	107	115
Labour force participation, adult female pop. (%)	36.6	37.0	37.2
Labour force participation, adult male pop. (%)	76.5	75.8	75.6
Mobile-cellular subscriptions (per 100 inhabitants)	6.0	7.0[d]	6.7[d]
Individuals using the Internet (%)[d]	1.1	1.3[e]	1.4

Social indicators		
Population growth rate (average annual %)	2010-2015	2.9
Urban population growth rate (average annual %)	2010-2015	3.8
Rural population growth rate (average annual %)	2010-2015	1.8
Urban population (%)	2013	38.7
Population aged 0-14 years (%)	2013	47.2
Population aged 60+ years (females and males, % of total)	2013	4.8/4.1
Sex ratio (males per 100 females)	2013	99.0
Life expectancy at birth (females and males, years)	2010-2015	56.5/53.3
Infant mortality rate (per 1 000 live births)	2010-2015	79.5
Fertility rate, total (live births per woman)	2010-2015	6.6
Contraceptive prevalence (ages 15-49, %)	2006-2012	14.6
International migrant stock (000 and % of total population)[fg]	mid-2013	24.6/0.2
Refugees and others of concern to UNHCR	mid-2013	1 144 309
Education: Primary-secondary gross enrolment ratio (f/m per 100)[h]	2006-2012	13.8/25.8
Intentional homicides (females and males, per 100 000)[f]	2008-2010	1.5/1.6
Seats held by women in national parliaments (%)	2014	13.8

Environmental indicators		
Threatened species	2013	164
Forested area (% of land area)	2011	10.6
CO_2 emission estimates (000 metric tons and metric tons per capita)	2010	608/0.1
Energy consumption per capita (kilograms oil equivalent)	2010	22.0[i]

a UN operational exchange rate. b September 2009. c April 2012. d ITU estimate. e 2011. f Estimates.
g Includes refugees. h UNESCO estimate. i UNSD estimate.

South Africa

Region	Southern Africa
Currency	Rand (ZAR)
Surface area (square kilometres)	1 221 037
Population in 2012 (estimated, 000)	52 386
Population density in 2012 (per square kilometre)	42.9
Capital city and population in 2011 (000)	Pretoria (1 501)[a]
United Nations membership date	7 November 1945

Economic indicators	2005	2010	2012
GDP: Gross domestic product (million current US$)	247 052	363 241	384 313
GDP: Growth rate at constant 2005 prices (annual %)	5.3	3.1	2.6
GDP per capita (current US$)	5 121.8	7 059.8	7 336.2
GNI: Gross national income per capita (current US$)	5 019.4	6 919.3	7 173.4
Gross fixed capital formation (% of GDP)	16.8	19.3	19.2
Exchange rates (national currency per US$)[b]	6.32	6.63	8.50
Balance of payments, current account (million US$)	−8 518	−7 023	−20 016
CPI: Consumer price index (2000=100)	128	179	198
Agricultural production index (2004-2006=100)	102	118	120
Food production index (2004-2006=100)	102	118	121
Unemployment (% of labour force)[c]	23.8	24.9	25.1
Employment in industrial sector (% of employed)[c]	25.6[d]	24.5[ef]	24.3[efg]
Employment in agricultural sector (% of employed)[c]	7.5[d]	4.9[ef]	4.6[efg]
Labour force participation, adult female pop. (%)	46.5	43.5	44.2
Labour force participation, adult male pop. (%)	62.2	59.9	60.0
Tourist arrivals at national borders (000)[hi]	7 369	8 074	9 188
Energy production, primary (000 mt oil equivalent)	132 694	136 342	...
Mobile-cellular subscriptions (per 100 inhabitants)	71.1	100.5	134.8[j]
Individuals using the Internet (%)	7.5	24.0[j]	41.0[j]

Total trade		Major trading partners			2012
	(million US$)		(% of exports)[k]		(% of imports)
Exports	86 712.0	China	11.7	China	14.4
Imports	101 610.6	Areas nes	10.4	Germany	10.1
Balance	−14 898.6	United States	8.7	Saudi Arabia	7.8

Social indicators

Population growth rate (average annual %)	2010-2015	0.8
Urban population growth rate (average annual %)	2010-2015	1.2
Rural population growth rate (average annual %)	2010-2015	−0.7
Urban population (%)	2013	62.9
Population aged 0-14 years (%)	2013	29.5
Population aged 60+ years (females and males, % of total)	2013	10.3/6.8
Sex ratio (males per 100 females)	2013	94.3
Life expectancy at birth (females and males, years)	2010-2015	59.1/54.9
Infant mortality rate (per 1 000 live births)	2010-2015	38.3
Fertility rate, total (live births per woman)	2010-2015	2.4
Contraceptive prevalence (ages 15-49, %)	2006-2012	59.9[l]
International migrant stock (000 and % of total population)[m]	mid-2013	2 399.2/4.6
Refugees and others of concern to UNHCR	mid-2013	295 675[n]
Education: Government expenditure (% of GDP)	2006-2012	6.0
Education: Primary-secondary gross enrolment ratio (f/m per 100)	2006-2012	100.8/102.7
Intentional homicides (females and males, per 100 000)	2008-2010	10.1/45.4
Seats held by women in national parliaments (%)[o]	2014	44.8

Environmental indicators

Threatened species	2013	461
Forested area (% of land area)	2011	7.6
CO_2 emission estimates (000 metric tons and metric tons per capita)	2010	459 748/9.2
Energy consumption per capita (kilograms oil equivalent)	2010	2 452.0
Precipitation in the capital city, total mean (millimetres)[p]		713[q]
Temperature in the capital city, mean °C (minimum and maximum)[p]		10.1/21.9[q]

a Pretoria is the administrative capital, Cape Town is the legislative capital and Bloemfontein is the judicial capital. b Principal rate. c Age group 15 to 64 years. d The indices are shown in terms of ISIC Rev. 3. e The indices are shown in terms of ISIC Rev.2. f Average of quarterly estimates. g 2011. h 1995-2008: Excludes arrivals for work and contract workers. i 2009: Methodology revised; data not strictly comparable. j ITU estimate. k See technical notes. l 2003-2004. m Includes refugees. n Refers to the end of 2012 in the absence of updated information provided by the Government of South Africa. o The figures on the distribution of seats do not include the 36 special rotating delegates appointed on an ad hoc basis, and all percentages given are therefore calculated on the basis of the 54 permanent seats. p Johannesburg. q Based on monthly averages for the period 1961-1990.

South Sudan

Region	Eastern Africa		
Currency	South Sudanese Pound (SSP)		
Population in 2012 (estimated, 000)	10 838		
Capital city and population in 2011 (000)	Juba (269)		
United Nations membership date	14 July 2011		

Economic indicators	2005	2010	2012
GDP: Gross domestic product (million current US$)	...	15 171	10 060
GDP: Growth rate at constant 2005 prices (annual %)	...	4.2	−53.0
GDP per capita (current US$)	...	1 526.1	928.3
GNI: Gross national income per capita (current US$)	...	846.1	549.7
Gross fixed capital formation (% of GDP)	...	10.7	7.2
Exchange rates (national currency per US$)[a]	...	...	3.05
Mobile-cellular subscriptions (per 100 inhabitants)	...	...	18.8

Social indicators		
Population growth rate (average annual %)	2010-2015	4.0
Urban population growth rate (average annual %)	2010-2015	4.2
Rural population growth rate (average annual %)	2010-2015	2.9
Urban population (%)	2013	18.4
Population aged 0-14 years (%)	2013	42.1
Population aged 60+ years (females and males, % of total)	2013	5.6/4.9
Sex ratio (males per 100 females)	2013	100.1
Life expectancy at birth (females and males, years)	2010-2015	56.0/53.9
Infant mortality rate (per 1 000 live births)	2010-2015	78.0
Fertility rate, total (live births per woman)	2010-2015	5.0
Contraceptive prevalence (ages 15-49, %)	2006-2012	3.5
International migrant stock (000 and % of total population)[b]	mid-2013	629.6/5.6
Refugees and others of concern to UNHCR	mid-2013	625 489[c]
Seats held by women in national parliaments (%)	2014	26.5

Environmental indicators		
Threatened species	2013	17

a UN operational exchange rate. b Includes refugees. c Includes 155,200 people who are in an internally displaced person-like situation.

Spain

Region	Southern Europe
Currency	Euro (EUR)
Surface area (square kilometres)	505 992
Population in 2012 (estimated, 000)	46 755 [a]
Population density in 2012 (per square kilometre)	92.4
Capital city and population in 2011 (000)	Madrid (6 574)
United Nations membership date	14 December 1955

Economic indicators	2005	2010	2012
GDP: Gross domestic product (million current US$)	1 130 799	1 384 845	1 322 126
GDP: Growth rate at constant 2005 prices (annual %)	3.6	−0.2	−1.6
GDP per capita (current US$)	26 062.8	29 986.7	28 278.0
GNI: Gross national income per capita (current US$)	25 692.7	29 602.8	27 948.8
Gross fixed capital formation (% of GDP)	29.3	23.7	21.1
Exchange rates (national currency per US$) [b]	0.85	0.75	0.76
Balance of payments, current account (million US$)	−83 388	−62 498	−15 142
CPI: Consumer price index (2000=100) [c]	114	128	135
Industrial production index (2005=100)	100	83	77
Agricultural production index (2004-2006=100)	95	103	90
Food production index (2004-2006=100)	94	104	90
Unemployment (% of labour force) [d]	9.2 [e]	20.1	25.0
Employment in industrial sector (% of employed) [fg]	29.7 [h]	23.1	20.7
Employment in agricultural sector (% of employed) [fg]	5.3 [h]	4.3	4.4
Labour force participation, adult female pop. (%)	45.8	51.4	52.6
Labour force participation, adult male pop. (%)	68.0	67.3	66.5
Tourist arrivals at national borders (000)	55 914	52 677	57 701
Energy production, primary (000 mt oil equivalent) [i]	15 604	17 885	...
Mobile-cellular subscriptions (per 100 inhabitants)	98.4	111.5	108.3 [jk]
Individuals using the Internet (%)	47.9 [l]	65.8 [m]	72.0 [d]

Total trade		Major trading partners			2012
	(million US$)		(% of exports)		(% of imports)
Exports	285 936.4	France	16.2	Germany	10.7
Imports	325 835.2	Germany	10.5	France	10.5
Balance	−39 898.8	Italy	7.4	China	7.0

Social indicators		
Population growth rate (average annual %) [a]	2010-2015	0.4
Urban population growth rate (average annual %) [a]	2010-2015	0.8
Rural population growth rate (average annual %) [a]	2010-2015	−<
Urban population (%) [a]	2013	77.7
Population aged 0-14 years (%) [a]	2013	15.4
Population aged 60+ years (females and males, % of total) [a]	2013	25.6/20.6
Sex ratio (males per 100 females) [a]	2013	97.7
Life expectancy at birth (females and males, years) [a]	2010-2015	85.2/78.8
Infant mortality rate (per 1 000 live births) [a]	2010-2015	3.1
Fertility rate, total (live births per woman) [a]	2010-2015	1.5
Contraceptive prevalence (ages 15-49, %)	2006-2012	65.7
International migrant stock (000 and % of total population) [a]	mid-2013	6 466.6/13.8
Refugees and others of concern to UNHCR	mid-2013	8 281 [n]
Education: Government expenditure (% of GDP)	2006-2012	5.0
Education: Primary-secondary gross enrolment ratio (f/m per 100)	2006-2012	116.3/116.0
Education: Female third-level students (% of total)	2006-2012	53.9
Intentional homicides (females and males, per 100 000)	2008-2010	0.6/1.2
Seats held by women in national parliaments (%)	2014	39.7

Environmental indicators		
Threatened species	2013	548
Forested area (% of land area)	2011	36.8
CO$_2$ emission estimates (000 metric tons and metric tons per capita)	2010	269 454/5.9
Energy consumption per capita (kilograms oil equivalent) [i]	2010	2 453.0
Precipitation in the capital city, total mean (millimetres)		436 [o]
Temperature in the capital city, mean °C (minimum and maximum)		9.7/19.5 [o]

a Includes Canary Islands, Ceuta and Melilla. b Market rate. c Index base 2001=100. d Age group 16 to 74 years. e Break in series; data not strictly comparable. f Age group 16 years and over. g European Labour Force Survey (Eurostat). h The indices are shown in terms of ISIC Rev.3. i Includes the Canary Islands. j Fourth quarter. k Incomplete coverage. l Age group 16 to 74 years using the Internet within the last 12 months. m Age group 10 years and over. n Refugee population refers to the end of 2012. o Based on monthly averages for the period 1971-2000.

Sri Lanka

Region	Southern Asia
Currency	Sri Lanka Rupee (LKR)
Surface area (square kilometres)	65 610
Population in 2012 (estimated, 000)	21 098
Population density in 2012 (per square kilometre)	321.6
Capital city and population in 2011 (000)	Colombo (693) [a]
United Nations membership date	14 December 1955

Economic indicators	2005	2010	2012
GDP: Gross domestic product (million current US$)	24 406	49 566	59 421
GDP: Growth rate at constant 2005 prices (annual %)	6.2	8.0	6.4
GDP per capita (current US$)	1 223.3	2 387.7	2 816.4
GNI: Gross national income per capita (current US$)	1 208.3	2 358.0	2 761.3
Gross fixed capital formation (% of GDP)	23.4	25.9	28.9
Exchange rates (national currency per US$) [b]	102.12	110.95	127.16
Balance of payments, current account (million US$)	−650	−1 075	−4 003
CPI: Consumer price index (2000=100) [c]	160	219 [d]	252 [d]
Agricultural production index (2004-2006=100)	102	124	121
Food production index (2004-2006=100)	102	125	123
Unemployment (% of labour force)	6.6 [e]	4.9	4.0 [f]
Employment in industrial sector (% of employed) [gh]	25.6 [i]	24.2 [j]	17.7 [k]
Employment in agricultural sector (% of employed) [gh]	30.7 [i]	32.7 [j]	39.4 [k]
Labour force participation, adult female pop. (%)	34.4	34.8	35.0
Labour force participation, adult male pop. (%)	76.2	76.5	76.4
Tourist arrivals at national borders (000) [l]	549	654	1 006
Energy production, primary (000 mt oil equivalent)	297	492	...
Mobile-cellular subscriptions (per 100 inhabitants)	16.9	83.2	95.8 [m]
Individuals using the Internet (%)	1.8 [n]	12.0	18.3 [n]

Total trade		Major trading partners			2012
	(million US$)	(% of exports)		(% of imports)	
Exports	9 369.8	United States	22.6	India	19.7
Imports	17 884.9	United Kingdom	11.3	China	14.4
Balance	−8 515.1	India	6.4	United Arab Emirates	7.2

Social indicators

Population growth rate (average annual %)	2010-2015	0.8
Urban population growth rate (average annual %)	2010-2015	1.4
Rural population growth rate (average annual %)	2010-2015	0.7
Urban population (%)	2013	15.2
Population aged 0-14 years (%)	2013	25.2
Population aged 60+ years (females and males, % of total)	2013	13.6/11.7
Sex ratio (males per 100 females)	2013	95.6
Life expectancy at birth (females and males, years)	2010-2015	77.4/71.1
Infant mortality rate (per 1 000 live births)	2010-2015	9.0
Fertility rate, total (live births per woman)	2010-2015	2.4
Contraceptive prevalence (ages 15-49, %)	2006-2012	68.0
International migrant stock (000 and % of total population) [op]	mid-2013	325.0/1.5
Refugees and others of concern to UNHCR	mid-2013	95 102
Education: Government expenditure (% of GDP)	2006-2012	2.0
Education: Primary-secondary gross enrolment ratio (f/m per 100)	2006-2012	99.4/98.4
Education: Female third-level students (% of total)	2006-2012	64.0
Intentional homicides (females and males, per 100 000)	2008-2010	</6.2
Seats held by women in national parliaments (%)	2014	5.8

Environmental indicators

Threatened species	2013	571
Forested area (% of land area)	2011	29.4
CO_2 emission estimates (000 metric tons and metric tons per capita)	2010	12 699/0.6
Energy consumption per capita (kilograms oil equivalent)	2010	205.0
Precipitation in the capital city, total mean (millimetres)		2 524 [q]
Temperature in the capital city, mean °C (minimum and maximum)		24.1/30.6 [q]

a Colombo is the commercial capital and Sri Jayewardenepura Kotte is the administrative and legislative capital. b Market rate. c Colombo. d Index base 2002=100. e 2006. f 2011. g Age group 10 years and over. h The indices are shown in terms of ISIC Rev.3. i Break in series; data not strictly comparable. j Excludes the Northern Province. k Average of quarterly estimates. l Excludes nationals residing abroad. m December. n ITU estimate. o Data refer to foreign citizens. p Includes refugees. q Based on monthly averages for the period 1961-1990.

State of Palestine

Region	Western Asia
Currency	New Sheqel (NIS)
Surface area (square kilometres)	6 020
Population in 2012 (estimated, 000)	4 219[a]
Population density in 2012 (per square kilometre)	700.8
Capital city and population in 2011 (000)	Ramallah (75)[b]

Economic indicators	2005	2010	2012
GDP: Gross domestic product (million current US$)	4 634	8 331	10 255
GDP: Growth rate at constant 2005 prices (annual %)	8.6	9.3	5.9
GDP per capita (current US$)	1 301.9	2 076.0	2 430.7
GNI: Gross national income per capita (current US$)	1 402.4	2 225.3	2 638.3
Gross fixed capital formation (% of GDP)	27.1	17.4	17.9
Exchange rates (national currency per US$)[c]	4.60	3.55	3.73
Balance of payments, current account (million US$)[d]	−1 152	−691	−2 205[e]
CPI: Consumer price index (2000=100)[d]	119	148	157
Industrial production index (2005=100)	100	87	103
Agricultural production index (2004-2006=100)	107	80	93
Food production index (2004-2006=100)	107	80	93
Unemployment (% of labour force)	23.5	23.7	23.0
Employment in industrial sector (% of employed)	26.3[f]	24.6[g]	26.3[g]
Employment in agricultural sector (% of employed)	14.6[f]	11.8[g]	11.5[g]
Labour force participation, adult female pop. (%)	14.2	14.7	15.2
Labour force participation, adult male pop. (%)	67.2	66.2	66.3
Tourist arrivals at national borders (000)[h]	88	522	490
Mobile-cellular subscriptions (per 100 inhabitants)	16.0	64.5	71.2[i]
Individuals using the Internet (%)[i]	16.0[j]	37.4[k]	41.1[ek]

Total trade		Major trading partners			2012
	(million US$)	(% of exports)			(% of imports)
Exports	782.4	Israel	81.7	Israel	71.3
Imports	4 697.4	Jordan	7.5	Turkey	5.0
Balance	−3 915.0	United Arab Emirates	1.9	China	4.2

Social indicators		
Population growth rate (average annual %)[a]	2010-2015	2.5
Urban population growth rate (average annual %)[a]	2010-2015	3.1
Rural population growth rate (average annual %)[a]	2010-2015	1.9
Urban population (%)[a]	2013	74.8
Population aged 0-14 years (%)[a]	2013	40.1
Population aged 60+ years (females and males, % of total)[a]	2013	4.8/4.3
Sex ratio (males per 100 females)[a]	2013	103.1
Life expectancy at birth (females and males, years)[a]	2010-2015	74.9/71.4
Infant mortality rate (per 1 000 live births)[a]	2010-2015	19.2
Fertility rate, total (live births per woman)[a]	2010-2015	4.1
Contraceptive prevalence (ages 15-49, %)	2006-2012	50.2
International migrant stock (000 and % of total population)[al]	mid-2013	256.5/5.9
Refugees and others of concern to UNHCR	mid-2013	0[m]
Education: Primary-secondary gross enrolment ratio (f/m per 100)	2006-2012	89.1/84.6
Education: Female third-level students (% of total)	2006-2012	57.6

Environmental indicators		
Threatened species	2013	20
Forested area (% of land area)	2011	1.5
CO$_2$ emission estimates (000 metric tons and metric tons per capita)	2010	2 363/0.6
Energy consumption per capita (kilograms oil equivalent)	2010	286.0

a Includes East Jerusalem. b Administrative Capital. c Market rate. d Refers to West Bank and the Gaza Strip. e 2011. f The indices are shown in terms of ISIC Rev.3. g The indices are shown in terms of ISIC Rev.2. h Arrivals of non-resident tourists in hotels and similar establishments. i ITU estimate. j Age group 10 years and over. k Refers to total population. l Refugees are not part of the foreign-born migrant stock in the State of Palestine. m Value is zero, not available or not applicable.

Sudan

Region	Northern Africa
Currency	Sudanese Pound (SDG)
Population in 2012 (estimated, 000)	37 195
Capital city and population in 2011 (000)	Khartoum (4 632)
United Nations membership date	12 November 1956

Economic indicators

	2005	2010	2012
GDP: Gross domestic product (million current US$)	35 183[a]	54 493	51 453
GDP: Growth rate at constant 2005 prices (annual %)	9.0[a]	7.2	−4.4
GDP per capita (current US$)	887.9[a]	1 528.5	1 383.3
GNI: Gross national income per capita (current US$)	853.9[a]	1 649.8	1 493.1
Gross fixed capital formation (% of GDP)	20.7[a]	22.3	22.5
Exchange rates (national currency per US$)[b]	2.31	2.48	4.43
Balance of payments, current account (million US$)	−2 487	−1 538	−6 341
Agricultural production index (2004-2006=100)[a]	101	99	...
Food production index (2004-2006=100)[a]	101	100	...
Labour force participation, adult female pop. (%)	30.2	30.9	31.2
Labour force participation, adult male pop. (%)	75.7	76.0	76.0
Tourist arrivals at national borders (000)[c]	246	495	536[d]
Energy production, primary (000 mt oil equivalent)	15 540	23 673	...
Mobile-cellular subscriptions (per 100 inhabitants)	4.8[e]	41.5	60.5
Individuals using the Internet (%)	1.3	16.7[f]	21.0[g]

Total trade

Total trade	Major trading partners		2012
(million US$)[d]	(% of exports)[d]		(% of imports)[d]
Exports 8 981.7	China	70.4	China 21.7
Imports 9 546.3	United Arab Emirates	10.5	United Arab Emirates 8.6
Balance −564.6	Japan	3.5	Saudi Arabia 8.1

Social indicators

Population growth rate (average annual %)	2010-2015	2.1
Urban population growth rate (average annual %)	2010-2015	2.6
Rural population growth rate (average annual %)	2010-2015	1.9
Urban population (%)	2013	33.5
Population aged 0-14 years (%)	2013	41.2
Population aged 60+ years (females and males, % of total)	2013	5.3/4.8
Sex ratio (males per 100 females)	2013	100.7
Life expectancy at birth (females and males, years)	2010-2015	63.8/60.2
Infant mortality rate (per 1 000 live births)	2010-2015	55.1
Fertility rate, total (live births per woman)	2010-2015	4.5
Contraceptive prevalence (ages 15-49, %)	2006-2012	9.0
International migrant stock (000 and % of total population)[h]	mid-2013	446.7/1.2
Refugees and others of concern to UNHCR	mid-2013	2 070 360[i]
Education: Female third-level students (% of total)[aj]	2006-2012	47.2[k]
Intentional homicides (females and males, per 100 000)[l]	2008-2010	16.7/31.6
Seats held by women in national parliaments (%)	2014	24.3

Environmental indicators

Threatened species	2013	127
CO_2 emission estimates (000 metric tons and metric tons per capita)	2010	14 161/0.3
Energy consumption per capita (kilograms oil equivalent)	2010	105.0
Precipitation in the capital city, total mean (millimetres)		121[m]
Temperature in the capital city, mean °C (minimum and maximum)		22.8/37.0[m]

a Former Sudan. b Principal rate. c 2005-2011: Includes nationals residing abroad. d 2011. e ITU estimate excludes Canar, which is counted as a fixed line. f ITU estimate. g Age group 15 years and over. h Includes refugees. i Includes 77,300 people who are in an internally displaced person-like situation. j UNESCO estimate. k 2000. l Estimates. m Based on monthly averages for the period 1971-2000.

Suriname

Region	South America
Currency	Surinamese Dollar (SRD)
Surface area (square kilometres)	163 820
Population in 2012 (estimated, 000)	535
Population density in 2012 (per square kilometre)	3.3
Capital city and population in 2011 (000)	Paramaribo (278)
United Nations membership date	4 December 1975

Economic indicators	2005	2010	2012
GDP: Gross domestic product (million current US$)	2 193	4 368	5 012
GDP: Growth rate at constant 2005 prices (annual %)	3.9	4.2	3.9
GDP per capita (current US$)	4 390.3	8 320.7	9 376.5
GNI: Gross national income per capita (current US$)	4 313.5	8 122.0	9 011.9
Gross fixed capital formation (% of GDP)	45.6	37.5	39.8
Exchange rates (national currency per US$)[a]	2.74	2.74	3.30
Balance of payments, current account (million US$)	−144	651	238
CPI: Consumer price index (2000=100)[bc]	171	249	307
Agricultural production index (2004-2006=100)	99	137	131
Food production index (2004-2006=100)	99	137	131
Employment in industrial sector (% of employed)	23.0[defgh]	...	...
Employment in agricultural sector (% of employed)	8.0[defgh]	...	...
Labour force participation, adult female pop. (%)	37.8	40.1	40.4
Labour force participation, adult male pop. (%)	67.3	68.7	68.8
Tourist arrivals at national borders (000)	161	205	240
Energy production, primary (000 mt oil equivalent)	715	865	...
Mobile-cellular subscriptions (per 100 inhabitants)	46.6	169.6[i]	182.9[i]
Individuals using the Internet (%)	6.4	31.6	34.7[i]

Total trade		Major trading partners			2012
	(million US$)[j]	(% of exports)[j]		(% of imports)[j]	
Exports	2 466.9	United Arab Emirates	26.1	United States	26.7
Imports	1 637.8	Canada	18.6	Trinidad and Tobago	25.4
Balance	829.1	United States	11.2	Netherlands	16.0

Social indicators		
Population growth rate (average annual %)	2010-2015	0.9
Urban population growth rate (average annual %)	2010-2015	1.4
Rural population growth rate (average annual %)	2010-2015	−0.5
Urban population (%)	2013	70.5
Population aged 0-14 years (%)	2013	27.4
Population aged 60+ years (females and males, % of total)	2013	10.9/8.6
Sex ratio (males per 100 females)	2013	100.4
Life expectancy at birth (females and males, years)	2010-2015	74.2/67.8
Infant mortality rate (per 1 000 live births)	2010-2015	17.4
Fertility rate, total (live births per woman)	2010-2015	2.3
Contraceptive prevalence (ages 15-49, %)	2006-2012	45.6
International migrant stock (000 and % of total population)[k]	mid-2013	41.7/7.7
Refugees and others of concern to UNHCR	mid-2013	3
Education: Primary-secondary gross enrolment ratio (f/m per 100)	2006-2012	104.4/95.0
Education: Female third-level students (% of total)	2006-2012	62.0[i]
Intentional homicides (females and males, per 100 000)	2008-2010	3.6/11.9
Seats held by women in national parliaments (%)	2014	11.8

Environmental indicators		
Threatened species	2013	75
Forested area (% of land area)	2011	94.6
CO_2 emission estimates (000 metric tons and metric tons per capita)	2010	2 382/4.5
Energy consumption per capita (kilograms oil equivalent)	2010	1 693.0

a Market rate. b Paramaribo. c Index base 2001=100. d 2004. e Population census. f The indices are shown in terms of ISIC Rev.3. g August. h Break in series; data not strictly comparable. i ITU estimate. j 2011. k Data refer to foreign citizens. l 2002.

Swaziland

Region	Southern Africa
Currency	Lilangeni (SZL)
Surface area (square kilometres)	17 363
Population in 2012 (estimated, 000)	1 231
Population density in 2012 (per square kilometre)	70.9
Capital city and population in 2011 (000)	Mbabane (66)[a]
United Nations membership date	24 September 1968

Economic indicators	2005	2010	2012
GDP: Gross domestic product (million current US$)	2 584	3 892	3 861
GDP: Growth rate at constant 2005 prices (annual %)	2.5	1.9	−1.5
GDP per capita (current US$)	2 339.3	3 261.6	3 136.7
GNI: Gross national income per capita (current US$)	2 500.7	3 274.1	3 363.0
Gross fixed capital formation (% of GDP)	15.0	9.7	9.5
Exchange rates (national currency per US$)[b]	6.32	6.63	8.50
Balance of payments, current account (million US$)	−103	−388	155
CPI: Consumer price index (2000=100)	140	121[cd]	...
Agricultural production index (2004-2006=100)	103	104	111
Food production index (2004-2006=100)	103	104	112
Labour force participation, adult female pop. (%)	42.9	43.5	43.8
Labour force participation, adult male pop. (%)	70.8	70.7	71.3
Tourist arrivals at national borders (000)	837	1 078	1 093
Energy production, primary (000 mt oil equivalent)	329	367[e]	...
Mobile-cellular subscriptions (per 100 inhabitants)	18.1	61.2	66.0
Individuals using the Internet (%)	3.7[f]	11.0	20.8[f]

Social indicators		
Population growth rate (average annual %)	2010-2015	1.5
Urban population growth rate (average annual %)	2010-2015	1.2
Rural population growth rate (average annual %)	2010-2015	1.4
Urban population (%)	2013	21.2
Population aged 0-14 years (%)	2013	37.8
Population aged 60+ years (females and males, % of total)	2013	6.1/4.7
Sex ratio (males per 100 females)	2013	97.4
Life expectancy at birth (females and males, years)	2010-2015	48.5/49.7
Infant mortality rate (per 1 000 live births)	2010-2015	64.6
Fertility rate, total (live births per woman)	2010-2015	3.4
Contraceptive prevalence (ages 15-49, %)	2006-2012	65.2
International migrant stock (000 and % of total population)[g]	mid-2013	25.5/2.0
Refugees and others of concern to UNHCR	mid-2013	927
Education: Government expenditure (% of GDP)	2006-2012	8.3
Education: Primary-secondary gross enrolment ratio (f/m per 100)	2006-2012	87.9/95.8
Education: Female third-level students (% of total)	2006-2012	50.6
Intentional homicides (females and males, per 100 000)[h]	2008-2010	13.3/69.9
Seats held by women in national parliaments (%)	2014	6.2

Environmental indicators		
Threatened species	2013	33
Forested area (% of land area)	2011	33.0
CO_2 emission estimates (000 metric tons and metric tons per capita)	2010	1 022/0.9
Energy consumption per capita (kilograms oil equivalent)	2010	354.0[e]
Precipitation in the capital city, total mean (millimetres)		1 442[i]
Temperature in the capital city, mean °C (minimum and maximum)		10.5/22.5[i]

a Mbabane is the administrative capital and Lobamba is the legislative capital. b Official rate. c 2009. d Index base 2007=100. e UNSD estimate. f ITU estimate. g Includes refugees. h Estimates. i Based on monthly averages for the period 1961-1990.

Sweden

Region	Northern Europe
Currency	Swedish Krona (SEK)
Surface area (square kilometres)	450 295
Population in 2012 (estimated, 000)	9 511
Population density in 2012 (per square kilometre)	21.1
Capital city and population in 2011 (000)	Stockholm (1 385)
United Nations membership date	19 November 1946

Economic indicators

	2005	2010	2012
GDP: Gross domestic product (million current US$)	370 580	463 062	523 804
GDP: Growth rate at constant 2005 prices (annual %)	3.2	6.6	1.0
GDP per capita (current US$)	41 038.0	49 354.9	55 071.7
GNI: Gross national income per capita (current US$)	41 332.8	50 464.5	56 303.6
Gross fixed capital formation (% of GDP)	17.9	18.0	19.0
Exchange rates (national currency per US$)[a]	7.96	6.71	6.50
Balance of payments, current account (million US$)	26 423	29 402	31 822
CPI: Consumer price index (2000=100)	108	116	120
Industrial production index (2005=100)	100	93	97
Agricultural production index (2004-2006=100)	100	94	96
Food production index (2004-2006=100)	100	94	96
Unemployment (% of labour force)[b]	7.8[c]	8.6	8.0
Employment in industrial sector (% of employed)	22.0[cdef]	19.9[bg]	19.5[bg]
Employment in agricultural sector (% of employed)	2.0[cdef]	2.1[bg]	2.0[bg]
Labour force participation, adult female pop. (%)	59.3	59.0	60.2
Labour force participation, adult male pop. (%)	68.1	68.1	68.1
Tourist arrivals at national borders (000)[h]	4 883	4 951	4 944
Energy production, primary (000 mt oil equivalent)	12 975	11 772	...
Mobile-cellular subscriptions (per 100 inhabitants)	100.8	117.2	122.6
Individuals using the Internet (%)	84.8[i]	90.0[j]	94.0[i]

Total trade		Major trading partners			2012
	(million US$)	(% of exports)			(% of imports)
Exports	172 756.0	Norway	10.2	Germany	17.3
Imports	164 113.5	Germany	9.6	Norway	9.1
Balance	8 642.5	United Kingdom	7.6	Denmark	8.5

Social indicators

Population growth rate (average annual %)	2010-2015	0.7
Urban population growth rate (average annual %)	2010-2015	0.7
Rural population growth rate (average annual %)	2010-2015	−0.5
Urban population (%)	2013	85.5
Population aged 0-14 years (%)	2013	16.9
Population aged 60+ years (females and males, % of total)	2013	27.2/23.8
Sex ratio (males per 100 females)	2013	99.4
Life expectancy at birth (females and males, years)	2010-2015	83.8/79.7
Infant mortality rate (per 1 000 live births)	2010-2015	2.3
Fertility rate, total (live births per woman)	2010-2015	1.9
Contraceptive prevalence (ages 15-49, %)[k]	2006-2012	75.2[l]
International migrant stock (000 and % of total population)	mid-2013	1 519.5/15.9
Refugees and others of concern to UNHCR	mid-2013	119 570[m]
Education: Government expenditure (% of GDP)	2006-2012	7.0
Education: Primary-secondary gross enrolment ratio (f/m per 100)	2006-2012	98.1/98.9
Education: Female third-level students (% of total)	2006-2012	59.1
Intentional homicides (females and males, per 100 000)	2008-2010	0.6/1.1
Seats held by women in national parliaments (%)	2014	45.0

Environmental indicators

Threatened species	2013	37
Forested area (% of land area)	2011	68.7
CO_2 emission estimates (000 metric tons and metric tons per capita)	2010	52 472/5.6
Energy consumption per capita (kilograms oil equivalent)	2010	2 951.0
Precipitation in the capital city, total mean (millimetres)		539[n]
Temperature in the capital city, mean °C (minimum and maximum)		3.6/10.0[n]

a Official rate. **b** Age group 15 to 74 years. **c** Break in series; data not strictly comparable. **d** The indices are shown in terms of ISIC Rev.3. **e** Age group 16 to 64 years. **f** Excludes conscripts. **g** European Labour Force Survey (Eurostat). **h** Arrivals of non-resident tourists in all types of accommodation establishments. **i** Age group 16 to 74 years. **j** Age group 16 to 75. **k** Age group 18 to 44 years. **l** 1996. **m** Refugee population refers to the end of 2012. **n** Based on monthly averages for the period 1961-1990.

Switzerland

Region	Western Europe
Currency	Swiss Franc (CHF)
Surface area (square kilometres)	41 285
Population in 2012 (estimated, 000)	7 997
Population density in 2012 (per square kilometre)	193.7
Capital city and population in 2011 (000)	Bern (353)
United Nations membership date	10 September 2002

Economic indicators	2005	2010	2012
GDP: Gross domestic product (million current US$)	384 755	549 105	631 183
GDP: Growth rate at constant 2005 prices (annual %)	2.7	3.0	1.1
GDP per capita (current US$)	51 933.5	70 123.6	78 923.6
GNI: Gross national income per capita (current US$)	56 722.5	74 716.7	81 607.7
Gross fixed capital formation (% of GDP)	22.0	20.0	20.1
Exchange rates (national currency per US$)[a]	1.31	0.94	0.92
Balance of payments, current account (million US$)	53 149	75 894	53 914
CPI: Consumer price index (2000=100)	104	109	109
Industrial production index (2005=100)	100	124	130
Agricultural production index (2004-2006=100)	99	103	104
Food production index (2004-2006=100)	99	103	104
Unemployment (% of labour force)[b]	4.4	4.5[c]	4.2
Employment in industrial sector (% of employed)	23.7[de]	21.1[cf]	20.3[f]
Employment in agricultural sector (% of employed)	3.8[de]	3.3[cf]	3.5[f]
Labour force participation, adult female pop. (%)	59.5	60.8	61.2
Labour force participation, adult male pop. (%)	75.0	75.3	75.3
Tourist arrivals at national borders (000)[gh]	7 229	8 628	8 566
Energy production, primary (000 mt oil equivalent)[i]	4 887	5 565	...
Mobile-cellular subscriptions (per 100 inhabitants)	92.2	125.8	135.3[j]
Individuals using the Internet (%)[k]	70.1	83.9	85.2

Total trade		Major trading partners			2012
	(million US$)[l]	(% of exports)[l]			(% of imports)[l]
Exports	225 948.8	Germany	19.8	Germany	29.6
Imports	197 786.9	United States	11.1	Italy	10.2
Balance	28 161.9	Italy	7.1	France	8.4

Social indicators		
Population growth rate (average annual %)	2010-2015	1.0
Urban population growth rate (average annual %)	2010-2015	0.5
Rural population growth rate (average annual %)	2010-2015	0.1
Urban population (%)	2013	73.8
Population aged 0-14 years (%)	2013	14.8
Population aged 60+ years (females and males, % of total)	2013	25.4/21.4
Sex ratio (males per 100 females)	2013	97.3
Life expectancy at birth (females and males, years)	2010-2015	84.9/80.1
Infant mortality rate (per 1 000 live births)	2010-2015	3.7
Fertility rate, total (live births per woman)	2010-2015	1.5
Contraceptive prevalence (ages 15-49, %)[m]	2006-2012	82.0[n]
International migrant stock (000 and % of total population)	mid-2013	2 335.1/28.9
Refugees and others of concern to UNHCR	mid-2013	71 772
Education: Government expenditure (% of GDP)	2006-2012	5.2
Education: Primary-secondary gross enrolment ratio (f/m per 100)	2006-2012	98.2/99.9
Education: Female third-level students (% of total)	2006-2012	49.3
Intentional homicides (females and males, per 100 000)	2008-2010	0.7/0.8
Seats held by women in national parliaments (%)	2014	31.0

Environmental indicators		
Threatened species	2013	62
Forested area (% of land area)	2011	31.1
CO_2 emission estimates (000 metric tons and metric tons per capita)	2010	38 725/5.0
Energy consumption per capita (kilograms oil equivalent)[i]	2010	2 459.0
Precipitation in the capital city, total mean (millimetres)[o]		1 086[p]
Temperature in the capital city, mean °C (minimum and maximum)[o]		4.9/12.7[p]

a Official rate. **b** Age group 15 to 74 years. **c** Break in series; data not strictly comparable. **d** Official estimates. **e** The indices are shown in terms of ISIC Rev.3. **f** European Labour Force Survey (Eurostat). **g** Arrivals of non-resident tourists in hotels and similar establishments. **h** Includes health establishments. **i** Includes Liechtenstein for oil statistics. **j** Estimate. **k** Age group 14 years and over using the Internet within the last 6 months. **l** Includes Liechtenstein. **m** Age group 20 to 49 years. **n** 1994-1995. **o** Zurich. **p** Based on monthly averages for the period 1961-1990.

Syrian Arab Republic

Region	Western Asia
Currency	Syrian Pound (SYP)
Surface area (square kilometres)	185 180
Population in 2012 (estimated, 000)	21 890
Population density in 2012 (per square kilometre)	118.2
Capital city and population in 2011 (000)	Damascus (2 650)
United Nations membership date	24 October 1945

Economic indicators	2005	2010	2012
GDP: Gross domestic product (million current US$)	28 397	60 465	46 540
GDP: Growth rate at constant 2005 prices (annual %)	6.2	3.4	1.6
GDP per capita (current US$)	1 563.1	2 808.1	2 126.1
GNI: Gross national income per capita (current US$)	1 493.4	2 744.9	2 083.5
Gross fixed capital formation (% of GDP)	23.0	20.8	21.0
Exchange rates (national currency per US$)[a]	52.00	46.58	74.37
Balance of payments, current account (million US$)	299	−367	...
CPI: Consumer price index (2000=100)	122	173	...
Agricultural production index (2004-2006=100)	100	89	88
Food production index (2004-2006=100)	99	92	92
Unemployment (% of labour force)	10.9[b]	8.6	14.9[c]
Employment in industrial sector (% of employed)[d]	28.3[ef]	32.7	32.7[c]
Employment in agricultural sector (% of employed)[d]	19.6[ef]	14.3	14.3[c]
Labour force participation, adult female pop. (%)	16.3	13.2	13.4
Labour force participation, adult male pop. (%)	76.1	72.7	72.7
Tourist arrivals at national borders (000)[gh]	3 571[i]	8 546	5 070[c]
Energy production, primary (000 mt oil equivalent)	28 521	28 672	...
Mobile-cellular subscriptions (per 100 inhabitants)	16.0	57.8	61.2
Individuals using the Internet (%)	5.7[j]	20.7	24.3[j]

Total trade		Major trading partners			2012
	(million US$)[k]	(% of exports)[k]			(% of imports)[k]
Exports	11 352.9	Iraq	20.2	Turkey	9.5
Imports	17 561.6	Italy	13.4	China	8.8
Balance	−6 208.7	Germany	13.0	Italy	7.4

Social indicators		
Population growth rate (average annual %)	2010-2015	0.7
Urban population growth rate (average annual %)	2010-2015	2.4
Rural population growth rate (average annual %)	2010-2015	0.8
Urban population (%)	2013	56.9
Population aged 0-14 years (%)	2013	35.1
Population aged 60+ years (females and males, % of total)	2013	6.5/6.1
Sex ratio (males per 100 females)	2013	103.8
Life expectancy at birth (females and males, years)	2010-2015	77.6/71.6
Infant mortality rate (per 1 000 live births)	2010-2015	17.7
Fertility rate, total (live births per woman)	2010-2015	3.0
Contraceptive prevalence (ages 15-49, %)	2006-2012	58.3
International migrant stock (000 and % of total population)[lm]	mid-2013	1 394.2/6.4
Refugees and others of concern to UNHCR	mid-2013	4 619 088[n]
Education: Government expenditure (% of GDP)	2006-2012	5.1
Education: Primary-secondary gross enrolment ratio (f/m per 100)	2006-2012	90.7/91.7
Education: Female third-level students (% of total)	2006-2012	48.8
Intentional homicides (females and males, per 100 000)	2008-2010	0.7/4.5
Seats held by women in national parliaments (%)	2014	12.0

Environmental indicators		
Threatened species	2013	85
Forested area (% of land area)	2011	2.7
CO₂ emission estimates (000 metric tons and metric tons per capita)	2010	61 808/3.0
Energy consumption per capita (kilograms oil equivalent)	2010	1 081.0
Precipitation in the capital city, total mean (millimetres)		134[o]
Temperature in the capital city, mean °C (minimum and maximum)		8.1/25.3[p]

a UN operational exchange rate. b 2008. c 2011. d The indices are shown in terms of ISIC Rev.2. e 2006. f Break in series; data not strictly comparable. g Arrivals of non-resident tourists in all types of accommodation establishments. h 2000-2011: Includes nationals residing abroad. i Excludes Iraqi nationals. j ITU estimate. k 2010. l Data refer to foreign citizens. m Includes refugees. n Refugee figures for Iraqis in the Syrian Arab Republic are government estimates. UNHCR has registered and is assisting 42,400 Iraqis at mid-2013. o Based on monthly averages for the period 1955-2004. p Based on monthly averages for the period 1956-2004.

Tajikistan

Region	Central Asia
Currency	Somoni (TJS)
Surface area (square kilometres)	143 100
Population in 2012 (estimated, 000)	8 009
Population density in 2012 (per square kilometre)	56.0
Capital city and population in 2011 (000)	Dushanbe (739)
United Nations membership date	2 March 1992

Economic indicators	2005	2010	2012
GDP: Gross domestic product (million current US$)	2 312	5 642	7 633
GDP: Growth rate at constant 2005 prices (annual %)	6.7	6.5	7.5
GDP per capita (current US$)	339.8	739.7	953.1
GNI: Gross national income per capita (current US$)	434.4	936.1	1 233.3
Gross fixed capital formation (% of GDP)	11.1	24.5	25.8
Exchange rates (national currency per US$) [a]	3.20	4.40	4.76
Balance of payments, current account (million US$)	−19	−370	−248
Agricultural production index (2004-2006=100)	99	124	144
Food production index (2004-2006=100)	99	138	159
Employment in industrial sector (% of employed)	17.9[bc]	...	...
Employment in agricultural sector (% of employed)	55.5[bc]	...	...
Labour force participation, adult female pop. (%)	57.7	58.3	58.7
Labour force participation, adult male pop. (%)	74.7	76.3	76.9
Tourist arrivals at national borders (000) [d]	325[e]	160	244
Energy production, primary (000 mt oil equivalent)	1 547	1 512	...
Mobile-cellular subscriptions (per 100 inhabitants)	4.1	86.4	92.2[f]
Individuals using the Internet (%)	0.3	11.6[f]	14.5[f]

Social indicators		
Population growth rate (average annual %)	2010-2015	2.4
Urban population growth rate (average annual %)	2010-2015	1.7
Rural population growth rate (average annual %)	2010-2015	1.4
Urban population (%)	2013	26.6
Population aged 0-14 years (%)	2013	35.9
Population aged 60+ years (females and males, % of total)	2013	5.2/4.5
Sex ratio (males per 100 females)	2013	100.8
Life expectancy at birth (females and males, years)	2010-2015	70.7/64.0
Infant mortality rate (per 1 000 live births)	2010-2015	56.8
Fertility rate, total (live births per woman)	2010-2015	3.9
Contraceptive prevalence (ages 15-49, %)	2006-2012	37.1
International migrant stock (000 and % of total population)	mid-2013	275.7/3.4
Refugees and others of concern to UNHCR	mid-2013	5 928
Education: Government expenditure (% of GDP)	2006-2012	3.9
Education: Primary-secondary gross enrolment ratio (f/m per 100)	2006-2012	86.5/94.7
Education: Female third-level students (% of total)	2006-2012	33.9
Intentional homicides (females and males, per 100 000)	2008-2010	1.5/2.1
Seats held by women in national parliaments (%)	2014	15.9

Environmental indicators		
Threatened species	2013	41
Forested area (% of land area)	2011	2.9
CO_2 emission estimates (000 metric tons and metric tons per capita)	2010	2 858/0.4
Energy consumption per capita (kilograms oil equivalent)	2010	329.0
Precipitation in the capital city, total mean (millimetres)		653[g]
Temperature in the capital city, mean °C (minimum and maximum)		8.1/22.0[g]

a Official rate. **b** 2004. **c** The indices are shown in terms of ISIC Rev.3. **d** Arrivals of non-resident visitors at national borders. **e** 2008. **f** ITU estimate. **g** Based on monthly averages for the period 1961-1990.

Thailand

Region	South-Eastern Asia
Currency	Baht (THB)
Surface area (square kilometres)	513 120
Population in 2012 (estimated, 000)	66 785
Population density in 2012 (per square kilometre)	130.2
Capital city and population in 2011 (000)	Bangkok (8 426)
United Nations membership date	16 December 1946

Economic indicators	2005	2010	2012
GDP: Gross domestic product (million current US$)	188 620	338 001	385 694
GDP: Growth rate at constant 2005 prices (annual %)	4.2	7.3	6.4
GDP per capita (current US$)	2 877.1	5 090.2	5 775.2
GNI: Gross national income per capita (current US$)	2 747.6	4 863.8	5 550.6
Gross fixed capital formation (% of GDP)	27.8	24.2	28.4
Exchange rates (national currency per US$)[a]	41.03	30.15	30.63
Balance of payments, current account (million US$)	−7 647	9 946	−1 431
CPI: Consumer price index (2000=100)	112	129	138[b]
Agricultural production index (2004-2006=100)	98	114	125
Food production index (2004-2006=100)	98	116	126
Unemployment (% of labour force)	1.9	1.1	0.7
Employment in industrial sector (% of employed)	20.2[cd]	20.6[ce]	20.9[ef]
Employment in agricultural sector (% of employed)	42.6[cd]	38.2[ce]	39.6[ef]
Labour force participation, adult female pop. (%)	66.1	64.4	64.4
Labour force participation, adult male pop. (%)	81.2	80.9	80.8
Tourist arrivals at national borders (000)	11 567[g]	15 936	22 354
Energy production, primary (000 mt oil equivalent)	35 688	51 037	...
Mobile-cellular subscriptions (per 100 inhabitants)	45.7	103.8	120.3
Individuals using the Internet (%)	15.0	22.4	26.5[h]

Total trade		Major trading partners			2012
	(million US$)		(% of exports)		(% of imports)
Exports	229 544.5	China	11.7	Japan	20.0
Imports	247 575.9	Japan	10.2	China	14.9
Balance	−18 031.4	United States	9.9	United Arab Emirates	6.3

Social indicators		
Population growth rate (average annual %)	2010-2015	0.3
Urban population growth rate (average annual %)	2010-2015	1.6
Rural population growth rate (average annual %)	2010-2015	−0.1
Urban population (%)	2013	34.8
Population aged 0-14 years (%)	2013	18.2
Population aged 60+ years (females and males, % of total)	2013	15.5/13.5
Sex ratio (males per 100 females)	2013	96.0
Life expectancy at birth (females and males, years)	2010-2015	77.7/71.0
Infant mortality rate (per 1 000 live births)	2010-2015	9.9
Fertility rate, total (live births per woman)	2010-2015	1.4
Contraceptive prevalence (ages 15-49, %)	2006-2012	79.6
International migrant stock (000 and % of total population)[i]	mid-2013	3 721.7/5.6
Refugees and others of concern to UNHCR	mid-2013	602 600
Education: Government expenditure (% of GDP)	2006-2012	5.8
Education: Primary-secondary gross enrolment ratio (f/m per 100)	2006-2012	89.4/87.5
Education: Female third-level students (% of total)	2006-2012	56.4
Intentional homicides (females and males, per 100 000)	2008-2010	2.3/18.0
Seats held by women in national parliaments (%)	2014	15.8

Environmental indicators		
Threatened species	2013	573
Forested area (% of land area)	2011	37.2
CO$_2$ emission estimates (000 metric tons and metric tons per capita)	2010	295 040/4.3
Energy consumption per capita (kilograms oil equivalent)	2010	1 287.0
Precipitation in the capital city, total mean (millimetres)		1 498[j]
Temperature in the capital city, mean °C (minimum and maximum)		24.1/32.7[j]

a Official rate. b Series linked to former series. c The indices are shown in terms of ISIC Rev.3. d Third quarter. e Average of quarterly estimates. f Break in series; data not strictly comparable. g Includes arrivals of nationals residing abroad. h Age group 6 years and over. i Includes refugees. j Based on monthly averages for the period 1961-1990.

The former Yugoslav Republic of Macedonia

Region	Southern Europe
Currency	Denar (MKD)
Surface area (square kilometres)	25 713
Population in 2012 (estimated, 000)	2 106
Population density in 2012 (per square kilometre)	81.9
Capital city and population in 2011 (000)	Skopje (499)
United Nations membership date	8 April 1993

Economic indicators	2005	2010	2012
GDP: Gross domestic product (million current US$)	5 987	9 339	9 576
GDP: Growth rate at constant 2005 prices (annual %)	4.4	2.9	−0.2
GDP per capita (current US$)	2 864.4	4 442.3	4 548.2
GNI: Gross national income per capita (current US$)	2 809.4	4 382.1	4 481.0
Gross fixed capital formation (% of GDP)	16.6	19.1	23.0
Exchange rates (national currency per US$)[a]	51.86	46.31	46.65
Balance of payments, current account (million US$)	−159	−198	−300
CPI: Consumer price index (2000=100)	109[b]	125[c]	...
Industrial production index (2005=100)	100	101	105
Agricultural production index (2004-2006=100)	100	117	110
Food production index (2004-2006=100)	99	117	111
Unemployment (% of labour force)[d]	36.0[e]	32.0	31.0
Employment in industrial sector (% of employed)	32.3[f]	31.3[fg]	29.9[h]
Employment in agricultural sector (% of employed)	19.5[f]	19.7[fg]	17.3[h]
Labour force participation, adult female pop. (%)	42.2	42.8	42.9
Labour force participation, adult male pop. (%)	63.8	68.6	67.3
Tourist arrivals at national borders (000)[i]	197	262	351
Energy production, primary (000 mt oil equivalent)	1 983	2 023	
Mobile-cellular subscriptions (per 100 inhabitants)	55.5	104.5	108.2[j]
Individuals using the Internet (%)	26.5[kl]	51.9[d]	63.2[l]

Total trade		Major trading partners			2012
	(million US$)	(% of exports)		(% of imports)	
Exports	4 001.9	Germany	29.4	Greece	12.3
Imports	6 510.9	Serbia	17.2	Germany	9.7
Balance	−2 509.0	Bulgaria	7.1	United Kingdom	8.6

Social indicators		
Population growth rate (average annual %)	2010-2015	0.1
Urban population growth rate (average annual %)	2010-2015	0.3
Rural population growth rate (average annual %)	2010-2015	−0.2
Urban population (%)	2013	59.5
Population aged 0-14 years (%)	2013	16.7
Population aged 60+ years (females and males, % of total)	2013	19.6/16.4
Sex ratio (males per 100 females)	2013	100.4
Life expectancy at birth (females and males, years)	2010-2015	77.5/72.9
Infant mortality rate (per 1 000 live births)	2010-2015	10.1
Fertility rate, total (live births per woman)	2010-2015	1.4
Contraceptive prevalence (ages 15-49, %)[m]	2006-2012	43.2[n]
International migrant stock (000 and % of total population)[o]	mid-2013	139.8/6.8
Refugees and others of concern to UNHCR	mid-2013	2 725
Education: Government expenditure (% of GDP)	2006-2012	3.5[p]
Education: Primary-secondary gross enrolment ratio (f/m per 100)	2006-2012	84.1/85.2
Education: Female third-level students (% of total)	2006-2012	53.2
Intentional homicides (females and males, per 100 000)	2008-2010	1.5/2.8
Seats held by women in national parliaments (%)	2014	34.1

Environmental indicators		
Threatened species	2013	99
Forested area (% of land area)	2011	39.8
CO_2 emission estimates (000 metric tons and metric tons per capita)	2010	10 864/5.3
Energy consumption per capita (kilograms oil equivalent)	2010	1 553.0
Precipitation in the capital city, total mean (millimetres)		504
Temperature in the capital city, mean °C (minimum and maximum)		6.0/18.2

a Market rate. **b** Annual average is the weighted mean of monthly data. **c** Series linked to former series. **d** Age group 15 to 74 years. **e** 2006. **f** The indices are shown in terms of ISIC Rev.3. **g** 2008. **h** European Labour Force Survey (Eurostat). **i** Arrivals of non-resident tourists in all types of accommodation establishments. **j** Fourth quarter. **k** Age group 16 to 74 years. **l** ITU estimate. **m** Age group 15 to 44 years. **n** 1970. **o** Includes refugees. **p** 2002.

Timor-Leste

Region	South-Eastern Asia
Currency	U.S. Dollar (USD)
Surface area (square kilometres)	14 919
Population in 2012 (estimated, 000)	1 114
Population density in 2012 (per square kilometre)	74.7
Capital city and population in 2011 (000)	Dili (180)
United Nations membership date	27 September 2002

Economic indicators	2005	2010	2012
GDP: Gross domestic product (million current US$)	1 801	4 216	5 387
GDP: Growth rate at constant 2005 prices (annual %)	53.3	−1.4	10.0
GDP per capita (current US$)	1 809.3	3 905.3	4 834.9
GNI: Gross national income per capita (current US$)	824.8	3 052.8	3 641.4
Gross fixed capital formation (% of GDP)	4.5	13.0	13.9
Balance of payments, current account (million US$)	541[a]	1 675	2 740
Agricultural production index (2004-2006=100)	98	121	114
Food production index (2004-2006=100)	98	126	122
Employment in industrial sector (% of employed)	...	9.2	...
Employment in agricultural sector (% of employed)	...	50.6	...
Labour force participation, adult female pop. (%)	32.0	25.0	24.7
Labour force participation, adult male pop. (%)	65.9	51.8	51.1
Tourist arrivals at national borders (000)[b]	14[a]	40	58
Energy production, primary (000 mt oil equivalent)[c]	7 395	7 418	...
Mobile-cellular subscriptions (per 100 inhabitants)	3.3	42.1	52.3[d]
Individuals using the Internet (%)	0.1	0.2[d]	0.9[d]

Total trade		Major trading partners			2012
	(million US$)[e]		(% of exports)[e]		(% of imports)[e]
Exports	53.3	China	26.8	Indonesia	28.9
Imports	339.7	Australia	24.6	Finland	20.2
Balance	−286.4	United States	20.1	China	17.8

Social indicators		
Population growth rate (average annual %)	2010-2015	1.7
Urban population growth rate (average annual %)	2010-2015	4.3
Rural population growth rate (average annual %)	2010-2015	2.4
Urban population (%)	2013	29.1
Population aged 0-14 years (%)	2013	45.8
Population aged 60+ years (females and males, % of total)	2013	5.7/4.9
Sex ratio (males per 100 females)	2013	103.4
Life expectancy at birth (females and males, years)	2010-2015	68.9/65.8
Infant mortality rate (per 1 000 live births)	2010-2015	39.3
Fertility rate, total (live births per woman)	2010-2015	5.9
Contraceptive prevalence (ages 15-49, %)	2006-2012	22.3
International migrant stock (000 and % of total population)	mid-2013	11.6/1.0
Refugees and others of concern to UNHCR	mid-2013	2
Education: Government expenditure (% of GDP)	2006-2012	9.7
Education: Primary-secondary gross enrolment ratio (f/m per 100)	2006-2012	89.8/92.3
Education: Female third-level students (% of total)	2006-2012	41.3
Intentional homicides (females and males, per 100 000)[f]	2008-2010	1.2/12.5
Seats held by women in national parliaments (%)	2014	38.5

Environmental indicators		
Threatened species	2013	21
Forested area (% of land area)	2011	49.2
CO_2 emission estimates (000 metric tons and metric tons per capita)	2010	183/0.2
Energy consumption per capita (kilograms oil equivalent)	2010	55.0[c]

a 2006. b Air arrivals at Dili Airport. c UNSD estimate. d ITU estimate. e 2011. f Estimates.

Togo

Region	Western Africa
Currency	CFA Franc (XOF)
Surface area (square kilometres)	56 785
Population in 2012 (estimated, 000)	6 643
Population density in 2012 (per square kilometre)	117.0
Capital city and population in 2011 (000)	Lomé (1 524)
United Nations membership date	20 September 1960

Economic indicators	2005	2010	2012
GDP: Gross domestic product (million current US$)	2 110	3 173	3 917
GDP: Growth rate at constant 2005 prices (annual %)	1.2	4.0	5.9
GDP per capita (current US$)	380.9	503.1	589.7
GNI: Gross national income per capita (current US$)	374.1	499.5	585.4
Gross fixed capital formation (% of GDP)	16.5	18.0	23.1
Exchange rates (national currency per US$)[a]	556.04	490.91	497.16
Balance of payments, current account (million US$)	−204	−200	...
CPI: Consumer price index (2000=100)[b]	114	134[c]	143
Industrial production index (2005=100)	100	124	141
Agricultural production index (2004-2006=100)	96	123	131
Food production index (2004-2006=100)	99	129	136
Employment in industrial sector (% of employed)	6.8[def]	...	...
Employment in agricultural sector (% of employed)	54.1[def]	...	...
Labour force participation, adult female pop. (%)	79.8	80.7	80.7
Labour force participation, adult male pop. (%)	80.4	81.0	81.2
Tourist arrivals at national borders (000)[g]	81	202	235
Energy production, primary (000 mt oil equivalent)	6	8	...
Mobile-cellular subscriptions (per 100 inhabitants)	8.0	40.7	56.0[h]
Individuals using the Internet (%)[h]	1.8	3.0	4.0

Total trade		Major trading partners			2012
	(million US$)	(% of exports)		(% of imports)	
Exports	900.4	Burkina Faso	16.7	China	13.8
Imports	1 665.1	Benin	12.3	France	9.4
Balance	−764.7	Nigeria	10.4	United States	8.1

Social indicators

Population growth rate (average annual %)	2010-2015	2.6
Urban population growth rate (average annual %)	2010-2015	3.3
Rural population growth rate (average annual %)	2010-2015	1.2
Urban population (%)	2013	39.0
Population aged 0-14 years (%)	2013	41.9
Population aged 60+ years (females and males, % of total)	2013	4.8/4.1
Sex ratio (males per 100 females)	2013	97.3
Life expectancy at birth (females and males, years)	2010-2015	57.3/55.5
Infant mortality rate (per 1 000 live births)	2010-2015	66.4
Fertility rate, total (live births per woman)	2010-2015	4.7
Contraceptive prevalence (ages 15-49, %)	2006-2012	15.2
International migrant stock (000 and % of total population)[i]	mid-2013	202.5/3.0
Refugees and others of concern to UNHCR	mid-2013	24 320
Education: Government expenditure (% of GDP)	2006-2012	4.5
Education: Primary-secondary gross enrolment ratio (f/m per 100)[j]	2006-2012	66.8/88.5
Education: Female third-level students (% of total)	2006-2012	21.4
Intentional homicides (females and males, per 100 000)[k]	2008-2010	5.2/16.6
Seats held by women in national parliaments (%)	2014	16.5

Environmental indicators

Threatened species	2013	62
Forested area (% of land area)	2011	4.9
CO_2 emission estimates (000 metric tons and metric tons per capita)	2010	1 539/0.3
Energy consumption per capita (kilograms oil equivalent)	2010	75.0
Precipitation in the capital city, total mean (millimetres)		877[l]
Temperature in the capital city, mean °C (minimum and maximum)		23.1/30.7[m]

a Official rate. b Lomé. c Series linked to former series. d 2006. e Core Welfare Indicators Questionnaire (World Bank). f The indices are shown in terms of ISIC Rev.2. g Arrivals of non-resident tourists in hotels and similar establishments. h ITU estimate. i Includes refugees. j UNESCO estimate. k Estimates. l Based on WMO Climatological Normals (CLINO) for the period 1960-1989. m Based on WMO Climatological Normals (CLINO) for the period 1961-1990.

Tonga

Region	Oceania-Polynesia
Currency	Pa'anga (TOP)
Surface area (square kilometres)	747
Population in 2012 (estimated, 000)	105
Population density in 2012 (per square kilometre)	140.5
Capital city and population in 2011 (000)	Nuku'alofa (25)
United Nations membership date	14 September 1999

Economic indicators	2005	2010	2012
GDP: Gross domestic product (million current US$)	264	374	465
GDP: Growth rate at constant 2005 prices (annual %)	1.6	3.3	0.9
GDP per capita (current US$)	2 612.9	3 589.5	4 429.4
GNI: Gross national income per capita (current US$)	2 615.6	3 623.8	4 524.3
Gross fixed capital formation (% of GDP)	21.9	29.6	33.1
Exchange rates (national currency per US$)[a]	2.06	1.81	1.74
Balance of payments, current account (million US$)	−21	−79	−95
CPI: Consumer price index (2000=100)[b]	160	210	225
Agricultural production index (2004-2006=100)	99	104	102
Food production index (2004-2006=100)	99	104	102
Labour force participation, adult female pop. (%)	53.3	53.6	53.5
Labour force participation, adult male pop. (%)	75.2	75.2	74.8
Tourist arrivals at national borders (000)[c]	42	47	49
Mobile-cellular subscriptions (per 100 inhabitants)[d]	29.6	52.2	53.4
Individuals using the Internet (%)[d]	4.9	16.0	34.9

Total trade		Major trading partners			2012
	(million US$)	(% of exports)			(% of imports)
Exports	15.6	New Zealand	26.3	New Zealand	30.0
Imports	199.2	United States	13.5	Singapore	22.9
Balance	−183.6	Japan	12.8	United States	13.0

Social indicators		
Population growth rate (average annual %)	2010-2015	0.4
Urban population growth rate (average annual %)	2010-2015	0.8
Rural population growth rate (average annual %)	2010-2015	0.3
Urban population (%)	2013	23.6
Population aged 0-14 years (%)	2013	37.2
Population aged 60+ years (females and males, % of total)	2013	9.2/6.8
Sex ratio (males per 100 females)	2013	100.5
Life expectancy at birth (females and males, years)	2010-2015	75.6/69.7
Infant mortality rate (per 1 000 live births)	2010-2015	20.5
Fertility rate, total (live births per woman)	2010-2015	3.8
International migrant stock (000 and % of total population)	mid-2013	5.4/5.2
Refugees and others of concern to UNHCR	mid-2013	3
Education: Government expenditure (% of GDP)	2006-2012	3.9[e]
Education: Primary-secondary gross enrolment ratio (f/m per 100)	2006-2012	101.3/99.6
Education: Female third-level students (% of total)	2006-2012	60.5[f]
Intentional homicides (females and males, per 100 000)	2008-2010	0.7/1.6
Seats held by women in national parliaments (%)	2014	3.6

Environmental indicators		
Threatened species	2013	74
Forested area (% of land area)	2011	12.5
CO$_2$ emission estimates (000 metric tons and metric tons per capita)	2010	158/1.5
Energy consumption per capita (kilograms oil equivalent)	2010	492.0[g]

a Official rate. b Excludes rent. c Air arrivals. d ITU estimate. e 2004. f 2003. g UNSD estimate.

Trinidad and Tobago

Region	Caribbean
Currency	Trinidad and Tobago Dollar (TTD)
Surface area (square kilometres)	5 130
Population in 2012 (estimated, 000)	1 337
Population density in 2012 (per square kilometre)	260.7
Capital city and population in 2011 (000)	Port of Spain (66)
United Nations membership date	18 September 1962

Economic indicators	2005	2010	2012
GDP: Gross domestic product (million current US$)	15 982	20 578	23 225
GDP: Growth rate at constant 2005 prices (annual %)	6.2	0.2	1.5
GDP per capita (current US$)	12 323.2	15 494.7	17 365.2
GNI: Gross national income per capita (current US$)	11 741.0	16 121.1	18 067.1
Gross fixed capital formation (% of GDP)	28.7	13.9	13.9
Exchange rates (national currency per US$)[a]	6.31	6.42	6.43
Balance of payments, current account (million US$)	3 881	4 172	2 899[b]
CPI: Consumer price index (2000=100)	126	196	206[b]
Industrial production index (2005=100)[c]	100	159	153
Agricultural production index (2004-2006=100)	99	97	98
Food production index (2004-2006=100)	99	98	98
Unemployment (% of labour force)	8.0	5.9	...
Employment in industrial sector (% of employed)[d]	31.0	32.2[e]	...
Employment in agricultural sector (% of employed)[d]	4.3	3.8[e]	...
Labour force participation, adult female pop. (%)	53.5	52.5	52.9
Labour force participation, adult male pop. (%)	76.2	75.4	75.5
Tourist arrivals at national borders (000)[f]	463	388	402[b]
Energy production, primary (000 mt oil equivalent)	34 428	49 311	...
Mobile-cellular subscriptions (per 100 inhabitants)	70.3	141.2	139.4
Individuals using the Internet (%)	29.0[g]	48.5[h]	59.5[g]

Total trade		Major trading partners			2012
	(million US$)[i]	(% of exports)[i]		(% of imports)[i]	
Exports	10 981.7	United States	48.1	United States	28.0
Imports	6 479.6	Jamaica	6.5	Gabon	12.9
Balance	4 502.1	Barbados	3.4	Colombia	9.5

Social indicators		
Population growth rate (average annual %)	2010-2015	0.3
Urban population growth rate (average annual %)	2010-2015	2.2
Rural population growth rate (average annual %)	2010-2015	0.0
Urban population (%)	2013	14.3
Population aged 0-14 years (%)	2013	20.8
Population aged 60+ years (females and males, % of total)	2013	14.8/12.4
Sex ratio (males per 100 females)	2013	97.8
Life expectancy at birth (females and males, years)	2010-2015	73.6/66.3
Infant mortality rate (per 1 000 live births)	2010-2015	24.2
Fertility rate, total (live births per woman)	2010-2015	1.8
Contraceptive prevalence (ages 15-49, %)	2006-2012	42.5
International migrant stock (000 and % of total population)	mid-2013	32.5/2.4
Refugees and others of concern to UNHCR	mid-2013	41
Education: Government expenditure (% of GDP)	2006-2012	3.2[j]
Education: Primary-secondary gross enrolment ratio (f/m per 100)[k]	2006-2012	94.5/93.5[l]
Education: Female third-level students (% of total)	2006-2012	55.4[l]
Intentional homicides (females and males, per 100 000)	2008-2010	5.5/72.2
Seats held by women in national parliaments (%)	2014	28.6

Environmental indicators		
Threatened species	2013	55
Forested area (% of land area)	2011	44.0
CO$_2$ emission estimates (000 metric tons and metric tons per capita)	2010	50 640/37.7
Energy consumption per capita (kilograms oil equivalent)	2010	17 587.0
Precipitation in the capital city, total mean (millimetres)		1 408[m]
Temperature in the capital city, mean °C (minimum and maximum)		22.0/31.9[m]

a Official rate. b 2011. c The indices are shown in terms of ISIC Rev.3. d The indices are shown in terms of ISIC Rev.2. e 2008. f Air arrivals. g ITU estimate. h Country estimate. i 2010. j 2003. k National estimate. l 2004. m Based on monthly averages for the period 1961-1990.

Tunisia

Region	Northern Africa
Currency	Tunisian Dinar (TND)
Surface area (square kilometres)	163 610
Population in 2012 (estimated, 000)	10 875
Population density in 2012 (per square kilometre)	66.5
Capital city and population in 2011 (000)	Tunis (790)
United Nations membership date	12 November 1956

Economic indicators	2005	2010	2012
GDP: Gross domestic product (million current US$)	32 272	44 321	45 132
GDP: Growth rate at constant 2005 prices (annual %)	4.0	3.2	4.2
GDP per capita (current US$)	3 210.7	4 168.7	4 150.1
GNI: Gross national income per capita (current US$)	3 045.3	3 974.2	3 942.5
Gross fixed capital formation (% of GDP)	21.5	24.4	23.1
Exchange rates (national currency per US$)[a]	1.36	1.44	1.55
Balance of payments, current account (million US$)	−299	−2 104	−3 773
CPI: Consumer price index (2000=100)	114	139[b]	152
Agricultural production index (2004-2006=100)	101	104	115
Food production index (2004-2006=100)	101	104	115
Unemployment (% of labour force)[c]	...	...	17.4
Employment in industrial sector (% of employed)	32.3[d]	32.7	33.5[e]
Employment in agricultural sector (% of employed)	18.7[d]	17.6	16.2[e]
Labour force participation, adult female pop. (%)	24.3	24.9	25.1
Labour force participation, adult male pop. (%)	68.4	70.1	70.6
Tourist arrivals at national borders (000)[f]	6 378	6 903	5 950
Energy production, primary (000 mt oil equivalent)	5 634	6 967	...
Mobile-cellular subscriptions (per 100 inhabitants)	57.3	106.0	120.0
Individuals using the Internet (%)	9.7	36.8	41.4[g]

Total trade		Major trading partners			2012
	(million US$)[e]	(% of exports)[e]			(% of imports)[e]
Exports	17 847.0	France	30.7	France	18.3
Imports	23 952.1	Italy	21.7	Italy	15.8
Balance	−6 105.1	Germany	9.1	Germany	7.4

Social indicators		
Population growth rate (average annual %)	2010-2015	1.1
Urban population growth rate (average annual %)	2010-2015	1.3
Rural population growth rate (average annual %)	2010-2015	0.4
Urban population (%)	2013	66.7
Population aged 0-14 years (%)	2013	23.2
Population aged 60+ years (females and males, % of total)	2013	11.5/10.2
Sex ratio (males per 100 females)	2013	98.3
Life expectancy at birth (females and males, years)	2010-2015	78.2/73.5
Infant mortality rate (per 1 000 live births)	2010-2015	15.5
Fertility rate, total (live births per woman)	2010-2015	2.0
Contraceptive prevalence (ages 15-49, %)	2006-2012	60.2
International migrant stock (000 and % of total population)[h]	mid-2013	36.5/0.3
Refugees and others of concern to UNHCR	mid-2013	1 338
Education: Government expenditure (% of GDP)	2006-2012	6.2
Education: Primary-secondary gross enrolment ratio (f/m per 100)	2006-2012	99.1/97.9
Education: Female third-level students (% of total)	2006-2012	60.4
Intentional homicides (females and males, per 100 000)[i]	2008-2010	</2.0
Seats held by women in national parliaments (%)	2014	28.1

Environmental indicators		
Threatened species	2013	80
Forested area (% of land area)	2011	6.6
CO_2 emission estimates (000 metric tons and metric tons per capita)	2010	25 857/2.5
Energy consumption per capita (kilograms oil equivalent)	2010	824.0
Precipitation in the capital city, total mean (millimetres)		466[j]
Temperature in the capital city, mean °C (minimum and maximum)		13.3/23.5[j]

a Market rate. b Series linked to former series. c 2011: Break in series; data not strictly comparable. d Break in series; data not strictly comparable. e 2011. f Excludes nationals residing abroad. g ITU estimate. h Data refer to foreign citizens. i Estimates. j Based on monthly averages for the period 1961-1990.

Turkey

Region	Western Asia
Currency	Turkish Lira (TRY)
Surface area (square kilometres)	783 562
Population in 2012 (estimated, 000)	73 997
Population density in 2012 (per square kilometre)	94.4
Capital city and population in 2011 (000)	Ankara (4 194)
United Nations membership date	24 October 1945

Economic indicators	2005	2010	2012
GDP: Gross domestic product (million current US$)	482 986	731 144	788 299
GDP: Growth rate at constant 2005 prices (annual %)	8.4	9.2	2.2
GDP per capita (current US$)	7 129.7	10 135.4	10 653.1
GNI: Gross national income per capita (current US$)	7 118.0	10 125.3	10 650.2
Gross fixed capital formation (% of GDP)	21.0	18.9	20.3
Exchange rates (national currency per US$)[a]	1.35	1.54	1.78
Balance of payments, current account (million US$)	−21 449	−45 447	−48 507
CPI: Consumer price index (2000=100)	381[b]	578	670
Industrial production index (2005=100)	100	116	131
Agricultural production index (2004-2006=100)	101	110	122
Food production index (2004-2006=100)	101	111	124
Unemployment (% of labour force)	10.6[c]	11.9	9.2
Employment in industrial sector (% of employed)	24.8[d]	26.2[e]	26.0[e]
Employment in agricultural sector (% of employed)	29.5[d]	23.7[e]	23.6[e]
Labour force participation, adult female pop. (%)	23.4	27.6	29.4
Labour force participation, adult male pop. (%)	70.3	70.7	70.8
Tourist arrivals at national borders (000)[f]	20 273	31 364	35 698
Energy production, primary (000 mt oil equivalent)	17 323	25 450	...
Mobile-cellular subscriptions (per 100 inhabitants)	64.0	84.9	90.8
Individuals using the Internet (%)[g]	15.5	39.8	45.1

Total trade	Major trading partners				2012
(million US$)	(% of exports)				(% of imports)
Exports	152 536.7	Germany	8.6	Russian Federation	11.3
Imports	236 544.5	Iraq	7.1	Germany	9.0
Balance	−84 007.8	Iran	6.5	China	9.0

Social indicators		
Population growth rate (average annual %)	2010-2015	1.2
Urban population growth rate (average annual %)	2010-2015	2.4
Rural population growth rate (average annual %)	2010-2015	−2.3
Urban population (%)	2013	73.4
Population aged 0-14 years (%)	2013	25.7
Population aged 60+ years (females and males, % of total)	2013	12.0/9.6
Sex ratio (males per 100 females)	2013	96.5
Life expectancy at birth (females and males, years)	2010-2015	78.5/71.7
Infant mortality rate (per 1 000 live births)	2010-2015	12.0
Fertility rate, total (live births per woman)	2010-2015	2.1
Contraceptive prevalence (ages 15-49, %)	2006-2012	73.0
International migrant stock (000 and % of total population)[h]	mid-2013	1 864.9/2.5
Refugees and others of concern to UNHCR	mid-2013	527 780[i]
Education: Government expenditure (% of GDP)	2006-2012	2.9
Education: Primary-secondary gross enrolment ratio (f/m per 100)	2006-2012	91.9/96.8
Education: Female third-level students (% of total)	2006-2012	45.2
Intentional homicides (females and males, per 100 000)	2008-2010	2.0/8.6
Seats held by women in national parliaments (%)	2014	14.4

Environmental indicators		
Threatened species	2013	182
Forested area (% of land area)	2011	14.9
CO_2 emission estimates (000 metric tons and metric tons per capita)	2010	297 759/4.1
Energy consumption per capita (kilograms oil equivalent)	2010	1 304.0
Precipitation in the capital city, total mean (millimetres)		383[j]
Temperature in the capital city, mean °C (minimum and maximum)		6.0/17.7[j]

a Market rate. **b** Series linked to former series. **c** Break in series; data not strictly comparable. **d** The indices are shown in terms of ISIC Rev.3. **e** European Labour Force Survey (Eurostat). **f** From 2007, Turkish citizens residing abroad are included. **g** Age group 16 to 74 years. **h** Includes refugees. **i** Refugee population for Syrians in Turkey is a government estimate. **j** Based on monthly averages for the period 1926-2000.

Turkmenistan

Region	Central Asia
Currency	Turkmen Manat (TMT)
Surface area (square kilometres)	488 100
Population in 2012 (estimated, 000)	5 173
Population density in 2012 (per square kilometre)	10.6
Capital city and population in 2011 (000)	Ashgabat (683)
United Nations membership date	2 March 1992

Economic indicators	2005	2010	2012
GDP: Gross domestic product (million current US$)	14 101	22 148	33 466
GDP: Growth rate at constant 2005 prices (annual %)	13.0	9.2	8.0
GDP per capita (current US$)	2 970.0	4 392.7	6 469.4
GNI: Gross national income per capita (current US$)	2 763.6	4 017.1	5 965.2
Gross fixed capital formation (% of GDP)	22.9	52.9	51.2
Exchange rates (national currency per US$)[a]	...	2.85[b]	...
Agricultural production index (2004-2006=100)	107	108	104
Food production index (2004-2006=100)	106	114	110
Labour force participation, adult female pop. (%)	47.0	46.4	46.7
Labour force participation, adult male pop. (%)	74.8	75.7	76.5
Tourist arrivals at national borders (000)	12	8[c]	...
Energy production, primary (000 mt oil equivalent)	66 956	50 502	...
Mobile-cellular subscriptions (per 100 inhabitants)	2.2[d]	63.4	76.5[d]
Individuals using the Internet (%)[d]	1.0	3.0	7.2

Social indicators		
Population growth rate (average annual %)	2010-2015	1.3
Urban population growth rate (average annual %)	2010-2015	1.9
Rural population growth rate (average annual %)	2010-2015	0.6
Urban population (%)	2013	49.4
Population aged 0-14 years (%)	2013	28.5
Population aged 60+ years (females and males, % of total)	2013	7.4/5.6
Sex ratio (males per 100 females)	2013	96.8
Life expectancy at birth (females and males, years)	2010-2015	69.7/61.3
Infant mortality rate (per 1 000 live births)	2010-2015	46.7
Fertility rate, total (live births per woman)	2010-2015	2.3
Contraceptive prevalence (ages 15-49, %)	2006-2012	61.8[e]
International migrant stock (000 and % of total population)	mid-2013	226.3/4.3
Refugees and others of concern to UNHCR	mid-2013	8 311
Intentional homicides (females and males, per 100 000)	2008-2010	3.3/20.6
Seats held by women in national parliaments (%)	2014	26.4

Environmental indicators		
Threatened species	2013	48
Forested area (% of land area)	2011	8.8
CO_2 emission estimates (000 metric tons and metric tons per capita)	2010	53 011/10.5
Energy consumption per capita (kilograms oil equivalent)	2010	4 459.0
Precipitation in the capital city, total mean (millimetres)		227[f]
Temperature in the capital city, mean °C (minimum and maximum)		10.4/23.2[f]

a UN operational exchange rate. b January 2009. c 2007. d ITU estimate. e 2000. f Based on WMO Climatological Normals (CLINO) for the period 1961-1990.

Tuvalu

Region	Oceania-Polynesia
Currency	Australian Dollar (AUD)
Surface area (square kilometres)	26
Population in 2012 (estimated, 000)	10
Population density in 2012 (per square kilometre)	379.2
Capital city and population in 2011 (000)	Funafuti (5)
United Nations membership date	5 September 2000

Economic indicators	2005	2010	2012
GDP: Gross domestic product (million current US$)	22	34	40
GDP: Growth rate at constant 2005 prices (annual %)	−3.9	−1.4	2.6
GDP per capita (current US$)	2 258.8	3 428.0	4 041.9
GNI: Gross national income per capita (current US$)	3 730.4	5 482.8	7 050.6
Gross fixed capital formation (% of GDP)	65.5	46.7	53.1
Exchange rates (national currency per US$)[a]	1.37	0.99	0.96
CPI: Consumer price index (2000=100)[b]	117	125[cd]	...
Agricultural production index (2004-2006=100)	101	111	106
Food production index (2004-2006=100)	101	111	106
Tourist arrivals at national borders (000)	1	2	1[e]
Mobile-cellular subscriptions (per 100 inhabitants)	13.4	16.3	28.4[f]
Individuals using the Internet (%)[f]	10.0[c]	25.0	35.0

Total trade		Major trading partners		2012
	(million US$)[g]	(% of exports)		(% of imports)[g]
Imports	26.5	...	Fiji	23.8
		...	Australia	18.1
		...	New Zealand	17.4

Social indicators		
Population growth rate (average annual %)	2010-2015	0.2
Urban population growth rate (average annual %)	2010-2015	1.0
Rural population growth rate (average annual %)	2010-2015	−0.6
Urban population (%)	2013	51.4
Population aged 0-14 years (%)[hi]	2013	32.8
Population aged 60+ years (females and males, % of total)[hi]	2013	10.8/7.4
Sex ratio (males per 100 females)[hi]	2013	103.7
Life expectancy at birth (females and males, years)[h]	2010-2015	67.8/64.8[jk]
Infant mortality rate (per 1 000 live births)[h]	2010-2015	23.4[jk]
Fertility rate, total (live births per woman)[h]	2010-2015	3.7[kl]
Contraceptive prevalence (ages 15-49, %)	2006-2012	30.5
International migrant stock (000 and % of total population)[m]	mid-2013	0.2/1.5
Education: Primary-secondary gross enrolment ratio (f/m per 100)[n]	2006-2012	96.9/86.3[o]
Seats held by women in national parliaments (%)	2014	6.7

Environmental indicators		
Threatened species	2013	93
Forested area (% of land area)	2011	33.3

a UN operational exchange rate. b Funafuti. c 2007. d Series linked to former series. e 2011. f ITU estimate. g 2008. h Data compiled by the Secretariat of the Pacific Community Demography Programme. i De facto estimate. j 2010-2012. k Preliminary. l 2012. m Data refer to foreign citizens. n National estimate. o 2001.

Uganda

Region	Eastern Africa
Currency	Uganda Shilling (UGX)
Surface area (square kilometres)	241 550
Population in 2012 (estimated, 000)	36 346
Population density in 2012 (per square kilometre)	150.5
Capital city and population in 2011 (000)	Kampala (1 659)
United Nations membership date	25 October 1962

Economic indicators	2005	2010	2012
GDP: Gross domestic product (million current US$)	10 040	17 181	21 736
GDP: Growth rate at constant 2005 prices (annual %)	10.0	6.2	4.4
GDP per capita (current US$)	349.5	505.5	598.0
GNI: Gross national income per capita (current US$)	340.1	494.7	584.2
Gross fixed capital formation (% of GDP)	21.3	22.8	24.5
Exchange rates (national currency per US$)[a]	1 816.86	2 308.30	2 685.95
Balance of payments, current account (million US$)	−26	−1 752	−2 222
CPI: Consumer price index (2000=100)	124	186	252
Agricultural production index (2004-2006=100)	100	112	110
Food production index (2004-2006=100)	100	112	110
Employment in industrial sector (% of employed)[bcde]	4.5[f]	6.0[g]	...
Employment in agricultural sector (% of employed)[bce]	71.6[f]	65.6[g]	...
Labour force participation, adult female pop. (%)	77.2	76.1	75.9
Labour force participation, adult male pop. (%)	80.0	79.4	79.3
Tourist arrivals at national borders (000)	468	946	1 197
Energy production, primary (000 mt oil equivalent)	156	103[h]	...
Mobile-cellular subscriptions (per 100 inhabitants)	4.6	38.4[i]	45.9
Individuals using the Internet (%)	1.7	12.5	14.7[j]

Total trade		Major trading partners				2012
	(million US$)	(% of exports)				(% of imports)
Exports	2 357.5	Sudan	17.2	India		20.9
Imports	6 044.1	Kenya	10.8	China		11.3
Balance	−3 686.6	Dem. Rep. of Congo	10.2	Kenya		9.8

Social indicators		
Population growth rate (average annual %)	2010-2015	3.3
Urban population growth rate (average annual %)	2010-2015	5.7
Rural population growth rate (average annual %)	2010-2015	2.6
Urban population (%)	2013	16.4
Population aged 0-14 years (%)	2013	48.4
Population aged 60+ years (females and males, % of total)	2013	3.9/3.5
Sex ratio (males per 100 females)	2013	100.5
Life expectancy at birth (females and males, years)	2010-2015	60.2/57.8
Infant mortality rate (per 1 000 live births)	2010-2015	57.0
Fertility rate, total (live births per woman)	2010-2015	5.9
Contraceptive prevalence (ages 15-49, %)	2006-2012	30.0
International migrant stock (000 and % of total population)[k]	mid-2013	531.4/1.4
Refugees and others of concern to UNHCR	mid-2013	265 860
Education: Government expenditure (% of GDP)	2006-2012	3.3
Education: Primary-secondary gross enrolment ratio (f/m per 100)[l]	2006-2012	82.4/83.8
Education: Female third-level students (% of total)	2006-2012	21.2
Intentional homicides (females and males, per 100 000)	2008-2010	1.0/15.5
Seats held by women in national parliaments (%)	2014	35.0

Environmental indicators		
Threatened species	2013	183
Forested area (% of land area)	2011	14.5
CO_2 emission estimates (000 metric tons and metric tons per capita)	2010	3 781/0.1
Energy consumption per capita (kilograms oil equivalent)	2010	38.0
Precipitation in the capital city, total mean (millimetres)		1 225[m]
Temperature in the capital city, mean °C (minimum and maximum)		17.7/27.8[m]

a Principal rate. b May of the current year to April of the following year. c Age group 14 to 64 years. d Refers to manufacturing only. e The indices are shown in terms of ISIC Rev.3. f Break in series; data not strictly comparable. g 2009. h UNSD estimate. i December. j ITU estimate. k Includes refugees. l UNESCO estimate. m Based on monthly averages for the period 1971-2000.

Ukraine

Region	Eastern Europe
Currency	Hryvnia (UAH)
Surface area (square kilometres)	603 500
Population in 2012 (estimated, 000)	45 530
Population density in 2012 (per square kilometre)	75.4
Capital city and population in 2011 (000)	Kiev (2 829)
United Nations membership date	24 October 1945

Economic indicators	2005	2010	2012
GDP: Gross domestic product (million current US$)	86 142	136 419	176 309
GDP: Growth rate at constant 2005 prices (annual %)	2.7	4.1	0.2
GDP per capita (current US$)	1 827.5	2 962.4	3 872.4
GNI: Gross national income per capita (current US$)	1 806.6	2 952.4	3 831.5
Gross fixed capital formation (% of GDP)	22.0	18.1	18.9
Exchange rates (national currency per US$)[a]	5.05	7.96	7.99
Balance of payments, current account (million US$)	2 534	−3 016	−14 777
CPI: Consumer price index (2000=100)	147	262[b]	...
Industrial production index (2005=100)[c]	100	94	99
Agricultural production index (2004-2006=100)	100	106	121
Food production index (2004-2006=100)	100	106	121
Unemployment (% of labour force)[d]	7.2	8.1	7.5
Employment in industrial sector (% of employed)[cd]	24.2	22.4[be]	20.7
Employment in agricultural sector (% of employed)[cd]	19.4	15.6[be]	17.2
Labour force participation, adult female pop. (%)	52.0	52.4	53.0
Labour force participation, adult male pop. (%)	65.3	66.1	66.6
Tourist arrivals at national borders (000)	17 631	21 203	23 013
Energy production, primary (000 mt oil equivalent)	65 324	60 635	...
Mobile-cellular subscriptions (per 100 inhabitants)	64.0	118.7	132.1
Individuals using the Internet (%)	3.8[f]	23.3[g]	33.7[h]

Total trade		Major trading partners			2012
	(million US$)	(% of exports)		(% of imports)	
Exports	68 694.5	Russian Federation	25.7	Russian Federation	32.4
Imports	84 656.7	Turkey	5.4	China	9.3
Balance	−15 962.2	Egypt	4.2	Germany	8.0

Social indicators

Population growth rate (average annual %)	2010-2015	−0.6
Urban population growth rate (average annual %)	2010-2015	−0.3
Rural population growth rate (average annual %)	2010-2015	−1.2
Urban population (%)	2013	69.3
Population aged 0-14 years (%)	2013	14.5
Population aged 60+ years (females and males, % of total)	2013	25.5/16.3
Sex ratio (males per 100 females)	2013	85.5
Life expectancy at birth (females and males, years)	2010-2015	74.3/62.8
Infant mortality rate (per 1 000 live births)	2010-2015	11.7
Fertility rate, total (live births per woman)	2010-2015	1.5
Contraceptive prevalence (ages 15-49, %)	2006-2012	66.7
International migrant stock (000 and % of total population)	mid-2013	5 151.4/11.4
Refugees and others of concern to UNHCR	mid-2013	39 821
Education: Government expenditure (% of GDP)	2006-2012	6.2
Education: Primary-secondary gross enrolment ratio (f/m per 100)[i]	2006-2012	100.1/100.9
Education: Female third-level students (% of total)	2006-2012	52.3
Intentional homicides (females and males, per 100 000)	2008-2010	2.9/10.1
Seats held by women in national parliaments (%)	2014	9.7

Environmental indicators

Threatened species	2013	88
Forested area (% of land area)	2011	16.8
CO$_2$ emission estimates (000 metric tons and metric tons per capita)	2010	304 555/6.7
Energy consumption per capita (kilograms oil equivalent)	2010	2 611.0
Precipitation in the capital city, total mean (millimetres)		648[j]
Temperature in the capital city, mean °C (minimum and maximum)		4.3/11.9[j]

a Official rate. **b** 2009. **c** The indices are shown in terms of ISIC Rev.3. **d** Age group 15 to 70 years. **e** Break in series; data not strictly comparable. **f** Age group 15 to 59 years using the Internet within the last 4 weeks. **g** Age group 5 years and over. **h** ITU estimate. **i** National estimate. **j** Based on monthly averages for the period 1961-1990.

United Arab Emirates

Region	Western Asia
Currency	United Arab Emirates Dirham (AED)
Surface area (square kilometres)	83 600
Population in 2012 (estimated, 000)	9 206
Population density in 2012 (per square kilometre)	110.1
Capital city and population in 2011 (000)	Abu Dhabi (942)
United Nations membership date	9 December 1971

Economic indicators	2005	2010	2012
GDP: Gross domestic product (million current US$)	180 617	287 422	383 799
GDP: Growth rate at constant 2005 prices (annual %)	4.9	1.7	4.4
GDP per capita (current US$)	43 534.0	34 048.5	41 691.7
GNI: Gross national income per capita (current US$)	44 229.6	35 099.0	43 206.5
Gross fixed capital formation (% of GDP)	18.4	24.9	21.9
Exchange rates (national currency per US$)[a]	3.67	3.67	3.67
Agricultural production index (2004-2006=100)	105	111	71
Food production index (2004-2006=100)	105	111	71
Employment in industrial sector (% of employed)[bc]	39.8[de]	23.1[fgh]	...
Employment in agricultural sector (% of employed)[bc]	4.9[de]	3.8[fgh]	...
Labour force participation, adult female pop. (%)	37.0	46.2	46.6
Labour force participation, adult male pop. (%)	91.7	89.5	91.0
Tourist arrivals at national borders (000)[ijk]	7 126	...	...
Energy production, primary (000 mt oil equivalent)	178 966	181 405	...
Mobile-cellular subscriptions (per 100 inhabitants)	111.4	145.5	169.9
Individuals using the Internet (%)	40.0[l]	68.0[m]	85.0[n]

Total trade		Major trading partners			2012
	(million US$)[o]	(% of exports)[op]			(% of imports)[op]
Exports	252 556.0	Asia nes	37.8	Areas nes	23.9
Imports	210 945.0	Areas nes	26.0	India	13.6
Balance	41 611.0	India	9.6	China	7.1

Social indicators		
Population growth rate (average annual %)	2010-2015	2.5
Urban population growth rate (average annual %)	2010-2015	2.5
Rural population growth rate (average annual %)	2010-2015	0.3
Urban population (%)	2013	85.0
Population aged 0-14 years (%)	2013	15.3
Population aged 60+ years (females and males, % of total)	2013	0.9/1.0
Sex ratio (males per 100 females)	2013	234.2
Life expectancy at birth (females and males, years)	2010-2015	78.1/76.1
Infant mortality rate (per 1 000 live births)	2010-2015	5.7
Fertility rate, total (live births per woman)	2010-2015	1.8
Contraceptive prevalence (ages 15-49, %)	2006-2012	27.5[q]
International migrant stock (000 and % of total population)[rs]	mid-2013	7 827.0/83.8
Refugees and others of concern to UNHCR	mid-2013	750
Education: Primary-secondary gross enrolment ratio (f/m per 100)	2006-2012	90.9/88.0[t]
Education: Female third-level students (% of total)	2006-2012	57.7
Intentional homicides (females and males, per 100 000)[u]	2008-2010	</<
Seats held by women in national parliaments (%)	2014	17.5

Environmental indicators		
Threatened species	2013	50
Forested area (% of land area)	2011	3.8
CO_2 emission estimates (000 metric tons and metric tons per capita)	2010	167 459/22.3
Energy consumption per capita (kilograms oil equivalent)	2010	9 151.0
Precipitation in the capital city, total mean (millimetres)		89[v]
Temperature in the capital city, mean °C (minimum and maximum)		20.2/33.7[v]

a Official rate. b The indices are shown in terms of ISIC Rev.3. c Break in series; data not strictly comparable. d Population census. e December. f 2009. g May. h Excludes labour camps. i Arrivals of non-resident tourists in hotels and similar establishments. j Arrivals in hotels only. k Includes domestic tourism and nationals residing abroad. l ITU estimate. m Refers to the total population. n Age group 15 to 74 years using the Internet within the last 3 months (excludes population living in working camps). o 2011. p See technical notes. q 1995. r Data refer to foreign citizens. s Includes refugees. t 1999. u Estimates. v Based on WMO Climatological Normals (CLINO) for the period 1982-1991.

United Kingdom

Region	Northern Europe
Currency	Pound Sterling (GBP)
Surface area (square kilometres)	242 495 [a]
Population in 2012 (estimated, 000)	62 783 [a]
Population density in 2012 (per square kilometre)	258.9
Capital city and population in 2011 (000)	London (9 005)
United Nations membership date	24 October 1945

Economic indicators	2005	2010	2012
GDP: Gross domestic product (million current US$)	2 321 358	2 295 523	2 471 600
GDP: Growth rate at constant 2005 prices (annual %)	3.2	1.7	0.1
GDP per capita (current US$)	38 502.3	36 985.0	39 367.3
GNI: Gross national income per capita (current US$)	39 193.3	37 265.9	39 248.5
Gross fixed capital formation (% of GDP)	16.8	14.9	14.3
Exchange rates (national currency per US$) [b]	0.58	0.64	0.63
Balance of payments, current account (million US$)	−59 406	−75 229	−92 383
CPI: Consumer price index (2000=100)	113	131	143
Industrial production index (2005=100)	100	91	88
Agricultural production index (2004-2006=100)	100	102	99
Food production index (2004-2006=100)	100	102	99
Unemployment (% of labour force) [c]	4.8	7.8	7.9
Employment in industrial sector (% of employed)	22.2 [def]	19.1 [g]	18.9 [g]
Employment in agricultural sector (% of employed)	1.3 [def]	1.2 [g]	1.2 [g]
Labour force participation, adult female pop. (%)	55.0	55.5	55.7
Labour force participation, adult male pop. (%)	69.3	68.6	68.8
Tourist arrivals at national borders (000)	28 039	28 295	29 282
Energy production, primary (000 mt oil equivalent) [h]	194 374	139 257	...
Mobile-cellular subscriptions (per 100 inhabitants)	108.8	130.8	130.8 [i]
Individuals using the Internet (%) [c]	70.0	85.0	87.0 [j]

Total trade		Major trading partners			2012
	(million US$)	(% of exports)			(% of imports)
Exports	481 225.8	United States	13.3	Germany	12.1
Imports	689 137.0	Germany	10.8	United States	8.9
Balance	−207 911.2	Netherlands	7.9	China	8.2

Social indicators

Population growth rate (average annual %)	2010-2015	0.6
Urban population growth rate (average annual %)	2010-2015	0.8
Rural population growth rate (average annual %)	2010-2015	−<
Urban population (%)	2013	79.9
Population aged 0-14 years (%)	2013	17.6
Population aged 60+ years (females and males, % of total)	2013	24.8/21.5
Sex ratio (males per 100 females)	2013	97.2
Life expectancy at birth (females and males, years)	2010-2015	82.4/78.5
Infant mortality rate (per 1 000 live births)	2010-2015	4.2
Fertility rate, total (live births per woman)	2010-2015	1.9
Contraceptive prevalence (ages 15-49, %) [k]	2006-2012	84.0
International migrant stock (000 and % of total population)	mid-2013	7 824.1/12.4
Refugees and others of concern to UNHCR	mid-2013	169 606 [l]
Education: Government expenditure (% of GDP) [m]	2006-2012	6.3
Education: Primary-secondary gross enrolment ratio (f/m per 100) [m]	2006-2012	101.9/101.4
Education: Female third-level students (% of total)	2006-2012	56.4
Intentional homicides (females and males, per 100 000)	2008-2010	0.8/1.7
Seats held by women in national parliaments (%)	2014	22.6

Environmental indicators

Threatened species	2013	83
Forested area (% of land area)	2011	11.9
CO_2 emission estimates (000 metric tons and metric tons per capita)	2010	493 101/7.9
Energy consumption per capita (kilograms oil equivalent) [h]	2010	3 143.0
Precipitation in the capital city, total mean (millimetres)		558 [n]
Temperature in the capital city, mean °C (minimum and maximum)		7.8/15.3 [n]

a Excludes Channel Islands (Guernsey and Jersey) and Isle of Man. b Market rate. c Age group 16 to 74 years. d The indices are shown in terms of ISIC Rev.3. e Age group 16 years and over. f Second quarter. g European Labour Force Survey (Eurostat). h Includes Jersey and Guernsey for oil statistics. Excludes these islands for electricity. i September. j ITU estimate. k Age group 16 to 49 years. l Refugee population refers to the end of 2012. m Includes Northern Ireland. n Based on monthly averages for the period 1981-2010.

United Republic of Tanzania

Region	Eastern Africa
Currency	Tanzania Shilling (TZS)
Surface area (square kilometres)	947 303
Population in 2012 (estimated, 000)	47 783[a]
Population density in 2012 (per square kilometre)	50.4
Capital city and population in 2011 (000)	Dodoma (226)
United Nations membership date	14 December 1961

Economic indicators	2005	2010	2012
GDP: Gross domestic product (million current US$)[b]	14 142	22 915	28 249
GDP: Growth rate at constant 2005 prices (annual %)[b]	7.4	7.0	6.9
GDP per capita (current US$)[b]	374.6	524.2	607.8
GNI: Gross national income per capita (current US$)[b]	369.7	522.5	603.5
Gross fixed capital formation (% of GDP)[b]	24.7	31.5	33.8
Exchange rates (national currency per US$)[c]	1 165.51	1 455.15	1 571.62
Balance of payments, current account (million US$)	−1 093	−1 960	−3 640
CPI: Consumer price index (2000=100)	128[b]	192[bd]	251
Agricultural production index (2004-2006=100)	97	122	140
Food production index (2004-2006=100)	96	123	140
Employment in industrial sector (% of employed)	4.3[befg]	...	...
Employment in agricultural sector (% of employed)	76.5[befg]	...	...
Labour force participation, adult female pop. (%)	88.5	88.3	88.1
Labour force participation, adult male pop. (%)	90.5	90.3	90.2
Tourist arrivals at national borders (000)	590	754	1 043
Energy production, primary (000 mt oil equivalent)	534	1 009	...
Mobile-cellular subscriptions (per 100 inhabitants)	7.6	46.8	57.1
Individuals using the Internet (%)[h]	1.1	2.9	4.0

Total trade		Major trading partners			2012
	(million US$)	(% of exports)		(% of imports)	
Exports	5 547.2	South Africa	17.7	Switzerland	13.5
Imports	11 715.6	Switzerland	14.4	China	9.9
Balance	−6 168.4	China	9.5	United Arab Emirates	8.8

Social indicators		
Population growth rate (average annual %)[a]	2010-2015	3.0
Urban population growth rate (average annual %)[a]	2010-2015	4.8
Rural population growth rate (average annual %)[a]	2010-2015	2.4
Urban population (%)[a]	2013	27.6
Population aged 0-14 years (%)[a]	2013	44.9
Population aged 60+ years (females and males, % of total)[a]	2013	5.3/4.5
Sex ratio (males per 100 females)[a]	2013	100.0
Life expectancy at birth (females and males, years)[a]	2010-2015	62.7/60.0
Infant mortality rate (per 1 000 live births)[a]	2010-2015	48.7
Fertility rate, total (live births per woman)[a]	2010-2015	5.2
Contraceptive prevalence (ages 15-49, %)	2006-2012	34.4
International migrant stock (000 and % of total population)[ai]	mid-2013	312.8/0.6
Refugees and others of concern to UNHCR	mid-2013	265 435
Education: Government expenditure (% of GDP)	2006-2012	6.2
Education: Primary-secondary gross enrolment ratio (f/m per 100)	2006-2012	69.3/69.6
Education: Female third-level students (% of total)	2006-2012	35.4
Intentional homicides (females and males, per 100 000)[j]	2008-2010	3.4/45.7
Seats held by women in national parliaments (%)	2014	36.0

Environmental indicators		
Threatened species	2013	914
Forested area (% of land area)	2011	37.3
CO$_2$ emission estimates (000 metric tons and metric tons per capita)	2010	6 841/0.2
Energy consumption per capita (kilograms oil equivalent)	2010	53.0
Precipitation in the capital city, total mean (millimetres)		607[k]
Temperature in the capital city, mean °C (minimum and maximum)		16.8/28.8[k]

a Includes Zanzibar. b Excludes Zanzibar. c Official rate. d Series linked to former series. e 2006. f The indices are shown in terms of ISIC Rev.2. g Break in series; data not strictly comparable. h ITU estimate. i Includes refugees. j Estimates. k Based on monthly averages for the period 1971-2000.

United States of America

Region	Northern America
Currency	U.S. Dollar (USD)
Surface area (square kilometres)	9 629 091
Population in 2012 (estimated, 000)	317 505
Population density in 2012 (per square kilometre)	33.0
Capital city and population in 2011 (000)	Washington, D.C. (4 705)
United Nations membership date	24 October 1945

Economic indicators	2005	2010	2012
GDP: Gross domestic product (million current US$)	13 095 400	14 958 300	16 244 600
GDP: Growth rate at constant 2005 prices (annual %)	3.4	2.5	2.8
GDP per capita (current US$)	43 919.9	47 905.3	51 163.3
GNI: Gross national income per capita (current US$)	44 346.8	48 426.7	52 013.3
Gross fixed capital formation (% of GDP)	22.8	18.0	18.6
Balance of payments, current account (million US$)	−739 802	−449 477	−440 423
CPI: Consumer price index (2000=100)[a]	113	127	133
Industrial production index (2005=100)	100	96	103
Agricultural production index (2004-2006=100)	100	106	102
Food production index (2004-2006=100)	100	107	103
Unemployment (% of labour force)[b]	5.1	9.6	8.1
Employment in industrial sector (% of employed)[b]	20.6[c]	16.7[d]	...
Employment in agricultural sector (% of employed)[b]	1.6[c]	1.6	...
Labour force participation, adult female pop. (%)	58.3	57.6	56.8
Labour force participation, adult male pop. (%)	72.0	69.8	69.3
Tourist arrivals at national borders (000)	49 206	59 796	66 969
Energy production, primary (000 mt oil equivalent)[ef]	1 455 431	1 559 291	...
Mobile-cellular subscriptions (per 100 inhabitants)	68.6[g]	91.9	98.2[h]
Individuals using the Internet (%)	68.0[h]	74.0	81.0[h]

Total trade		Major trading partners			2012
	(million US$)[e]	(% of exports)[e]		(% of imports)[e]	
Exports	1 545 565.3	Canada	18.9	China	19.0
Imports	2 333 805.3	Mexico	14.0	Canada	14.0
Balance	−788 240.0	China	7.2	Mexico	12.0

Social indicators		
Population growth rate (average annual %)	2010-2015	0.8
Urban population growth rate (average annual %)	2010-2015	1.1
Rural population growth rate (average annual %)	2010-2015	−0.6
Urban population (%)	2013	82.9
Population aged 0-14 years (%)	2013	19.6
Population aged 60+ years (females and males, % of total)	2013	21.3/18.0
Sex ratio (males per 100 females)	2013	96.9
Life expectancy at birth (females and males, years)	2010-2015	81.2/76.4
Infant mortality rate (per 1 000 live births)	2010-2015	6.1
Fertility rate, total (live births per woman)	2010-2015	2.0
Contraceptive prevalence (ages 15-49, %)[i]	2006-2012	78.6
International migrant stock (000 and % of total population)	mid-2013	45 785.1/14.3
Refugees and others of concern to UNHCR	mid-2013	288 409[j]
Education: Government expenditure (% of GDP)	2006-2012	5.6
Education: Primary-secondary gross enrolment ratio (f/m per 100)	2006-2012	96.3/95.9
Education: Female third-level students (% of total)	2006-2012	57.0
Intentional homicides (females and males, per 100 000)	2008-2010	1.9/6.6
Seats held by women in national parliaments (%)	2014	18.3

Environmental indicators		
Threatened species[k]	2013	1 278
Forested area (% of land area)	2011	33.3
CO_2 emission estimates (000 metric tons and metric tons per capita)[ef]	2010	5 428 612/17.3
Energy consumption per capita (kilograms oil equivalent)[ef]	2010	6 501.0
Precipitation in the capital city, total mean (millimetres)		1 055[l]
Temperature in the capital city, mean °C (minimum and maximum)		6.7/19.1[l]

a All urban consumers. b Age group 16 years and over. c The indices are shown in terms of ISIC Rev.3. d Excludes electricity, gas, steam and air conditioning supply and water supply. e Includes Puerto Rico and the U.S. Virgin Islands. f Includes American Samoa, Guam, Northern Mariana Islands, Johnston Atoll, Midway Islands and Wake Island. g Methodology revised. h ITU estimate. i Age group 15 to 44 years. j Excludes individuals whose decisions on their asylum claims with the Executive Office for Immigration Review are pending. k Excludes United States Minor Outlying Islands. l Based on monthly averages for the period 1981-2010.

United States Virgin Islands

Region	Caribbean
Currency	U.S. Dollar (USD)
Surface area (square kilometres)	347
Population in 2012 (estimated, 000)	106
Population density in 2012 (per square kilometre)	306.8
Capital city and population in 2011 (000)	Charlotte Amalie (60)

Economic indicators	2005	2010	2012
Agricultural production index (2004-2006=100)	98	118	123
Food production index (2004-2006=100)	98	118	123
Labour force participation, adult female pop. (%)	54.9	55.2	54.4
Labour force participation, adult male pop. (%)	76.1	73.9	72.8
Tourist arrivals at national borders (000)	593	590	580
Mobile-cellular subscriptions (per 100 inhabitants)	73.4[a]	...	...
Individuals using the Internet (%)[a]	27.3	31.2	40.6

Social indicators		
Population growth rate (average annual %)	2010-2015	0.1
Urban population growth rate (average annual %)	2010-2015	−0.1
Rural population growth rate (average annual %)	2010-2015	−3.6
Urban population (%)	2013	95.8
Population aged 0-14 years (%)	2013	20.7
Population aged 60+ years (females and males, % of total)	2013	23.5/21.6
Sex ratio (males per 100 females)	2013	91.3
Life expectancy at birth (females and males, years)	2010-2015	82.9/77.2
Infant mortality rate (per 1 000 live births)	2010-2015	9.4
Fertility rate, total (live births per woman)	2010-2015	2.5
Contraceptive prevalence (ages 15-49, %)[b]	2006-2012	78.4[c]
International migrant stock (000 and % of total population)	mid-2013	63.3/59.3

Environmental indicators		
Threatened species	2013	43
Forested area (% of land area)	2011	57.4

a ITU estimate. b Age group 18 to 44 years. c 2002.

Uruguay

Region	South America
Currency	Uruguayan Peso (UYU)
Surface area (square kilometres)	176 215
Population in 2012 (estimated, 000)	3 395
Population density in 2012 (per square kilometre)	19.3
Capital city and population in 2011 (000)	Montevideo (1 672)
United Nations membership date	18 December 1945

Economic indicators	2005	2010	2012
GDP: Gross domestic product (million current US$)	17 363	38 846	49 919
GDP: Growth rate at constant 2005 prices (annual %)	7.5	8.9	3.9
GDP per capita (current US$)	5 221.7	11 520.3	14 702.5
GNI: Gross national income per capita (current US$)	5 071.4	11 074.7	14 271.5
Gross fixed capital formation (% of GDP)	16.6	19.3	22.1
Exchange rates (national currency per US$)[a]	24.10	20.09	19.40
Balance of payments, current account (million US$)	42	−753	−2 626
CPI: Consumer price index (2000=100)[b]	162	230	270
Agricultural production index (2004-2006=100)	101	116	128
Food production index (2004-2006=100)	101	117	130
Unemployment (% of labour force)[c]	10.9[de]	7.2	6.5
Employment in industrial sector (% of employed)[f]	21.9[cgh]	21.2	21.1[i]
Employment in agricultural sector (% of employed)[fj]	4.6[cgh]	11.8	10.9[i]
Labour force participation, adult female pop. (%)	52.7	55.2	55.5
Labour force participation, adult male pop. (%)	74.1	76.7	76.8
Tourist arrivals at national borders (000)	1 808	2 353	2 711
Energy production, primary (000 mt oil equivalent)	575	733	...
Mobile-cellular subscriptions (per 100 inhabitants)	34.8	131.7[k]	147.3
Individuals using the Internet (%)	20.1	46.4[l]	55.1[m]

Total trade	Major trading partners				2012
	(million US$)	(% of exports)[n]			(% of imports)
Exports	8 709.2	Brazil	19.4	Brazil	18.0
Imports	11 652.1	Free zones	16.3	Argentina	14.9
Balance	−2 942.9	China	9.1	China	14.3

Social indicators

Population growth rate (average annual %)	2010-2015	0.3
Urban population growth rate (average annual %)	2010-2015	0.5
Rural population growth rate (average annual %)	2010-2015	−0.9
Urban population (%)	2013	92.7
Population aged 0-14 years (%)	2013	21.9
Population aged 60+ years (females and males, % of total)	2013	21.4/15.9
Sex ratio (males per 100 females)	2013	93.4
Life expectancy at birth (females and males, years)	2010-2015	80.5/73.6
Infant mortality rate (per 1 000 live births)	2010-2015	11.5
Fertility rate, total (live births per woman)	2010-2015	2.1
Contraceptive prevalence (ages 15-49, %)[o]	2006-2012	77.0[p]
International migrant stock (000 and % of total population)	mid-2013	73.5/2.2
Refugees and others of concern to UNHCR	mid-2013	237
Education: Government expenditure (% of GDP)	2006-2012	4.5
Education: Primary-secondary gross enrolment ratio (f/m per 100)	2006-2012	103.1/99.0
Education: Female third-level students (% of total)	2006-2012	62.5
Intentional homicides (females and males, per 100 000)	2008-2010	3.2/7.9
Seats held by women in national parliaments (%)	2014	13.1

Environmental indicators

Threatened species	2013	104
Forested area (% of land area)	2011	10.2
CO_2 emission estimates (000 metric tons and metric tons per capita)	2010	6 639/2.0
Energy consumption per capita (kilograms oil equivalent)	2010	820.0
Precipitation in the capital city, total mean (millimetres)		1 101
Temperature in the capital city, mean °C (minimum and maximum)		12.4/21.4

a Market rate. b Montevideo. c Age group 14 years and over. d 2006. e Break in series; data not strictly comparable. f The indices are shown in terms of ISIC Rev.3. g Urban areas. h Excludes conscripts. i 2011. j Includes mining and quarrying. k Includes data dedicated subscriptions. l Age group 6 years and over. m ITU estimate. n See technical notes. o Age group 15 to 50 years. p 2004.

Uzbekistan

Region	Central Asia
Currency	Uzbekistan Sum (UZS)
Surface area (square kilometres)	447 400
Population in 2012 (estimated, 000)	28 541
Population density in 2012 (per square kilometre)	63.8
Capital city and population in 2011 (000)	Tashkent (2 227)
United Nations membership date	2 March 1992

Economic indicators	2005	2010	2012
GDP: Gross domestic product (million current US$)	14 396	39 526	51 414
GDP: Growth rate at constant 2005 prices (annual %)	7.0	8.5	7.4
GDP per capita (current US$)	552.8	1 423.4	1 801.4
GNI: Gross national income per capita (current US$)	551.8	1 465.3	1 213.3
Gross fixed capital formation (% of GDP)	22.0	26.2	30.9
Exchange rates (national currency per US$)[a]	1 177.00	1 640.00	1 980.00
Agricultural production index (2004-2006=100)	100	127	139
Food production index (2004-2006=100)	99	135	151
Labour force participation, adult female pop. (%)	47.5	47.6	47.9
Labour force participation, adult male pop. (%)	72.6	74.5	75.2
Tourist arrivals at national borders (000)	242	975	...
Energy production, primary (000 mt oil equivalent)	61 736	60 443	...
Mobile-cellular subscriptions (per 100 inhabitants)	2.8	76.3[b]	72.2
Individuals using the Internet (%)	3.3	20.0[b]	36.5[b]

Social indicators		
Population growth rate (average annual %)	2010-2015	1.4
Urban population growth rate (average annual %)	2010-2015	1.3
Rural population growth rate (average annual %)	2010-2015	1.1
Urban population (%)	2013	36.3
Population aged 0-14 years (%)	2013	28.6
Population aged 60+ years (females and males, % of total)	2013	7.3/5.8
Sex ratio (males per 100 females)	2013	99.0
Life expectancy at birth (females and males, years)	2010-2015	71.6/64.9
Infant mortality rate (per 1 000 live births)	2010-2015	44.0
Fertility rate, total (live births per woman)	2010-2015	2.3
Contraceptive prevalence (ages 15-49, %)	2006-2012	64.9
International migrant stock (000 and % of total population)	mid-2013	1 266.3/4.4
Refugees and others of concern to UNHCR	mid-2013	141
Education: Primary-secondary gross enrolment ratio (f/m per 100)	2006-2012	100.0/102.4
Education: Female third-level students (% of total)	2006-2012	38.6
Intentional homicides (females and males, per 100 000)	2008-2010	1.6/5.6
Seats held by women in national parliaments (%)	2014	22.0

Environmental indicators		
Threatened species	2013	54
Forested area (% of land area)	2011	7.7
CO$_2$ emission estimates (000 metric tons and metric tons per capita)	2010	104 358/3.8
Energy consumption per capita (kilograms oil equivalent)	2010	1 716.0
Precipitation in the capital city, total mean (millimetres)		419
Temperature in the capital city, mean °C (minimum and maximum)		8.3/21.0

a UN operational exchange rate. b ITU estimate.

Vanuatu

Region	Oceania-Melanesia
Currency	Vatu (VUV)
Surface area (square kilometres)	12 189
Population in 2012 (estimated, 000)	247
Population density in 2012 (per square kilometre)	20.3
Capital city and population in 2011 (000)	Port Vila (47)
United Nations membership date	15 September 1981

Economic indicators	2005	2010	2012
GDP: Gross domestic product (million current US$)	393	680	752
GDP: Growth rate at constant 2005 prices (annual %)	5.2	1.6	2.0
GDP per capita (current US$)	1 878.3	2 875.8	3 039.8
GNI: Gross national income per capita (current US$)	1 746.2	2 710.2	2 868.8
Gross fixed capital formation (% of GDP)	19.7	27.8	28.0
Exchange rates (national currency per US$)[a]	112.33	93.15	91.73
Balance of payments, current account (million US$)	−34	−35	−50
CPI: Consumer price index (2000=100)	112	133	134[b]
Agricultural production index (2004-2006=100)	100	132	134
Food production index (2004-2006=100)	100	132	134
Employment in industrial sector (% of employed)	...	7.0[cde]	...
Employment in agricultural sector (% of employed)	...	60.5[cde]	...
Labour force participation, adult female pop. (%)	65.3	61.5	61.5
Labour force participation, adult male pop. (%)	81.7	80.6	80.3
Tourist arrivals at national borders (000)	62	97	108
Energy production, primary (000 mt oil equivalent)	0[f]	1	...
Mobile-cellular subscriptions (per 100 inhabitants)	6.0	70.9	54.4
Individuals using the Internet (%)	5.1	8.0	10.6[g]

Total trade		Major trading partners			2012
	(million US$)[b]	(% of exports)[b]			(% of imports)[b]
Exports	63.5	Malaysia	20.5	Australia	29.7
Imports	280.6	Philippines	18.1	Singapore	18.2
Balance	−217.1	Australia	11.3	New Zealand	12.7

Social indicators		
Population growth rate (average annual %)	2010-2015	2.2
Urban population growth rate (average annual %)	2010-2015	3.6
Rural population growth rate (average annual %)	2010-2015	2.0
Urban population (%)	2013	25.5
Population aged 0-14 years (%)	2013	37.1
Population aged 60+ years (females and males, % of total)	2013	6.2/6.0
Sex ratio (males per 100 females)	2013	103.0
Life expectancy at birth (females and males, years)	2010-2015	73.6/69.6
Infant mortality rate (per 1 000 live births)	2010-2015	23.9
Fertility rate, total (live births per woman)	2010-2015	3.4
Contraceptive prevalence (ages 15-49, %)	2006-2012	38.4
International migrant stock (000 and % of total population)	mid-2013	3.1/1.2
Refugees and others of concern to UNHCR	mid-2013	2
Education: Government expenditure (% of GDP)	2006-2012	5.0
Education: Primary-secondary gross enrolment ratio (f/m per 100)	2006-2012	90.3/91.8
Education: Female third-level students (% of total)[h]	2006-2012	36.1[i]
Intentional homicides (females and males, per 100 000)[j]	2008-2010	</1.3
Seats held by women in national parliaments (%)	2014	0.0

Environmental indicators		
Threatened species	2013	137
Forested area (% of land area)	2011	36.1
CO$_2$ emission estimates (000 metric tons and metric tons per capita)	2010	117/0.5
Energy consumption per capita (kilograms oil equivalent)	2010	169.0
Precipitation in the capital city, total mean (millimetres)		2 222[k]
Temperature in the capital city, mean °C (minimum and maximum)		21.5/28.2[k]

a Official rate. b 2011. c 2009. d Population census. e November. f UNSD estimate. g ITU estimate. h UNESCO estimate. i 2004. j Estimates. k Based on monthly averages for the period 1961-1990.

Venezuela (Bolivarian Republic of)

Region	South America
Currency	Bolívar (VEF)
Surface area (square kilometres)	912 050
Population in 2012 (estimated, 000)	29 955
Population density in 2012 (per square kilometre)	32.8
Capital city and population in 2011 (000)	Caracas (3 242)
United Nations membership date	15 November 1945

Economic indicators	2005	2010	2012
GDP: Gross domestic product (million current US$)	145 513	393 808	382 424
GDP: Growth rate at constant 2005 prices (annual %)	10.3	−1.5	5.5
GDP per capita (current US$)	5 444.7	13 559.3	12 766.7
GNI: Gross national income per capita (current US$)	5 362.3	13 392.1	12 483.4
Gross fixed capital formation (% of GDP)	20.3	18.7	19.9
Exchange rates (national currency per US$)[a]	2.15	2.59	4.29
Balance of payments, current account (million US$)	25 053	8 812	11 016
CPI: Consumer price index (2000=100)	255[bc]	156[d]	238[d]
Agricultural production index (2004-2006=100)	101	105	116
Food production index (2004-2006=100)	101	105	116
Unemployment (% of labour force)	12.2	8.5	7.8
Employment in industrial sector (% of employed)[e]	20.8[f]	22.1	21.2[gh]
Employment in agricultural sector (% of employed)[e]	9.7[f]	8.7	7.7[gh]
Labour force participation, adult female pop. (%)	51.6	50.5	50.9
Labour force participation, adult male pop. (%)	81.5	79.3	79.2
Tourist arrivals at national borders (000)	706	526	710
Energy production, primary (000 mt oil equivalent)	200 168	186 138	...
Mobile-cellular subscriptions (per 100 inhabitants)	46.9	96.2	102.1[i]
Individuals using the Internet (%)	12.6	37.4[j]	44.1[k]

Total trade		Major trading partners			2012
	(million US$)[l]	(% of exports)[lm]			(% of imports)[l]
Exports	91 338.3	S. America nes	31.1	United States	27.9
Imports	36 387.6	Areas nes	29.8	China	12.0
Balance	54 950.7	N & C Ame nes	18.0	Brazil	8.6

Social indicators		
Population growth rate (average annual %)	2010-2015	1.5
Urban population growth rate (average annual %)	2010-2015	1.7
Rural population growth rate (average annual %)	2010-2015	−1.6
Urban population (%)	2013	93.9
Population aged 0-14 years (%)	2013	28.5
Population aged 60+ years (females and males, % of total)	2013	10.0/8.9
Sex ratio (males per 100 females)	2013	100.6
Life expectancy at birth (females and males, years)	2010-2015	77.6/71.7
Infant mortality rate (per 1 000 live births)	2010-2015	15.0
Fertility rate, total (live births per woman)	2010-2015	2.4
Contraceptive prevalence (ages 15-49, %)	2006-2012	70.3[n]
International migrant stock (000 and % of total population)	mid-2013	1 171.3/3.9
Refugees and others of concern to UNHCR	mid-2013	206 893
Education: Government expenditure (% of GDP)	2006-2012	6.9
Education: Primary-secondary gross enrolment ratio (f/m per 100)	2006-2012	95.7/93.5
Education: Female third-level students (% of total)[o]	2006-2012	62.1
Intentional homicides (females and males, per 100 000)	2008-2010	4.7/87.6
Seats held by women in national parliaments (%)	2014	17.0

Environmental indicators		
Threatened species	2013	305
Forested area (% of land area)	2011	52.1
CO$_2$ emission estimates (000 metric tons and metric tons per capita)	2010	201 582/7.0
Energy consumption per capita (kilograms oil equivalent)	2010	2 593.0
Precipitation in the capital city, total mean (millimetres)		913[p]
Temperature in the capital city, mean °C (minimum and maximum)		16.0/30.3[p]

a Official rate. b Metropolitan areas. c Caracas. d Index base 2008=100. e The indices are shown in terms of ISIC Rev.2. f Second semester. g Average of bi-annual estimates. h Break in series; data not strictly comparable. i Preliminary. j Country estimate. k ITU estimate. l 2011. m See technical notes. n 1998. o National estimate. p Based on monthly averages for the period 1964-1990.

Viet Nam

Region	South-Eastern Asia
Currency	Dong (VND)
Surface area (square kilometres)	330 957
Population in 2012 (estimated, 000)	90 796
Population density in 2012 (per square kilometre)	274.3
Capital city and population in 2011 (000)	Hanoi (2 955)
United Nations membership date	20 September 1977

Economic indicators	2005	2010	2012
GDP: Gross domestic product (million current US$)	57 633	115 932	155 820
GDP: Growth rate at constant 2005 prices (annual %)	12.0	6.4	5.3
GDP per capita (current US$)	678.5	1 301.9	1 716.2
GNI: Gross national income per capita (current US$)	666.0	1 252.3	1 640.6
Gross fixed capital formation (% of GDP)	31.3	32.6	24.2
Exchange rates (national currency per US$)[a]	15 916.00	18 932.00	20 828.00
Balance of payments, current account (million US$)	−560	−4 276	9 062
CPI: Consumer price index (2000=100)[b]	126	208	...
Industrial production index (2005=100)	100[c]	156[c]	174[d]
Agricultural production index (2004-2006=100)	100	120	129
Food production index (2004-2006=100)	100	119	128
Unemployment (% of labour force)	...	...	1.8
Employment in industrial sector (% of employed)[e]	20.2[fgh]	...	21.1[i]
Employment in agricultural sector (% of employed)[e]	51.7[fgh]	...	47.4[i]
Labour force participation, adult female pop. (%)	72.6	72.3	72.8
Labour force participation, adult male pop. (%)	81.9	81.3	81.9
Tourist arrivals at national borders (000)[j]	3 477	5 050	6 848
Energy production, primary (000 mt oil equivalent)	50 528	57 425	...
Mobile-cellular subscriptions (per 100 inhabitants)	11.5	127.0	149.4[k]
Individuals using the Internet (%)	12.7	30.7	39.5[k]

Total trade		Major trading partners			2012
	(million US$)	(% of exports)		(% of imports)	
Exports	114 529.2	United States	17.2	China	25.5
Imports	113 780.4	Japan	11.4	Republic of Korea	13.7
Balance	748.8	China	11.2	Japan	10.2

Social indicators		
Population growth rate (average annual %)	2010-2015	1.0
Urban population growth rate (average annual %)	2010-2015	3.0
Rural population growth rate (average annual %)	2010-2015	0.1
Urban population (%)	2013	32.3
Population aged 0-14 years (%)	2013	22.7
Population aged 60+ years (females and males, % of total)	2013	11.6/7.7
Sex ratio (males per 100 females)	2013	97.7
Life expectancy at birth (females and males, years)	2010-2015	80.4/71.2
Infant mortality rate (per 1 000 live births)	2010-2015	14.1
Fertility rate, total (live births per woman)	2010-2015	1.8
Contraceptive prevalence (ages 15-49, %)	2006-2012	77.8
International migrant stock (000 and % of total population)[lm]	mid-2013	68.3/0.1
Refugees and others of concern to UNHCR	mid-2013	11 500
Education: Government expenditure (% of GDP)	2006-2012	6.9
Education: Primary-secondary gross enrolment ratio (f/m per 100)	2006-2012	78.3/84.4[n]
Education: Female third-level students (% of total)	2006-2012	49.4
Intentional homicides (females and males, per 100 000)	2008-2010	0.5/2.6
Seats held by women in national parliaments (%)	2014	24.3

Environmental indicators		
Threatened species	2013	523
Forested area (% of land area)	2011	45.0
CO_2 emission estimates (000 metric tons and metric tons per capita)	2010	150 107/1.7
Energy consumption per capita (kilograms oil equivalent)	2010	481.0
Precipitation in the capital city, total mean (millimetres)		1 676[o]
Temperature in the capital city, mean °C (minimum and maximum)		20.9/27.0[o]

a Market rate. b Series linked to former series. c The index is shown in terms of ISIC Rev.3. d The index is shown in terms of ISIC Rev.4. e Break in series; data not strictly comparable. f 2006. g Living standards survey. h The indices are shown in terms of ISIC Rev.2. i Average of quarterly estimates. j Arrivals of non-resident visitors at national borders. k ITU estimate. l Data refer to foreign citizens. m Includes refugees. n 1998. o Based on monthly averages for the period 1898-1990.

Western Sahara

Region	Northern Africa	
Currency	Morocco Dirham (MAD)	
Surface area (square kilometres)	266 000 [a]	
Population in 2012 (estimated, 000)	549	
Population density in 2012 (per square kilometre)	2.1	
Capital city and population in 2011 (000)	El Aaiún (237)	

Economic indicators	2005	2010	2012
Exchange rates (national currency per US$) [b]	9.25	8.36	8.43
Agricultural production index (2004-2006=100)	100	102	102
Food production index (2004-2006=100)	100	102	102

Social indicators		
Population growth rate (average annual %)	2010-2015	3.2
Urban population growth rate (average annual %)	2010-2015	3.5
Rural population growth rate (average annual %)	2010-2015	2.1
Urban population (%)	2013	82.4
Population aged 0-14 years (%)	2013	26.6
Population aged 60+ years (females and males, % of total)	2013	4.4/5.1
Sex ratio (males per 100 females)	2013	110.8
Life expectancy at birth (females and males, years)	2010-2015	69.8/65.9
Infant mortality rate (per 1 000 live births)	2010-2015	37.2
Fertility rate, total (live births per woman)	2010-2015	2.4
International migrant stock (000 and % of total population) [c]	mid-2013	4.9/0.9

Environmental indicators		
Threatened species	2013	37
Forested area (% of land area)	2011	2.7
CO_2 emission estimates (000 metric tons and metric tons per capita)	2010	238/0.4
Energy consumption per capita (kilograms oil equivalent)	2010	149.0[d]

a Comprises the Northern Region (former Saguia el Hamra) and Southern Region (former Rio de Oro). b Official rate. c Estimates. d UNSD estimate.

Yemen

Region	Western Asia
Currency	Yemeni Rial (YER)
Surface area (square kilometres)	527 968
Population in 2012 (estimated, 000)	23 852
Population density in 2012 (per square kilometre)	45.2
Capital city and population in 2011 (000)	Sana'a (2 419)
United Nations membership date	30 September 1947

Economic indicators	2005	2010	2012
GDP: Gross domestic product (million current US$)	19 041	31 167	32 831
GDP: Growth rate at constant 2005 prices (annual %)	5.1	5.7	2.0
GDP per capita (current US$)	945.5	1 369.2	1 376.4
GNI: Gross national income per capita (current US$)	868.8	1 293.9	1 326.9
Gross fixed capital formation (% of GDP)	18.3	19.7	19.7
Exchange rates (national currency per US$)[a]	195.08	213.80	214.89
Balance of payments, current account (million US$)	624	−1 381	−1 029[b]
CPI: Consumer price index (2000=100)	174	292[c]	384
Agricultural production index (2004-2006=100)	98	136	141
Food production index (2004-2006=100)	98	137	142
Employment in industrial sector (% of employed)[d]	16.3[efg]	18.8[hi]	...
Employment in agricultural sector (% of employed)[d]	31.0[efg]	24.7[hi]	...
Labour force participation, adult female pop. (%)	23.5	24.8	25.2
Labour force participation, adult male pop. (%)	71.0	71.2	71.8
Tourist arrivals at national borders (000)[j]	336	1 025	1 174
Energy production, primary (000 mt oil equivalent)	20 080	20 104	...
Mobile-cellular subscriptions (per 100 inhabitants)	11.0	46.1	54.4
Individuals using the Internet (%)	1.1[k]	12.4	17.5[k]

Total trade		Major trading partners			2012
	(million US$)	(% of exports)			(% of imports)
Exports	7 062.1	China	41.0	United Arab Emirates	9.8
Imports	11 259.6	Thailand	19.2	Switzerland	8.8
Balance	−4 197.5	India	11.4	Netherlands	7.9

Social indicators		
Population growth rate (average annual %)	2010-2015	2.3
Urban population growth rate (average annual %)	2010-2015	4.8
Rural population growth rate (average annual %)	2010-2015	2.2
Urban population (%)	2013	33.5
Population aged 0-14 years (%)	2013	40.2
Population aged 60+ years (females and males, % of total)	2013	4.8/4.4
Sex ratio (males per 100 females)	2013	101.7
Life expectancy at birth (females and males, years)	2010-2015	64.4/61.7
Infant mortality rate (per 1 000 live births)	2010-2015	56.2
Fertility rate, total (live births per woman)	2010-2015	4.2
Contraceptive prevalence (ages 15-49, %)	2006-2012	27.7
International migrant stock (000 and % of total population)[lm]	mid-2013	314.7/1.3
Refugees and others of concern to UNHCR	mid-2013	655 104
Education: Government expenditure (% of GDP)	2006-2012	5.2
Education: Primary-secondary gross enrolment ratio (f/m per 100)	2006-2012	63.0/81.9
Education: Female third-level students (% of total)	2006-2012	29.9
Intentional homicides (females and males, per 100 000)[n]	2008-2010	0.6/3.5
Seats held by women in national parliaments (%)	2014	0.3

Environmental indicators		
Threatened species	2013	286
Forested area (% of land area)	2011	1.0
CO_2 emission estimates (000 metric tons and metric tons per capita)	2010	21 834/0.9
Energy consumption per capita (kilograms oil equivalent)	2010	270.0

a Official rate. b 2011. c Series linked to former series. d Break in series; data not strictly comparable. e 2004. f Population census. g The indices are shown in terms of ISIC Rev.3. h Child labour survey. i Age group 15 to 65 years. j From 2006, includes nationals residing abroad. k ITU estimate. l Data refer to foreign citizens. m Includes refugees. n Estimates.

Zambia

Region	Eastern Africa
Currency	Zambia Kwacha (ZMW)
Surface area (square kilometres)	752 612
Population in 2012 (estimated, 000)	14 075
Population density in 2012 (per square kilometre)	18.7
Capital city and population in 2011 (000)	Lusaka (1 802)
United Nations membership date	1 December 1964

Economic indicators	2005	2010	2012
GDP: Gross domestic product (million current US$)	7 179	16 190	21 490
GDP: Growth rate at constant 2005 prices (annual %)	5.3	7.6	7.3
GDP per capita (current US$)	625.9	1 225.0	1 526.8
GNI: Gross national income per capita (current US$)	570.8	1 121.8	1 402.6
Gross fixed capital formation (% of GDP)	22.4	21.1	26.6
Exchange rates (national currency per US$)[a]	3.51	4.80	5.15
Balance of payments, current account (million US$)	−600	1 206	−1
CPI: Consumer price index (2000=100)	251	420	475[b]
Agricultural production index (2004-2006=100)	101	143	157
Food production index (2004-2006=100)	98	148	156
Employment in industrial sector (% of employed)	7.1[cde]	...	...
Employment in agricultural sector (% of employed)	72.2[cde]	...	...
Labour force participation, adult female pop. (%)	73.6	73.3	73.2
Labour force participation, adult male pop. (%)	86.2	85.9	85.7
Tourist arrivals at national borders (000)	669	815	859
Energy production, primary (000 mt oil equivalent)	852	970	...
Mobile-cellular subscriptions (per 100 inhabitants)	8.3	41.6	75.8
Individuals using the Internet (%)	2.9[f]	10.0	13.5[f]

Total trade		Major trading partners		2012
	(million US$)[g]	(% of exports)[g]		(% of imports)[g]
Exports	9 000.9	Switzerland	48.9	South Africa	35.7
Imports	7 177.8	China	16.7	Dem. Rep. of Congo	18.5
Balance	1 823.1	South Africa	9.3	China	9.8

Social indicators		
Population growth rate (average annual %)	2010-2015	3.2
Urban population growth rate (average annual %)	2010-2015	4.2
Rural population growth rate (average annual %)	2010-2015	2.3
Urban population (%)	2013	40.0
Population aged 0-14 years (%)	2013	46.6
Population aged 60+ years (females and males, % of total)	2013	4.2/3.6
Sex ratio (males per 100 females)	2013	99.5
Life expectancy at birth (females and males, years)	2010-2015	59.5/55.9
Infant mortality rate (per 1 000 live births)	2010-2015	65.5
Fertility rate, total (live births per woman)	2010-2015	5.7
Contraceptive prevalence (ages 15-49, %)	2006-2012	40.8
International migrant stock (000 and % of total population)[h]	mid-2013	98.9/0.7
Refugees and others of concern to UNHCR	mid-2013	52 306
Education: Government expenditure (% of GDP)	2006-2012	1.4
Education: Primary-secondary gross enrolment ratio (f/m per 100)	2006-2012	106.3/111.6
Education: Female third-level students (% of total)[i]	2006-2012	31.6[j]
Intentional homicides (females and males, per 100 000)	2008-2010	0.8/3.0
Seats held by women in national parliaments (%)	2014	10.8

Environmental indicators		
Threatened species	2013	75
Forested area (% of land area)	2011	66.3
CO_2 emission estimates (000 metric tons and metric tons per capita)	2010	2 426/0.2
Energy consumption per capita (kilograms oil equivalent)	2010	117.0
Precipitation in the capital city, total mean (millimetres)		843[k]
Temperature in the capital city, mean °C (minimum and maximum)		14.9/26.4[k]

a Official rate. **b** Series linked to former series. **c** The indices are shown in terms of ISIC Rev.2. **d** November to December. **e** Break in series; data not strictly comparable. **f** ITU estimate. **g** 2011. **h** Includes refugees. **i** UNESCO estimate. **j** 2000. **k** Based on monthly averages for the period 1970-2000.

Zimbabwe

Region	Eastern Africa
Surface area (square kilometres)	390 757
Population in 2012 (estimated, 000)	13 724
Population density in 2012 (per square kilometre)	35.1
Capital city and population in 2011 (000)	Harare (1 542)
United Nations membership date	25 August 1980

Economic indicators	2005	2010	2012
GDP: Gross domestic product (million current US$)	6 223	7 433	9 802
GDP: Growth rate at constant 2005 prices (annual %)	−4.1	9.6	4.4
GDP per capita (current US$)	489.6	568.4	714.2
GNI: Gross national income per capita (current US$)	481.7	562.0	697.4
Gross fixed capital formation (% of GDP)	2.0	14.0	16.0
Exchange rates (national currency per US$)[a]	80.77	...	...
CPI: Consumer price index (2000=100)	1 117[bcd]	103[e]	111[e]
Agricultural production index (2004-2006=100)	93	94	103
Food production index (2004-2006=100)	91	93	96
Employment in industrial sector (% of employed)	9.3[fghi]	...	...
Employment in agricultural sector (% of employed)	64.8[fgh]	...	...
Labour force participation, adult female pop. (%)	83.1	83.0	83.2
Labour force participation, adult male pop. (%)	90.1	89.5	89.7
Tourist arrivals at national borders (000)[j]	1 559	2 239	1 794
Energy production, primary (000 mt oil equivalent)	2 836	2 337	...
Mobile-cellular subscriptions (per 100 inhabitants)	5.2	61.3	96.9
Individuals using the Internet (%)	8.0	11.5	17.1[k]

Total trade		Major trading partners			2012
	(million US$)	(% of exports)		(% of imports)	
Exports	3 882.4	South Africa	68.9	South Africa	42.2
Imports	7 362.5	United Arab Emirates	12.4	United Kingdom	17.2
Balance	−3 480.1	Mozambique	7.3	United States	7.6

Social indicators		
Population growth rate (average annual %)	2010-2015	2.8
Urban population growth rate (average annual %)	2010-2015	3.4
Rural population growth rate (average annual %)	2010-2015	1.3
Urban population (%)	2013	39.6
Population aged 0-14 years (%)	2013	39.5
Population aged 60+ years (females and males, % of total)	2013	6.4/5.0
Sex ratio (males per 100 females)	2013	97.5
Life expectancy at birth (females and males, years)	2010-2015	60.8/58.8
Infant mortality rate (per 1 000 live births)	2010-2015	37.2
Fertility rate, total (live births per woman)	2010-2015	3.5
Contraceptive prevalence (ages 15-49, %)	2006-2012	58.5
International migrant stock (000 and % of total population)[l]	mid-2013	361.0/2.6
Refugees and others of concern to UNHCR	mid-2013	63 333
Education: Government expenditure (% of GDP)	2006-2012	2.5
Education: Primary-secondary gross enrolment ratio (f/m per 100)	2006-2012	69.2/71.8[m]
Education: Female third-level students (% of total)	2006-2012	44.0
Intentional homicides (females and males, per 100 000)[n]	2008-2010	4.3/24.5
Seats held by women in national parliaments (%)	2014	31.5

Environmental indicators		
Threatened species	2013	58
Forested area (% of land area)	2011	39.5
CO$_2$ emission estimates (000 metric tons and metric tons per capita)	2010	9 420/0.7
Energy consumption per capita (kilograms oil equivalent)	2010	265.0
Precipitation in the capital city, total mean (millimetres)		841[o]
Temperature in the capital city, mean °C (minimum and maximum)		12.3/25.5[o]

a Official rate. b 2006. c Index base 2005=100. d Annual average is calculated as the geometric mean of monthly indices. e Index base 2009=100. f 2004. g The indices are shown in terms of ISIC Rev.3. h June. i Excludes electricity, gas and water supply. j Arrivals of non-resident visitors at national borders. k ITU estimate. l Includes refugees. m 2003. n Estimates. o Based on monthly averages for the period 1961-1990.

Technical notes

Below are brief descriptions of the indicators presented in the country profiles. The terms are arranged in alphabetical order.

Agricultural production index: The indices are calculated by the Laspeyres formula based on the sum of price-weighted quantities of different agricultural commodities produced. The commodities covered in the computation of indices of agricultural production are all crops and livestock products originating in each country. Practically all products are covered, with the main exception of fodder crops. Production quantities of each commodity are weighted by the average international commodity prices in the base period and summed for each year. To obtain the index, the aggregate for a given year is divided by the average aggregate for the base period 2004-2006. Indices are calculated without any deductions for feed and seed and are referred to as "gross" by the Food and Agriculture Organization of the United Nations (FAO).
Source of the data: FAOSTAT database of the Food and Agriculture Organization of the United Nations, available at http://faostat3.fao.org/faostat-gateway/go/to/download/Q/QI/E (7 February 2014 update).

Balance of payments is a statement summarizing the economic transactions between the residents of a country and non-residents during a specific period, usually a year. It includes transactions in goods, services, income, transfers and financial assets and liabilities. Generally, the balance of payments is divided into two major components: the current account and the capital and financial account. The data on balance of payments presented in the *World Statistics Pocketbook* correspond to the current account category. The current account is a record of all transactions in the balance of payments covering the exports and imports of goods and services, payments of income, and current transfers between residents of a country and non-residents.
Source of the data: International Monetary Fund, *Balance of Payments (BOP)* database (last accessed 31 January 2014).

Capital city and population: The designation of any specific city as a capital city is done solely on the basis of the designation as reported by the country or area. The city can be the seat of the government as determined by the country. Some countries designate more than one city to be a capital city with a specific title function (e.g., administrative and/or legislative capital). The data refer to the year 2011.
Source of the data: The United Nations Population Division, *World Urbanization Prospects: The 2011 Revision*, Table 13, available at http://esa.un.org/unpd/wup/CD-ROM/Urban-Agglomerations.htm (last accessed 7 November 2013).

CO$_2$ emission estimates represent the volume of carbon dioxide (CO$_2$) produced during the combustion of solid, liquid, and gaseous fuels, from gas flaring and the manufacture of cement. Original data were converted to CO$_2$ emissions by using the conversion formula: 1 gram Carbon = 3.664 grams CO$_2$, as per http://cdiac.ornl.gov/pns/convert.html#3.
Source of the data: Global, Regional, and National Fossil-Fuel CO$_2$ Emissions, Carbon Dioxide Information Analysis Center, National (All countries) file, available at http://cdiac.ornl.gov/trends/emis/overview_2010.html (last accessed 14 November 2013).

Contraceptive prevalence refers to the percentage of women married or in-union aged 15 to 49 who are currently using, or whose sexual partner is using at least one method of contraception, regardless of the method used. Contraceptive methods include modern methods such as sterilization, oral hormonal pills, intra-uterine devices, condoms, injectables, implants, vaginal barrier methods and emergency contraception and traditional methods such as the rhythm, withdrawal, lactational amenorrhea method and folk methods. The data contain the most recent estimates of contraceptive prevalence between the years 2006 and 2012.
Source of the data: United Nations, Department of Economic and Social Affairs, Population Division, Fertility and Family Planning Section, *World Contraceptive Use 2012*, Survey-based Observations 1950-2012, available at http://www.un.org/esa/population/publications/WCU2012/MainFrame.html.

CPI: Consumer price index measures changes over time in the general level of prices of goods and services that a reference population acquires, uses or pays for consumption. A consumer price index is estimated as a series of summary measures of the period-to-period proportional change in the prices of a fixed set of consumer goods and services of constant quantity and characteristics, acquired, used or paid for by the reference population. Each summary measure is constructed as a weighted average of a large number of elementary aggregate indices. Each of the elementary aggregate indices is estimated using a sample of prices for a defined set of goods and services obtained in, or by residents of, a specific region from a given set of outlets or other sources of consumption goods and services. Unless otherwise noted, the indices here generally refer to "all items" and to the country as a whole.
Source of the data: LABORSTA Internet, International Labour Organization (ILO) database, Consumer Price Indices, Main statistics (monthly): General Indices, food indices, Table: B9, available at http://laborsta.ilo.org/data_topic_E.html (last accessed 12 December 2013).

Currency refers to those notes and coins in circulation that are commonly used to make payments. The official currency names and the ISO currency codes are those officially in use, and may be subject to change.
Source of the data: United Nations Treasury's website, available at http://treasury.un.org/operationalrates/OperationalRates.aspx (data as of 1 November 2013).

Education: Female third-level students: The number of female students at the third-level of education is expressed as a percentage of the total number of students (males and females) at the same level in a given school year. Third-level education is that which is provided at university, teachers' college, higher professional school, and which requires, as a minimum condition of admission, the successful completion of education at the second level, or evidence of the attainment of an equivalent level of knowledge. Unless otherwise indicated, the data refer to the latest available year between 2006 and 2012.
Source of the data: UNESCO Institute of Statistics website, Education, Table 14: Tertiary indicators, available at http://stats.uis.unesco.org/unesco/ (October 2013 release).

Education: Government expenditure (% of GDP): Unless otherwise indicated, the data refer to the latest available year between 2006 and 2012. They show the trends in general government expenditures for educational affairs and services at pre-primary, primary, secondary and tertiary levels and subsidiary services to education, expressed as a percentage of the gross domestic product.
Source of the data: UNESCO Institute for Statistics website, Education, Table 19: Finance indicators by ISCED level, available at http://stats.uis.unesco.org/ unesco/ (October 2013 release).

Education: Primary and secondary gross enrolment ratio is the total enrolment in first and second levels of education, regardless of age, expressed as a percentage of the eligible official school-age population corresponding to the same level of education in a given school year. Education at the first level provides the basic elements of education (e.g. at elementary school or primary school). Education at the second level is provided at middle school, secondary school, high school, teacher-training school at this level and schools of a vocational or technical nature. Enrolment is at the beginning of the school or academic year. The gross enrolment ratio at the first and second level should include all pupils whatever their ages, whereas the population is limited to the range of official school ages. Therefore, for countries with almost universal education among the school-age population, the gross enrolment ratio will exceed 100 if the actual age distribution of pupils extends beyond the official school ages. Unless otherwise indicated, the data refer to the latest available year between 2006 and 2012.

Technical notes (*continued*)

Source of the data: UNESCO Institute of Statistics website, Education, Table 5: Enrolment ratios by ISCED level, available at http://stats.uis.unesco.org/unesco/ (October 2013 release).

Employment in agricultural and in industrial sectors: The "employed" comprise all persons above a specified age who, during a specified brief period, either one week or one day, were in "paid employment" or in "self-employment" as defined below. "Persons in paid employment" comprise all persons in the following categories: (a) "at work": persons who during the reference period performed some work for wages, salary or related payments, in cash or in kind; or (b) "with a job but not at work": persons who, having already worked in their present job, were absent during the reference period and continued to have a strong attachment to their job. "Persons in self-employment" comprise all persons (a) "at work": persons who during the reference period performed some work for profit or family gain, in cash or in kind; or (b) "with an enterprise but not at work": persons with an enterprise, which may be a business enterprise, a farm or a service undertaking, who were temporarily not at work during the reference period for any specific reason. Employers, own-account workers and members of producers' co-operatives should be considered as in self-employment and should be classified as "at work" or "not at work", as the case may be. (See ILO's *Current International Recommendations on Labour Statistics*). Unless otherwise indicated, the data refer to the 15 years and over age group who perform any work at all in the reference period, for pay or profit in industry (mining, manufacturing, electricity, gas and water and construction) and in agriculture. Agriculture comprises the following divisions of the International Standard Industrial Classification of All Economic Activities (ISIC), Rev. 4: crop and animal production, hunting and related service activities, forestry and lodging, and fishing and aquaculture. Data sources include the World Bank's Core Welfare Indicators Questionnaire, Eurostat's European Labour Force Survey, household income and expenditure surveys, household or labour force surveys, living standards surveys, official estimates and population censuses. The most common source of the data shown is the household or labour force survey; if other sources have been used they are indicated with a footnote.

Source of the data: The Key Indicators of the Labour Market database, International Labour Organization (ILO), available at http://www.ilo.org/empelm/what/WCMS_114240/lang--en/index.htm (last accessed 8 January 2014).

Energy consumption per capita: Data on consumption refers to "apparent consumption", which is derived from the formula "production + imports - exports - bunkers +/- stock changes".

Source of the data: The *Energy Statistics Yearbook* (information provided by the Industrial and Energy Statistics Section of the United Nations Statistics Division as of 18 December 2013).

Technical notes (*continued*)

Energy production, primary, refers to the first stage of production of various forms of energy (from sources that involve only extraction or capture, with or without separation from contiguous material, cleaning or grading, before the energy embodied in that source can be converted into heat or mechanical work, converted into a common unit (metric ton of oil equivalent) (see United Nations publication *Concepts and Methods in Energy Statistics, with Special Reference to Energy Accounts and Balances*, 1982). The data refer to the following commercial primary energy sources: hard coal, lignite, peat, oil shale, crude petroleum, natural gas liquids, biodiesel, alcohol, natural gas, primary steam/heat, and electricity generated from hydro, nuclear, geothermal, wind, tide, wave and solar sources.

Source of the data: The *Energy Statistics Yearbook* (information provided by the Industrial and Energy Statistics Section of the United Nations Statistics Division as of 18 December 2013).

Exchange rates are shown in units of national currency per US dollar and refer to end-of-period quotations. The exchange rates are classified into broad categories, reflecting both the role of the authorities in the determination of the exchange and/or the multiplicity of exchange rates in a country. The market rate is used to describe exchange rates determined largely by market forces; the official rate is an exchange rate determined by the authorities, sometimes in a flexible manner. For countries maintaining multiple exchange arrangements, the rates are labelled principal rate, secondary rate, and tertiary rate.

Source of the data: The International Monetary Fund, *International Financial Statistics* database (last accessed 6 January 2014). For those currencies for which the IMF does not publish exchange rates, non-commercial rates derived from the year-end operational rates of exchange for United Nations programmes are shown, as published by the United Nations Treasury, available at http://www.un.org/Depts/treasury/ (last accessed 6 January 2014).

Fertility rate: The total fertility rate is a widely used summary indicator of fertility. It refers to the number of children that would be born per woman, assuming no female mortality at child bearing ages and the age-specific fertility rates of a specified country and reference period. Unless otherwise indicated, the data are the five-year average for the reference period 2010-2015.

Source of the data: United Nations, Department of Economic and Social Affairs, Population Division (2013), *World Population Prospects: The 2012 Revision*, available at http://esa.un.org/unpd/wpp/Excel-Data/population.htm; supplemented by official national statistics published in the *United Nations Demographic Yearbook 2012*, Table 4, available at http://unstats.un.org/unsd/demographic/products/dyb/dyb2012.htm; and data compiled by the Secretariat of the Pacific Community (SPC) Statistics and Demography Programme, Population and demographic indicators, available at http://www.spc.int/sdp.

Technical notes (*continued*)

Food production index covers commodities that are considered edible and contain nutrients. Accordingly, coffee and tea are excluded because they have practically no nutritive value. The index numbers shown may differ from those produced by countries themselves because of differences in concepts of production, coverage, weights, time reference of data, and methods of evaluation. The data include estimates made by FAO in cases where no official or semi-official figures are available from the countries.

Source of the data: FAOSTAT database of the Food and Agriculture Organization of the United Nations, available at http://faostat3.fao.org/faostat-gateway/go/to/download/Q/QI/E (7 February 2014 update).

Forested area refers to the percentage of land area occupied by forest. Forest is defined in the Food and Agriculture Organization's *Global Forest Resources Assessment* as land spanning more than 0.5 hectares with trees higher than 5 metres and a canopy cover of more than 10 percent, or trees able to reach these thresholds in situ. It does not include land that is predominantly under agricultural or urban land use. Data are derived from the forest estimates divided by the land area for 2011.

Source of the data: The FAOSTAT database of the Food and Agriculture Organization of the United Nations, available at http://faostat3.fao.org/faostat-gateway/go/to/download/R/RL/E (last accessed 14 November 2013).

GDP: Gross domestic product is an aggregate measure of production equal to the sum of gross value added of all resident producer units plus that part (possibly the total) of taxes on products, less subsidies on products, that is not included in the valuation of output. It is also equal to the sum of the final uses of goods and services (all uses except intermediate consumption) measured at purchasers' prices, less the value of imports of goods and services, and equal to the sum of primary incomes distributed by resident producer units (see *System of National Accounts 2008*). The data in the *World Statistics Pocketbook* are in current United States (US) dollars and are estimates of the total production of goods and services of the countries represented in economic terms, not as a measure of the standard of living of their inhabitants. In order to have comparable coverage for as many countries as possible, these US dollar estimates are based on official GDP data in national currency, supplemented by national currency estimates prepared by the Statistics Division using additional data from national and international sources. The estimates given here are in most cases those accepted by the United Nations General Assembly's Committee on Contributions for determining United Nations members' contributions to the United Nations regular budget. The exchange rates for the conversion of GDP national currency data into US dollars are the average market rates published by the International Monetary Fund, in *International Financial Statistics*. Official exchange rates are used only when free market rates are not available. For non-members of the Fund, the conversion rates used are the average of United Nations operational rates of exchange. It should be noted that the conversion from local currency into US dollars introduces deficiencies in comparability over

Technical notes (*continued*)

time and among countries which should be considered when using the data. For example, comparability over time is distorted when exchange rate fluctuations differ substantially from domestic inflation rates.

Source of the data: The *National Accounts Main Aggregates Database,* available at http://unstats.un.org/unsd/snaama/dnllist.asp (December 2013 update) and the *National Accounts Statistics: Analysis of Main Aggregates*, compiled from national data provided to the United Nations Statistics Division.

GDP: Growth rate at constant 2005 prices is derived on the basis of constant price series in national currency. The figures are computed as the geometric mean of annual rates of growth expressed in percentages for the years indicated.

Source of the data: The *National Accounts Main Aggregates Database,* available at http://unstats.un.org/unsd/snaama/dnllist.asp (December 2013 update) and the *National Accounts Statistics: Analysis of Main Aggregates*, compiled from national data provided to the United Nations Statistics Division.

GDP per capita estimates are the value of all goods and services produced in the economy divided by the population.

Source of the data: The *National Accounts Main Aggregates Database* available at http://unstats.un.org/unsd/snaama/dnllist.asp (December 2013 update) and the *National Accounts Statistics: Analysis of Main Aggregates*, compiled from national data provided to the United Nations Statistics Division.

GNI: Gross national income per capita estimates are the aggregate value of the balances of gross primary incomes for all sectors in the economy divided by the population. GNI is equal to GDP less primary incomes payable to non-resident units plus primary incomes receivable from non-resident units. In other words, GNI is equal to GDP less taxes (less subsidies) on production and imports, compensation of employees and property income payable to the rest of the world plus the corresponding items receivable from the rest of the world. Thus GNI at market prices is the sum of gross primary incomes receivable by resident institutional units/sectors. It is worth noting that GNI at market prices was called gross national product in the 1953 SNA, and it was commonly denominated GNP. In contrast to GDP, GNI is not a concept of value added, but a concept of income (see *System of National Accounts 2008*).

Source of the data: The *National Accounts Main Aggregates Database,* available at http://unstats.un.org/unsd/snaama/dnllist.asp (December 2013 update) and the *National Accounts Statistics: Analysis of Main Aggregates*, compiled from national data provided to the United Nations Statistics Division.

Gross fixed capital formation is measured by the total value of a producer's acquisitions, less disposals, of fixed assets during the accounting period plus certain specified expenditure on services that adds to the value of non-produced assets (see *System of National Accounts 2008*). The data are based on the percentage distribution of GDP in current prices.

Source of the data: The *National Accounts Main Aggregates Database*, available at http://unstats.un.org/unsd/snaama/dnllist.asp (December 2013 update) and the *National Accounts Statistics: Analysis of Main Aggregates*, compiled from national data provided to the United Nations Statistics Division.

Individuals using the Internet refer to the percentage of people who used the Internet from any location and for any purpose, irrespective of the device and network used. It can be via a computer (i.e. desktop or laptop computer, tablet or similar handheld computer), mobile phone, games machine, digital TV, etc. Access can be via a fixed or mobile network. Data are obtained by countries through national household surveys and are either provided directly to the International Telecommunication Union (ITU) by national statistical offices (NSO), or ITU carries out necessary research to obtain data, for example, from NSO websites. There are certain data limits to this indicator, insofar as estimates have to be calculated for many developing countries which do not yet collect information and communications technology household statistics.

Source of the data: The World Telecommunication/ICT Indicators Database 2013 (17th Edition) of the International Telecommunication Union, Time series by country, available at http://www.itu.int/en/ITU-D/Statistics/Pages/stat/default.aspx (last accessed 23 January 2014).

Industrial production index: The data shown here generally cover, unless otherwise noted, the International Standard Industrial Classification of All Economic Activities, Revision 4 (ISIC Rev. 4) sections B, C, D and E (i.e., mining and quarrying; manufacturing; electricity, gas, steam and air conditioning supply; and water supply, sewerage, waste management and remediation activities). The data that are footnoted as referring to ISIC Rev. 3 cover Tabulation Categories C, D and E (mining and quarrying; manufacturing; and electricity, gas and water supply).

Source of the data: United Nations *Monthly Bulletin of Statistics*, Table 5, available at http://unstats.un.org/unsd/mbs/ (last accessed 28 January 2014).

Infant mortality rate (per 1 000 live births) is the ratio of infant deaths (the deaths of children under one year of age) in a given year to the total number of live births in the same year. Unless otherwise noted, the rates are the five-year projected averages for the reference period 2010-2015.

Source of the data: United Nations, Department of Economic and Social Affairs, Population Division (2013), *World Population Prospects: The 2012 Revision,* available at http://esa.un.org/unpd/wpp/Excel-Data/population.htm and supplemented by data compiled by the Secretariat of the Pacific Community (SPC) Statistics and Demography Programme, Population and demographic indicators, available at http://www.spc.int/sdp.

Technical notes (*continued*)

Intentional homicides: The rates are the annual number of unlawful deaths purposefully inflicted on a person by another person, reported by sex for the year per 100 000. The data refer to the latest available year between 2008 and 2010. For most countries, country information on causes of death is not available for most causes. Estimates are therefore based on cause of death modelling and death registration data from other countries in the region. Further country-level information and data on specific causes was also used.

Source of the data: United Nations Office on Crime and Drugs, Homicide Statistics - Homicides by sex, available at https://www.unodc.org/unodc/en/data-and-analysis/homicide.html (last accessed 27 March 2014).

International migrant stock generally represents the number of persons born in a country other than that in which they live. When information on country of birth was not recorded, data on the number of persons having foreign citizenship was used instead. In the absence of any empirical data, estimates were imputed. Data refer to mid-2013. Figures for international migrant stock as a percentage of the population are the outcome of dividing the estimated international migrant stock by the estimated total population and multiplying the result by 100.

Source of the data: The United Nations Population Division, *Trends in International Migrant Stock: The 2013 Revision- Migrants by age and sex*, Total International Migrant Stock (Tables 1 and 3), available at http://esa.un.org/unmigration/TIMSA2013/migrantstocks2013.htm?mhome (last accessed 8 November 2013).

Labour force participation rate is calculated by expressing the number of persons in the labour force as a percentage of the working-age population. The labour force is the sum of the number of persons employed and the number of unemployed (see ILO's *Current International Recommendations on Labour Statistics*). The working-age population is the population above a certain age, prescribed for the measurement of economic characteristics. Unless otherwise noted, the data refer to the age group of 15 years and over.

Source of the data: The Key Indicators of the Labour Market database, International Labour Organization (ILO), available at http://www.ilo.org/empelm/what/WCMS_114240/lang--en/index.htm (last accessed 8 January 2014).

Life expectancy at birth is the average number of years of life at birth (age 0) for males and females according to the expected mortality rates by age estimated for the reference year and population. Unless otherwise indicated, the data are the five-year projected averages for the reference period 2010-2015.

Source of the data: United Nations, Department of Economic and Social Affairs, Population Division (2013), *World Population Prospects: The 2012 Revision*, available at http://esa.un.org/unpd/wpp/Excel-Data/population.htm; supplemented by official national statistics published in the *United Nations Demographic Yearbook 2012*, Table 21, available at http://unstats.un.org/unsd/demographic/products/dyb/dyb2012.htm; and data compiled by the Secretariat of the Pacific

Technical notes (*continued*)

Community (SPC) Statistics and Demography Programme, Population and demographic indicators, available at http://www.spc.int/sdp.

Major trading partners show the three largest trade partners (countries of last known destination and origin or consignment) in international merchandise trade transactions. In some cases a special partner is shown (i.e. Areas nes, bunkers, etc.) instead of a country and refers to one of the following special categories. Areas not elsewhere specified (Areas nes) is used (a) for low value trade, (b) if the partner designation was unknown to the country or if an error was made in the partner assignment and (c) for reasons of confidentiality. If a specific geographical location can be identified within Areas nes, then they are recorded accordingly (i.e. Other Europe nes, South America nes, North and Central America nes, Oceania nes, Other Africa nes, and Other Asia nes). Bunkers are ship stores and aircraft supplies, which consists mostly of fuels and food. Free zones belong to the geographical and economic territory of a country but not to its customs territory. For the purpose of trade statistics the transactions between the customs territory and the free zones are recorded, if the reporting country uses the Special Trade System. Free zones can be commercial free zones (duty free shops) or industrial free zones. Data are expressed as percentages of total exports and of total imports of the country, area or special partner.

Source of the data: The United Nations Statistics Division's Commodity Trade Statistics Database (COMTRADE), available at http://comtrade.un.org and the United Nations *International Trade Statistics Yearbook.*

Mobile-cellular telephone subscriptions, per 100 inhabitants refer to the number of mobile cellular telephone subscriptions in a country for each 100 inhabitants. It is calculated by dividing the number of mobile cellular telephone subscriptions by the total population and multiplied by 100.

Source of the data: The World Telecommunication/ICT Indicators Database 2013 (17th Edition) of the International Telecommunication Union, Time series by country, available at http://www.itu.int/en/ITU-D/Statistics/Pages/stat/default.aspx (last accessed 13 December 2013).

Population aged 0-14 years refers to the population aged 0-14 years of both sexes as a percentage of total population. Unless otherwise indicated, the data refer to the year 2013.

Source of the data: United Nations, Department of Economic and Social Affairs, Population Division (2013), *World Population Prospects: The 2012 Revision,* available at http://esa.un.org/unpd/wpp/Excel-Data/population.htm; supplemented by official national statistics published in the *United Nations Demographic Yearbook 2012,* Table 7, available at http://unstats.un.org/unsd/demographic/products/dyb/dyb2012.htm; and data compiled by the Secretariat of the Pacific Community (SPC) Statistics and Demography Programme, Population and demographic indicators, available at http://www.spc.int/sdp.

Technical notes (*continued*)

Population aged 60 years and over refers to the percentage of the female population who are 60 years and older and the percentage of the male population who are 60 years and older, respectively. Unless otherwise indicated, the data refer to the year 2013.

Source of the data: United Nations, Department of Economic and Social Affairs, Population Division (2013), *World Population Prospects: The 2012 Revision,* available at http://esa.un.org/unpd/wpp/Excel-Data/population.htm; supplemented by official national statistics published in the *United Nations Demographic Yearbook 2012*, Table 7, available at http://unstats.un.org/unsd/demographic/products/dyb/dyb2012.htm; and data compiled by the Secretariat of the Pacific Community (SPC) Statistics and Demography Programme, Population and demographic indicators, available at http://www.spc.int/sdp.

Population density refers to population per square kilometre of surface area. Data are derived from the population estimates for 2011 divided by the surface area. See also *population estimates* and *surface area*.

Population estimates: Data for "Population in 2012" refer to de facto population as of 1 July 2012. The total population of a country may comprise either all usual residents of the country (de jure population) or all persons present in the country (de facto population) at the time of the census; for purposes of international comparisons, the de facto definition is recommended.

Source of the data: United Nations, Department of Economic and Social Affairs, Population Division (2013), *World Population Prospects: The 2012 Revision,* available at http://esa.un.org/unpd/wpp/Excel-Data/population.htm (last accessed 16 December 2013).

Population growth rate is the average annual percentage change in total population size. Unless otherwise indicated, the data refer to the period 2010-2015.

Source of the data: United Nations, Department of Economic and Social Affairs, Population Division (2013), *World Population Prospects: The 2012 Revision*, available at http://esa.un.org/unpd/wpp/Excel-Data/population.htm.

Precipitation in the capital city refers to the total mean of rain and/or snow, computed by adding average monthly measurements from the weather stations in the capital city, unless otherwise noted. The data are official climatological information supplied by national meteorological and hydrological services. Since the definition of mean precipitation and averaging periods may be different for different countries, care should be taken when comparing city climatologies.

Source of the data: The World Meteorological Organization website, available at http://www.worldweather.org/ (last accessed 10 February 2014).

Technical notes (*continued*)

Refugees and others of concern to the Office of the United Nations High Commissioner for Refugees (UNHCR): The 1951 United Nations Convention relating to the Status of Refugees states that a refugee is someone who, owing to a well-founded fear of being persecuted for reasons of race, religion, nationality, political opinion or membership in a particular social group, is outside the country of his or her nationality and is unable to, or owing to such fear, is unwilling to avail himself or herself of the protection of that country; or who, not having a nationality and being outside the country of his or her former habitual residence, is unable or, owing to such fear, unwilling to return to it. In this series, refugees refer to persons granted a humanitarian status and/or those granted temporary protection. Included are persons who have been granted temporary protection on a group basis. The series also includes returned refugees, asylum-seekers, stateless persons and persons displaced internally within their own country and others of concern to the UNHCR.

Source of the data: The *UNHCR Mid-Year Trends 2013*, Table 1: Refugees, asylum-seekers, internally displaced persons (IDPs), returnees (refugees and IDPs), stateless persons, and others of concern to UNHCR by country/territory of asylum, mid-2013 (or latest available estimates), available at http://www.unhcr.org/statistics.html (last accessed 8 January 2014). See also the website of the Internal Displacement Monitoring Centre (IDMC) for further information.

Region: Macro geographical regions arranged according to continents and component geographical regions used for statistical purposes.

Source of the data: The S*tandard Country or Area Codes and Geographical Regions for Statistical Use, Revision 4* (United Nations publication), Composition of macro geographical (continental) regions, geographical sub-regions, and selected economic and other groupings available at http://unstats.un.org/unsd/methods/m49/m49regin.htm (last accessed 26 November 2013).

Rural population growth rate data are based on the number of persons defined as rural according to national definitions of this concept. In most cases these definitions are those used in the most recent population census.

Source of the data: The United Nations Population Division, *World Urbanization Prospects: The 2011 Revision, File 7,* available at http://esa.un.org/unpd/wup/CD-ROM/Urban-Rural-Population.htm (last accessed 8 November 2013).

Seats held by women in national parliaments refer to the number of women in the lower chamber of national parliaments expressed as a percentage of total occupied seats in the lower or single House.

Source of the data: The Inter-Parliamentary Union, Women in National Parliaments, Situation as of 1 January 2014, available at http://www.ipu.org/wmn-e/classif-arc.htm (last accessed 20 March 2014).

Technical notes (*continued*)

Sex ratio is calculated as the ratio of the number of men to that of 100 women. Unless otherwise indicated, the data refer to the year 2013.

Source of the data: United Nations, Department of Economic and Social Affairs, Population Division (2013), *World Population Prospects: The 2012 Revision* ,available at http://esa.un.org/unpd/wpp/Excel-Data/population.htm; supplemented by official national statistics published in the *United Nations Demographic Yearbook 2012*, Table 7, available at http://unstats.un.org/unsd/demographic/products/dyb/dyb2012.htm; and data compiled by the Secretariat of the Pacific Community (SPC) Statistics and Demography Programme, Population and demographic indicators, available at http://www.spc.int/sdp.

Surface area, unless otherwise noted, refers to land area plus inland water.

Source of the data: The United Nations *Demographic Yearbook 2012*, Table 3, available at http://unstats.un.org/unsd/demographic/products/dyb/dyb2012.htm (last accessed 11 December 2013).

Temperature in the capital city, mean °C (minimum and maximum): Data were computed from average monthly measurements from the weather stations in the capital city, unless otherwise noted. The data are official climatological information supplied by national meteorological and hydrological services worldwide. Since the definition of mean temperature and averaging periods may be different for different countries, care should be taken when comparing city climatologies.

Source of the data: The World Meteorological Organization website, available at http://www.worldweather.org/ (last accessed 10 February 2014).

Threatened species represents the number of plants and animals that are most in need of conservation attention and are compiled by the World Conservation Union IUCN/ Species Survival Commission (SSC).

Source of the data: The IUCN Red List of Threatened Species version 2013.2: Table 5, available at http://www.iucnredlist.org/about/summary-statistics#Tables_5_6 (last accessed 10 January 2014).

Total trade: exports and imports show the movement of goods out of and into a country. Goods simply being transported through a country (goods in transit) or temporarily admitted (except for goods for inward processing) do not add to the stock of material resources of a country and are not included in the international merchandise trade statistics. In the "general trade system", the definition of the statistical territory of a country coincides with its economic territory. In the "special trade system", the definition of the statistical territory comprises only a particular part of the economic territory, mainly that part which coincides with the free circulation area for goods. "The free circulation area" is a part of the economic territory of a country within which goods "may be disposed of without Customs restrictions". In the case of exports, the transaction value is the value at which the goods were sold by the exporter, including the cost of transportation and insurance, to bring the goods onto the transporting vehicle at the frontier of the exporting country (an FOB-type valuation). In the case of imports, the transaction value is the value at which the goods were purchased by the importer plus the cost of transportation and insurance to the frontier of the importing country (a CIF-type valuation). Both imports and exports are shown in United States dollars. Conversion from national currencies is made by means of currency conversion factors based on official exchange rates (par values or weighted averages).

Source of the data: The United Nations Statistics Division's Commodity Trade Statistics Database (COMTRADE), available at http://comtrade.un.org and the United Nations *2012 International Trade Statistics Yearbook*.

Tourist arrivals at national borders: An international tourist is any person who travels to a country other than that in which he or she has his or her usual residence but outside his/her usual environment for a period not exceeding 12 months and whose main purpose of visit is other than the exercise of an activity remunerated from with the country visited, and who stays at least one night in a collective or private accommodation in the country visited (see *Recommendations on Tourism Statistics* of the United Nations and the World Tourism Organization). Unless otherwise indicated, the data refer to arrivals of non-resident tourists at national borders.

Source of the data: The United Nations World Tourism Organization *Compendium of Yearbook Statistics* (information provided by the United Nations World Tourism Organization as of 20 December 2012).

Unemployment refers to persons above a specified age who during a specified reference period were: "without work", i.e. were not in paid employment or self-employment as defined under employment; "currently available for work", i.e. were available for paid employment or self-employment during the reference period; and "seeking work", i.e. had taken specific steps in a specified recent period to seek paid employment or self-employment. In circumstances where employment opportunities are particularly limited and where persons not working do not have easy access to formal channels for seeking employment or face social and cultural barriers when looking for a job, the "seeking work" criterion should be relaxed. National definitions of unemployment often differ from the recommended international standard definitions and thereby limit international comparability. Inter-country comparisons are also complicated by the different types of data collection systems used to obtain information on unemployed persons. Unless otherwise indicated, the data refer to the 15 years and over age group and are national employment office statistics, usually labour force surveys, compiled by the ILO. (See ILO's *Current International Recommendations on Labour Statistics*, 2000 Edition).

Technical notes (*continued*)

Source of the data: The LABORSTA Internet ILO database, Short term indicators, Unemployment rate by sex, available at http://www.ilo.org/ilostat/faces/home/ statisticaldata/data_by_subject?_adf.ctrl-state=hhcnozbjq_110&_afrLoop= 1400953161591832 (last accessed 23 April 2014).

United Nations membership dates: The United Nations is an intergovernmental organization whose members are the countries of the world. Currently there are 192 Member States of the United Nations, some of which joined the UN by signing and ratifying the Charter of the United Nations in 1945; the other countries joined the UN later, through the adoption of a resolution admitting them to membership. The process usually follows these steps: first, the country applies for membership and makes a declaration accepting the obligations of the Charter; second, the Security Council adopts a resolution recommending that the General Assembly admit the country to membership and finally the General Assembly adopts a resolution admitting the country.

Source of the data: The List of Member States, available at http://www.un.org/en/members/ (accessed 4 November 2013).

Urban population is based on the number of persons defined as urban according to national definitions of this concept. In most cases these definitions are those used in the most recent population census.

Source of the data: United Nations Population Division, *World Urbanization Prospects: The 2011 Revision*, CD-ROM Edition, File 21, available at http://esa.un.org/unpd/wup/CD-ROM/Urban-Rural-Population.htm.

Urban population growth rate is based on the number of persons defined as urban according to national definitions of this concept. In most cases these definitions are those used in the most recent population census.

Source of the data: United Nations Population Division, *World Urbanization Prospects: The 2011 Revision*, File 6, available at http://esa.un.org/unpd/wup/CD-ROM/Urban-Rural-Population.htm (last accessed 8 November 2013).

Statistical sources and references

Statistical sources

Carbon Dioxide Information Analysis Center, Oak Ridge, Tennessee, *Global, Regional, and National Fossil-Fuel CO_2 Emissions*, available at http://cdiac.ornl.gov/trends/emis/overview_2010.html /.

Food and Agriculture Organization of the United Nations, Rome, FAOSTAT database, available at http://faostat3.fao.org/faostat-gateway/go/to/home/E.

International Labour Organization, *Key Indicators of the Labour Market, 7th edition* software, available at http://www.ilo.org/empelm/what/WCMS_114240/lang--en/index.htm.

_____, LABORSTA Internet database, available at http://laborsta.ilo.org/data_topic_E.html.

International Monetary Fund (IMF), Washington, Balance of Payments (BOP) database.

_____, International Financial Statistics (IFS) database.

Inter-Parliamentary Union, Women in National Parliaments, available at http://www.ipu.org/wmn-e/classif.htm.

International Telecommunication Union (ITU), Geneva, the World Telecommunication/ICT Indicators Database 2013 (17th Edition) database, available at http://www.itu.int/ITU-D/ict/publications/world/world.html.

International Union for Conservation of Nature (IUCN), *The 2013 IUCN Red List of Threatened Species*, available at http://www.iucnredlist.org/.

Secretariat of the Pacific Community (SPC) Statistics and Demography Programme, Population and demographic indicators, available at http://www.spc.int/sdp.

United Nations Educational, Scientific and Cultural Organization (UNESCO) Institute for Statistics, Montreal, UNESCO statistics database, available at http://stats.uis.unesco.org.

United Nations High Commissioner for Refugees, Geneva, UNHCR Mid-Year Trends 2013, available at http://www.unhcr.org/statistics.html.

United Nations, Department of Economic and Social Affairs, Population Division, New York, *Trends in International Migrant Stock: The 2013 Revision* (United Nations publication POP/DB/MIG/Stock/Rev.2013/Age), available at http://esa.un.org/unmigration/TIMSA2013/migrantstocks2013.htm?mhome.

_____, Fertility and Family Planning Section, *World Contraceptive Use 2012*, available at http://www.un.org/esa/population/publications/WCU2012/MainFrame.html.

_____, *World Population Prospects. The 2012 Revision,* available at http://esa.un.org/unpd/wpp/index.htm.

_____, *World Urbanization Prospects: The 2011 Revision,* available at http://esa.un.org/unpd/wup/index.htm.

United Nations, Department of Economic and Social Affairs, Statistics Division, New York, Commodity Trade Statistics Database (COMTRADE), available at http://comtrade.un.org/db/default.aspx.

_____, *Demographic Yearbook 2012* (United Nations Publication, ST/ESA/STAT/SER.R/42), available at http://unstats.un.org/unsd/demographic/products/dyb/dyb2.htm.

_____, *Energy Statistics Yearbook* (Series J, United Nations publication), available at http://unstats.un.org/unsd/energy/yearbook/default.htm.

_____, *International Trade Statistics Yearbook* (Series G, United Nations publication), available at http://comtrade.un.org/pb/.

_____, *Monthly Bulletin of Statistics* (Series Q, United Nations publication), available at http://unstats.un.org/unsd/mbs/.

_____, *National Accounts Statistics: Analysis of Main Aggregates* (Series X, United Nations publication), available at http://unstats.un.org/unsd/snaama/introduction.asp.

_____, *Standard Country or Area Codes for Statistical Use* (ST/ESA/STAT/SER.M/49/Rev.4) and http://unstats.un.org/unsd/methods/m49/m49.htm.

United Nations, Department of Management, Office of Programme Planning, Budget and Accounts, New York, Treasury website, available at http://www.un.org/Depts/treasury.

United Nations Member States website, available at http://www.un.org/en/members/.

United Nations Office on Drugs and Crime, Vienna, Homicide Statistics website, available at http://www.unodc.org/unodc/en/data-and-analysis/homicide.html.

United Nations World Tourism Organization (UNWTO), Madrid, UNWTO statistics database, *Yearbook of Tourism Statistics* available at http://www.unwto.org.

World Meteorological Organization (WMO), available at http://www.worldweather.org/.

Statistical sources and references *(continued)*

References

Food and Agriculture Organization of the United Nations (2010). *Global Forest Resources Assessment 2010* (Rome), available at http://www.fao.org/forestry/fra/fra2010/en/.

International Labour Organization (2000). *Current International Recommendations on Labour Statistics*, 2000 Edition (Geneva), available at http://www.ilo.org/public/english/bureau/stat/publ/currrec.htm.

United Nations (1951 and 1967). Convention relating to the Status of Refugees of 1951 (United Nations, Treaty Series, vol. 189 (1954), No. 2545, p. 137), art. 1) and Protocol relating to the Status of Refugees of 1967 (United Nations, Treaty Series, vol. 606 (1967), No. 8791, p. 267).

United Nations (1982). Concepts and Methods in Energy Statistics, with Special Reference to Energy Accounts and Balances: A Technical Report. Statistical Office, Series F, No. 29 and Corr. 1 (United Nations publication, Sales No. E.82.XVII.13 and corrigendum), available at http://unstats.un.org/unsd/publication/SeriesF/SeriesF_29E.pdf.

United Nations (2008). *Principles and Recommendations for Population and Housing Censuses Rev. 2*. Statistics Division, Series M, No. 67, Rev. 2 (United Nations publication, Sales No. E.07.XVII.8), available at http://unstats.un.org/unsd/publication/SeriesM/Seriesm_67rev2e.pdf.

United Nations (2008). *International Standard Industrial Classification of All Economic Activities (ISIC), Rev. 4*. Statistics Division, Series M, No. 4, Rev.4 (United Nations publication, Sales No. E.08.XVII.25), available at http://unstats.un.org/unsd/publication/SeriesM/seriesm_4rev4e.pdf.

United Nations (2004). *International Merchandise Trade Statistics: Compilers Manual,* Statistics Division, Series F, No. 87 (United Nations publication, Sales No. E.02.XVII.17), available at http://unstats.un.org/unsd/publication/SeriesF/seriesf_87e.pdf.

United Nations (2010).*International Merchandise Trade Statistics: Concepts and Definitions*, Statistics Division, Series M, No.52, Rev.3, (United Nations publication, Sales No. E.10.XVII.13), available at http://unstats.un.org/unsd/trade/EG-IMTS/IMTS%202010%20(English).pdf.

United Nations European Commission, International Monetary Fund, Organisation for Economic Cooperation and Development and World Bank (2009). *System of National Accounts 2008 (SNA 2008),* available at http://unstats.un.org/unsd/nationalaccount/sna2008.asp.

United Nations and World Tourism Organization (2008). International Recommendations for Tourism Statistics 2008, Series M, No. 83/Rev.1 (United Nations publication, Sales No. E.08.XVII.28).

Statistical sources and references (*continued*)

World Health Organization (WHO, 2007). International Statistical Classification of Diseases and Related Health Problems, Tenth Revision (ICD-10), (Geneva), available at http://www.who.int/classifications/icd/en/.